DISABILITY, SOCIETY,
AND THE INDIVIDUAL

DISABILITY, SOCIETY, AND THE INDIVIDUAL

THIRD EDITION

JULIE SMART
PhD, LPC, CRC (ret.), LVRC, NCC

pro·ed
An International Publisher

8700 Shoal Creek Boulevard
Austin, Texas 78757-6897
800/897-3202 Fax 800/397-7633
www.proedinc.com

© 2016, 2009, 2001 by PRO-ED, Inc.
8700 Shoal Creek Boulevard
Austin, Texas 78757-6897
800/897-3202 Fax 800/397-7633
www.proedinc.com

Permission granted by The Associated Press and YGS Group to reprint Exhibit 1.1.
Permission granted by Ann Landers and Creators Syndicate to reprint Exhibits 3.1, 3.2, 5.1, and 5.2.

LIBRARY OF CONGRESS CATALOGING-IN-PUBLICATION DATA

Smart, Julie, author.
  Disability, society, and the individual / Julie Smart. — Third edition.
      pages cm
  Includes bibliographical references and index.
  ISBN 978-1-4164-1000-3 — ISBN 978-1-4164-1001-0 (e-book)
1. People with disabilities—Social conditions. 2. Discrimination against people with disabilities. 3. Sociology of
disability. I. Title.
  HV1568.S63 2016
  305.9'0816—dc23
                          2015025865

Art Director: Jason Crosier
Designer: Bookbright Media

Printed in the United States of America

2 3 4 5 6 7 8 9 10   25 24 23 22 21 20 19 18 17

This book is dedicated to the memory of my dear parents,
Helen and Ben Fishler.

CONTENTS

ACKNOWLEDGMENTS

I have been amazed and pleased at the reception this book has received. *Disability, Society, and the Individual* has been used as an introductory course on disability by many academic disciplines, including sociology, social work, counseling, psychology, and rehabilitation counseling. I am so pleased and grateful for all those who have used the first two editions of my book.

I have used many excerpts from various writers, people with disabilities, and disability scholars, and there probably would be no book (or second and third editions) without their contributions. I have long respected the ideas and scholarship of these individuals, and their work certainly strengthens and broadens the scope of this book. Also, I don't think the work of these individuals has received the recognition and consideration it deserves. Many of my sources are books from university presses, typically small and esoteric publishers who publish books that very few students read and study. Therefore, I have tried to bring many of these authors together in a single book and give a broader context to this oft-hidden scholarship.

Finally, I wish to thank my students. Over the years, I have taught a course titled "Psychosocial Aspects of Disability" in a master's degree program in rehabilitation counseling, during which the students and I have discussed the ideas in this book. Also at Utah State University, this book is used for a General Education Social Sciences undergraduate course titled, "Society and Disability." In this course, students of any major are provided some introductory understanding of disability. If I have managed to present many sides of a single issue, much of this is a result of these classroom discussions. In addition, students and graduates send me articles, e-mails, and other materials, knowing that I am deeply interested in issues related to disability. Many of these materials have been used in this book. As I re-read what I have written, I am struck by—and feel grateful for—the many contributions of my students.

Julie Smart
Utah State University
March 2015

ABBREVIATIONS AND TERMS

ADA	Americans with Disabilities Act
ADAAA	Americans with Disabilities Act Amendments Act
ADL	Activities of daily living, such as eating, bathing, grooming, doing household maintenance tasks, conducting necessary business, and shopping
ASL	American Sign Language
CRAB	Currently regarded as able-bodied
IL	Independent Living
PWD	Person or people with disabilities
PWOD	Person or people without disabilities
TAB	Temporarily able-bodied
UNCRPD	United Nations Convention on the Rights of Persons with Disabilities

Note: *"Deaf" with a capital "D" indicates the Deaf Culture (sometimes referred to as the Deaf community), while "deaf" with a small "d" refers to the disability of deafness. Individuals who are Deaf do not consider themselves to have a disability; instead, they view themselves as part of another culture that speaks another language. Indeed, the symbol of their oppression—sign language—has evolved into a symbol of unity and community.[*]*

---

[*]See *Deaf Empowerment: Emergence, Struggle, and Rhetoric*, by K. A. Jankowski, 1997, Washington, DC: Gallaudet University.

DISABILITY, SOCIETY,
AND THE INDIVIDUAL

INTRODUCTION

On the first day of class, I ask my students: "When you walk into any major chain bookstore, do you find any books about people with disabilities?" All of my students are smart, but it takes them a bit of time to think about this. Eventually, they answer: Helen Keller, Christopher Reeve, and the blind guy who climbed Mt. Everest. But all of these individuals are considered to be *disabled heroes*, individuals with many more resources than the typical person with a disability. Given the fact that nearly one fifth (18%) of the American population has a disability (NOD/Harris Survey, 2004), it is surprising that there isn't a section in the bookstore devoted to "Disability History."

I ask my students this question because I want them to think about the invisibility of people with disabilities in our society and culture. People with disabilities, and their experiences, knowledge, and accumulated wisdom, are invisible in our society and culture; furthermore, this invisibility is not noticed or discussed. No one questions why there are no books written by people with disabilities, or better stated, why books written by people with disabilities are not widely available.

John Hockenberry, a journalist with a spinal cord injury, describes the invisibility of people with disabilities in textbooks and the curriculum:

> Why is it that a person would not be considered educated or privileged if he went through school and never learned there was a France or a French language? But if a person went through school and knew nothing about disability, never met a disabled person [*sic*], never heard of American Sign Language, he might be considered not only educated, but also lucky? (cf. Fleischer & Zames, 2001, p. 205)

In spite of this invisibility, disability is being redefined as a social construct; people with disabilities are developing a collective identity, and the number of those with disabilities continues to climb. Furthermore, "We want more disabled people [*sic*], not fewer" (Stalcup, 1997, p. 175). Perhaps most important, all of us have the possibility of acquiring a disability, or marrying someone with a disability, or having a child with a disability.

The Purpose of This Book

The threefold purpose of this book is to look at the disability experience from the perspective of the individual who has a disability, to discuss how disabilities are viewed by society, and to consider the relationship between these two viewpoints. As this book emphasizes, a perfect world is not a world without disabilities; it is a world in which accommodations for people with disabilities (PWDs) are provided and artificial barriers are removed. It is also a world that does not stigmatize or discriminate against those with disabilities, a world that accords basic human rights to PWDs. (Note: the acronyms PWD and PWOD, and their plurals, will be used throughout the book for the purposes of clarity and brevity. PWD denotes a person or people *with* disabilities, and PWOD denotes a person or people *without* disabilities.)

I wanted to write a book that, in a single place, would consider the overall, broad, comprehensive experience of disability. It was important for me that readers gain an introductory understanding of the way in which three broad areas relate to each other. These areas are as follows: definitions of disability, societal response to PWDs, and the experience of disability. To my knowledge, such a book has not been available. Of course, there are excellent books on each of the three broad areas, and I have used these works in my research and writing and have referenced each, to which the reader may refer for more depth and detail. Therefore, I have deliberately sacrificed detail and depth to provide a broad overview of the disability experience. Some sort of organization and conceptualization, even if artificial, is necessary. Hence, these three sections of the book (and the *sequence* of the sections) are provided to facilitate learning. Whenever possible, these interrelationships are noted.

Clearly, the most important section of this book deals with the experience of the PWD. It may appear counterintuitive that the most important section of the book is also the final section. After much consideration, I decided that it is impossible to understand the experiences of PWDs without first learning about the differing definitions and models of disability and how these affect the daily lives of PWDs. The services PWDs receive, whether they live in the community or in an institution, or whether they *live* at all, are all determined by definitions and models of disability. Hence, the first section defines disability. The second section deals with societal responses to disability. The PWD is greatly affected by the way in which society views him or her and the disability. Indeed, many PWDs declare that coping with prejudice and discrimination is a greater concern than the disability itself. Furthermore, because everyone's self-identity is partially determined by one's culture and society, it makes sense to consider the way in which society views (and has viewed) PWDs before discussing the experience of PWDs.

Do these well-defined sections represent the reality of any one person? Of course not. No book can truly communicate someone's experience. Moreover, there are no neat divisions between defining disability, society's response, and the individual's experience of living with a disability. Certainly, all three of these concepts interact with each other, and no one truly conceives of his or her life in these three neat, clean paradigms.

In contrast to most textbooks on disability, this book is not organized by the various diagnostic categories of disability, with each chapter discussing a specific disability, such as blindness, mental illness, paraplegia, or intellectual disabilities. Rather, broad similarities and differences across a wide range of disabilities are considered. There are many psychosocial issues, responses, and tasks required of PWDs; therefore, this book discusses these broad issues. Society's view of disability and PWDs are also discussed in terms of a wide spectrum of disabilities, rather than discussing society's view of and response to each disability type.

Section 1: Definitions of Disability

The first section defines disability and normality and the various models of disability. Normality and disability are defined in relation to each other, and the definition of neither is straightforward or clear-cut. (I recently saw a bumper sticker on a car that read, "Normal at our house is just a setting on the clothes dryer.") Some of this section is devoted to what a disability is *not*. Models of disability, at first glance, appear to be theoretical abstractions; however, these models determine the daily lives of PWDs. Six reasons why there are more disabilities than ever before are discussed in addition to the Americans With Disabilities Act (ADA). The ADA was passed in 1990, leading many in the Disability Rights Movement to term PWDs as the "last and least minority." Certainly, most other minority groups in the United States were accorded their civil rights before 1990. These first two chapters also present the rationale underlying the correct terminology for describing disability and PWDs. Much of the research for this section is focused on demographic data and legal scholarship.

Section 2: Society and Disability (or, the Best Way to Teach Social Justice Is to Teach the History of Social Injustice)

The second section of the book discusses society's responses to disability and PWDs—most of which have included prejudice and discrimination. Chapters 3, 4, and 5 discuss sources of prejudice and discrimination. Each PWD, regardless of his or her achievements, economic resources, or privilege, understands that he or she belongs to a devalued group. PWDs are often faced with the need to negotiate a relationship with a society that, in many cases, rejects them. The focus of these three chapters is on the effect of prejudice on PWDs; however, the way in which people without disabilities (PWODs) pay for their prejudice is also reviewed. Prejudice is expensive. Prejudice against any group costs the larger group, and eliminating prejudice against the minority group improves the economy. By systematically refusing to allow members of one group the right to fulfill their potential, the larger group forfeits economic benefits. Furthermore, PWODs pay for their prejudice by losing the creativity and diversity of ideas that PWDs could provide, if allowed. For example, most universities offer women's studies courses and African American (Black American) courses, but the incorporation into the undergraduate curriculum of disability history or disability studies lags far behind. Finally, PWODs pay for their prejudice against PWDs by losing an opportunity to grow because of the fear of acquiring a disability. If PWDs and their experiences were socially validated, PWODs could understand the disability experience and not fear it as much.

Some concepts in this second section are difficult to understand. First, as a society, we have never viewed disability as an ordinary human experience. Indeed, many PWDs report that they would not wish to be cured of their disability; instead, they would rather simply be treated as individuals whose disability does not make them unordinary or less than fully human. When the public views disability as heroic or tragic, not only is this an inaccurate perception of the lives of PWDs, but it also does not allow PWDs to be regarded as and judged like everyone else. Second, the idea that disability is a collective concern may appear illogical; nonetheless, these chapters attempt to show that disability concerns everyone. Finally, and most difficult, many readers have questioned my arguments against telethons, simulation exercises, and other "well-intentioned handicapism." I think it is important to think about the *results* of some of these practices. Without question, the *motives* of those who support telethons and simulations are well-intentioned; however, the costs to PWDs and the *results* have set the Disability Rights Movement back. Indeed, many PWDs point out that there are no telethon or simulation exercises for other minority groups. Many PWDs consider charity of any type, including telethons, to have relieved general society of any need to provide civil rights for PWDs. Titles of many books stress the contradiction between civil rights and charity, including Shapiro's (1993) *No Pity: People With Disabilities Forging a New Civil Rights Movement*; Fleischer and Zames's (2001) *The Disability Rights Movement: From Charity to Confrontation*; and Scotch's (1984) *From Good Will to Civil Rights: Transforming Federal Disability Policy*. Much of the literature for this section was taken from works on the sociological view of disability and books on disability rights.

Section 3: The Individual and Disability

The focus changes in Chapters 6, 7, 8, and 9. In these chapters, the individual's response to disability is considered, especially considering the factors of the disability itself and factors in the environment. Types of onset, varied courses, levels of severity, degree of visibility, the presence of chronic pain, and the degree of stigma and prejudice directed toward that particular disability are all known to have an effect on the individual's response. Disability scholars recognize that factors in the environment have an important impact on the individual's response to the disability. Of course, most PWDs think of the disability as a personal attribute, not as a tragic problem. For many PWDs, the disability is not the single most important self-identifier. Furthermore, the only shared identity is the prejudice and discrimination PWDs experience. Other than this devalued position in society, it is safe to state that there is no single disability experience.

There are many blogs and YouTube sources that show PWDs relating their experiences and viewpoints and allowing viewers to see PWDs in many different settings: in their homes, in hospitals, at work, with their friends, or in school. Some of these videos follow a PWD for a long period of time, providing viewers with a long-term perspective of a disability. In other videos, family members, friends, and professional caregivers, in addition to the PWD, discuss their responses to the PWD and the disability. This provides a multifaceted picture of the disability experience. Some videos show historical scenes of hospitals and institutions that have been closed for decades, and two videos show the institutions in Nazi Germany where PWDs were murdered. In other videos, major players in the Disability Rights Movement recount their experiences and the difficulties in obtaining basic civil rights for Americans with disabilities. It is my hope that this book will provide the foundation and background for viewing these videos; moreover, it is clear that these videos will add richness, detail, and immediacy in understanding disabilities and the people who experience them. Sources include the magazine *Ragged Edge* (http://raggededgemagazine.com) and many others. The *Ragged Edge* blog consists of PWDs discussing their experiences with prejudice and discrimination and presents current disability rights information. In contrast, the second website is an academic, research-oriented journal, *Disability Studies Quarterly* (http://dsq-sds.org/), which provides articles on international disability law and policy.

As a society, we are increasingly understanding the pervasiveness, significance, and value of the disability experience. I hope that this book will lend support to a transformation of the way in which we view ourselves.

SECTION 1

DEFINITIONS OF DISABILITY

It may seem unnecessary to devote two chapters to defining disabilities. Nonetheless, the concept and diagnosis of disability are complicated, based on which government agency or large standardized medical or psychiatric system is used; based on the historical period in which the disability occurs; and based on ethnic, cultural, linguistic, and personal considerations. For example, the World Health Organization (WHO) has changed the underlying focus of the *International Classification of Impairments, Disabilities, and Handicaps* (1960) to reflect the way in which the functioning of the individual interacts with the disabilities. This radical change resulted in a new system, *The International Classification of Functioning, Disability, and Health* (2001). Thus, the most standardized, objective, and widely used medical diagnostic system has changed the fundamental definition of disability, clearly illustrating that the definition of disability changes throughout time.

Readers may also find it surprising that there are more people with disabilities (PWDs) than ever before in the history of humankind, and, furthermore, these increases are viewed as progress, both as societal progress and progress for the individuals who experience the disability. Of course, it is better to avoid disability altogether, and safety laws are enacted and enforced, such as the use of safety belts and helmets, in order to avoid disability (and death.) However, when the choice is between death or living with a disability, most of us would choose to live with a disability. Therefore, neonatal medicine, which saves many newborns, or emergency medicine, which saves accident and trauma victims, or combat veterans, are seen as advances. Before medical, scientific, and technological advances, there were fewer PWDs, but much higher death rates.

The second chapter defines and describes *models of disability*. For most readers, these models, which define and describe disability differently, will be new concepts. Basically, models describe and define disability in five different ways:

1. the religious or moral viewpoint
2. the medical, biological, organic viewpoint
3. the environmental viewpoint
4. the functional viewpoint
5. the civil rights viewpoint

Most PWODs view disability from the medical viewpoint, not being aware that there are other ways (models) to view disability. For example, most bioethical debates concerning PWDs—debates over assisted suicide, infanticide of newborns with severe disabilities, and abortion of fetuses with severe disabilities—would be more fully informed by considering more than the medical viewpoint. Seeing PWDs as more than a medical condition, illness, or disability would help us to understand these bioethical dilemmas.

CHAPTER 1

DEFINING DISABILITY

✧ Is disability truly a universal concern?

✧ Does anyone know what "normal" is?

✧ Why is it necessary to define or categorize disabilities?

✧ Why are labels and diagnoses depersonalizing for the individual?

✧ Does everybody have a disability of some sort?

✧ If medicine and medical technology have made such great advances, why are there more disabilities than ever before?

✧ Why is the increase in disabilities considered to be progress?

The Universality of Disability, or Disability Is a Natural Part of Everyone's Life

In this section, look for—

- ✧ why disability is an "equal opportunity situation"
- ✧ how many PWODs choose to deny or minimize the possibility of acquiring a disability
- ✧ how disability concerns all of us

Disability has been present throughout human history in every culture and society, and yet there never has been a universal definition of disability (Hiranandani, 2005). Disability is a permanent part of human history, and the number of people with disabilities continues to increase. Of course, not everyone has a disability or will have a disability, but everyone has the potential to acquire a disability, and every child born has the potential for a congenital disability—a disability present at birth. Clay Haughton, director of Civilian Equal Opportunity for the Department of Defense, explained:

> No one is immune to developing a disability, and almost no one, regardless of race, gender, religion or economic status, will go through life without suffering from some form of physical impairment. It's truly the equal opportunity situation, and those of us who are disabled are a constant visual reminder of the frailty of each member of the human race. And so, accepting this possibility and adjusting to disability, those are matters that concern us all. (Fleischer & Zames, 2001, p. 109)

While Haughton termed the acquisition of a disability an "equal opportunity situation," Berube (1998), a university professor, referred to the potential for anyone to acquire a disability as follows:

> A category whose constituency is contingency itself. Any of us who identify as "nondisabled" must know that our self-designation is inevitably temporary, and that a car crash, a virus, a degenerative genetic disease, or a precedent-setting legal decision would change our status in ways over which we have no control whatsoever. (p. viii)

Ironically, disability is the only "open" minority group, but many PWODs deny this reality. One mother of a child with a disability asked the following:

> What is our fear of disability about? Of course, there is more work and more costs for everyone. But, time and money are insufficient explanations for

the terror of disability. Few things are as difficult to face as disabilities they themselves have. Few differences, such as race, gender, religion, are as threatening to a person's sense of worth . . . the able-bodied can be turned into the disabled at the next turn of the road. You would think that prejudice would be contained, because at any time, I could turn into them. (National Public Radio, 1998c)

So, rather than thinking of disability as something abnormal, exotic, or marginal to our interests, we see that disability concerns all of us (J. F. Smart, 2004). Everyone will have a family member with a disability, attend school with students with a wide range of disabilities, work with colleagues and supervisors who have disabilities, and marry or form long-term relationships with PWDs.

Does Anyone Know What "Normal" Is?

In this section, look for—

- ✧ Is the concept of normalcy fixed and unchanging?
- ✧ the idea that normalcy is a changing, elastic concept
- ✧ Does normalcy always imply progress for human kind?
- ✧ Is normalcy solely the absence of deviance, illness, or disability?
- ✧ the reasons why "diagnoses of exclusion" are frequently ambiguous
- ✧ Is normalcy an ideal or standard of evaluation?
- ✧ Does abnormalcy always imply deficit, pathology, or inferiority?

The questions that head this section are important ones because the answers have a great impact on the self-concepts of individuals, on how people treat each other, and on the allocation of public resources for services and benefits. In some societies, the definition of *normal* determined if PWDs lived or died. Other questions follow: Is it always positive to be labeled normal? Where can we see pictures of normal people? Is *abnormal* always a negative label, indicating someone as inferior, deviant, or deficient? Is there one fixed, correct pattern of human development? Or, is the concept of normalcy a dynamic, changing concept (in contrast to a fixed, unchanging idea)? Does the concept of normalcy always imply progress for humankind? A disability scholar stated that normalcy was "a dynamic concept for a changing and progressing world, the premise of which was that one could discern from observation of human behavior the direction of human evolution" (Baynton, 1997a, p. 83). Indeed, disabilities or people with disabilities were either absent or invisible in the futuristic books of the 1950s that envisioned the great scientific and technological advances of the 21st century.

Often, normal is defined solely as the absence of deviance, illness, or disability, so that the definition becomes a definition of exclusion. In other words, if deviance, illness, or disability is not present, the person is judged to be normal. No definition of exclusion is very helpful. After all, only eliminations are made, usually of those factors considered to be undesirable; no further guidelines or clarifications are given. Diagnoses of exclusion, including the determination of normalcy, are frequently given as a result of the ambiguity and lack of specificity of these types of diagnoses. Consequently, there are more clear-cut, standardized, measurable, and objective guidelines for the definition of abnormal than there are for the definition of normal.

Conceptualizing normalcy as the ideal, as the standard against which everything is measured, is another invalid assumption. For many, normal means perfect. Assumptions, accurate or not, can remain intact throughout centuries of human history. Davis (1997a) summarized the long history of the concept of normalcy: "A common assumption would be that some concept of the norm must have always existed. After all, people seem to have an inherent desire to compare themselves to others" (p. 9). Those who subscribe to this assumption believe that anything or anyone that does not meet all the prescribed criteria, guidelines, and standards is abnormal. Indeed, Wolfensberger (1972) stated, "Normalcy is often confused with humanity." In the third section of this book, we will see that PWDs often redefine normalcy, and the way in which PWODs define normalcy is often not valued by PWDs.

Defining power is the authority to determine who or what is normal. Normalcy is, in many ways, in the eyes of the beholder; indeed, the determination of normalcy and abnormalcy may tell us more about the people making the determinations than about the people being judged. The most clear-cut example of defining power is the example of Nazi Germany and the Holocaust. The Nazis defined the criteria of being normal and then killed those who did not meet these criteria, including German children and adults with disabilities (Friedlander, 1995). Nazi pseudoscientists "confirmed" these criteria with "data."

In the original sense of the word, *normal* carries no value judgment; normal is neither good nor bad. Normal simply means typical, prevalent, customary, routine, commonplace, in the middle, and to be expected (Davis, 1997a). Normal means average, ordinary, and common. Nonetheless, most people aspire to be normal but not average! Remember the radio program "A Prairie Home Companion," which tells of a fictional town called Lake Wobegon, in which all of the children are "above average"? Both normal and abnormal, therefore, can also be good or bad. Here is an example of abnormalcy: "I am abnormal because I am extremely beautiful, I am an Olympic athlete, and I have a genius-level IQ." Consider this example: "It is normal for 500 murders to be committed each year in the City of Oz." Accordingly, the determination of normalcy or abnormalcy is not an evaluation or value judgment because these concepts have no inherent value; rather, it is a simple determination based on how typical an event, a characteristic, or a behavior is. Normalcy, then, is more of a statistical concept, which includes the ideas of "most commonly occurring and most likely to happen."

One disability scholar stated: "There is no flesh-and-bones human body that is normal; the only 'normal body' is the one constructed from the 'bare bones' of statistics. . . . This is the fiction presented to disabled people [*sic*]" (Michalko, 2002, p. 32). Of course, PWODs, people who consider themselves to be normal, often do not realize that these categories exist. Murphy, a university anthropology professor who became paralyzed because of a spinal tumor, explained that the identity of normal is an elite category, just as White is thought to often be the valued category in racial and ethnic classifications, and therefore neither the "Normals" nor the "Whites" are required to think of themselves as being in these categories. Murphy recalled a discussion with a Black anthropology colleague in which the colleague stated, "I always think of myself as being Black just as you always think of yourself as being White." With Murphy's disability came a realization that "I would no more have thought of myself as White than I would have thought of myself as walking on two legs" (Murphy, 1990, pp. 102–103). In other words, when an individual is within the so-called *normal* group, the individual is often unaware that there is a classification system of normalcy versus abnormalcy. Indeed, while most PWDs think of themselves as someone with a disability, most PWODs would not describe themselves as able-bodied persons.

Confusing Normalcy With the Ideal

According to Davis, eugenics had the effect of making the physical body the individual's most important source of identity. The individual became his or her body, an organic entity, a mechanical machine that either functioned correctly and efficiently or did not function. With the appearance of statistics, the normal curve, and eugenics, the concept of normalcy was enshrined as the desired status. Disability scholars (Davis, 1997a; Wendell, 2006) assert that society has confused normalcy with the ideal. With the concept of normalcy, society confers a desirable status on some people (the "normal" ones). In contrast, with the concept of the ideal, everyone falls short. No one has the ideal characteristics (or is supposed to). Indeed, the concept of the ideal often embodied spiritual, philosophical, mythical, or religious meanings in which divine beings are ideal. In some belief systems, humans can become ideal but only in some sort of afterlife. Further, in many spiritual orientations, the individual is not his or her body—the main identity of the individual is his or her eternal spirit. Therefore, in these belief systems the spirit could not be measured (as the body can be in statistics). The idea that humans (rather than deity) have the capability to measure the worth of an individual (such as eugenics) would seem without reason in many religious or spiritual belief systems.

The Social Construction of Normalcy and Disability

The increasing proportion of the population with disabilities adds a new dimension to the concept of normalcy. If normalcy is based on numbers, with those in the numerical majority considered to be normal and those in the numerical minority considered to be abnormal, then as more individuals acquire the identification of having a disability, will the definitions of normalcy and disability change? An unusual example of a substantial number of individuals having a disability (albeit not a majority) and not being perceived as having a disability because of their large proportion in the population is described in Groce's (1985) book, *Everyone Here Spoke Sign Language: Hereditary Deafness on Martha's Vineyard*. In 1694, the first D/deaf resident of Martha's Vineyard, Jonathan Lambert, arrived. Lambert was an English sailor who brought an inherited trait that causes D/deafness. Geographic isolation and intermarriage resulted in D/deafness for many individuals; many families had members who were D/deaf. By 1850, 1 in 25 residents of the town of Chilmark was D/deaf, and in one neighborhood, the ratio was 1 in 4. What is truly unusual about the story is the lack of a disability identity on the island. On Martha's Vineyard, D/deafness was a natural part of human existence. D/deafness was unremarkable; marriages took place between D/deaf individuals and hearing individuals and the birth of a D/deaf baby was not regarded as a tragedy. Moreover, as the title of Groce's book suggests, the use of sign language was not regarded as an accommodation, and, indeed, the widespread use of a communication system that everyone could understand probably contributed to the lack of a disability identity. Also, because telecommunications had not yet been introduced, most long-distance communication used the written word. Thus, people who were D/deaf were not disadvantaged, socially or economically. People who were D/deaf were viewed as different but not as deviant or pathological. Researchers asked residents on Martha's Vineyard if there were any people with disabilities on the island. All of the respondents answered "yes," giving examples of people who were blind or had orthopedic impairments. No one described a D/deaf person as a person with a disability. Many disability advocates have theorized that it is not biological conditions that make disabilities; rather, it is the lack of accommodations (Higgins, 1992b; Liachowitz, 1988; Scott, 1969). The story of Martha's Vineyard lends support to this theory.

The theoretical model of everyone in a community having the same disability helps us to understand the social construction of disability. For example, if no one could walk, the community would be completely accessible for wheelchairs. Even more important, there would be no stigma, prejudice, or stereotypes about people who could not walk. The community would adjust to the inability to walk, with both universal accessibility and the corresponding absence of prejudice and discrimination.

If a spaceship from another planet landed in our imaginary community and the aliens could walk, they would find all the drinking fountains in this community to be too low because the fountains would be at wheelchair height. Also, the aliens would probably experience a great deal of prejudice, discrimination, and stereotyping because of their deviance (their ability to walk). If, instead of the ability to walk, the universal disability was D/deafness, there would be the same conditions: (a) universal accommodations and (b) lack of prejudice and discrimination against people who are D/deaf, which, of course, would be everybody. A third result occurs: the identity of people who are D/deaf then becomes a cultural and sociolinguistic identity and not a disability identity.

Five Factors That Determine the Definition of Normalcy

In spite of the complexities of defining normalcy and abnormalcy, some widely accepted standards of normalcy must be established, depending on both the characteristic(s) and the environment. How can society operate without some broad guidelines to provide services that are most appropriate? Naturally, determination of normalcy and abnormalcy must (occasionally) be made, but it is important when making these types of assessments to consider the following:

1. value judgments that may mistakenly interfere
2. the environment in which the person functions
3. who is making the determination and what their motives are (Remember, it is Normals who have defining power. Normals define nonnormals, not the other way around, so it is not a matter of equal differences. "Normal" people, whoever they might be, have power, and "nonnormal" people, whoever they might be, do not have power.)
4. the purpose of the assessment
5. the diagnostic tools, instruments, and classification system used

All five of these considerations are subject to adaptation and revision. We may like to think that our value systems are fixed and unchanging, but societal values do shift, environments evolve, clinicians change their diagnostic criteria and methods, and policymakers pass in and out of power. What is considered to be normal today might not be normal tomorrow (S. C. Brown, 1991; D. W. Smart & J. F. Smart, 1997; J. F. Smart, 2005b).

It is important to understand, especially with intellectual disabilities and mental and emotional disabilities, that the diagnostic instruments and tools and the classification systems are very much linked to the environment or culture in which they are developed and implemented. D. W. Smart and J. F. Smart (1997), for example, studied the *Diagnostic and Statistical Manual of Mental Disorders–Fourth Edition* (DSM-IV) published by the American Psychiatric Association (APA, 1994). The DSM-IV was the classification system used to diagnose psychoses, personality disorders, intellectual disorders, and other types of mental illness. Many professionals are required to render a diagnosis of some sort from the DSM-IV to be paid for services. As described by D. W. Smart and J. F. Smart, the DSM-IV did not take into account the individual's culture or religious or spiritual background. Indeed, Kirk and Kutchins (1992) detailed a highly critical account of the DSM as a *political* rather than a *scientific* classification system.

They labeled the DSM-IV as "lily white" (p. 103), questioning the validity of using DSM diagnoses for people of color. Seem and Hernandez (1997, as cited in Ivey & Ivey, 1998) conducted an analysis of the DSM-IV and determined that more attention should be paid to feminist issues. This is not to advocate that the use of the DSM-IV should have been discontinued. These cautions, however, clearly point out the necessity of a critical awareness that every diagnosis based on DSM criteria always occurs in the broad sociocultural context of the North American culture. As Allen Frances, the chief architect of the APA's Diagnostic and Statistical Manual, DSM–IV, said, "The special features (of the new edition) are . . . elimination of the term 'organic mental disorder' because it incorrectly implied that other psychiatric disabilities did not have a biological contribution" ("Mental Disorders," 2000, para. 9). In other words, it took 42 years for the APA to acknowledge that biological and physical factors contribute to the causality of mental illnesses and other psychiatric disabilities.

Having discussed the most widely used classification system for intellectual disability and mental illness (the DSM), it is important to make a brief statement about the diagnostic tools and instruments used to make these types of diagnoses. Many psychological tests have a "fundamental negative bias" (as cited in H. McCarthy, 1993) in that only pathology is noted and described. Many widely used instruments, such as the *Minnesota Multiphasic Personality Inventory–Second Edition* (MMPI-2; Butcher, Dahlstrom, Graham, Tellegen, & Kaemmer, 2001), tap only negative traits and do not give a picture of the individual's adaptive functioning. Surely, if the tools clinicians use are based on deficit and pathology, disability diagnoses will be given. Further, groups considered to be inferior, such as women, gay men and lesbians, and racial and ethnic minorities, will be given diagnoses of pathology more often than individuals who are not considered inferior.

Finally, the reason why the assessment of normalcy is made is important. We like to think that society is committed to providing the best services for those with disabilities; however, occasionally the considerations of convenience, cost, and the comfort of those without disabilities receive first priority (Hahn, 1988b, 1991). Managed-care reforms, cost-containment efforts, and financial risk-shifting may work together to more narrowly define both disability and normalcy (Vernellia, 1994). It should also be remembered that there are many situations in which such assessments of normal and abnormal are unnecessary and irrelevant.

Both the importance of the determination of *normal* and the difficult questions raised by scientific and medical advances were presented in an article in *The Atlantic* magazine, found in the "Technology" section entitled, "Making Babies: Five Predictions about the Future of Reproduction" (Madrigal, 2014). The following excerpt shows that the concept of *normal* can be expanded or narrowed.

> Here's a final paradox: even as reproductive freedom increases, enabling more types of parents to have children, these parents may choose children who fit a narrower and narrower notion of normal.

A British infertility doctor gave a disturbing preview of where we may be headed. "You start out offering these prenatal screenings for certain conditions that everybody agrees are very severe. It is not particularly eugenic, but about alleviating the suffering of the child and the parents. But there is slippage. The more you can test for and screen out, the more people do. And the example this person gave was the high number of people who will abort a fetus that is found to have an extra digit." (p. 34)

The general discussion of a woman's right to an abortion is not questioned here. What is questioned is the availability of abortions based solely on small, easily treatable conditions (such as an extra finger). It is difficult to foresee the future determination of normal as medicine and science advances.

It is important to discuss the concept of normalcy and abnormalcy early in this book because everything that follows—the categorization of disability, the individual's adjustment to disability, and society's reaction to those with disabilities—will directly relate to these ideas.

Large Classifications and Diagnostic Systems

In the previous section, we discussed the DSM-IV and some of its limitations in order to illustrate the point that judgments and diagnoses of normalcy and abnormalcy are the products of an historical period of time and a particular culture. In 2013, the DSM-5 replaced the DSM-IV-TR (APA, 2000), again redefining mental disorders as both scientific and cultural views changed.

For our purposes, we shall discuss the two standard classification and diagnostic systems used for PWDs. The first is *the International Statistical Classification of Diseases and Related Health Problems, Tenth Revision* (ICD-10) published by the World Health Organization (WHO, 2015) in Geneva, Switzerland. The second system is the *Diagnostic and Statistical Manual of Mental Disorders–Fifth Edition* (DSM-5) published by the APA (2013). Obviously, each of these systems is a serial process, with ongoing revisions. The ICD-10 is the 10th revision, and revision for the 11th edition is underway. The DSM-5 is the fifth edition, with the first edition published in 1952. These ongoing revisions and editions are necessary as medical knowledge becomes more advanced and societal and cultural needs change. However, with each new edition the clinicians who use these systems are required to be trained in its use.

The ICD-10 provides diagnostic codes which are generally organized around specific body systems. For example, F00–F90 is Mental and Behavioural Disorders, G00–G99 is Diseases of the Nervous System, and M00–M99 is Diseases of the Musculoskeletal System and Connective Tissue. Information on level of severity and the cause and source of the condition is part of the diagnostic coding. Medical practitioners use the ICD-10.

In 2001, the WHO published a comprehensive classification system, the *International Classification of Functioning, Disability and Health* (ICF; WHO, 2001). Indeed, the ICF appears to have surmounted many of the conceptual inadequacies of the *International Classification of Impairments, Disabilities, and Handicaps* (or ICIDH, as it was previously known). In Chapter 2, when we discuss the Functional Model of disability, features of the ICF will be presented.

The DSM-5 is a 947-page manual that describes hundreds of mental disorders, used throughout the world, often being referred to as the "bible of psychiatry." Sections include "Neurodevelopmental Disorders," "Schizophrenia Spectrum and Other Psychotic Disorders," "Mood Disorders," and "Anxiety Disorders." The APA noted that, in spite of efforts to be exhaustive, there may be mental disorders that are not listed in the DSM-5.

The fifth edition of the DSM was published after 14 years of debate by medical professionals and is considered to be a "radical shift" rather than an "incremental change." Basically, the DSM-5 has shifted somewhat to a dimensional system, viewing mental disorders as existing on a continuum from mild to severe (rather than in distinct, separate categories); it has eliminated some diagnoses, added diagnoses, and revised some of the names of diagnoses (Dailey, Gill, Karl, & Minton, 2014; Frances, 2013; Morrison, 2014).

Morrison (2014) quoted one of his professors in medical school, who spoke about the then-in-use edition of the DSM, the DSM-III. The professor summarized his judgment of the diagnostic criteria: "The Bible may tell us so, but the criteria don't. They are better than what we had, but they are still a long way from perfect" (p. 15). Morrison concluded, "In the DSM-5, those statements are still true" (p. 15).

Categorizing Disabilities

In this section, look for—

- ✧ Reasons why it is necessary to categorize disabilities:
  - • to provide benefits and services
  - • to allocate resources
  - • to provide diagnoses for third-party payers

- ✧ How labels and diagnoses can be depersonalizing for individuals:
  - • how diagnoses often affect self-image
  - • how categorization can increase prejudice and discrimination
  - • why classification systems may be more useful for administrative purposes than for providing care
  - • the short leap from categorization to stereotyping

Categorization of disabilities is necessary to provide benefits and services to those who need them. Government agencies must design some sort of counting and data collection system to estimate the resources necessary to serve the needs of their mandated populations and also to establish policy (Thompson-Hoffman & Storck, 1991). The determination of eligibility for services and benefits, the agencies from which applicants are allowed to receive services, and the settings in which individuals live (institutions or in the community) are closely related to the categorization of the disability. In the move toward managed care and cost containment (which often includes benefit limitations), the categorization, diagnosis, and definition of disability are important, but complex and detailed. Simply stated, without a diagnosis, third-party payers will not reimburse, nor will government agencies provide, services and benefits (Ivey & Ivey, 1998). Advocacy groups, usually individuals with disabilities, need information in understandable categories to represent their legislative and judicial interests.

Categorization of disabilities also exerts a powerful effect on the type of prejudice and discrimination directed toward individuals with disabilities (Szymanski & Trueba, 1994). The relationship between disability categorization and societal responses will be discussed in a later chapter. Finally, and most importantly, the categorization of the disability affects the self-identity of the individual with the disability, as will be seen in Chapter 5. Professional vocabulary, including diagnoses, often affects self-images of those who are given these diagnoses. Physicians, psychologists, and other clinicians know that a diagnosis describes a condition a person has and not the person himself or herself. However, diagnosis often sculpts the self-image of those who receive the diagnosis. A textbook for nursing students illustrates the effect of a diagnosis on the individual:

> When a veterinarian diagnoses a cow's condition as an illness, he does not merely, by diagnosis, change the cow's behavior . . . but when a physician diagnoses a human's condition as an illness, he changes the man's behavior by diagnosis: a social state is added to a biophysiological state by assigning the meaning. (Lubkin & Larsen, 2006, p. 23)

Furthermore, one disability scholar (E. J. Langer, 1983) found that labels affected the performance of those who received them and, moreover, the clinicians formed their expectations of patients based on the label given. Those individuals who received labels of low competence performed poorly (as expected by their physicians), and those individuals who received labels of high competence performed well. This process is known as a self-fulfilling prophecy (Hannah & Midlarsky, 1987).

Categorization of these diagnoses, while necessary, is also fraught with difficulties, and no classification system truly represents the reality and experience of the individual with the disability. Categorization may lead to false stereotypes, such as the stereotype that all or most individuals with the same disability share important characteristics, experiences, or perceptions (e.g., "Most people who are D/deaf are shy" or, "Most little people are feisty"). It is a short leap from categorization to stereotyping (H. McCarthy, 1993; B. A. Wright, 1991). Also, in theory, these are classifications and categories of disabilities that people experience and not classifications of people themselves. In practice, however, many individuals with disabilities are consigned to categorization. Indeed, to be perceived as a person with a disability is to be immediately, and often incorrectly, categorized (e.g., a rehabilitation counselor who disrespectfully states, "I have four quads on my caseload"). Any categorization scheme tends to emphasize differences *between* categories and emphasizes the similarities *within* categories (Schmelkin, 1988). Furthermore, simply because the focus of most categorization systems is on the disability, the strengths, abilities, assets, and resources of the individual are not considered. Finally, and most importantly, these categorization schemes of disability do not take into account the self-identities of the individuals with disabilities. Two people who experience the same type and severity of disability have differing circumstances, resources, values, interests, and abilities.

An example of the way in which *removing* a diagnostic category affects the self-identity is shown in the case of John Elder Robison, who had been diagnosed with Asperger's syndrome. Robison had felt such relief in his diagnosis of Asperger's, in his words, finding "tribal solidarity with other Aspies," after years of isolation and loneliness. However, in the fifth edition of the DSM, the APA eliminated the diagnosis of Asperger's. In the following excerpt, Robison compared the APA to "corrupt referees":

> For John Elder Robison, the revision amounts to an abrupt and unwelcome assault on an all-important identity. "Just like that, Asperger's was gone," he wrote in an essay on *New York* magazine's Web site. "You can do things like that when you publish the rules. Like corrupt referees at a rigged college football game, the APA removed Asperger's from the field of play and banished the term to the locker room of psychiatric oblivion." Robison, who grew up feeling under siege in a deeply dysfunctional family in the 1960s, champions the label and the tribal protection it offers in a "neurotypical" world that he is sure will always stigmatize and misunderstand people like him—and his son. (Rosin, 2014, para. 1)

Everyone has multiple identities, and for people with disabilities, the disability is only one aspect of their identity. Finally, the diagnosis may not fit the individual's self-concept, and these individuals may be surprised or resentful that they are considered to have a particular diagnosis. In summary, having explained (a) the necessity for categorization and (b) the effects of categorization, it is important to emphasize that categories are only abstractions and never can fully describe or capture anyone's reality.

Although there is no one universally accepted categorization of disabilities, the most widely accepted categorization is organized by the symptoms and manifestations of disabilities and not by the cause (etiology) or the source (pathogenesis) of the disability. For example, schizophrenia is considered to be a psychiatric disability, but if disabilities were categorized according to etiology, schizophrenia, and many other mental illnesses, would be considered a physical disability because it has been shown that many mental illnesses are caused by physical factors. Defining or categorizing disability by the etiology or pathogenesis would be difficult because (a) for many disabilities, such as mental illness, the cause is not known; (b) for some disabilities, there are multiple causes (Kiesler, 1999); (c) clinicians may change their hypotheses concerning the cause of a specific disability; and (d) for some disabilities, the same treatments might apply, regardless of cause. It should also be noted that while professionals know that diagnoses do not carry any implications about cause, many nonprofessionals—including individuals who are given these diagnoses—are unaware that most diagnoses are based only on symptoms and other clinical features, saying nothing about possible causes. Certainly, the categorization of disabilities by their symptoms, whether they are physical, intellectual, cognitive, or psychiatric, has the longest history in both medicine and the social sciences. An advantage of this categorization system is the treatment and management plans that result from looking at the course, type, and severity of symptoms. Notwithstanding the present wide acceptance of categorization of disabilities by their symptoms, efforts to refine these classification systems continue. This book will use this categorization of disabilities according to symptoms, unless otherwise noted.

Thus, there are three broad categories of disability—physical, neurocognitive, and psychiatric—all of which are based on symptoms. Individuals with physical disabilities experience physical symptoms; those with neurocognitive disabilities have cognitive manifestations; and psychiatric symptoms are present in those individuals who have been diagnosed as having a psychiatric disability. Many individuals have more than one disability, and, in these cases, one disability is typically labeled the "primary" disability, the other disabilities are labeled "secondary," and so on.

Injuries may or may not result in disabilities. If, after medical stabilization, there are no limitations or impairments, then the individual is not considered to have a disability. However, many injuries do result in life-long, chronic disabilities. Therefore, breaking a leg skiing, which heals completely, would not be considered a disability, either legally or clinically. However, an injury that severs the spinal cord and results in paralysis would be considered a disability.

Physical Disabilities

Physical disabilities include mobility impairments; neurological impairments, such as cerebral palsy and seizure disorders; traumatic brain injuries; musculoskeletal conditions, such as muscular dystrophy; and arthritis, sensory loss, and health disorders. Most people are surprised to learn that many experts consider arthritis to be the most frequently occurring disability in the United States (LaPlante, 1991, 1993, 1996, 1997). In Chapter 3, the societal prejudice, discrimination, and stigma directed toward individuals with disabilities will be discussed, and we will see that of the three broad neurodevelopmental categories of disabilities (physical, neurocognitive, and psychiatric), individuals with physical disabilities experience the least amount of prejudice and discrimination. Because government policymakers are subject to the same flawed human perceptions as the general public, we will learn that individuals with intellectual, cognitive, and psychiatric disabilities were not declared eligible for government funding for benefits and services long after those with physical disabilities. Tragically, intellectual, cognitive, and psychiatric disabilities were not considered to be disabilities until the 20th century. The longer history of service provision and allotment of resources to individuals with physical disabilities has resulted in the development of more professional experience and knowledge in dealing with physical disabilities (DeJong & Lifchez, 1983). This longer history of self-identification has resulted in stronger advocacy groups, such as the National Federation for the Blind (NFB), established in 1940.

Physical disabilities lend themselves to objective, quantifiable diagnoses, often with standardized laboratory procedures. In contrast, the diagnosis of intellectual, cognitive, or psychiatric disabilities requires more subjective, impressionistic, clinical judgment. Indeed, some disability advocates regard many psychiatric diagnoses as thinly veiled moral judgments (Szasz, 1961). The most clear-cut illustration of a diagnosis of pathology (not a disability) reflecting society's moral judgment is outlined in Clendinen and Nagourney's (1999) book, *Out for Good: The Struggle To Build a Gay Rights Movement in America*. The authors devote a chapter to describing the struggle to remove homosexuality as a diagnosis of pathology from the APA's *Diagnostic and Statistical Manual of Mental Disorders*.

Mobility Impairments

Mobility impairments interfere with one's movement and coordination. Examples of such impairments are spina bifida; cerebral palsy; spinal cord injuries; paraplegia; quadriplegia; muscular dystrophy; and amputations, including congenital limb deficiencies.

Many of these conditions are the result of heredity; others occur before or during birth; and still others occur because of injury or infection. For example, the single largest cause of amputation in the United States is therapeutic surgical procedures necessitated by complications and secondary infections resulting from diabetes. Spinal cord injuries, which often result in paraplegia (paralysis of the lower limbs) or quadriplegia (paralysis of all four limbs and the trunk), are caused by automobile accidents, falls, gunshot wounds, and stabbing, among others. More than 80% of individuals with spinal cord injuries are male. Thus, spinal cord injuries are the only physical disability that is more prevalent among one sex.

Mobility impairments are visible to others, and many individuals with these conditions also experience other disabilities, such as hearing loss, intellectual deficits, and general perceptual difficulties. Some mobility impairments, such as muscular dystrophy, will eventually result in death, but most are stabilized after the acute phase.

Visual Impairments

Visual impairments include total blindness from birth; the gradual loss of vision; muscular disorders, such as strabismus, or "crossed eyes"; and loss of acuity across the visual field, such as tunnel vision. People who wear eyeglasses or contact lenses are not considered to have a visual impairment, simply because the use of a common and easily obtainable device, such as eyeglasses, restores the individual to full functioning. Indeed, to be considered a visual impairment, the condition must be severe enough to limit daily functioning. Degenerative conditions, affecting the retina or optic nerve, include retinitis pigmentosa, retinal detachment, and glaucoma (Carroll, 1961). Visual impairments may also be caused by genetic factors, such as malformations, or may be acquired from infections, inflammations, accidents, or tumors (Panek, 1992). However, a large percentage of visual impairments have unknown causes. LaPlante (1991) estimated that approximately 1.5 million individuals of all ages have visual impairments.

The age distribution of visual impairments is different from that of other disabilities inasmuch as these impairments occur, for the most part, at the beginning of life (before the age of 1 year) or at the end of life (after the age of 70 years). Indeed, it is estimated that 60% of all visual impairments occur before the age of 1. Two factors that, in the past, led to thousands of cases of blindness in newborn infants have now been virtually eliminated. These two factors are maternal rubella and excess oxygen administered to premature infants, which resulted in retrolental fibroplasia. The rubella vaccine and incubators introduced in the 1960s, which control the amount of oxygen, have almost eliminated these causes of blindness. However, many adults born before the 1960s experienced lifelong blindness as a result of these two causes.

There is a larger percentage of visual impairments than ever before in the United States because of the larger percentage of elderly people. The prevalence of visual impairments is positively correlated with age, and as the population ages, the number of people with visual impairments increases. Advances in medicine and medical technology have greatly decreased the number of infants born with blindness and yet have also indirectly increased the number of elderly individuals who are blind. Because medical advances have lengthened the life span of elderly individuals, they now survive with disabilities, many of which are visual impairments.

Individuals with visual impairments, especially those who have been blind since birth, often have been educated in specialized residential schools. Although these residential schools are being replaced with specialized programs in regular schools, there are many adults today who were educated in these segregated schools. Most people with other types of disabilities, except for hearing impairments and intellectual disabilities, were not educated in schools that required them to live apart from their families. Before the advent of special education programs in the public schools, parents had little choice other than to send their children to boarding schools that were equipped with the educational resources, including teachers, to help their children reach their academic potential. Nonetheless, the emotional cost—for the child sent to school, for the parents, and for the siblings—was high. In Chapter 2 we will discuss the effects of segregation on the individual and the costs to society of segregating groups.

Historically, people who are blind have been viewed as receiving preferential treatment (Berkowitz, 1987) inasmuch as more services and benefits have been accorded to them. Individuals with visual impairments, as a group, have been the beneficiaries of legislation that offered services exclusively to those who are blind. The original Social Security Act allowed only those who were blind to qualify for public assistance (welfare), and today, individuals who are blind automatically qualify for Social Security benefits. The Randolph-Sheppard Act allowed only people who were blind to operate vending stands in federal buildings, and the Wagner O'Day Act of 1938 required the federal government to purchase products produced in workshops by people who are blind. No other disability group has had legislation and policy written exclusively for it. An additional example of this exclusivity is seen in the box on federal income tax forms where taxpayers can indicate if they are blind. Most states (approximately 32) have separate agencies for individuals who are blind. (People with all other types of disabilities are served by a single agency—Vocational Rehabilitation.)

Hearing Impairments

Most people have viewed closed-captioned television programs and watched sign language interpreters at meetings and in the classroom, and many have had to make accommodations for elderly relatives and friends with hearing loss. Indeed, according to Livneh and Antonak (1997), hearing impairments are among the most prevalent types of physical disability in the United States. Because of their prevalence, then, individuals with hearing impairments have achieved a measure of visibility and integration within the broader American culture.

Hearing loss is measured in decibels, but in defining the exact level of loss, two other factors are considered: age of onset and site of the loss. Prelingual D/deafness occurs before the individual develops speech, usually before the age of 2 years, and postlingual D/deafness occurs after the age of 2. Obviously, the functional limitations of prelingual D/deafness are greater than those of postlingual D/deafness because with the latter, the individual usually has the capacity to speak. The site of the loss often determines treatment, such as surgery or the use of hearing aids. Estimates of the prevalence of hearing loss in the United States are as high as 28 million people, or 11% of the population.

The cause of more than 25% of all hearing loss is unknown. Nonetheless, hearing impairments are often the result of many known conditions, which are divided into two broad categories: congenital and acquired. Congenital, meaning existing at birth, includes hereditary factors, such as those that cause otosclerosis, and prenatal disease, such as rubella. Acquired hearing loss includes postnatal infections, such as scarlet fever, measles, mumps, influenza, typhoid fever, meningitis, and otitis media. As would be expected, the development of antibiotics has greatly decreased the number of individuals with postlingual D/deafness (Higgins, 1992a). Environmental factors, such as physical abuse and exposure to prolonged loud noise, can also cause hearing loss.

The presence of hearing loss in a child often requires parents to make important decisions early in the child's life. The type of education, the means of communication, and the use of technology, such as cochlear implants and hearing aids, are decisions that will have lifelong effects, yet these decisions must be made early on, when the child is too young to be accorded a great deal of input.

Nonetheless, many individuals with hearing impairments and D/deafness consider themselves to be part of a different culture—D/deaf Culture—claiming individual identity as members of a linguistic culture, rather than as individuals with a disability (Bauman & Drake, 1997; Stokoe, Croneberg, & Casterline, 1965; Van Cleve & Crouch, 1989). Individuals in no other disability category consider themselves to be a different culture. Those who advocate for the identification of a D/deaf Culture cite the use of a different language, American Sign Language (ASL), and the fact that individuals who are D/deaf tend to marry other individuals who are deaf. The fact that many of these individuals were educated at residential schools may also contribute to their self-identity as a separate culture. Certainly, their unwillingness to accept "the disabled role" of impairment, deviance, and inferiority plays a large part in the D/deaf Culture movement. The impetus for D/deaf Culture came from within the group of people who are D/deaf and was motivated, for the most part, by the need for solidarity and mutual support. In addition, many D/deaf Culture scholars assert that it is impossible to understand the motivations behind the D/deaf Culture without understanding the tragic history of oralism, in which D/deaf children were not allowed to use sign language and were forced to use oral communication (speaking). Alexander Graham Bell, the inventor of the telephone, was a teacher of D/deaf children, an oralist, and a eugenicist. Although he believed that D/deaf people should be allowed to live, Bell did not believe that D/deaf people should be allowed to marry and have children. In Bell's time, it was not widely known that most D/deaf parents have hearing children.

D/deaf Culture does not view D/deafness as pathology or disability. Jankowski (1997), in her book, *Deaf Empowerment: Emergence, Struggle and Rhetoric*, emphasized that those in the D/deaf Culture have been opposed to cochlear implants, devices that have the capability to restore some hearing. Jankowski told of a hearing mother in Canada who claimed the right to have her D/deaf child implanted with this device, giving her reason as "it would make him more like her, a hearing person." A former Ontario legislator, Gary Malkowski, replied, "Then you presumably have no objection to D/deaf parents requesting surgery to make their hearing child D/deaf" (Jankowski, 1997, p. 145). The D/deaf Culture, at its most extreme, refuses services, accommodations, and cochlear implants and did not support the passage of the Americans With Disabilities Act (ADA).

Acceptance into the D/deaf Culture can be narrowly defined. Heather Whitestone, Miss America of 1995, is D/deaf. Whitestone's parents insisted that she learn to speak, and, therefore, she was not fluent in American Sign Language. Ironically, in 1992,

Ms. Whitestone competed in the Miss Deaf Alabama competition, "where she was trounced because . . . [she was] unable to fully understand the ASL of the interviewer (or the judges)—and their inability to understand her ironically 'handicapped' Whitestone . . . (Burch, 2007, p. 255). As Whitestone wrote in her autobiography, "Just because I spoke . . . they [Miss Deaf Alabama pageant officials] decided that I could not fit into the deaf culture, that I was not an 'ideal' deaf person" (Burch, 2007, p. 255). So, while Whitestone was not considered "deaf enough" in the D/deaf Culture, the Miss America Pageant considered her to be D/deaf.

Dual Sensory Loss: D/deaf–Blindness

As would be expected, individuals who are both D/deaf and blind experience severe communication deficits. Another obstacle to the education and rehabilitation of individuals who are D/deaf–blind is the fact that this type of disability is a low-incidence category. Simply because there are so few people whose disabilities fall within this category, it is difficult to provide services and benefits. A biographer of Helen Keller explained the disability of D/deaf–blindness:

> Today, relatively few deaf-blind people suffer [*sic*] from Helen Keller's condition—that is, being completely deaf and blind from an early age. The life-threatening childhood infections such as meningitis and scarlet fever have been for the most part eradicated, and the simultaneous onset of blindness and deafness seldom occurs. . . . In general, deafness precedes blindness. Today 50 percent of the deaf-blind population suffer [*sic*] from Usher syndrome, a genetic condition characterized by hearing loss and by retinitis pigmentosa, an irreversible condition causing . . . eventual total blindness in middle age. (Herrmann, 1998, p. 340)

As with simple D/deafness or blindness, time of onset has an important impact on the functional limitations of the individual, and learning to speak is a difficult task for these people. D/deaf children were often educated in residential schools, far from their homes. Communication is an overriding issue. Helen Keller, probably the most well-known person with dual sensory loss, reported a lifetime of difficulty in distinguishing between her own ideas and the ideas of others because most of what she learned she received literally "secondhand." Information was finger-spelled into her hand (Herrmann, 1998).

Health Disorders and Chronic Illness

Health disorders such as diabetes, seizure disorders, multiple sclerosis, hemophilia, sickle cell anemia, AIDS, and cystic fibrosis are considered to be disabilities because they limit functioning; require treatment, care, and management; and often cause individuals with these conditions to be the target of discrimination and prejudice. However, health disorders are different from sensory loss or orthopaedic disabilities in some important aspects. For example, some health disorders are invisible, and thus the individual must balance the costs of disclosure against the need for accommodation (Livneh & Antonak, 1997). Some health disorders, such as diabetes, are asymptomatic, and the individual may not be aware that he or she has the disorder. Indeed, some health disorders may be somewhat "invisible" to the individual who has the condition because when symptoms subside, the individual may no longer continue treatment or management, feeling that he or she no longer has the condition. Lifelong management needs and quality-of-life issues are important to individuals with health disorders. The terminal course of some health disorders (meaning the individual will eventually die from the disorder or complications from the disorder) renders these disabilities different from other disabilities that are stable. Another difference in course or progression of the disability is the episodic nature of many health disorders. Relapses, seizures, or flare-ups are often unpredictable and frequently are exacerbated by stress. So, at the exact time when the individual wants to be symptom-free, such as for job interviews or in social situations, stress may help to bring on an episode of the health disorder.

Neurodevelopmental Disabilities

Cognitive disabilities impair perception, memory, information processing, reasoning, sensory discrimination (auditory and visual), and attention. Neurodevelopmental disabilities can impair all of these cognitive functions but differ from late-onset dementia or Alzheimer's because symptoms appear in the individual's early developmental period. Nonetheless, all of these disabilities are considered to be lifelong conditions, and individuals do not outgrow these disabilities. Indeed, some health demographers believe that the majority of individuals with Autism Spectrum Disorder (ASD) are adults because their numbers have progressively grown as people age over the lifespan.

As stated previously, these disabilities are grouped together because of their similar symptoms or manifestations, yet the range of these symptoms is broad. Government funding for education and services for individuals with intellectual disabilities was initiated only recently. Special education in neighborhood schools began in the 1970s (Hardman, Drew, Egan, & Wolf, 1993). Therefore, today there are many adults with these types of disabilities born before these changes who either remained at home in the care of the family or were institutionalized. Now, there are both community services and specialized education in community schools for individuals with these disabilities, allowing the majority to live at home with their families while they receive an education.

It is estimated that approximately 6 million people in the United States (3% of the population) can be classified as having intellectual disability, with 90% of these classified as having a mild intellectual disability (Joseph P. Kennedy, Jr. Foundation, 1991). Intellectual disability is more than seven times as prevalent as blindness or D/deafness and 10 times as prevalent as physical disabilities. Causes of intellectual disabilities include maternal infection during pregnancy, most often congenital rubella or fetal alcohol syndrome; birth trauma (most often lack of oxygen); postnatal infections such as encephalitis or metabolic problems that result in the body's inability to process certain substances; and chromosomal abnormalities.

Learning disabilities are different from intellectual disabilities; most people with learning disabilities have average or above-average intellectual abilities. The first indication that a child may have a learning disability usually occurs when parents or teachers notice a discrepancy between the child's achievement in school and his or her measured intelligence or potential. The child with a learning disability scores lower on achievement tests than his or her classmates, but also scores lower than would be expected given his or her assessed level of intelligence or potential (i.e., IQ scores). These discrepancies are a result of the fact that school achievement tests, on subjects such as spelling, arithmetic, and handwriting, require skill and facility in the cognitive areas of perception, visual discrimination, auditory discrimination, and information processing (Houck, 1984). Often, individuals with learning disabilities are clumsy, are unable to distinguish their right from their left, have no sense of direction, transpose numbers, are unable to distinguish between sounds of different words, and have poor handwriting skills.

Once considered to be a disability that an individual outgrew or, at a minimum, to be a disability only in academic settings, learning disabilities are now known to be lifelong impairments (Johnston, 1987). It is difficult for adults to totally avoid tasks that require reading, writing, or math skills, and, furthermore, the individual knows that he or she is intelligent but is unable to explain his or her difficulties in academic areas (even to himself or herself). Often, spouses of adults with learning disabilities undertake the financial responsibilities for the family and all other family tasks that require writing and math. Also, adults with learning disabilities are frequently underemployed, meaning they work in jobs that do not utilize their full potential.

Hypotheses of the causation generally fall into two categories: neurological causes or genetic causes. Damage to the central nervous system, usually occurring at birth, such as anoxia or abnormal fetal position, or infections are thought to be associated with learning disabilities. Genetic abnormalities are also thought to be linked to learning disabilities. Traumatic brain injuries can be caused by accidents, strokes, or infections. Traumatic brain injuries are the leading cause of death and disability among children and adolescents; these injuries occur most frequently to individuals aged 15 to 24 years. Of those who sustain traumatic brain injuries, 80% are male.

Psychiatric Disabilities

Psychiatric disabilities, the disability category that was the last to receive government funding for services and benefits, includes mental illness and chemical and substance abuse. The disabilities in this category are often viewed by the general public as self-imposed and being caused, or at least exaggerated, by the individual's lack of character or willpower.

Indeed, more than any other disability group, the families of individuals with psychiatric disabilities are often blamed for the disability. The combination of societal stigma and a short history of government funding for services renders the category of psychiatric disabilities vulnerable to reduction in social services and discontinuity of care.

Mental illness includes schizophrenia, delusional disorders, bipolar affective disorders, major depression, and anxiety and panic disorders (APA, 2013). The treatment of mental illness underwent a dramatic shift with the introduction of psychotropic medications. Before the introduction of these medications, individuals with severe psychoses were institutionalized for decades; many individuals lived in institutions for their entire lives. Medications, although certainly not without problems, triggered the deinstitutionalization movement and allowed many of these former patients to integrate into the community. Perhaps even more important than community integration, the success of psychotropic medication has "humanized" the disability, helping the general public to understand the role of organic and biological factors in the causation of these mental illnesses (Deegan, 1997).

Does Everyone Have a Disability of Some Sort?

In this section, look for—

- ✧ the Americans With Disabilities Act definition of disability
- ✧ how *disadvantage* is not *disability*
- ✧ examples of perceived disabilities

The answer to the question "Does everyone have a disability of some sort?" will affect an individual's self-concept, determine funding and benefits for government services, and assist individuals without disabilities to better understand those who do have disabilities. It is often stated that everyone has limitations, challenges, and problems. This is true. However, disadvantage is not disability. The American with Disabilities Act (ADA, 1990) clearly defined disability by providing three general guidelines, all of which are necessary to complete the definition: (a) the presence of a physical, cognitive, intellectual, or psychiatric condition, or a combination of conditions; (b) pervasive impairment in social and occupational functioning; and (c) individuals with these impairments are the target of prejudice, discrimination, stigma, and reduced opportunities. So, it can be seen that disability is a combination of the condition, limitations in functioning, and societal prejudice and discrimination.

Are prejudice and discrimination always inherent in the definition of disability? Societal negative response to individuals with disabilities will be discussed in detail in Chapter 3. However, the example of facial disfigurement will illustrate this relationship. There are no functional limitations in many individuals with facial disfigurements, but, not surprisingly, these disabilities are among the most limiting simply because of the marked reaction of others to the individual with the disfigurement. So, in spite of the fact that the individual has no functional limitations, he or she is often not employed and lives a life of isolation and reduced opportunity. "Perceived" disabilities, such as obesity and stuttering, usually do not involve functional limitations, but individuals who experience these conditions are subject to reduced opportunity, prejudice, and discrimination. The ADA provides protection to people who are "*regarded* as having a disability." Other well-documented examples of visible physical conditions leading to reduced opportunities are lack of height for boys and men and obesity for girls and women. Looking at the newspaper article that described a lon-

GIRLS' WEIGHT, BOYS' HEIGHT AFFECT EARNING POWER

CHICAGO (AP)—Obese teenage girls and short teenage boys make less money when they become young adults than others their age, a study of thousands of British youths found.

The study doesn't indicate whether the culprit is discrimination or some internal factor such as low self-esteem, but it suggests appearance can have a big effect on teens' transition from school to work, the research said in the July issue of the *Archives of Pediatrics and Adolescent Medicine*.

Dr. James D. Sargent, lead author of the study, said obesity needs to be prevented by teaching children to eat properly. But he said he is also concerned that women are starving themselves or purging to achieve the ideal of thinness prized in British and U.S. society.

Previous studies, including a recent survey of more than 10,000 Americans ages 16 to 24, found that overweight people, especially women, are far less likely to get married or make a comfortable living when they get older.

Dr. William H. Dietz, who led that study, said that the new work "provides once again pretty compelling evidence that obesity is a major social handicap as well as physical handicap."

He said it matters little whether discrimination or factors such as low self-esteem were behind the findings, because both result from societal attitudes.

The new study looked at 12,537 people in England, Scotland, and Wales, where all children born between March 3 and 9, 1958, were enrolled in a national child development study and have been tracked ever since.

The study found that girls in the heaviest 10 percent of their age group at age 16 earned 7.4 percent less than their non-obese peers by the time they reached 23, and those in the heaviest 1 percent earned 11.4 percent less at age 23.

For boys, obesity did not appear to affect earnings, but height did. For every four inches less height at age 16, boys earned 2 percent less at age 23, the researchers found.

Exhibit 1.1

gitudinal study in Great Britain (B. C. Coleman, 1994; see Exhibit 1.1), it can be seen that, over their lifetimes, short men and overweight women earned less money. Therefore, individuals with both of these physical traits, the majority of whom experience no functional limitations, fight long-standing prejudice and discrimination. Many of these individuals, as high school students, probably did not get dates for the prom and then continued to be devalued through their lifetimes. This study quantifies the devaluation in terms of lifetime salaries. For the individuals whose daily lives were summarized, categorized, and interpreted in this study, the low salaries and the lack of occupational success and opportunities are probably less hurtful than the social discrimination and alienation they have been forced to endure. There is an interesting aspect to the prejudice and discrimination directed toward height and weight in that the prejudice seems to be gender-specific. Lack of height among women is not generally considered as negative (short women are described by the positive term "petite"), and obesity in men is more accepted by the general public than obesity in women. Men who are overweight are described by such positive terms as *stocky* or *husky*.

Another clear-cut example of a disability with few, if any, functional limitations is provided by Shapiro (1993) in his book, *No Pity*. Shapiro told the story of Paul Steven Miller, a top graduate of Harvard Law School and a dwarf. Miller was told by a law firm in Philadelphia that, although the firm was impressed with his credentials, they would not hire Mr. Miller, because clients, on meeting Mr. Miller, would, in the words of the interviewer, "think we're running some sort of circus freak show" (p. 28). Miller was the Commissioner of the Equal Employment Opportunity Commission (EEOC) in Washington, DC, for 10 years.

Also, a severe case of flu is not comparable to the experience of a disability. Although the flu can limit an individual's activities and is an unpleasant and painful episode, it is not a long-term condition. Furthermore, people who have or have had the flu or similar illness are not the target of prejudice and discrimination, and finally, a bout with the flu has little effect on a person's self-identity. Extreme fear of speaking in public is certainly a limitation, but it is not considered to be a disability, because, in addition to the difficulty in documenting a physical condition, people with stage fright experience little functional impairment because they can simply avoid the need to speak in public. Disadvantage is not a disability.

There Are More Disabilities Than Ever Before

In this section, look for—

✦ how medical and societal advances have eliminated some disabilities and reduced the rates of other types of disabilities

✦ how society enacts laws to reduce the rate of disability

✦ how it is common knowledge that it is best (for society and the individual) to avoid acquiring a disability

Certainly there have been societal advances that have eliminated some disabilities and reduced the number of other types of disabilities. Workplace safety, public sanitation, and more widely available health insurance are all examples of societal advances that have reduced the number of disabilities. Large-scale epidemics, such as polio epidemics, have been eradicated in the Western, developed world; however, there are probably more disabilities caused by recreational and sports injuries than in the past. Wars continue to produce disabilities, and, indeed, the combat survival rates continue to climb along with the disability rate.

Governments enact laws, such as seatbelt and helmet laws and laws that prohibit driving while drunk, to prevent disabilities (and deaths). Some citizens view these laws as infringements on personal freedom; nonetheless, most citizens understand that costs for most disabilities are paid from the public purse (insurance and government support).

Challenges in Counting Disabilities

In this section, look for—

    ✧ why there is no single uniform definition of disability

    ✧ why each government agency defines disability a little differently

    ✧ why medical organizations, such as the World Health Organization (WHO) and the American Psychiatric Association (APA) define disability differently than government agencies do

    ✧ why all government censuses of numbers of PWDs are underestimations of the true number

There is no uniform definition of disability because government agencies define disability differently (Zola, 1993). Further clouding the picture is the fact that some health demographers (people who count and categorize the number of health conditions and disabilities) do not define disability as completely as do rehabilitation demographers. For example, while rehabilitation demographers define alcohol abuse and learning disorders as disabilities, health demographers do not. Finally, rehabilitation demographers are also concerned about health conditions such as obesity, diabetes, and hypertension, which, if not defined as disabilities, are disposing factors that lead to disability.

Some federal programs such as the Social Security Disability Insurance (SSDI) and Supplemental Security Income (SSI) define disability in terms of activity limitations, either in major life activities or work limitations. This functional limitation definition of a disability, especially with regard to work limitations, is economically motivated. Children younger than age 16 and individuals older than age 65 are not typically included in these surveys, because they are thought to be excused from work. Medical organizations and the diagnostic manuals they produce, such as the ICD-10 and the DSM-5 define disabilities in terms of pathology, losses, disorders, impairments, defects, and abnormalities in physical, psychological, or anatomical structure or function.

A disability scholar, Walkup (2000), viewed the "definitional diversity" of disability as necessary and as an ascendant trajectory because when both professionals and the public understand the various factors in the definition of disability, deeper understandings will result. Rather than simply viewing disability as a physical impairment, disability is now defined much more broadly, taking interactional factors, such as the environment and the individual's resources, into account. Walkup pointed out that more consistent, standardized communication among professionals, policymakers, and the public is "no mere 'housekeeping' task":

> Although not posing any problem in principle, standardization of concepts and measures is no mere "housekeeping" task. Definitional diversity is partly maintained because, even under the best of circumstances, extensive amounts of hard thought and labor are required to operationalize a concept. Moreover, even when all parties can agree that new concepts or measures are needed, disability definitions carry consequences for agencies, professionals, advocates, and politicians. (Walkup, 2000, p. 411)

There is no way to know the exact number of disabilities. Surveys are a major undertaking, both expensive and time-consuming. It is necessary to design and develop a questionnaire, implement accurate sampling procedures, and create interviewing and coding procedures. Field testing of procedures is lengthy and expensive. Data analysis is complex. However, there are surveys that seek to learn the number and types of disabilities. There are three major sources of federal data, and, although none of these sources allows for a determination of causality, all three surveys have different purposes (Thompson-Hoffman & Storck, 1991). The goals of some of these survey programs are simply to gather economic and social data on the *entire* population and include some questions about disability. The goal of the second type of national survey is to collect data on the health status of all Americans, and we have seen that health demographers define disability differently than disability programs do. The goal of the third type of national survey is to assess the number of individuals who are receiving benefits and services from federal disability agencies and programs; therefore, only recipients are surveyed. Obviously, there are many PWDs who are not recipients of services; therefore, these types of surveys would grossly underestimate the number of disabilities. Advocacy groups (nonprofit, consumer-driven groups that typically represent one type of disability) use government survey data because such groups would not have the resources to undertake large-scale national surveys.

In addition to the logistical challenges of collecting data, the prevalence of disability is underreported because some disabilities are still considered to be stigmatizing and individuals are reluctant to report family members who have these disabilities. In addition, there are many individuals who have disabilities, such as learning disabilities, but are not aware that they do, in fact, have a disability.

Six Reasons for Increases in Disability Rates

In this section, look for—

❖ The six reasons why there are more disabilities than ever before:

1. advances in neonatal medicine

2. advances in emergency medicine and trauma care

3. aging of the population

4. longer life spans of PWDs

5. liberalization and expansion of the definition of disability

6. more accurate counting

❖ The increase in disability is progress—both for individuals with disabilities and society.

It is probably safe to assume that the narrow definitions and the lack of consistency among agencies and different demographic methods result in underestimations and underreporting of the prevalence of disability. Nonetheless, it is widely understood that the higher rates of disability result from the six factors explained in the following section (Jones, Sanford, & Bell, 1997; H. S. Kaye, LaPlante, Carlson, & Wenger, 1997; Pope & Tarlov, 1991).

Considering only disability costs:

in the United States, annual disability costs have doubled in the past 10 years to approximately $23 billion a year. During this time, the number of beneficiaries of public disability income support has increased by 57% from 4 million to 5.3 million citizens. (Kouzis & Eaton, 2000, p. 908)

Advances in Neonatal Medicine

There are more congenital disabilities (disabilities present at birth) than ever before as a result of the capabilities of neonatal medicine to sustain life. Neonatal medicine is a specialty that concerns itself with newborn infants. Infants who in the past would have died now undergo treatment in the uterus and receive better monitoring and care during the birth process and advanced treatment during the first few months of life. As a result, more babies are born, and more babies live, with cerebral palsy, spina bifida, and intellectual disabilities. In a cover article, *Time* magazine (Kluger, 2014) described neonatal intensive care units (NICUs) in large metropolitan hospitals as "round-the-clock SWAT teams of nearly 300 nutritionists, pulmonary specialists, surgeons, nurses, and dieticians and, for when the need arises, a pair of chaplains" (p. 26).

In 2012, the American Academy of Pediatrics standardized the requirements of NICUs, specifying the sophisticated equipment necessary and the professionals of differing subspecialties needed to care for preemies. Currently, there are four levels of NICUs: Levels 1–4. Forty weeks of gestation is considered to be full-term, and the earlier the birth occurs, the smaller the baby. Smaller and smaller preemies are surviving today, and the smaller and earlier the infant, the greater the possibility of developmental delays and vision, hearing, cardiac, and respiratory problems as children and adults (Kluger, 2014, p. 28). This does not mean that all preemies who survive have lifelong disabilities; nonetheless, studies how shown that intellectual disabilities among preemies increase anywhere from 1.4 fold to 22 fold. Kluger (2014) summarized:

> Stanford University researchers recently found that people born prematurely stand a 38% greater risk of dying in young adulthood than full-terms, typically from heart problems. University of Rhode Island studies found a 32% greater risk of asthma and vision problems. Overall, about 66% of preemies born before 27 weeks have some kind of disability at age 3, and many may never recover. (p. 31)

Today, it is commonplace for infants as small as 1.5 pounds to survive. The increasing number of births to teenage mothers also contributes to greater incidence of congenital disabilities because teenage mothers have higher rates of babies who are premature or have low birthweight, or both (Himmelstein, Woolhandler, & Wolfe, 1992). Medical advances and technology, such as fertility enhancement, have brought about multiple births. This increased prevalence of multiple births has also augmented the number of congenital disabilities. For example, there is a fourfold increase in the probability of an infant having cerebral palsy if the infant is part of a multiple birth. The strides of neonatology have resulted in higher rates of cerebral palsy, intellectual disability, and spina bifida.

Advances in Emergency Medicine and Trauma Care

The Vietnam War was a great impetus to the development of emergency medicine and trauma care; the larger medical community incorporated these military methods of evacuating people with injuries and providing trauma care while en route to the hospital. As a result of these advances, victims of accidents or trauma experience high survival rates because they are evacuated from the scene quickly, treated, and stabilized while being transported to a hospital. Fewer individuals die before they reach the hospital. In 1980, for example, fewer than 10% of individuals with traumatic brain injury or spinal cord injuries survived. Today, the survival rate for individuals with these disabilities is higher than 90%.

The Vietnam War was a defining point in emergency medicine, just as World War II introduced the widespread use of antibiotics to save lives. In Gawande's book, *Better: A Surgeon's Note on Performance* (2007), the author, who is a civilian surgeon, asked military medical personnel how they were able to save so many lives. Dr. Gawande gave his opinion on the reasons for the success of military medicine:

> I asked everyone I met who had worked on medical teams in the war. And what they described revealed an intriguing effort to do something we in civilian medicine do spottily at best: to make a science of performance, to investigate and improve how well they use the knowledge and technologies they already have at hand. The doctors told me of simple, almost banal changes that produced enormous improvements. (pp. 55–56)

Examples included faster transport of wounded soldiers to hospitals. In World War II, it took 11 hours to evacuate soldiers to hospitals; in Vietnam, with helicopter transport, evacuation time was reduced to under an hour, thus increasing survival rates, but increasing disability rates. Since World War II, the ratio of wounded soldiers to soldiers who died has increased. This means that for every soldier killed, higher numbers survive, but many of these survivors will live with a lifelong disability. According to the *Christian Science Monitor* (Knickerbocker, 2006), citing a University of Pennsylvania study, 24% of American troops died in Vietnam, compared to 13% in Iraq and Afghanistan.

Another innovation, resulting from the war in Afghanistan and the Gulf Wars, is the advances in artificial limbs. In these wars, body armor and flak jackets were used to protect the trunk of the body. These protections saved soldiers' lives; but, due to blast injuries, many soldiers survived with limb amputations. The military pushed the prostheses industry to produce more technologically useful, lightweight artificial limbs, which improved the lives of both military veterans and civilians. Advances in military medicine lead to advances in civilian medicine as the progress in emergency medicine shows. Fewer individuals die at the site of their accident, but they often survive with a disability due to innovations and success of military medicine.

Aging of the Population

It is clear that as an individual ages, he or she has a greater probability of acquiring a disability, most often a chronic illness. It is also clear that as a large proportion of a population ages, such as is occurring in the United States presently, the population becomes more disabled. Two social workers summarized the aging of the American population in this way: "The aging are coming and they are us" (Galambos & Rosen, 2000, p. 13). In the 20th century, "the percentage of Americans ages 65 and older . . . more than tripled and the number . . . increased 11 times" (Galambos & Rosen, 2000, p. 13). In the year 2030, more than 1 in 5 people will be older than age 65, and by the year 2050, if current trends continue, the percentage of older adults in the population will exceed the percentage of children (Conway-Giustra, Crowley, & Gorin, 2002).

Medicine and medical technology have lengthened the life span of Americans. For example, since the 1970s, stroke *mortality rates* have decreased significantly, but the *incidence* of stroke has not decreased. Obviously, more individuals survive strokes, many with disabilities.

Arthritis is very common among older individuals, but arthritis, although disabling, is rarely fatal. Of all therapeutic amputations performed in the United States today, 75% are performed on people older than age 65. Most of these amputations are the result of complications of diabetes. Diabetes, a condition often associated with old age, is the leading cause of blindness in the United States. Mobility impairments and sensory loss are prevalent among elderly people. As Americans live longer, they will continue to experience higher disability rates. Indeed, by the year 2040, when the younger baby boomers are 85 years old, the number of Americans with disabilities will be triple what it is today. Also, those individuals with congenital disabilities or disabilities acquired early in life are experiencing longer life spans.

Nonetheless, it is now thought that the rate of disability among older Americans has been overestimated (Jacoby, 2002). Health demographers are not quite sure what is contributing to these lower disability rates among older people, but they consider the lower rates of smoking and drinking, healthier lifestyles, and medications for heart disease and high blood pressure to be contributing factors. The U.S. Census, citing 2010 data, summarized:

> At 70.5 percent, people in the oldest age group (people 80 years and older) were about 8 times as likely to have a disability as the youngest age group (children less than 15 years old), at 8.4 percent. Between 2005–2010, disability rates *decreased* for people 55 to 64 years old and for people 65 to 69 years old.
>
> Severe disability and the need for personal assistance also increased with age. The probability of severe disability was 1-in-20 for people aged 15 to 24, while 1-in-4 for those aged 65 to 69. (Brault, 2012, p. 5)

People With Disabilities Live Longer

Not only are there more people with disabilities, but people with disabilities live longer with the disabilities than before. For example, individuals with spinal cord injuries experience permanent paralysis and other health problems such as decubitus ulcers or pressure sores (bed sores) and respiratory and bladder complications. Antibiotics that treat, and cure, these secondary infections allow individuals with spinal cord injuries (and amputations) to experience long life spans. After World War I, there were 400 American men with battle injuries that paralyzed them from the waist down. Of these men, 90% died before they reached home, most as a consequence of secondary infections. After World War II and the discovery and accelerated production of antibiotics, there were 2,000 veterans with paraplegia, and 85% were alive 20 years later (Shapiro, 1993). A surgeon reported, "Even as late as 1940, the nation only had enough penicillin to treat ten patients" (Rutkow, 2010, p. 223). Indeed, most individuals today with paraplegia or quadriplegia consider themselves to be healthy (some consider themselves athletes), controlling infections and other complications with the use of antibiotics.

The overall increase in the life span contributes to the longer lives of people with disabilities; but even more important are the scientific, technological, and medical advances in the management and treatment of chronic disabilities. To cite a single example, 50 years ago, many parents of infants with disabilities were told by physicians that their babies would not survive to adulthood. Fifty years ago, this was an accurate prognosis. Now, the situation is very different, and most infants with congenital or early-onset disabilities survive to adulthood. Indeed, more than 90% of children with disabilities survive into adulthood (P. H. White, 2002).

Living longer with a disability has implications for the individual, the family, and the larger society. For example, individuals with Down syndrome (a genetic condition that causes intellectual disability) are living twice as long as they did 20 years ago. The average life span of someone with Down syndrome in 2007 was 56 years, while in 1983, the average life span was 25 years. Better medical care and advances in surgery have led to these longer life spans. Before the 1980s, there were no programs for adults with Down syndrome simply because there were very few adults with this condition.

Harriet McBryde Johnson, a 39-year-old lawyer, was born with muscular dystrophy. Her parents were told that she would die in her teenage years. In an article entitled "Too Late to Die Young," she said of her childhood, "The death sentence hangs over my childhood like a cloud" (Johnson, 2005, p. 46). Johnson described her life:

> As my body continues to deteriorate, my life looks more and more normal. At 25 I leave the cozy comfort of home to go to law school. I figure I'll be 27 when I finish; if I go now I can probably practice for a couple of years. By this time, the thought is almost subconscious: when I die I might as well die a lawyer. (p. 99)

She concluded, "My plan to die young hasn't worked out. . . . It's too late to die young." Ms. Johnson died in 2007 at the age of 50.

Nearly 30 years ago, a disability scholar (Trieschmann, 1987) questioned the training and competence of physicians to treat PWDs who were aging.

> Aging is synonymous with living. . . . The issue of aging with a disability is a new problem for western societies, one that has caught our health care system by surprise. Currently, individuals who have lived with spinal injury, polio, and other disabilities for 30, 40, and 50 years are arriving in physicians' offices with a variety of complaints that the physicians have not been taught to handle. (p. 1)

The combination of the longer lives of PWDs and the survival rates of individuals with certain types of disability results in challenges for newly trained medical professionals. In a study entitled *Health and Wellness: People with Disabilities Discuss Barriers and Facilitators to Well Being* (Putnam et al., 2003), researchers stated:

> A common complaint was the lack of knowledge medical professionals have in general about disabilities, such as spinal cord injuries, polio, multiple sclerosis, cerebral palsy, and amputation. One participant said, "We have doctors now that are so young they've never even seen a case of polio. And several of my doctors, I've had to educate them and send them materials and talk to them about it because they have no experience." Another stated, "In my condition as a paraplegic, I find that the medical profession is . . . ignorant in most things, dealing with a person who's a paraplegic because they have no concept of what I can or cannot do, and they're afraid to ask." (p. 42)

Stubbins (1988) asserted that medical science has not only increased the number of people with disabilities but also changed the experience and personal significance of disability: "Medical advances have transformed the central meaning of disability from physical survival to the search for meaning when one is socially isolated, unemployed, or underemployed, and lacking essential environmental accommodations" (p. 24). Furthermore, the health care financing system and federal agencies and programs have not kept pace with the increased life spans of PWDs. Additionally, there are young adults with disabilities who want to become independent and obtain education, jobs, and marriage, and there are few policies or agencies in place to assist them.

Liberalization and Expansion of the Definition of Disability

The expansion and liberalization of the definition of disability has resulted in higher numbers of disabilities. This is termed a statistical cause because the number of people with these types of disabilities did not increase; rather, the way in which their disability was defined or diagnosed changed. Nonetheless, changes in definition result in greater numbers of people to be served and more people who consider themselves to have a disability.

Disability used to be thought of as only physical disability by both the general public and government policymakers. Even today there are many who think of disability solely in terms of physical disabilities. Nonetheless, such impairments as mental illness, learning disabilities, and alcohol dependence and substance abuse are defined as disabilities, and individuals who experience these conditions are eligible for services and accommodations. It should be noted that while it was formerly questioned, there were few experts who did not consider conditions such as alcoholism to be diseases or disabilities (Fingarette, 1988; Peele, 1989). Last to be legally recognized as disabilities, psychiatric and cognitive disabilities are the first to be eliminated in government agency guidelines. For example, in 1997 the Social Security Administration ruled that individuals with alcohol or chemical dependency were no longer eligible for benefits (Watkins & Podus, 2000).

In addition to the liberalization of the definition of disability, it is safe to state that there has also been an expansion in the definition of disability. Examples such as AIDS, post-polio syndrome, and chronic fatigue syndrome illustrate that the number and types of disabilities are expanding.

The increasing rates of autism spectrum disorders (ASD) provide a clear-cut example of the liberalization and expansion of defining disabilities. In 2010, the Centers for Disease Control and Prevention showed a 30% increase in ASD diagnoses over the last 4 years. In 2000, 1 in 150 children was diagnosed with ASD; in 2010, 1 in 110 individuals were given the ASD diagnosis, and today, the prevalence rate is 1 in 68. White children are 30% more likely to be diagnosed with ASD than Black children. In addition to this large racial disparity, states vary widely in their incident rates of ASD. Alabama has an ASD rate of 1 in 175, while New Jersey has a rate of 1 in 45. Health demographers understand that *actual* prevalence rates have not increased as much as these statistics indicate. Two factors must be considered. First, physicians know that patients without a diagnosis do not receive services, and, therefore, they give an ASD diagnosis that may not be entirely appropriate. Second, in earlier times, children with the same set of symptoms were not given any diagnosis, were diagnosed as schizotypal, or were misdiagnosed as having an intellectual disability. Interestingly, the diagnostic category of autism was not widely known among doctors in the United States until 30–40 years after the term *autism* was introduced. In 1943, an Austrian psychiatrist, Dr. Leo Kanner, saw symptoms in children that he recognized as different from childhood schizophrenia. Dr. Kanner named this syndrome of symptoms "autism" and wrote papers about autism and the children he had diagnosed and treated. The problem was that Dr. Kanner wrote in the German language and it was not until the 1970s that his work was translated into English.

Learning disabilities provide an illustration of the liberalization of the definition of disability and the way in which such definitions reduce stigmatization and allow for accommodations. John R. Horner flunked out of the University of Montana six times, but later "his brilliant synthesis of evidence . . . forced paleontologists to revise their ideas about dinosaur behavior, physiology, and evolution" (West, 1997, p. 344; cf. Gerber & D. S. Brown, 1997). Horner related the stigma of learning disabilities: "Back in the days when I was growing up, nobody knew what dyslexia was. . . . So everybody thought you were lazy or stupid or both. And I didn't think I was, but I wasn't sure" (Gerber & D. S. Brown, 1997). Horner has served as a technical advisor for all the *Jurassic Park* films.

Not everyone accepts some of the more recently defined disabilities as legitimate disabilities that are protected under the Americans With Disabilities Act and therefore require accommodations:

Barbara Bateman . . . , one of the most respected leaders in the field of learning disabilities, noted that even after a quarter of a century of evolution in this field, we still find individuals who believe that learning disabilities do not exist. Unfortunately, there are still individuals directing universities, graduate schools, medical schools, and corporate training programs who think that a learning disability is just another fancy excuse for getting special attention. (Brinckerhoff, 1997, p. 145)

More Accurate Counting

As both the general public and government policymakers become more clear on the definitions of disability, the numbers of all individuals *reported* to have disabilities continue to climb. Essentially, more accurate counting is another statistical cause for the higher disability rates because the number of people with disabilities did not increase, only the number of people who are counted or reported as having a disability. Further, disability and health demographers consider the reported number of disabilities to be an underestimation, simply because there are many individuals who do not wish to identify themselves as having a disability. Another illustration showing increased numbers of individuals reporting disabilities concerns the inverse relationship between the economy and disability rates (Yelin, 1992). During economic slumps and depressions, more individuals claim disabilities; most of these individuals are unemployed and need to claim their disability to receive financial benefits. In times of prosperity, the number of disability claims decreases. Therefore, the number of people with disabilities did not increase, but rather the number of people *reporting* disabilities.

The following is a summary of the data of the number of civilian, noninstitutionalized Americans with disabilities (Brault, 2012). These data do not include military personnel with disabilities or PWDs who live in long-term care facilities. The latest date for which census data are available is 2010.

- Approximately 56.7 million Americans had a disability, representing almost one fifth of the American population (18.7%).
- Approximately 38.3 million or 12.6% of Americans reported having a *severe* disability.
- In a five-year period, the total number of PWDs increased by 2.3 million from 54.4 million in 2005 to 56.7 million in 2010. The percentage of PWDs in the American population remained unchanged.
- Of the 62.2 million American children under the age of 15, about 5.2 million or 8.4% had some kind of disability. Among children aged 6 to 14, disability was defined more broadly. About 4.5 million had a disability, representing 12.2%.
- Approximately 2.3 million children had difficulty in doing regular schoolwork (6.2%), including 1.6 million who received special education services.

(text continues on p. 44)

Table 1.1

Prevalence of Disability for Selected Age Groups: 2005 and 2010 (Numbers in thousands)

Category	2005[1]				2010				Difference	
	Number	Margin of error (±)[2]	Percent	Margin of error (±)[2]	Number	Margin of error (±)[2]	Percent	Margin of error (±)[2]	Number	Percent
All ages	291,099	*****	100.0	(X)	303,858	*****	100.0	(X)	**12,760	(X)
With a disability	54,425	894	18.7	0.3	56,672	905	18.7	0.3	*2,247	–
Severe disability	34,947	601	12.0	0.2	38,284	654	12.6	0.2	*3,337	*0.6
Aged 6 and older	266,752	84	100.0	(X)	278,222	88	100.0	(X)	*11,469	(X)
Needed personal assistance	10,996	336	4.1	0.1	12,349	386	4.4	0.1	*1,353	*0.3
Aged 15 and older	230,391	*****	100.0	(X)	241,682	*****	100.0	(X)	**11,291	(X)
With a disability	49,069	794	21.3	0.3	51,454	838	21.3	0.3	*2,385	–
Severe disability	32,771	567	14.2	0.2	35,683	631	14.8	0.3	*2,912	*0.5
Difficulty seeing	7,793	350	3.4	0.2	8,077	354	3.3	0.1	284	–
Severe	1,783	129	0.8	0.1	2,010	139	0.8	0.1	*228	0.1
Difficulty hearing	7,809	325	3.4	0.1	7,572	320	3.1	0.1	-237	*-0.3
Severe	993	103	0.4	–	1,096	122	0.5	0.1	103	–
Aged 21 to 64	170,349	185	100.0	(X)	177,295	193	100.0	(X)	*6,945	(X)
With a disability	28,141	622	16.5	0.4	29,479	705	16.6	0.4	*1,338	0.1
Employed	12,838	495	45.6	1.2	12,115	432	41.1	1.0	*-723	*-4.5

Severe disability	18,705	469	11.0	0.3	20,286	566	11.4	0.3	*1,581	*0.5
Employed	5,738	277	30.7	1.2	5,570	261	27.5	1.0	-167	*-3.2
Nonsevere disability.	9,436	403	5.5	0.2	9,193	374	5.2	0.2	-243	*-0.4
Employed.	7,100	356	75.2	1.6	6,544	311	71.2	1.6	*-556	*-4.1
No disability.	142,208	636	83.5	0.4	147,816	733	83.4	0.4	*5,607	-0.1
Employed.	118,707	678	83.5	0.3	116,881	862	79.1	0.4	*-1,826	*-4.4
Aged 65 and older	**35,028**	*****	**100.0**	[X]	**38,599**	*****	**100.0**	[X]	**3,571	[X]
With a disability.	18,132	324	51.8	0.9	19,234	327	49.8	0.8	*1,102	*-1.9
Severe disability.	12,942	273	36.9	0.8	14,138	276	36.6	0.7	*1,196	-0.3

— Represents or rounds to zero.

(X) Not applicable.

* Denotes a statistically significant difference at the 90% confidence level.

** Denotes a difference between two controlled estimates. By definition, this difference is statistically significant.

**** Indicates (in margin of error column) that the estimate is controlled to independent population estimates. A statistical test for sampling variability is not appropriate.

1 Estimates of disability prevalence for 2005 may differ from the estimates presented in Americans With Disabilities: 2005 (Brault, 2008) due to changes in the survey weighting since the report's publication. Furthermore, the margins of error in the 2005 report were calculated using the generalized variance formula method. The estimates of variance shown here use the successive differences replication method.

2 A margin of error is a measure of an estimate's variability. The larger the margin of error in relation to the size of the estimate, the less reliable the estimate. The margins of error shown in this table are for the 90% confidence level. For more information about the source and accuracy of the estimates, including margins of error, standard errors, and confidence intervals, see the Source and Accuracy Statement (http://www.census.gov/sipp/sourceac/S&A08_W1toW6(S&A-13).pdf).

Note. From U.S. Census Bureau, Survey of Income and Program Participation, June–September 2005 and May–August 2010. Retrieved from https://www.census.gov/people/disability/publications/disab10/table_1.pdf

- Approximately 3.4 million children (9.3%) had one or more selected mental, emotional, or developmental disability. About 692,000 had a learning disability, 1.9 million had Attention Deficit Hyperactivity Disorder (ADHD), and 1.7 million had an intellectual or developmental disability or condition.

Table 1.1 shows the prevalence of disabilities by age groups for 2005 and 2010 (Brault, 2012). Each number in this table represents one thousand. We see that the horizontal rows show the numbers for (a) all ages, (b) those age 6 and older, (c) those age 15 and older, (d) those age 21 to 64, and (e) those age 65 and older. The vertical columns show the number and percentage of PWDs for two time periods, 2005 and 2010, and the final column shows the difference between 2005 and 2010.

In Figure 1.1, disability is divided into two categories (*any disability* and *severe disability*), and a third category (*needs assistance*) is also included. This figure is arranged by age categories. It is easy to see that individuals in the older age categories have more disabilities, or as stated by the U.S. Census Bureau (Brault, 2012):

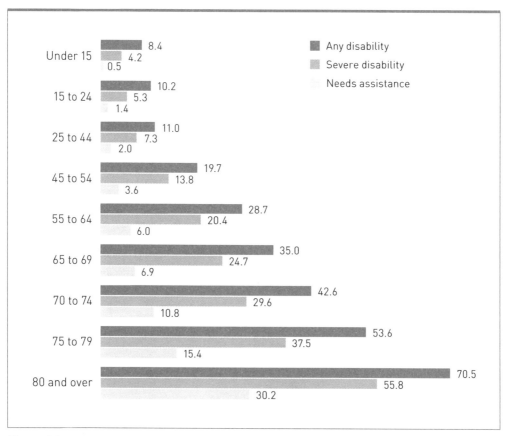

Figure 1.1. *Disability prevalence and the need for assistance by age: 2010 (in percent).*
Note. The need for assistance with activities of daily living was not asked of children under 6 years. From U.S. Census Bureau, Survey of Income and Program Participation, May–August 2010. Retrieved from http://www.census.gov/people/disability/publications/disab10/figure_2.pdf

Table 1.2

Age-Adjusted and Unadjusted Disability Rates by Gender, Race, and Hispanic Origin: 2005 and 2010

| | Age-adjusted disability rate[1] | | | | | Unadjusted disability rate | | | | |
| | 2005 | | 2010 | | | 2005 | | 2010 | | |
Category	Estimate	Margin of error (±)[2]	Estimate	Margin of error (±)[2]	Difference	Estimate	Margin of error (±)[2]	Estimate	Margin of error (±)[2]	Difference
All people	18.6	0.3	18.1	0.3	*-0.5	18.7	0.3	18.7	0.3	–
Male	17.9	0.4	17.6	0.4	-0.3	17.3	0.4	17.4	0.4	0.2
Female	19.0	0.3	18.3	0.4	*-0.7	20.1	0.3	19.8	0.4	-0.2
White alone	17.9	0.3	17.4	0.3	*-0.5	18.6	0.3	18.5	0.3	–
Not Hispanic	18.1	0.4	17.6	0.4	-0.4	19.7	0.4	19.8	0.4	0.1
Black alone	23.2	0.7	22.2	0.7	-1.0	20.4	0.7	20.3	0.7	-0.2
Not Hispanic	23.3	0.7	22.3	0.7	*-1.0	20.7	0.7	20.7	0.7	–
Asian alone	14.5	1.3	14.5	1.1	–	12.4	1.2	13.0	1.0	0.6
Not Hispanic	14.6	1.3	14.4	1.1	-0.2	12.5	1.2	13.0	1.1	0.5
Hispanic or Latino	18.4	0.9	17.8	0.7	-0.6	13.1	0.7	13.2	0.6	0.1

– Represents or rounds to zero.

* Denotes a statistically significant difference at the 90% confidence level.

1 Age-adjustments followed the methodology described in Anderson and Rosenberg (1998) using the year 2000 standard population by 5-year age groups from Day (1996).

2 A margin of error is a measure of an estimate's variability. The larger the margin of error in relation to the size of the estimate, the less reliable the estimate. The margins of error shown in this table are for the 90% confidence level. For more information about the source and accuracy of the estimates, including margins of error, standard errors, and confidence intervals, see the Source and Accuracy Statement (http://www.census.gov/content/dam/Census/programs-surveys/sipp/tech-documentation/source-accuracy-statements/2008/SIPP%202008%20Panel%20Waves%201-16%20Source%20and%20Accuracy%20Statement.pdf).

Note. From U.S. Census Bureau, Survey of Income and Program Participation, June–September 2005 and May–August 2010. Retrieved from https://www.census.gov/people/disability/publications/disab10/table_1.pdf

As a generally accepted understanding of prevalence, the risk of having a disability increased with successively older age groups. At 70.5%, people in the oldest age groups (people 80 years and older) were about 8 times as likely to have a disability as people in the youngest age group (children less than 15 years old). (p. 5)

Until age 45, the percentage of any disability increases by only a few percentage points. At age 45, the disability percentage (both "any disability" and "severe disability") of each age category increased by larger increments, with an almost 20% increase between those age 75 to 79 and those 80 or older.

Table 1.2 shows the percentages of disability in the US categorized by gender and four racial categories (Brault, 2012). First, it is evident that females (of all ages) experience more disabilities (19%) than males (17.9%). Looking at the four racial categories, it can be seen that some American ethnic groups are not represented, such as Native Americans, Pacific Islanders, or those of mixed racial groups. However, this chart shows that Asian Americans have the lowest rate of disabilities (14.5%) whereas Black Americans have the highest rate, at 23.3%. White Americans who are not Hispanic have an 18.1% prevalence rate.

These tables and charts are only a starting point when learning about the prevalence of disability. If we were to change the definitions of the variables, such as disability, or the various ethnic groups, these numbers would change. For example, if chronic illness were deleted from the definition of disability, the disparity between male and female rates of disability would be decreased. It is well known that women experience more chronic illness than men. Females also tend to live longer than males, so it can be assumed that this raises the disability rate of females. Women survive longer, but with a disability.

Summary

We began this chapter by noting that everyone has the potential to be born with a disability or to acquire a disability because disability is part of life and humanity. No one aspires to have a disability; but, it is also true that few prepare for the possibility of a disability. Most PWODs seem to deny this possibility, probably because:

- they (wrongly) think that the disability is tragic, helpless, and hopeless; and
- some PWODs may consider themselves a "special" minority and that disability happens to "other people."

These two misconceptions hurt PWDs because the natural response of PWODs is to shield themselves from thinking about this possibility, and this includes segregating people who have disabilities or, at minimum, avoiding personal contact. In a book entitled, *Extraordinary Bodies: Figuring Physical Disability in American Culture and Literature*, Thomson (1997a) wrote:

> The physically disabled body becomes a repository for social anxieties about such troubling concerns as vulnerability, control, and identity. The body is usually unobtrusive and is taken for granted. All of this is changed by seeing a person with a disability. (p. 6)

However, such unwarranted attitudes and behaviors may hurt PWODs more than PWDs. If PWODs were to have more natural, equal social status relationships with PWDs, they would see that for most PWDs, disability is not an unbearable tragedy. Certainly, disability is difficult and expensive and changes lives; however most PWODs really do not understand what life is with a disability, and this fear of the unknown leads to misconceptions and prejudice.

Because of such an avoidance of PWDs, when a PWOD acquires a disability, has a baby with a congenital disability, or is diagnosed with a chronic illness, *the individual becomes the target of his or her own prejudice and lack of knowledge*. In a later chapter, we will read of a woman who acquired a disability and stated, "I always thought that people with disabilities were weirdos and creeps and that I should feel sorry for them." Another example is of a mother of a newborn infant who is a dwarf who stated, "It never occurred to me, not even in my wildest disaster scenarios, that I would have a child different enough to elicit stares." Andrew Solomon spent 10 years interviewing more than 300 families of PWDs, culminating in the book *Far From the Tree: Parents, Children, and the Search for Identity.* He summarized his feelings as follows:

> I grew up afraid of illness and disability, inclined to avert my gaze from anyone who was too different....This book helped me kill that bigoted impulse, which I had always known to be ugly. (Solomon, 2012, p. 677)

Indeed, PWDs often state: "We have a lot to teach the normies (PWODs)".

Demographers and trend analysts have alerted the public to such important population trends as the aging of the Baby Boom cohort, the decline in the number of "traditional" marriages, the redefinition of marriage, and declining birth rates. However, one population trend these scholars and experts have missed is the rising number of PWDs. Even more surprising, health demographers have not alerted the popular media to the rising disability rates (both in proportion of the population and numbers). For example, many PWDs point out that physicians are not trained to treat PWDs. Medical offices are often not physically accessible or do not have equipment to treat PWDs. Temple Grandin is a university professor who designs animal and food production facilities and is perhaps the most famous person with ASD. Her mother wrote about Temple's childhood. "Why didn't doctors know as much as I did?" (Solomon, 2012, p. 274). One disability scholar summarized, "Social planning was based on the concept that there were no people with disabilities" (Wendell, 2006, p. 243).

CHAPTER **2**

MODELS OF DISABILITY

The Religious–Moral Model, the Biomedical Model, the Environmental Model, the Functional Model, and the Sociopolitical Model

- ✧ What are models of disability?
- ✧ What are the five models of disability?
- ✧ Is there one complete model of disability?
- ✧ How do interactive models compare with the Biomedical Model?
- ✧ Why are most bioethical questions based in the Biomedical Model?
- ✧ What are five titles of the ADA?
- ✧ Why were amendments to the Americans With Disabilities Act enacted in 2008?
- ✧ Why shouldn't we use words such as *cripples*, *victims*, or *handicapped*? Regardless of which words are used, isn't the meaning the same?

In the preceding chapter, we learned about the difficulty of determining normalcy and the reasons why there are more disabilities than ever in history. In this chapter, we will discuss the ways in which normalcy is defined and regulated—both clinically and legally. To gain some understanding of both society's response to disability (the second section of this book) and PWD's response to disability (the third section of this book), it is necessary to discuss the various models of disability.

What Are Models of Disability?

In this section, look for—

- ✧ why models of disability are important
- ✧ how models define our world and influence our attitudes and actions
- ✧ functions of models

One way to conceptualize disability relates to the different models for disability that can be implemented. A model is a set of guiding assumptions, concepts, and propositions about the nature of phenomena or human experience. Models have often been defined as human-made tools for understanding and human-made guidelines for action. As would be expected, treatment and intervention strategies are guided by the type of disability model used. There are five basic models of conceptualizing disability: (a) the Religious–Moral Model, (b) the Biomedical Model, (c) the Environmental Model, (d) the Functional Model, and (e) the Sociopolitical Model. Different models of disability have different uses, and each model has its advantages and disadvantages. However, all models are, to some extent, incomplete and subject to error, simply because models are *human-made representations* of experiences and phenomena.

Many people unknowingly think of disabilities in terms of these models without being aware that they are doing so. Understanding these models brings clarity and understanding to the experience of disability. Nonetheless, these models are important both to individuals with disabilities and to those without disabilities. It is essential to be clear and explicit—especially to ourselves—about the models we use. Occasionally, we should question and examine models to which we subscribe, and we should question our ways of explaining the world. Indeed, models define our world and influence our attitudes and actions. Each of the following models formed the basis for the development of different types of government-sponsored services (Bickenbach, 1993).

Functions of Models of Disability

- to provide definitions of disability
- to identify the location of the "problem"

- to serve as a "starting point" for government laws, policies and guidelines
- to determine which academic disciplines study disability
- to determine causal attribution
- to determine responsibility attribution
- to determine the needs of PWDs
- to serve as a starting point for research on disability issues and the development of psychometric instruments

Models of disability provide definitions of disability. Because each model defines disability in a narrow fashion, each model answers the question, "What is a disability?" A second function of models of disability is to help identify the location of the "problem" and, subsequently the third function, identify who is to be held responsible for the solution. Determination of the location of the problem is referred to as the *causal attribution,* and determination of who is to solve the problem is referred to as the *responsibility attribution.* A fourth function of models of disability is to determine needs. For example, if all needs of a PWD are considered to be medical, then all resources will be allocated to meet only medical needs. Fifth, models guide the formulation and implementation of policy. Laws such as the Social Security laws, the Vocational Rehabilitation Acts, the Individuals with Disabilities Education Act, and the Americans With Disabilities Act (ADA) all derive from different models. Sixth, models determine which academic disciplines study and learn about the experience of disability. If disability is thought to be a social construction, then the social sciences and political sciences would teach about disability, whereas if disability is thought to be solely a medical phenomenon, only those in the health sciences will learn about disability.

Linton (1998), a disability scholar, wrote *Claiming Disability: Knowledge and Identity,* in which she looked at the various university curricula, such as the humanities and the behavioral sciences, and described the way in which knowledge of the experience and history of PWDs could be incorporated into each of these college majors. But first, Linton succinctly summarized the current state of university study on PWDs, concluding that the little disability study available is worse than no information about PWDs. Linton believed that the little available material is "patronizing and distorted":

> Even a cursory review of the [university] curricula reveals only patronizing and distorted representations of disability, and these are left largely unexamined and unchallenged. But minor housecleaning will not rid out the deeper structural elements, the scholarly conventions, and theoretical underpinnings within which those representations are deemed valid and useful. A closer look reveals problems in both the structure and content of the curriculum, predicated on a narrowly conceived interpretation of disability. (p. 4)

Perhaps what Linton referred to as "deeper structural elements," "theoretical under-pinning," and "interpretation of disability," are what we are terming *models of disability*.

Seventh, models provide the basis for research because research tries to find cause-and-effect relationships and the causal attribution is defined by the model used. It is safe to state that most research on PWDs has focused on the individual and the disability, ignoring the resources available to the PWD and stigma and prejudice directed toward the PWD and his or her particular type of disability. In the book, *Medical Statistics* (Feinstein & Chapman, 2002), the authors asserted that a great deal of research "has been done with biases that destroy the scientific credibility of the results" (p. 3). Eighth, most psychometric tests, such as personality tests, have negative biases because they provide "diagnoses of exclusion" and often compare the test taker to psychiatric patient groups.

Models shape the self-identity of those with disability. Because models provide definitions, diagnoses, and theories of causation and responsibility, based on seemingly authoritative and prestigious sources, PWDs often accept these concepts as self-identifiers.

Finally, models can cause prejudice and discrimination. Three of the models—the Religious–Moral, the Biomedical, and the Functional models—have a normative basis, meaning that the absence of a disability is considered to be better than the presence of a disability, and because of this normative basis, prejudice results.

Models of disability are abstractions or theories and do not exist in reality. However, they are *not* harmless abstractions. Models guide legislation and determine the service settings for PWDs and where PWDs live (or if they live at all). Models guide the training of professionals who serve PWDs, and models have a significant impact on the popular media. Most of all, models determine the daily, lived experience of having a disability.

The Religious–Moral Model of Disability

In this section, look for—

- ✧ The Religious–Moral Model
  - considered sin, wrongdoing, or evil to be the *causes* of disability;
  - considered disability to be the *result* of sin, wrongdoing, or evil;
  - considered the "treatment" for disability to be repentance, prayer, and segregation from "good" people who do not have disabilities;
  - was a non-interactional model because both the cause and the response are the responsibility of the PWD;
  - is the model with the longest history;
  - relied on the expertise of priests, clergy, or other native healers to "diagnose," interpret, and "treat" disability;

- provided the basis for the societal response of charity to PWDs; and
- provided the basis for the institutionalization, segregation, and marginalization of PWDs.

In the first two editions of this book, I did not describe the Religious–Moral Model of disability, because I thought this model no longer exercised any power of definition or treatment. Indeed, I wrote one sentence to describe this model: "in the Religious/Moral Model disability was thought to be the result of sin and evil." I have decided to write a more complete description in this edition for the following reasons: (a) to give more context to the Biomedical Model, showing that the Biomedical Model was considered an improvement over the Religious–Moral Model; (b) to show the ways that remnants or vestiges of the Religious–Moral Model are found in the modern world, especially in the popular media; (c) to provide an explanation of the strength and longevity of the charity movement as the sole, or the most important, response to disability; (d) to show the resilience of the idea that disability is an individual tragedy, something to be ashamed of; and (e) to counter the shame and stigma that often follows instances of assumed moral failure. Issues of right and wrong are deeply imbedded in human thinking, and moral and ethical failure can bring strong condemnation.

One clarification is necessary. The Religious–Moral Model should not be confused with the positive response and adaptation to disability in finding meaning and strength in spirituality or religion; indeed, many PWDs consider religious or spiritual meaning, strength, and comfort to be their greatest resources. The Religious–Moral Model considers disability to be a *punishment* from God, while some PWDs may feel that their disability is a *gift* from God.

Humankind has always believed that disability and disfigurement were objective, realistic facts, and we must keep this in mind when we discuss the Religious–Moral Model. Today, it may appear to us that the Religious–Moral Model is misconceived, even laughable, but throughout thousands of years, everyone, including PWDs, thought that this model *was* reality and, therefore, not to be questioned. Indeed, they believed in this explanation of disability as much as our society believes in the ICD-10 or the DSM-5 today.

The Religious–Moral Model of disability has the longest history of all the models; it relied on authoritative and prestigious professionals, and considered disability and disfigurement to be the result of moral defect or sin of the PWD or his or her parents or ancestors. Disability was considered to be a punishment for the PWD. In the Judeo-Christian tradition, especially in the Old Testament, PWDs were not allowed inside the Temple, because they were "unclean," but were allowed to beg at the gates of the Temple. Begging at the gates of the Temple also served as a warning for PWODs to avoid sin and evil or they, or their children, could acquire a disability. These PWDs served as living morality lessons.

St. Augustine broadened the possibility of acquiring a disability to all of human-kind, but still considered disability to be a punishment when he stated that disability was retribution for the fall of Adam and other sins. Even more extreme, it was often thought that the PWD was the embodiment of the devil. This was especially true for individuals with seizure disorders or with mental illness.

As with all models, the assumed "cause" of the disability dictates the treatment and response. For PWDs who were thought to be possessed by the devil, death was often the response. If the individual was not killed, he or she was beaten and tortured in other ways. A third societal response was to pray for and bless the PWD in order to cure or drive out an evil spirit. A fourth societal response was to segregate these sinners from "good" people, PWODs. Evil and sin were thought to be contagious, and, therefore, PWDs were often hidden or institutionalized in order to "protect" PWODs. Even today, debate about institutionalization and segregated facilities for PWDs begins with a discussion of the rationale of such treatment. Proponents of institutionalization often state that it is for the good of PWDs, providing a restful retreat from the world. Opponents of institutionalization find the roots of institutionalization in the Religious–Moral Model of disability in which the sole purpose was to protect PWODs from PWDs.

The personal response to disability included repentance, prayer, and adhering to the religious authority's counsel and care. The PWD's family was often ostracized because they may have been part of the sin and evil. Enforced humility was often the result because PWDs were consigned to beg for a living. PWODs could give coins to these beggars and feel very good about themselves. In all types of charity, it is clear who the good person is—the giver.

The Religious–Moral Model was in force for thousands of years, and it equated biological norms with moral norms. Biological wholeness was thought to be a reli-gious reward for virtue simply because the opposite was considered true (biological unwholeness was thought to be the result of sin and evil.) There is still a tendency to associate moral values with biological wholeness. A former commissioner of the Reha-bilitation Services Administration, a presidential appointee, Nell Carney, stated, "It's not quite respectable to have a disability." Ms. Carney was born blind. Today, in the developed world, there is a "religious syndrome" of social value and moral worth that includes intelligence, achievement, earning capacity, and appearance. In the book, *Far From the Tree*, Solomon (2012) concluded: "Much of this [disability] history is a nar-rative of suffering and abuse. Unusual bodies have been described through-out his-tory as reflections of sin, as omens from the gods, as the basis for laughter or charity or punishment."

In this model, it was both right and natural that PWDs and their families should feel shame about the disability and accept the blame. This is a vestige of the Religious–Moral Model that is found today. While society, as a whole, does not think that sin or evil causes disabilities, PWDs have often felt that society makes them feel ashamed of their disabilities. Jan Little, who used a wheelchair since her childhood, recalled that in the

1940s, "being in a wheelchair carried a fair amount of shame," and after her parents took her to a local concert, one of their neighbors chastised them for "taking a child like that out in public" (Wilson, 1990, pp. 178–179). Many of those who contracted polio during the American polio epidemics stated, "It felt un-American to get polio" (Shell, 2005, p. 53).

Many disability scholars have drawn attention to the number of villains and wicked people in books, movies, and television programs who are PWDs.

> Numerous other stories associating disability and disfigurement with sin. Similar associations permeate secular Western literature, in which "bodily intactness and glowing health have been almost exclusively characteristics of the good and noble, while physical infirmities are reserved for the evil and malevolent." We grow up hearing tales of disabled and wicked characters such as Rumpelstiltskin, Captain Hook, Long John Silver, or the dwarves, giants and gnomes in the Brothers Grimm fairy tales. In adult literature, the common literary device of the "twisted mind in the twisted body" appears in as exalted a writer as Shakespeare, who depicted Richard III as a hunchback in order to provide a physical embodiment of his supposedly warped soul. Captain Ahab's body-length scar and wooden leg serve as convenient metaphors for his traumatized and monomaniacal character in Moby Dick. ("Long and Sorry History," 2000, sec. 2, ¶)

This quote shows the way in which PWDs were portrayed as sinister, evil, and dangerous. Today, our media are showing more accurate depictions of PWDs as normal people with disabilities. The media portrayals include PWDs who have families, jobs, friends, and are often the hero of the story.

The Biomedical Model of Disability

In this section look for—

- ✧ The strengths of the Biomedical Model are
  - its long history;
  - the use of objective, standardized tests and diagnoses;
  - its alliance with prestigious professions, such as physicians, scientists, and nurses; and
  - it is the model most understood by society.

The Biomedical Model is the most familiar and best understood conception of disease and disability, probably because this model has the second longest history. The Biomedical Model uses objective, clear-cut, standardized measures and, as the name suggests, uses experts, such as physicians, to provide defining characteristics, causes, prognoses, and methods of treatment. There are two dimensions of this model, normal and pathological, with the diagnosis of normal often defined as the absence of any pathology. As would be expected, the Biomedical Model focuses on the anatomy and physiology of the individual and uses standardized procedures to make diagnoses. These standardized procedures allow different medical experts to arrive at the same diagnosis. Because of the high levels of skill and knowledge necessary to render both diagnoses and treatment, the Biomedical Model of disability relies on the use of experts, usually physicians. It was medicine that challenged and discredited the Religious–Moral Model. Furthermore, physicians and other medical professionals declare that diagnoses do not involve moral judgments, blame, or a judgment on the worth of the individual with the diagnosis or disability. While the contributions of the profession of medicine cannot be overstated, there are deficiencies in the Biomedical Model; however, conscious wrongdoing on the part of medical professionals is not implied. After all, it is society who has endowed the medical professions with these responsibilities.

Most medical professionals are hardworking humanitarians who are providing services based upon their education and training, meeting board and licensing standards, following the ethical guidelines of medical specialty organizations, and working in accredited hospitals. These practitioners rely on large classification and diagnostic systems (the ICD-10 and the DSM-5) in order to render diagnoses and develop treatment plans so that large businesses (insurance companies) will pay for treatment. Finally, until fairly recently, no other profession provided services to PWDs. The only other profession to serve PWDs was created with the enactment, in 1920, of the Civilians Rehabilitation Act, which established the state–federal system of rehabilitation.

You will remember that it was the professions of medicine and science that produced advances that resulted in the demographic surge of large numbers of PWDs. Neonatal medicine allowed infants to survive, and many of these newborns had disabilities. Emergency medicine resulted in many survivors of accidents, many with disabilities. Advances in longevity have increased the number of PWDs. If medical practitioners and scientists allowed so many PWDs to live, why are any PWDs dissatisfied with the way the Biomedical Model defines and treats PWDs? Perhaps Atul Gawande (2014), surgeon and author, explained it best: "Medicine has been slow to confront the very changes that it has been responsible for—or to apply the knowledge we have" (p. 36).

In the Biomedical Model, pathology, abnormality, and deviance are present in the individual. Bickenbach (1993) described this definition of disability as deviance:

> The most commonly held belief about [this model of] disablement is that it involves a defect, deficiency, dysfunction, abnormality, failing or medical "problem" that is located in an individual. We think it is so obvious as to be beyond serious dispute that disablement is a characteristic of a *defective person*, someone who is functionally limited or anatomically abnormal, diseased, or

pathoanatomical, someone who is neither whole nor healthy, fit nor flour-ishing, someone who is biologically inferior or subnormal. The essence of disablement, in this view, is that there are things *wrong* with people with dis-abilities. (p. 61)

As a result of the deficit orientation of this model, an individual with a disability understands that he or she is a member of a devalued group—the disabled—regardless of any personal qualities, resources, or advantages of the individual (J. F. Smart, 2006). This also means that society often considers that the life of a PWD is worth less invest-ment than the life of a PWOD (H. McCarthy, 1993). Indeed, taken to an extreme, society could endow the medical profession with the mandate to eliminate disabilities and the people who experience them (P. Singer, 1981, 2000).

Therefore, disability is viewed as an individual tragedy (Shell, 2005). Society is ef-fectively absolved of all responsibility for disability because society relinquished au-thority to the medical profession. Conrad (2004) described the way in which society has endowed the medical professions with the power to remove the experience of dis-ability from attention and concern of the general public:

Because of the way the medical profession is organized and the mandate it receives from society, decisions related to medical diagnoses and treatment are virtually controlled by the medical professions. . . . By defining a problem as medical, it is removed from the public realm where there can be discus-sion by ordinary people and put on a plane where only medical people can discuss it. (p. 22)

It is only within the last 100 years that physicians have faced the challenge of help-ing patients to manage and treat conditions over their life span. For centuries, medical treatment had two outcomes: a total cure or the death of the person. Hahn (2005) stated that in this two-outcome paradigm, diagnosis was straightforward—the patient was either dead or cured. Of course, there were exceptions to this, such as mental ill-ness or sensory loss. The flu epidemics illustrate the two outcomes: individuals either died of the flu (500,000 died in the United States), or they recovered completely. However, the polio epidemics were different because they produced three outcomes: the individual died, the individual recovered completely, or he or she lived with an orthopedic disability. Thus, the polio epidemics resulted in tens of thousands of in-dividuals with disabilities. For many conditions, such as diabetes, there wasn't any management or treatment available, and individuals with diabetes died. People with amputations did not survive long after the procedure, because, before the advent of antibiotics, infections, which are secondary to amputations, killed them. People today live with many conditions, both physical and emotional, that are neither acute nor curable but that could result in death or further disablement if the conditions are not managed and controlled.

The lingering effects of this two-outcome paradigm of the Biomedical Model are experienced by people with disabilities today. For example, many individuals with disabilities are very healthy and do not require referral to medical specialists when they have commonplace illnesses that are not related to their disabilities or even when they need routine physical or dental examinations. Yet, many physicians refer patients with disabilities to treatment by specialists. Indeed, many individuals with disabilities must undergo hospitalization needlessly to have simple dental work performed. Another example of the vestiges of the two-outcome paradigm is found in insurance policies that do not provide payment for services after medical stabilization has been reached. Therefore, such services as marriage counseling to deal with the adjustment to a disability, treatment for secondary conditions and complications, and medical services to deal with the interaction of the aging process and the disability are typically not funded (J. F. Smart, 2005a). After medical stabilization, most insurance policies do not fund services.

The focus of the Biomedical Model on pathology and on the biology and physiology of the patient has, for the most part, ignored the individual's role functioning and his or her environmental demands (J. F. Smart, 2012b). Disability concerns are divorced from social factors in the Biomedical Model. Indeed, the Biomedical Model conceived the problem as existing entirely within the individual and focused all efforts on fixing the individual, rarely acknowledging the social construction of and societal reaction to disability. The Biomedical Model places the responsibility for rehabilitation on the individual in two different ways. First, the PWD was expected to comply with all treatments and management techniques, and second, the PWD must respond to the challenge of the disability. Many PWODs tell PWDs that they are challenged by their disability. Thinking of PWDs as challenged relieves society of the responsibility to dismantle long-term, institutionalized prejudice and discrimination, and, furthermore, when the PWDs *appears* to fail, he or she is considered lazy or "chicken." Thirty years ago ("The Problem With 'Challenge'," 1985), a PWD wrote about the phrase, "physically challenged":

> I don't like it, though. It ignores a crucial fact—the reason we can't do lots of things is not because we're lazy, or because we won't accept a challenge (isn't it implied when you won't accept a challenge that you're 'chicken'?) but because many things are simply beyond our control. That's admitting a political truth. Admitting a truth is the first step toward changing it. (para. 5)

The PWD concluded, "A challenge is something you can solve by yourself." But lack of accommodations, transportation, and prejudice and discrimination are societal issues and cannot be solved by a single individual.

Overcoming, having a good attitude, and meeting the challenge are not possible, because of the disability itself. A middle-aged man who became quadriplegic wrote:

I thought that if I had a good attitude and worked really hard—I'm someone who's used to being an achiever—I'd overcome problems. So I went into this program and I thought, "Get out of my way. I'm really going to set this world on fire. I'm going to be the hardest working patient they've ever had. I'm going to have the best attitude." I never skipped a therapy session. I never cut out early. But then I would see someone next to me with the worst attitude in the world—wouldn't go, didn't care, whined, sat in the corner. And they got better and walked out of the place. And I didn't get better and I was stuck there. Then I realized that your body gets better when your body wants to get better, and it doesn't when it doesn't. Attitude doesn't make up for everything. And working hard doesn't make up for everything. And you cannot just will yourself where you want to go. (Close, 1993, p. 19)

Others, instead of the PWD, judge when the PWD has met these goals. The individual with a disability, however severe the disability, is not recognized as a complete person with family, work, and community responsibilities, all of which affect the diagnosis of the disability. To cite a single common example, in order to determine level of benefits, physicians often render a numerical rating of a disability, such as 25% or 35%, not taking into account such factors as the degree of stigma toward the disability, the individual's family support, or the individual's coping resources. Two clear-cut examples of disabilities that are very limiting, but not from any functional or organic limitations, are the disabilities of Paul Steven Miller, found in Chapter 1, and the disabilities of individuals with facial disfigurements. The Biomedical Model, with its emphasis solely on the individual, is not broad enough to describe these individuals' experiences or generate plans to change their situations. Two people with the same diagnosis, at the same numerical rating, may have different prognoses. The solution, of course, is multidisciplinary case management in which disability professionals, with their complementary knowledge, skills, and perspectives, provide a complete range of services, including medical, educational, and vocational.

The perspective of the Biomedical Model often objectified people with disabilities because these individuals were viewed as a body part, a specific organ, or a type of disability. The PWD becomes a quad, a schizophrenic, a diabetic, or a chronic. Clearly, some of this objectification and impersonal treatment of the PWD assists physicians in maintaining an objectivity and emotional detachment. It appears that, rather than easing the discomfort of the patient, physicians have chosen to respond to their own discomfort. The Biomedical Model, in its most extreme form, holds that if physicians view patients as whole people and as collaborators in the diagnosis and treatment of their conditions, the effectiveness of physicians will be compromised. As technology and laboratory diagnostic procedures proliferate, less emphasis will be placed on history-taking and learning about the patient from the patient. Thus, in the name of medical pragmatism, the individual and his or her environment are ignored

(Cameron, 1982). Leonard Kriegel, who contracted polio, effectively captured the power of the Biomedical Model and the objectification it brings. Notice that Kriegel compared himself to a monster, the creation of Dr. Frankenstein:

> Filled with pride in their technological prowess, the three of them (bracemakers) stood in front of me, admiring their skills. Had I been created in the laboratory of Mary Shelley's Dr. Frankenstein, I could not have felt myself any more the creature of scientific pride. (Kriegel, 1997, p. 41)

The Biomedical Model is often perceived to be that of experts delivering services to passive recipients who are expected to be compliant and to whom little information and few treatment options are provided. This "expert-in-control" is referred to as the "omniscience of the experts" (DeLoach & Greer, 1981). Paternalism probably began in the Biomedical Model (J. F. Smart, 2004). A practicing attorney with a severe congenital disability stated, "Doctors never bothered asking me what my life could become" (Mikata, 1995). Disability advocates report stories of experts and physicians who did not listen to individuals with disabilities and their family members; other experts who viewed the individuals' disabilities as tragic flaws; and experts who did not have the experience of living with disabilities 24 hours a day, 7 days a week. In the National Public Radio (NPR) Disability History Project, "Tomorrow's Children," a parent of a child with spina bifida stated, "Parents endow the doctors with more understanding than they often have" (NPR, 1998c).

Solomon (2012) spent years interviewing PWDs and parents of children with disabilities. He summarized the reasons why parents often submit their children to numerous treatments and surgeries.

> No one knows that a given child will require 20 surgeries over four years; the question of what to do is resolved one procedure at a time. It can be hard for parents who haven't been down this route to understand the gradualism of it, and while the cumulative effect of all these interventions may become brutal, to deny any single one can seem murderous. (p. 368)

Although these patterns are changing, many individuals with disabilities have felt devalued and treated as inferior by medical professionals and were allowed very little control over their treatment (J. F. Smart, 2005a, 2005b). Today, some adults with disabilities feel resentment toward their parents, believing that the parents unquestioningly submitted them to all the treatments, procedures, hospitalizations, and institutionalizations prescribed by doctors. However, at that time, parents had few options.

A pediatrician, Perri Klass, has described a possible result of the Biomedical Model:

> If we are at war, then who is the enemy? Rightly the enemy is the disease, and even if that is not your favorite metaphor, it is a rather common way to

think of medicine: we are combating these deadly processes for the bodies of our patients. They become battlefields, lying there passively in bed while the evil armies of pathology and the resplendent forces of modern medicine fight it out. Still, there are some very good doctors who seem to think that way, who take disease as a personal enemy and battle it with fury and dedication. The real problem arises because all too often the patient comes to personify the disease and somehow the patient becomes the enemy. (Klass, as cited in Couser, 1997, pp. 26–27)

One of the greatest leaders in the disability rights movement was Ed Roberts. However, physicians saw little value in his life when he was a teenager and contracted polio. Roberts internalized those views. He was respirator-dependent. With others, Roberts later founded the independent living movement and the World Institute on Disability. He fought to graduate from high school and to be admitted to the University of California at Berkeley, where he organized the "Rolling Quads" to fight for the right to live outside the campus hospital. Roberts was later appointed by Governor Jerry Brown to be director of the California State Department of Rehabilitation. He died in 1995.

Shapiro (1993) described the effect of the Biomedical Model of disability on Roberts:

> Roberts saw himself as a "helpless cripple" overwhelmed by depression, powerlessness, and self-hatred. He asked his parents if he would ever go to college, marry, or hold a job. The answer, based on what doctors, nurses, and counselors had said, was always no. It would have been more humane, a doctor had told his mother, if the high fever of polio had killed him quickly. (p. 42)

Because of its long history, most of which was involved with the treatment of physical conditions, the Biomedical Model does not lend itself well to intellectual, cognitive, or psychiatric disabilities (Helms, 1992). Only recently have neurodevelopmental, cognitive, and psychiatric disabilities been recognized as disabilities. Furthermore, these disabilities are conditions that are, for the most part, managed and treated over the life span of the individual. The Biomedical Model, with its emphasis on finding, treating, and curing a problem that exists solely within the individual (without taking the environment into consideration) does not address cognitive, intellectual, or psychiatric disabilities well. Cases of polio illustrate the Biomedical Model's complete lack of interest in the psychological and sociological aspects of disability. Wilson (1990), a polio survivor, collected and studied hundreds of first-person accounts of polio in the United States and Canada. He summarized:

> While physicians, surgeons, physical therapists, and nurses focused on rehabilitating the body, the polio survivors of whatever age were largely left alone to deal with the significant emotional and psychological responses to

physical crippling and extended rehabilitation hospitalization. The cost was tremendous. (p. 67)

Polio survivors, many of them young children, had endured months of separation from their families and had experienced many treatments and therapies. They had also seen their roommates die and had wondered if they would survive to leave the hospital. When they returned home, many had orthopedic disabilities. Most difficult, these polio survivors returned to a society in which there were no accommodations, no peer support groups, and little assistive technology. One polio survivor (Mee, 1999) told of his father's only reference to his polio: "The world is not going to change for you." Yet, in spite of obvious needs, professionals never saw the necessity for emotional or psychological counseling and support for polio survivors or their families.

Also, concerning the dominance of the Biomedical Model in shaping the polio experience, authors have noted that Franklin Delano Roosevelt, the president of the United States who was a polio survivor and a consummate politician, regarded polio as a personal tragedy for which society should provide charity. Rather than seeking to bring about national legislation that would provide civil rights, services, and public accommodations for polio survivors, Roosevelt began the first nationwide charity drives, and the first poster children were the creation of the March of Dimes. Indeed, many disability scholars refer to Roosevelt as a "handicapitalist" and the father of the charity telethons, such as Jerry Lewis's Muscular Dystrophy telethon. Of course, it should be remembered that FDR provided millions of dollars for the treatment and care of individuals with polio, and, perhaps most important, he served as a role model for Americans with all types of disabilities. Nevertheless, charity drives cannot take the place of permanent civil rights legislation, public accommodations, and fully funded services, many of which had to await passage of the ADA many decades later.

It is not extreme to state that the Biomedical Model forms the basis for most bioethical concerns regarding disability, such as the automatic abortions of fetuses with disabilities, allowing newborn infants with disabilities to die, and assisting in the suicide of individuals with severe and multiple disabilities. In all of these situations, the individuals, whether elderly or still in the womb, have only one identity—the disability. The individual *becomes* the disability. No other resources or solutions are considered, such as the individual's strengths or resources, treatments, assistive technology available, or the provision of civil rights. The Disability Rights Movement has a derisive phrase to describe the Biomedical Model solution to these ethical concerns—*"Cure 'em or kill 'em."*

Medicalization and Pathologization

Before we leave our discussion of the Biomedical Model, two practices that have resulted from this model should be defined. The first practice is medicalization and occurs when social, human experiences or conditions are *unjustifiably* defined as medical problems, which then allow medical professionals to diagnose and treat the problem. Previously, these conditions had been considered normal. The second practice is pathologization and occurs when normal human behaviors and experiences are treated as sickness and deviance. The most clear cut example of pathologization was the inclusion of homosexuality in the DSM as deviance and sickness and a condition which required fixing. In 1973, after lobbying efforts of LGBT (Lesbian, Gay, Bisexual, Transgendered Persons) organizations, the American Psychiatric Association voted to eliminate a normal human behavior, homosexuality, from the DSM. The vote was 5,853 for excluding and 3,810 for retention. Pathologizing an experience simply means that we as a society believe that something is wrong and needs fixing.

Both of these practices are the results of the changing social construction of diagnoses and normality. PWDs, and their families, have always been aware of medicalization and pathologization; but it has been only in the last 30 years that PWODs have begun to recognize these practices.

The practices of pathologization and medicalization are most often defined in negative ways, but these practices are easier to understand when models of disability are considered. Also, there are benefits to pathologization and medicalization. First, the Biomedical Model supplanted the Religious–Moral Model, and society has transferred many of the roles of religious leaders to medical professionals, especially the friendly family doctor. The Biomedical Model provides objective explanations to conditions rather than thinking that the cause of the condition is an individual's moral failing. For example, is it more helpful to define ADHD as a neurocognitive developmental disability rather than accusing the parents of bad parenting and the child as being oppositional?

Advances in medications, medical technology, genetics, and surgery coupled with the increase in the number of medical specialties enlarge the medical professions' scope of practice and, in turn, result in greater influence over both PWDs and PWODs. However, PWDs have experienced a much longer and pervasive history of medicalization and pathologization than PWODs. For example, most residential schools for children who were blind or deaf were headed by a physician rather than an educational administrator, a teacher, or someone who was deaf or blind. The primary function of these schools was educational, and the students did not have long-term illnesses; most were healthy, but nonetheless, because these children had disabilities, it was thought that only a physician should have authority to educate them. One author summarized, "The institutions, even when they were benign, existed because people with medical authority could decide what is best for PWDs" (Byrom, 2004, p. 27).

PWDs have had a long and tragic history of being subjected to pathologization. A disability scholar summarized:

> Disability research consistently finds that health care professionals have as negative or more negative attitudes toward living with a disability than the general public and far more negative opinions than disabled people hold. A leading psychologist researching disabilities calls the findings on this discrepancy of views consistent and stunning. (Longmore, 2003, p. 179)

This tendency to pathologize the experience of disability, combined with the often unchallenged authority of physicians, and the lack of oversight, often resulted in the death of PWDs. The Nazi genocide of 200,000 Germans with disabilities is a horrific example of pathologization. Another illustration of pathologization is told by a mother of a child, Jacob, who has ASD: "The doctors say that Jacob hits his older brother because Jacob has ASD. But, I think Jacob hits his brother because all brothers (at a young age) hit each other. Not every misbehavior is the result of the ASD" (Rosin, 2014, para. 7).

Physicians as the Cultural Interpreters of the Disability Experience

In the past, only physicians wrote about the experience of disability, making them "cultural interpreters" of disability to the general public. There are few exceptions (such as Helen Keller); however, because of their knowledge and expertise, and the fact that history in general is written by winners, successes, and those in power, physicians wrote the little available disability history we have. One PWD summarized the irony that those living with disability 24/7 did not write their history as, "It's like having White people writing about the African American experience."

Interactive Models: Disability as a Personal Tragedy or a Collective Responsibility?

Both the Religious–Moral and Biomedical models of disability are non-interactive because the cause and treatment of disability are considered to be the sole responsibility of the individual. In non-interactive models, no other source of the disability is of interest, nor are the PWD's environment, strengths, social role demands, resources, or the political and social time period considered. In the Religious–Moral Model, disability is viewed as a personal tragedy, and in the Biomedical Model, disability is viewed as "individual bad luck." Disability, and the people who experience them, are viewed as strange outsiders. In these models, PWDs should not ask or require anything of society, such as civil rights, accommodations, dignity, or respect.

Non-interactional models tend to look for a single field of expertise, and society relinquishes power to these professions. In the Religious–Moral Model, spiritual and religious authorities were the experts on disability, and in the Biomedical Model of disability, medical professionals are the experts. Non-interactional models provide clear, unambiguous judgments, and according to one sociologist, "We create clear and unambiguous categories into which people fall, ignoring the fact that definition of disability changes all the time and is riddled with inconsistencies and overlapping boundaries" (A. G. Johnson, 2001, pp. 22–23). Because non-interactional models give power of definition and treatment to professional experts, PWDs become passive recipients of treatment, with little input into the types of services they receive.

In summary, non-interactional models seem to be neat, seem to be easily understood by everybody, and seem to relieve the broader culture of any responsibility for PWDs because disability is only a religious or medical "problem."

The use of non-interactional models is also a more straightforward way to design and conduct research studies. The most important requirements of research are control of confounding variables, and non-interactional models of disability provide more control because of their simplicity. At first glance, these "advantages" appear appealing and desirable. Interactional models, on the other hand, do not provide neat, easily understood categories. These models require a shift in perspective because in these models: (1) the services of many types of professionals are used, (2) disability is conceptualized as a social construction that evolves, (3) the individual PWD is considered to be the expert on his or her disability, and (4) society is viewed as part of the problem of disability. Therefore, society is required to be part of the solution to disability because there are so many variables. Interactional models are not clear cut or neat, but they do represent the daily, lived lives of most PWDs, more than non-interactional models.

The next three models that we will discuss are interactive models of disability in which disability is being increasingly viewed as a collective, public responsibility. These interactive models are environmental, functional, and sociopolitical. PWDs are viewed as normal people, with the same motivations, feelings, and goals as PWODs. With what does an individual's disability interact? First, the PWD's strengths and resources are considered; second, the prejudice and discrimination found in the larger society (which is not inherent in the disability itself) are acknowledged and addressed; and third, the environment and the individual's functional demands are taken into account.

The Environmental Model of Disability

In this section look for—

⬦ how prejudice and discrimination are not an inherent aspect of a disability

⬦ how the environment can cause, define, or exaggerate disability

The Environmental Model posits that the individual's environment—both social and physical—can cause, define, or exaggerate disability. It is easy to see the relationship between disability and the physical environment. "Disability is viewed as . . . a product of a disabling, unresponsive, or insensitive environment" (Hursh, 1995, p. 322). Essentially, environments can limit physical access and opportunities for work, education, and social participation. If a person with paraplegia does not have a wheelchair, then the impact of the paraplegia is greater. Barriers in the physical environment can hinder the individual with a disability, and the ADA is helping to make the environment accessible for all citizens. We shall see in Chapter 5 that the physical world has been designed on the (false) assumption that everyone can walk, everyone can hear, and everyone can see.

It is a little more difficult to understand the relationship between disability and the social and cultural environment. For example, in Manchurian China, infant girls from upper-class homes had their feet bound tightly until the bones were broken and twisted; as a result, these girls and women were unable to walk. Furthermore, to most people today who look at photographs of these Manchurian girls and women, the feet of the girls and women appear to be deformed. The Manchurian people considered the feet of these women to be beautiful, however, and, moreover, judged the inability to walk or stand to be a sign of prestige and status because these girls and women came from rich homes and therefore were not required to work. This is an unusual example, but it does illustrate that disability is not only a biological construction; it is also the result of social and cultural definitions.

Another example of a disability that is often environmentally defined is a learning disability. Learning disabilities, the result of neurological malfunction, probably were not noticeable in preliterate societies. In modern times, individuals with learning disabilities are often called "6-hour retardates" by others and by themselves because their learning disabilities seem environmentally specific during the 6 hours they are in school. Another example of environmental factors defining disability, rather than anything related to the disability itself, is described by Sobsey (1994). Sobsey recounted that many men with disabilities left institutions during World War I and World War II to fight in the United States military. One institution in Connecticut, Southbury Training School, released 13 men who then enlisted to fight in World War II. Four of these 13 men were wounded in combat, and seven were promoted to higher ranks. When the war ended, most of these soldiers were returned to institutions.

While there is an environmental factor to all types of disability, the Environmental Model may more completely provide a solution to psychiatric disabilities. Stefan (2001), a legal scholar, explained psychiatric disabilities as follows:

> Episodic, highly responsive to context and environment, and exist along a spectrum, which theoretically can be cause for hope—people with mental disabilities are frequently strong, talented, competent, and capable, and their environments can be structured in a way to support and increase their strengths, talents, competence, and capabilities. (p. 10)

Today, there are many environmental changes that have transformed the definition of disability. For example, the introduction of psychotropic medications, which allow many individuals with mental illnesses to control their symptoms, has dramatically changed the ways in which both society and the individual view mental illness. Of course, these medications do not work for everyone, and there are many side effects, but nonetheless, these medications have brought about many changes. We can see that this is an environmental change and not a change in mental illness. Other environmental changes that have affected the definition of disability include supported employment and supported living. Used primarily for individuals with intellectual disabilities and individuals with mental illness, these types of community jobs and apartment living are supervised and assisted by professional service providers. Individuals who in the past would not have been thought to be capable of working or living outside an institution now do both. Once again, these types of professional services are environmental changes and are not changes in the disabilities. Finally, the accordance of civil rights to PWDs by the ADA is another straightforward example of environmental shifts that have transformed the meaning of disability.

Before the advent of industrialized, urban society, disability was defined and treated differently. In small, rural communities in which members of families worked side by side, day after day, and everyone in the small community knew everyone else, PWDs had their basic needs met and were accorded a place in their community. As described by a noted disability scholar: "In small scale societies, nondisabled citizens knew disabled citizens. People many of us take to be 'bizarre' or 'disturbed' in today's urban areas would often have become familiar, accepted (if not well understood) neighbors of rural communities" (Higgins, 1992a, p. 191).

For everyone in these small communities, with or without disabilities, home and family were the basis of everyday life. Everyone was perceived as a unique individual, with both a history and place in the community before the standardization and anonymity of large cities. It was the environment that influenced the status and perception of PWDs and not anything inherent in the disabilities. Another disability scholar described the place of the PWD in these small communities:

> [In preindustrial communities] rigid separation had not yet been made between home and work and where travel was difficult for anyone, citizens with disabilities may not have been exposed to some of the egregious inequities that have subsequently become apparent in highly impersonal autonomous cultures. . . . Deviant or atypical personal characteristics that may have become familiar in a small community seemed bizarre or disturbing in an urban milieu. (Hahn, 1997, pp. 177–178)

The impact on a PWD of moving from a small community to a larger, more anonymous community also occurs today. Casey Roberts Dunham, former Miss South Central Georgia, who has Tourette's syndrome, a neuropsychiatric disability that causes involuntary behaviors, explained:

> I was brought up in a small town and went to school with the same kids for years. They took it as something I always did—grunted and made facial expressions. But by the time I was 13 or 14 years old and went to Wayne

County, where there was a bigger and more diverse crowd of kids, it was harder. They made smart remarks and I had no ammo for fighting back. . . . My confidence was beat to the dirt. ("A Family Portrait," 2005, p. 3)

Scheer and Groce (1988) summarized the negative effect: "Americans have lost familiarity with disabled [*sic*] people so common in small-scale societies" (p. 33). It is interesting that Scheer and Groce viewed this loss to be greater for PWODs than for PWDs.

Prejudice, discrimination, and stigma are not an inherent part of a disability; instead, they are part of the environment. These attitudes needlessly hinder PWDs. More relevant today as examples are individuals with mental illness who manage their illnesses with medications and, yet, because of societal prejudice, discrimination, and stigma, are unnecessarily hindered.

Society has created many barriers, both physical and attitudinal, for people with disabilities. For example, in the United States, the attributes of health, strength, youth, fitness, and beauty are highly valued (Buss, 2014), and the emphasis on these attributes increases the impact of disability. In the chapter on society's response to disability, the societal and cultural construction of disability will be discussed more thoroughly.

The Functional Model of Disability

In this section look for—

⬥ the relationship between disability and society's roles and functions

⬥ the relationship between disability and the individual's roles and functions

⬥ the way in which assistive technology can change the definition of disability

The Functional Model of disability theorizes that the functions of the individual influence the definition of disability. Individuals who enjoy physical activities would probably be more affected by a mobility impairment than those who do not care for such activities. Individuals whose work does not require physical strength, movement, or stamina would be less affected by a mobility impairment. The example most often used to illustrate the Functional Model of disability is that of the professional pianist who has one finger amputated. The loss of one finger would probably not be considered a disability for most people, and yet, because of the impairment in occupational functioning for the concert pianist, the amputation would be a life-changing disability. Individuals who are visual learners and lose their vision probably experience a greater sense of loss than auditory learners who lose their sight. The relationship between functioning and disability can be very specific to the individual. For example, Stephen Hawking, professor of physics at Cambridge University and world-famous theoretical physicist, considers his disability, amyotrophic lateral sclerosis (ALS), which greatly limits mobility and impairs speech, to be an advantage because it allows him more time to think. Two people can have the same type and degree of disability, but because of their functions and environments, they have a very different disability experience.

Judy Gilliam, a Government Service 15 (top-level) manager at the Defense Department, was described by her supervisor as follows:

> She's a quadriplegic, Phi Beta Kappa, and she says it this way, "I can't dress myself. I can't walk. I can't drive. I can't pick up a glass of water. But I can work." And her work, I am here to tell you, is consistently characterized by superior quality and productivity. (Fleischer & Zames, 2001, p. 131)

Another example of the way in which the vocational environment may change the definition of disability concerns learning disabilities. In the same way that machines replaced the need for human muscle power during the Industrial Revolution, computers may replace the need for many human clerical skills.

> Over the lifetime of today's students, many of the basic verbal and clerical skills that have long dominated education at all levels will cease to be important in an economy and marketplace where these tasks will be increasingly taken over by semi-intelligent machines. With these changes, the visual-spatial talents, global thinking mental models, pattern recognition, creative problem solving and other nonverbal abilities often associated with dyslexia are expected to become increasingly important in tomorrow's workplace, as greater use is made of data visualization, computer graphics, and interactive multi-sensory technologies to understand and communicate information about complex systems and discontinuous trends. As everyone struggles to accommodate themselves to deep changes in thinking and working, some dyslexics [sic] will doubtless play, once again, their oft-repeated role—working creatively at the edge of a new frontier, reading little but learning much, experimenting, innovating, establishing a path forward—learning from direct experience, anticipating where things are going, taking risks. (West, 1997, p. 350)

Weisgerber (1991) told of a man named Manny Guitierrez, with Down syndrome, who works with archaeologists from the University of Arizona. Mr. Guitierrez tags all the artifacts unearthed on the digs. Weisgerber summarized: "His work does not entail intellectual tasks but rather the ability to label archaeological artifacts, a task at which he excels" (p. 179).

Three scholars and researchers who study the sources of attitudes toward people with disabilities (Langer, Bashner, & Chanowitz, 1985) found that children can understand disability from a functional model. After speaking to a group of children about disabilities and discussing the various jobs at which PWDs are successful, the researchers showed the children two pictures of male newscasters; one newscaster was in a wheelchair, and the other newscaster did not have a visible disability. The children rated both newscasters as equally qualified to perform the job. The children could see that the mobility impairment would not impede the newscaster on the job.

In 1997, a syndicated newspaper article addressed the problem of disability insurance fraud and illustrated the lengths to which fraudsters will go to fake a disability. One example clearly shows the Functional Model of disability, when a dentist is able to collect disability insurance for the loss of a single finger, his right index finger, "a crucial digit."

> A 38-year-old Florida dentist, for instance, had his own finger chopped off to collect on a $72,000-a-year disability policy, which would have continued, with annual increases, through age 65.
>
> Dr. John Rende agreed to have a pair of brothers, Robert and Kenneth Alberton, chop off his right index finger with an ax. The Jacksonville dentist got $1.3 million from the Albertons' homeowners insurance company for the "wood-cutting accident."
>
> Because he could no longer practice dentistry without the crucial digit, Dr. Rende was set to collect disability for nearly three decades. But he got frightened when the Albertons began black-mailing him for a bigger cut, and Rende went running to confess to the FBI. (Anderson & Moller, 1997)

Another unusual example of idiosyncratic meaning of both function and disability concerns the publisher, Charles Scribner, Jr. In the book, *The Mind's Eye,* Oliver Sacks relates Scribner's experience.

> [Charles Scribner] presided over the publishing house established by his great-grandfather in the 1840s. In his sixties, he developed a visual alexia—probably as a result of a degenerative process in the visual parts of the brain. It was a devastating problem for a man who had published the work of Hemingway and others, a man whose life was centered on reading and writing. (Sacks, 2010, p. 64)

It took some time and a great deal of practice, but Scribner was able to switch to audio books, and he resumed his career.

Ryan and Thomas (1980) explained the way in which industrialization altered the definition of intellectual disability: "The speed of factory work, the enforced discipline, the timekeeping and production norms—all of these were a highly unfavourable change from the slower, more self-determined and flexible methods of work into which many handicapped [*sic*] people had been integrated" (p. 101).

The shift of the economy of the United States from an economy that depended on physical labor such as farming, mining, and manufacturing to an economy based on service and information processing has influenced the definition of disability. In an economy based on physical labor, many individuals with cognitive disabilities, such as learning disabilities or mild intellectual disabilities, were successful workers. In contrast, in that economy, an individual (especially a man) with a physical disability would have been severely limited. In today's economy, a cognitive disability is much more limiting than a physical disability because service jobs and technological and information-processing jobs require high levels of cognitive functioning. Today, an individual with a physical disability who has the use of assistive technology has many employment options (J. F. Smart & D. W. Smart, 2006).

Thirty years ago, Farber and his colleagues (Farber, 1968; Farber & Lewis, 1976; Heiney, 1976) incorporated the Functional Model of disability into their label for people with disabilities: "surplus populations." People with disabilities, according to these disability scholars, are thought of as surplus populations by the general public because they are not considered to be necessary for institutional efficiency and progress.

Changes in social role functioning also alter the definition of disability. For example, elderly people today live far more active lives than their counterparts did 100 years ago, with many today working until age 75 and many more engaging in active community work and physical activity in their retirement years. Today, an older person who experiences a disability, such as blindness or a mobility impairment, probably considers the disability to be limiting rather than simply an expected outcome of aging. As can be seen from these examples, large-scale changes in functioning alter the definition of disability.

Should nonessential functions such as leisure and sports be included in the Functional Model of disability? Most functional models, at present, include only work activities and activities of daily living (ADLs), which assist PWDs in getting to jobs. As a result of this exclusive focus on work and ADLs, many individuals in the Disability Rights Movement regard the Functional Model of disability as an economic model. According to these advocates, the Functional Model is primarily concerned with the earning capacity of the PWD. Wheelchair sports are an example of a non-work function of PWDs. Yet, there were no wheelchair sports until a particular wheelchair was developed in the 1980s.

The Functional Model of disability, of course, is closely related to the availability of adaptive technology and the capability of such technology to assist in role functioning (Spechler, 1996). A professor in a wheelchair can perform his or her occupational functions; an individual who is blind who uses a computer with a speech synthesizer, a brailler (braille typewriter), and other assistive technology can perform successfully in many vocational roles. Mobility devices include power wheelchairs, sonic guides, vision enhancement devices, and functional electronic stimulation (FES). In FES, successive bursts of low-level, controlled electricity stimulate paralyzed muscles to contract according to patterns programmed into a computer. This allows the return of coordinated movement to paralyzed muscles, such as those needed for walking. It is used with persons whose muscles have not been damaged and with persons, such as those with spinal cord injuries, whose movements have been blocked by the inability of messages from the brain to get through the spinal cord and to the muscles (Scherer, 1993, p. 18).

Assistive technology (AT) not only increases functioning, but, according to many PWDs, also gives them freedom and independence. A 2004 National Organization on Disability (NOD) national survey reported that one third of PWDs stated that they would lose their independence if they did not have AT. Many PWDs clearly remember the day they received a piece of technology, such as a scooter, wheelchair, or computer. Perhaps these memories can be compared to memories of obtaining a driver's license or a first car. The world suddenly becomes much larger.

There are also augmentative and alternative communication devices that help the individual to communicate; environmental control devices that allow the individual to lock doors, operate the thermostat, and operate other household appliances; and sensory devices that read for people who are blind.

Scherer (1993) explained the rapid increase in the use of assistive technology:

> Each passing year has seen the numbers of assistive technologies in use increase exponentially. . . . As recently as the early 1960s, most equipment available to individuals with disabilities was only of a mechanical nature. Wheelchairs were literally chairs on wheels. Artificial limbs were plastic or, earlier, metal and wooden replacements for lost arms or legs. (p. 19)

The story of Amy Purdy, age 34, provides a final example of a very specialized type of function and the way in which very specialized assistive technology met these needs. Ms. Purdy was a competitor in the Paralympics in Sochi, Russia, and won a Bronze medal in snowboarding. While in Sochi, she began rehearsals for ABC's televised dance competition, *Dancing with the Stars*. There was no time to waste between the Paralympics and *Dancing with the Stars*; every minute of dance rehearsal was important. Unexpectedly, she found that her prosthetic walking legs would not work for dancing. Ms. Purdy had had two lower limb amputations at age 19 due to a case of bacterial meningitis. The article in *USA Today*, related:

> During her first day of rehearsal, she realized her walking legs wouldn't work for dancing. "My calf muscles were wanting to expand, but they couldn't because they're in carbon fiber. So it was painful." Luckily, there was a prosthetic shop at the Sochi Paralympics. "They rounded out the insides of my legs for my calves to expand." And now, she says, she's not in any pain. "At this point,

my legs fit well enough to do what I'm going to be doing. I'm snowboarding and dancing, and in between, I'm walking really far." (Oldenburg, 2014, para. 13)

Some might think, "Isn't it wonderful that someone without real legs would be allowed to participate in an international sports competition and dance on national television?" However, it is the highly technologized prosthesis that gave Ms. Purdy these opportunities. She could not have participated if her prosthetics had been wooden legs.

The Sociopolitical Model of Disability

In this section, look for—

- ✧ The Sociopolitical Model considers disability to be a collective concern.
- ✧ The Sociopolitical Model is a reaction against the Biomedical Model.
- ✧ The Sociopolitical Model includes prejudice and discrimination as causal factors in disability.
- ✧ The Sociopolitical Model advocates for an accommodating society rather than requiring the PWD to "take the world as it is."
- ✧ The Sociopolitical Model advocates for civil rights rather than charity or pity.
- ✧ Proponents of this model want to form a group identity and identity politics.
- ✧ PWDs want their civil rights as American citizens while at the same time maintaining their identity as PWDs.

This model is a radical shift and, at first glance, may be difficult to understand. Proponents of this model posit that disability is a societal concern (May, 2005). Society causes disability, and it is society, rather than the individual, who should bear the responsibility for dealing with disability. A disability scholar explained:

The idea that disability is a collective issue, however, is not easy to grasp. It seems to run counter to the traditional Western social and political philosophies, influenced by the Enlightenment, that place tremendous importance on the individual. Combine this emphasis with belief in the superiority of reason and mind over the passions and vicissitudes of the body, also a legacy of the Enlightenment, and we can begin to understand why the disability has long been conceived of as only an individual issue. (Michalko, 2002, p. 6)

If we review the six reasons why there are more disabilities than ever before, not *in spite of* medical advances but *because* of medical advances, the idea that society plays a part in causing disabilities becomes clearer.

Thinking in terms of large populations (demographics), it has long been acknowledged that societal influences such as lack of health insurance, lack of education, and poverty are associated with higher rates of disability. Those without insurance, those with less than an eighth-grade education, those who work in dangerous and physically demanding jobs, and those who live below the poverty line are at greater risk for acquiring a disability (J. F. Smart & D. W. Smart, 1997). It is clear that all of these societal problems can be eliminated, or, at minimum, improved.

The Sociopolitical Model, because of its emphasis on demographics and large groups, has the capability to consider other social identities of the individual with a disability, such as gender, religion, sexual orientation, or racial, ethnic, and cultural identity. Such recognition of these other statuses can more completely describe the individual's experience of disability. On a demographic level (looking at large populations of people), the Sociopolitical Model recognizes that those of racial and ethnic minority status have a greater probability of experiencing a disability (with the exceptions of Asians and Pacific Islanders). An excellent summary is provided by disability demographers Thompson-Hoffman and Storck (1991):

> There is a higher concentration of disability among blacks, and, in most cases, there is a lower concentration among Hispanics. Where breakdowns are available on Native Americans, they consistently form the subgroup with the largest percentage of disabled persons. Disability prevalence rates for Asians and Pacific Islanders are markedly below national estimates. (p. 25)

Disability demographers have posited some possible causes for these higher rates of disability, including less insurance coverage, higher employment rates in physically demanding and dangerous jobs, lower educational levels, and high rates of poverty. Disabilities for which in utero testing is available, such as Down syndrome, may become "low-income disabilities" if low-income pregnant women do not have insurance to pay for expensive prenatal testing. On the other hand, higher income pregnant women who can afford prenatal testing might choose to abort a fetus when the tests reveal the presence of a disability. Using the example of Down syndrome, if these disparities in insurance coverage persist, far more babies with Down syndrome would be born to low-income families. It can be seen that *all* of these hypothesized causes are the result of societal conditions. If these societal conditions could be changed, reduced, or improved, it stands to reason that the higher rates of disabilities for minorities and lower socioeconomic groups would be reduced.

Proponents of the Sociopolitical Model assert that many of the difficulties PWDs experience are caused by society. Disability is not a private concern, because disability is defined as a social and political construction. We can recall the example of

Martha's Vineyard, in which people who were deaf were not considered to be socially different and did not experience lives of reduced opportunity, and most important, PWODs accommodated the Deaf by learning sign language. Isolation of PWDs, reduced opportunities for PWDs, and legalized discrimination against PWDs are all socially constructed and not related to any biological or emotional condition of the individual.

A Canadian disability scholar summarized, "As a society, we allow handicaps to exist by refusing to pay the price to remove them. Therefore, disabilities are social responsibilities" (Bickenbach, 1993, p. 161). Bickenbach is defining handicaps as societal obstacles and not as disabilities. He also quotes the Canadian Bill of Human Rights: "All Canadians are responsible for the necessary changes which will give disabled persons the same choices of participation that are enjoyed by those who are not disabled." Included in Bickenbach's quotation is the idea that we, as a society, *choose* to allow societal obstacles to persist, such as inaccessible environments, lack of accommodations, or provision of limited choices. Bickenbach also shows that handicapping societal conditions are not inevitable or unchangeable. Disabilities are natural and inevitable, but handicapping conditions are not.

The Sociopolitical Model recognizes that there is a biological component to disability, but also holds that there is nothing in the disability or the PWD that warrants prejudice or discrimination (J. F. Smart, 2004). Any inferiority experienced by PWDs is the inferiority conferred on them by society. There is a wide range of disadvantages and barriers experienced by PWDs, probably far more than society recognizes or acknowledges; none of which has to do with disabilities themselves or the individuals who have disabilities. Some of these barriers have been supported by federal legislation, or better stated, PWDs experienced the lack of federal protection under the law. Indeed, PWDs often state that their experiences with prejudice and discrimination are far more limiting than the impairments of their disabilities.

While the Biomedical Model may seek to address disability by eliminating, preventing, or curing disability, the Sociopolitical Model seeks to address the lack of civil rights and accommodations for PWDs. In contrast to the Sociopolitical Model, the shortcomings of the Biomedical Model are seen in the following statement:

> Society sees its responsibility to disability in the provision of preventive, curative, and rehabilitative measures. Disability must be prevented; failing this, it must be cured; if it can be neither prevented nor cured, society must see that the person is rehabilitated, the "final solution." These responses are in keeping with the biomedical version of what it means to be human. This version, which emphasizes adjustment and adaptation, plays a dominant role in the contemporary understanding of disability. Unfortunate as it is, disability is something that *happens* to some of us and it is up to us to take advantage of what society gives us in the form of medical and rehabilitation programs— and adjust. (Michalko, 2002, pp. 6–7)

Here is an exercise that might help us to understand the difference between the models of disability. Identify which statement is *most* true.

- Louisa's problem is her deafness.
- Louisa's problem is the lack of sign language interpreters.

Now, identify the problem that is more easily solved. Here are two more statements.

- Dr. Brilliant cannot perform surgery in small hospitals because of his paraplegia.
- Dr. Brilliant cannot perform surgery in small hospitals because these hospitals do not have elevators.

Prestigious professions, labels, and diagnoses can shape self-identities. One woman asked:

> When are we ever going to believe, in our hearts—truly believe—that our problems are not things we are given by God, to solve ourselves, but are things that we have a right to require our society to change—because the problem isn't our disabilities but inaccessible environment which society built in the first place. ("The Problem With 'Challenge'," 1985, para. 12)

The Sociopolitical Model has three advantages over the other models. First, the Sociopolitical Model more accurately and completely describes the daily lives of PWDs. Second, the Sociopolitical Model has the potential to mobilize PWDs to assert their rights. Third, this model allows individuals with all types of disabilities to form a group identity.

The ADA is based on the Sociopolitical Model. Much of the impetus (and methodology) of the Sociopolitical Model is derived from the Civil Rights Movement of the 1960s. While the advocates of this model recognize that not every PWD, or even most PWDs, will become political activists, they also understand that collective gains will result in individual successes. In the NPR Disability History Project, *Tomorrow's Children,* a mother of a child with a disability related:

> When my daughter was young, people would ask, "Is she going to school?" I feel that I owe a debt to the older generation for creating the cultural and educational opportunities that my daughter has. They insured the basic human rights for people [PWDs] whose very existence was not acknowledged. (National Public Radio, 1998c)

American citizens should not be required to ask for their rights. Rights should be automatically given. Furthermore, every American citizen should have legal protection provided by law to redress infringements on his or her civil rights.

Comparison of the Five Models

Each of these models contributes to the understanding of the disability experience and provides guidelines for action. In the Religious–Moral Model, because disability is defined as an individual's sin, wrongdoing, or character weakness, treatment is based on religious practices, such as prayer and repentance. In the Biomedical Model, treatment methods are concerned with changing the individual; in the Functional Model, intervention methods are aimed at adapting the functions of the individual; in the Environmental Model, professionals seek to change both the physical and social environments of the individual; and in the Sociopolitical Model, the provision of civil rights and equal social status is the goal. In only two of the five models, the Religious–Moral Model and the Biomedical Model, is the "problem" viewed as entirely within the individual. Nonetheless, biology and organic functioning are important. No one would advocate that individuals who are blind should be bus drivers. The clear point, however, is that biology is not as important as it was previously thought to be.

No one today subscribes to a single disability model, although it is safe to state that for centuries there was only one model, the Religious–Moral Model. There is a purpose for each model, and comparison and combination of models can result in greater accuracy and detail in understanding the disability experience. It is important to understand how these models of disability relate to each other. For instance, the most clear-cut example of differing models of disability concerns deafness. For some, deafness is viewed from the Biomedical Model as a biological loss or dysfunction that requires some sort of treatment to the individual. In contrast, the Deaf Community views deafness from the Environmental Model and regards individuals who are deaf as members of a different culture who use a different language. In fact, many in the Deaf Community feel more identification with those who speak a different language from the majority, such as Spanish-speakers in a predominately English-speaking area.

Research Is Only as Good as the Model on Which It Is Based

The research that has sought to understand the individual's adaptation and response to a disability has been grounded in the Biomedical Model. As you remember, the Biomedical Model posits that the problem lies entirely within the individual, and, therefore, the responsibility for resolution and adaptation lies with that individual. Psychological instruments that have been used to assess a person's adjustment to a disability have not attempted to assess (1) the availability of resources to the individual, (2) the degree of stigma directed toward the type of disability that the individual experiences, or (3) the functions that are affected by the disability. The Biomedical Model deals with the treatment and rehabilitation of PWDs and does not usually consider such interventions as changing the social and physical environments.

Disability scholars (Anson, Stanwyck, & Krause, 1993; Krause, 1998a, 1998b; Krause & Anson, 1997; Krause, Coker, Charlifue, & Whiteneck, 1999) incorporate measures such as the *Life Situations Questionnaire* (LSQ; Krause, 1998b) and the *Reciprocal Support*

Scale (RSS; Krause & Anson, 1997) in their studies of the ways in which individuals respond to disabilities. The LSQ and the RSS ask questions about the individual's finances, career opportunities, living circumstances (whether he or she lives in an institution or at home), level of education, and degree of social interaction and emotional support. The Environmental and Functional models of disability are the bases of these types of questionnaires. Instruments such as these are used *in addition to* instruments that assess the individual's emotional response to the disability. As would be expected, by incorporating three models of disability—Biomedical, Functional, and Environmental—a more complete and accurate picture of the individual's response to the disability can be obtained.

Linton (1998) summarized the tension between research based in the Biomedical Model and research based in the interactive models, especially the Sociopolitical Model:

> Scientists and society at large are unused to disabled people as assertive, active, and, at times, aggressive. They are not used to disabled people who have little interest in being cured or in eliminating disability. If scientists reckon with that active voice, they may begin to see the disabled subject as less passive and controllable. The active voice of disabled people and the activated subject have a place in a comprehensive and representative science curriculum. (p. 96)

Equal Opportunity Under the Law: The Americans With Disabilities Act

In this section, look for—

  ✧ the rationale and intent of the 1990 ADA
  ✧ why the ADA (and the Amendments) do not require preferential treatment
  ✧ how court decisions weakened the intent and rationale of the ADA

In 1972, the 92nd Congress failed to add a disability provision to the 1964 Civil Rights Act. However, the Americans with Disabilities Act (ADA) was signed into law in July 1990 by President George H. W. Bush, thus enacting the first federal law that mandated and protected the civil rights of Americans with disabilities. Although the ADA is a separate disability civil rights act, much of the language of the 1964 Civil Rights Act was adapted and inserted in the ADA. While PWDs consider the ADA of 1990 to be a great step forward for the nation, one disability activist focused attention on the 200 years required to pass a civil rights law for a group of Americans:

It is a tremendously tragic commentary that . . . disabled people came to have enough hope to protest. It took two hundred years after this country was formed—*two hundred years*—for these people (PWDs) to begin to have hope. (Bowe, 1993, p. xi)

The Intent and Rationale of the Americans With Disabilities Act

The ADA clearly states the rationale of this statute: "Individuals with disabilities are a discrete and insular minority who have been faced with restrictions and limitations, subjected to a history of purposeful unequal treatment and relegated to a position of political powerlessness in our society" (Title I, §2(7)). A bill much like the Civil Rights Act of 1964 was needed to extend legal protection against discrimination to citizens with disabilities. People with disabilities often jokingly refer to the intent of the ADA as "boldly going where everybody else goes." Before the passage of the ADA, it was legal to discriminate against a qualified job applicant solely on the basis of disability. Employers could, and did, candidly inform applicants with disabilities that they did not obtain a job simply because of the presence of a disability, and individuals who acquired a disability while they were employed, which did not render them unqualified or incapable of performing the functions of a job, often were terminated. These individuals had no legal recourse.

Two disability analysts (Batavia & Schriner, 2001) described the *intent* of the ADA; however, they also point out the need for further laws to mandate specific needs of PWDs. Notice within this quote the words "in the mainstream of our society." These analysts are pointing out that "separate is not equal" and that the intent of the law is to minimize segregation and institutionalization.

> Although the ADA was intended to achieve social reform primarily on a case-by-case basis, it does provide some insight into how broader issues should be addressed. It indicates, through the general intent of Congress, that a major goal of disability policy in this country is to ensure the inclusion of people with disabilities in the mainstream of our society, and that people with disabilities are to be treated as first-class citizens. Using the ADA as a philosophical statement reflecting our national disability policy provides guidance and is valuable to keep us focused on ultimate policy goals. However, legally, it is no substitute for the laws needed to achieve such goals as access to health insurance, personal assistance services, employment, smoke-free environments, and the electoral process. (p. 690)

The ADA and ADAAA Do Not Require Preferential Treatment for People With Disabilities or Lowering of Standards

The ADA and ADAAA (Americans with Disabilities Act Amendments Act of 2008) are federal laws, although they are not totally universal in their application, because private organizations, religious organizations, and Native American tribes are not required to comply. Much of the general public mistakenly believes that the ADA designates Americans with disabilities as eligible for preferential treatment such as lowering or waiving requirements. The ADA clearly states that the individual must be qualified, or, stated another way, must be able to perform the essential functions of the job (with or without accommodations) and is not exempted from any legitimate requirement or qualification. In Chapter 4, on societal response to disability, a discussion of the differences between ensuring equal opportunity and extending preferential treatment will be presented. The ADA ensures equal opportunity for qualified individuals, based on their American citizenship, and does not require or encourage preferential treatment for people with disabilities.

The Five Titles of the ADA and AADA

In this section, look for—

  ✧ The five titles of the ADA
   1. Title I: Employment
   2. Title II: Transportation
   3. Title III: Public Accommodations and Services
   4. Title IV: Telecommunications
   5. Title V: Miscellaneous

The ADA has five main sections, or titles, each addressing a particular issue and each with different enforcing bodies. In addition to the enforcement by federal bodies, individuals can file lawsuits. A brief summary of each of the five titles of the ADA follows.

Title I: Employment

All employment aspects, including hiring, pay, benefits, job training, promotion, tenure, and termination, are covered in Title I. It is important to understand that current users of illegal drugs are not protected by the ADA. No employer with 15 or more employees can discriminate against an individual with a disability who is qualified and capable of performing the essential functions of the job. Further, employers must provide "reasonable accommodations," such as adaptations in employment testing procedures, assistive technology, job restructuring, provision of written materials in alternative formats such as Braille, provision of sign language interpreters, time off for visits to therapists, and architectural access for their employees with disabilities. Employment-testing accommodations include extra time for taking the test, someone to read the test, sign language interpreters, oral tests, large print, allowing the use of a magnifying glass, assisting in marking the answer sheet, and Braille presentations. The rationale behind the provision of these accommodations is to allow the test-taker to demonstrate his or her skill and knowledge level while still maintaining the validity of the test. (Of course, for some jobs, such as air traffic controller, speed of response is an integral part of the job, and, therefore, some accommodations on pre-employment tests, such as extended time, cannot be given.) Applicants or employees who pose a direct threat to the health and safety of other individuals may be refused a job or may be fired. Employers cannot make blanket inquiries about the presence of disabilities, such as health checklists on application forms, nor are they allowed to ask, verbally or in writing, if the applicant has a disability. Also, employers are allowed to require pre-employment medical examinations only after a conditional offer of employment has been made. Of course, individuals whose disabilities are readily visible, such as those who use a sign language interpreter or individuals who use wheelchairs, would not have the option of disclosing the presence of a disability.

Employers must pay employees with disabilities at the same rate as comparable employees without disabilities. This equal pay provision extends to benefits, including health insurance, and health insurance is very important to people with disabilities. The ADA also prohibits employers from assigning employees who have disabilities to the "back room." In other words, employers are not allowed to segregate an employee because of his or her disability. The Equal Employment Opportunity Commission enforces this title. Private clubs, organizations and churches, and Native American tribes are exempt from this title.

Title II: Transportation

Public entities, such as airplanes, buses, and trains, must provide vehicles that are accessible to people with disabilities. These accessible vehicles must be of a comparable level and comparable response time as vehicles used for people without disabilities. Therefore, accessible public transportation must provide the same schedules and routes that are available to everyone. The Architectural and Transportation Barriers Compliance Board, with members appointed by the President, devises standards for compliance, and the Department of Transportation enforces this title.

Title III: Public Accommodations and Services

Individuals with disabilities cannot be denied full and equal enjoyment of public accommodations solely on the basis of their disability. Public accommodations are hotels, motels, restaurants, theaters, art galleries, libraries, shopping malls, banks, professional offices, recreational facilities, parks, and zoos. For example, many movies are audio-described for people who are blind and closed-captioned for people who are deaf, allowing many PWDs to go to the movies if the theater is physically accessible. Private organizations and religious organizations are exempt. The Attorney General enforces this title.

Title IV: Telecommunications

Individuals with speech and hearing disabilities have the right to rapid, efficient, nationwide telephone and telecommunications systems (Equal Access to Software and

Information, 1999). Therefore, all telephone companies must provide public telephones that are accessible to people with speech and hearing impairments 24 hours a day, 7 days a week, to and from the United States, at no extra cost to the user. These devices include TDDs (telecommunication devices for the deaf). Federally funded public service announcements must include closed captions.

Bowe (1993) described accessibility to television:

> The Television Decoder Circuitry Act of 1990 (P.L. 100-431) requires that all 13-inch or larger television sets sold or manufactured in the United States after July 1993 include built-in chips enabling the set to receive and display captions or subtitles. The chips themselves cost under $10 to manufacture and are included as part of the purchase price of the set. Broadcasters, advertisers, and others pay the cost of producing the captions themselves. (p. xii)

This title is enforced by the Federal Telecommunications Commission. Electronic databases, Web sites, and e-mail must be available in alternative formats for individuals who are blind or who have learning disabilities.

Title V: Miscellaneous

Guidelines for making historical sites and wilderness accessible to individuals with disabilities are included. Accessible wilderness areas, including hunting and fishing locations, were mandated under Section 502 of the Rehabilitation Act of 1973 (Sullivan, 1998). The government must ensure that Americans with disabilities are able to engage in outdoor activities in the national parks and all other federal lands. The ADA strengthened and reinforced this mandate.

Resistance to the ADA

In this section, look for—

- ✧ Hospitals, colleges, universities, and state and local governments were required to make their buildings accessible.
- ✧ Public transportation companies were required to make all of their vehicles accessible.
- ✧ The nursing home lobby feared losing residents and, therefore, income.
- ✧ Employers feared rising health insurance costs.

Some of the criticisms of the ADA are humorous and ill-informed. Brian Doherty (1997), a senior editor for *Reason*, a monthly libertarian periodical, wrote an article entitled, "ADA Compliance Is Too Expensive." Doherty stated, "Sometimes it makes more sense to help a person in a wheelchair up a step or two than to spend thousands of dollars on ramps" (p. 53). We have learned that the provision of civil rights is never based on cost and, therefore, such statements are without basis. Moreover, there are many people in wheelchairs who would need help with those one or two steps. Bovard (1997), in an article entitled, "The ADA Defines Disability Too Broadly," made the following statements: "The ADA is also exploding like a series of cluster bombs across the budgets of local governments across the country" (p. 54); "The ADA is sometimes said to stand for 'Attorneys' Dreams Answered'" (p. 59); and "At colleges, the ADA has been a godsend to shirking students" (p. 60).

On the one hand, it would seem reasonable that everyone (including businesses, state governments, and nursing home administrators) would support a civil rights law for a portion of the population. On the other hand, it would seem reasonable that businesses, including public transportation, hotels, and movie theaters would welcome another source of income if PWDs were able to access their services.

Money, however, became the focus of resistance. It was thought that the ADA was too expensive to enforce. Many of the criticisms were the result of a civil rights clause in the 1973 Rehabilitation Act. This service law (which guided and funded the state-federal Rehabilitation agency) may be considered the forerunner of the ADA, but it only applied to businesses and government entities, including colleges and universities, which received federal funds. Also, this civil rights clause was not well known among the general population. Nonetheless, whether under the Rehabilitation Act of 1973 or the ADA, those entities which were required to comply with this law resisted.

Greyhound Bus refused to add wheelchair lifts to their buses; many municipal bus companies refused to train their drivers in the use of wheelchair lifts, and when these lifts broke down, they were not repaired or replaced. Polling places did not install wheelchair ramps. The nursing home industry had built too many facilities and knew that the ADA would mandate that PWDs could live in "the least restrictive environments,' their homes, and the industry would lose millions of dollars. Nursing home beds would be empty. A New York City attorney who is deaf, Michael Chatoff, sued the NYC Police Department on behalf of more than 200,000 New Yorkers who are deaf for failing to make the 911 emergency system available to teletype users (the telephone system people who are deaf used at the time.) "Chatoff sued in U.S. District Court, arguing that the issue was a matter of life and death" (Fleischer & Zames, 2001, p. 99). In a class action law suit against Boston University, *Elizabeth Guckenberger v. Boston University,* students with learning disabilities claimed that Boston University had systematically refused to provide accommodations to them and other students with learning disabilities. They brought their suit to federal court in July 1996. Elizabeth Guckenberger was a third-year law student. Boston University lost the case.

The ADA legal definition of disability showed that it is possible to both widen and narrow this definition. Early critics of the ADA wrongly thought the PWDs (and their lawyers) would interpret the ADA definition very broadly. Instead, the definition of disability was narrowed, and often the main focus of the lawsuit, discrimination against PWDs, was deflected while lawyers argued if the plaintiff had a disability. This is probably the single greatest problem of enforcing the ADA.

In the first edition of this book, I quoted a University of Chicago economics professor and Nobel Prize winner who wrote an editorial entitled, "Are We Hurting or Helping the Disabled?" in the magazine *Business Week*. He pointed out a potential weakness of the ADA:

> Congress allowed the definition of disability in the act to be vague. I predicted in this magazine that the vagueness of the ADA and the litigious nature of the judicial system would encourage lawyers and workers to widen the concept of disability to absurd extremes. (Becker, 1999, p. 9)

Eighteen years of implementing the ADA showed Becker to be right on two counts: first, the definition of disability did require clarification, and second, there were many ADA lawsuits because of the "litigious nature of the judicial system." However, Becker got it wrong on an important point: The vague definition of disability did not widen; the definition narrowed. Lawyers and employers, not workers, successfully narrowed the definition of disability, thus defeating the intent and purpose of the ADA.

In three employment cases (*Toyota v. Williams, 2002; Murphy v. United Parcel Service, Inc.;* and *Albertsons, Inc. v. Kirkenburg*) the Supreme Court ruled that anyone whose disability could be controlled or managed did not have a disability. Therefore, these cases were not heard. Murphy had high blood pressure that was controlled by medication, Kirkenburg had monocular vision, and Williams had carpal tunnel syndrome.

Results of the ADA

In this section, look for—

⬦ why the ADA has spurred advances in assistive technology
⬦ why the ADA has contributed to a collective identity for PWDs
⬦ how the ADA has increased the employment rate of PWDs

As expected, the ADA facilitated the access of people with disabilities into many aspects of public life. In addition, the ADA has spurred many advances in telecommunications, assistive technology, and job restructuring. Many of these advances have also benefited people without disabilities. For example, closed-captioned television, originally developed for viewers who are deaf, has also been helpful for elderly individuals or people who are learning English, and much of the assistive technology developed for people who are blind is used as memory aids for forgetful people who are not blind. Ramps into buildings that facilitate access for people who use wheelchairs also facilitate access for anyone or anything on wheels, such as strollers, carts, and wheeled suitcases. The first use of the transistor tube, which led to the computer revolution, was in hearing aids.

The ADA has also contributed to a collective identity of people with disabilities. Although this group identity did not begin with the ADA, the ADA has fostered the growth, pride, and awareness of the rights and responsibilities of PWDs under the law. For example, in the state of Utah, a man named Robert Irons undertook a project to contact people with disabilities and assist them in becoming registered to vote. Mr. Irons helped 900 people to register and then organized telephone committees to ensure that each of these 900 people had transportation to the polls on voting days. Mr. Irons simply informed individuals with disabilities about their large numbers and their ability to vote on legislation that would be favorable to them. It is safe to state that the ADA has increased group solidarity of Americans with disabilities.

In 2015, most young adults with disabilities do not remember the pre-ADA history, and many disability scholars refer to PWDs born after 1990 to be the "post-ADA generation." Adults with disabilities who acquired their disabilities before 1990 and the families of children who were born with disabilities before the ADA view the ADA as a watershed event in their lives. Grandparents with long-term disabilities might tell their amazed grandchildren about the "bad old days" (or pre-ADA history) when people who used wheelchairs were not allowed on airline flights!

Changes Enacted in the ADAAA

In this section, look for—

- ◈ more broadly defining disability
- ◈ clarification that disabilities that are episodic or in remission are considered disabilities
- ◈ why "ameliorative" effects of disabilities should NOT be considered
- ◈ academic requirements in higher education outlined

Robert Burgdorf (2002) is a professor of law who wrote the original draft of the ADA. In 2004 Burgdorf wrote:

> As I drafted the original version of the Americans with Disabilities Act, I never dreamed that this landmark civil rights law would become so widely misunderstood and my words so badly misinterpreted particularly by the body meant to protect the very rights guaranteed by the law. (para. 1)

After 18 years of witnessing the intent of the ADA being eroded, the Amendments to the ADA were passed in 2008. One legal expert described the results as "a litany of cases, a crazy quilt of decisions, narrowly defined, on issue after issue." In order to publicize the need for amendments to the ADA, buses called "The Road to Freedom Days" toured the U.S. To make a clear-cut comparison between the African American Civil Rights movement and the ADA, the buses stopped at the Martin Luther King Library, the Southern Poverty Law Center, and Lorraine Motel in Memphis (where King was assassinated), and the Brown v. Board of Education National Historical site (Fleischer & Zames, 2001). The purposes of the Amendments were to (a) facilitate a PWD seeking protection under the ADA; (b) to apply "a less demanding standard" by the courts in defining disability; and (c) to mandate reasonable modifications in policies, practices, or procedures in institutions of higher education.

Some specific guidelines for broadening the definition included episodic conditions. An individual who manages an episodic disability and is symptom-free would be considered to have a disability if the condition in its active state is considered a disability. The same guideline applies to relapsing and remitting disabilities such as multiple sclerosis or lupus. Often, these types of disabilities can be managed and controlled by medication and other treatments. Nonetheless, even while symptom-free, individuals with these types of conditions would be defined as having a disability and would be protected under the ADA. The sole exception to this guideline is the use of eyeglasses and contacts.

The ADA defined disability as a condition which "substantially limits a major life activity." The Amendments mandate that broader, more liberal definitions are given to both "major life activity" and "substantially limits." In academic institutions of higher education, "reasonable modifications" are required unless these modifications would alter the nature of the education. Modifications in policies, practices, or procedures are required unless the college or university can prove that these changes compromise the quality of education. Until the 2008 Amendments, many academic administrators thought that the ADA required the lowering of academic standards (or preferential treatment for students with disabilities.) This was never the intent of the ADA; however, the Amendments clearly spell out the modifications required and place the burden of proof upon the academic institution. Students with disabilities are to be held to the same academic standards as students without disabilities.

Several Supreme Court decisions were struck down. Disability lawyers asserted that the U.S. Supreme Court was treating Congress as a lower court rather than an equal government branch. By redefining the ADA's disability definition, the Supreme Court had unlawfully usurped power from Congress.

Talking About Disability

In this section, look for—

  ✧ how language can be demeaning, distancing, and polarizing

✧ how language can determine job opportunities, educational opportunities, and social participation for PWDs

✧ how language can communicate deficit

Using language that conveys respect for people with disabilities is, at times, cumbersome and awkward, and for most of us, there is new terminology to be learned. Language is more than political correctness or semantics. Listening to the NPR Disability
History Project, especially the segment "Tomorrow's Children," we can learn the way
in which the words used to describe people directly resulted in their deaths.

> Newspapers and medical journals of 1915 referred to people with disabilities
> as 'defective,' 'idiot,' and 'imbecile.' These were incredible value judgments.
> They didn't see the hostility, the contempt, the subjectivity. They thought
> they were making technically valid, objective decisions. Chloroform unfit
> children. Show them the mercy we show beasts that are no longer fit to live.
> (National Public Radio, 1998c)

Assumptions about the value of lives often derive from the life's perceived value to
society and to itself. Often, the language used to refer to PWDs implies that their lives
are not worth living (Marks, 1999, p. 38).

Language is powerful, and the use of words clearly communicates attitudes toward
people. For example, there are many unacceptable words for individuals of various
racial, cultural, and ethnic groups. If a parent were to hear his or her child use one
of these words, the parent would automatically correct the child, explaining why the
word the child used is offensive and what the correct word is.

Language is a mirror that reflects society's views toward certain groups, and the
words that are used very accurately reveal social and cultural history. There are many
words that are offensive, demeaning, and out of date and lead to inaccurate stereotypes. Indeed, much of the objection to many words used to describe PWDs is derived from the history of their use, rather than from their actual meaning. Much of the
language used to describe the disability experience comes from the Bible, illustrating
the long history of underlying attitudes toward people with disabilities. Indeed, in
reviewing the history of any group of people that has been the target of prejudice, discrimination, and reduced opportunity, we find that the language used by the broader
society to speak about these people has these characteristics:

- The words used to describe these people are both offensive and demeaning.
- The identifying words that are used to set these people apart from the
  broader society make very clear that these people do not belong with everybody else (this is called *distancing* or *polarization*).
- Usually the language is not a self-identification—people don't use these terms
  to describe themselves.

- The language usually lumps all the people perceived to be in the group together regardless of individual differences.
- The labels used to describe people with disabilities describe, often inaccurately, only one aspect of an individual's identity (this is called *reductionism*).
- Society is very reluctant to change individual language use, using the defense of ease of use or freedom of speech.

Legislation cannot control language, but educating the public about the correct way to discuss disability and the underlying rationale behind this language is a first step in integrating people with disabilities into society.

In the newest edition of the Diagnostic and Statistical Manual-5, the names of a few diagnoses have been changed in order to eliminate stigma and negative connotations. For example, *stuttering* is now referred to as *childhood-onset fluency disorder*, and *intellectual disability* has replaced *mental retardation* (Dailey et al., 2014).

In the case of people with disabilities, the language used can determine job opportunities, educational opportunities, and social participation. Before behavior and attitudes can be changed, language must be changed. In the chapters on society and disability, it will become clear that people with disabilities have experienced pervasive, systematic, institutionalized prejudice and discrimination, and, naturally, the language used by society very clearly reflected these attitudes (Rossides, 1990). Language forces people into pejorative categories.

Language That Communicates Deficit, Inferiority, and Pathology

The language used to describe disabilities and the people who experience disabilities communicates deficit and inferiority. The prefixes *dis-* and *dys-* mean *difficult, impaired,* or *absent*. Words such as *disorder, disability, disease, dyslexia, dystrophy,* and *dysfunction* reflect these meanings. The prefixes *im-* and *in-* mean *absence* or *lack*; therefore, the word *invalid* means *without value or validity*; *impairment* means *without strength or quality* (or *spoiled*); and *infirm* means *without strength*. The prefix *para-* (in *Paralympics*) means *subsidiary*. (Note: Paralympics are competitions for athletes with physical disabilities, and the Special Olympics are competitions for people with intellectual disabilities.) It is not surprising that most PWODs think of disabilities as deficits and inferiority, because language shapes our attitudes. The Veterans Administration (VA) no longer uses the term *Disabled Veterans*. Instead, they use the term *Wounded Warriors*. This is probably, at least in part, to remind the nation of its responsibility to these men and women.

In Chapters 6, 7, 8, and 9, we will see that many PWDs do not think of their disabilities as losses or as the absence of something. Moreover, many PWDs consider their disabilities to be assets and an integral part of their self-identities. For example, Dr. Irving King Jordan, former president of Gallaudet University, who is deaf, made this statement: "If there are 1,000 aspects of being deaf, 998 are good and 2 are bad." By quantifying the experience of deafness, Dr. Jordan is making the point that his disability has been an asset and not a deficit.

Person-First Language

There are some basic guidelines. The first, and most well known, is the "people-first" approach. It is the *Americans With Disabilities Act* and not the *Disabled Americans Act* because this federal legislation is based on people's American citizenship and not their disability. They are Americans first. Also, it is correct to say "individual with a disability," not "a disabled individual." It is correct to say "a person who is blind," not "a blind person." It is "an athlete with a disability" or, even better, simply "an athlete." In spite of this, the term *disabled athletes* often is used. Person-first language may appear to be more cumbersome, but it serves the purpose of emphasizing that the individual is a person first and the disability is secondary. In the past, it was legal in many places to institutionalize, sterilize, and even kill people with disabilities because they were not considered to be fully human. Therefore, the importance of person-first language can be seen. However, individuals who are deaf, especially those in the Deaf Culture, prefer to be referred to as "a Deaf person" (Stalcup, 1997). You will see that the word "Deaf" is capitalized. This insistence on putting the word "Deaf" before the word "person" is based on the Deafs' identity as a culture, as a group not unified by a disability, but rather unified by shared experiences and a common language. Incidentally, the use of the expression "the Deaf" is acceptable. However, it is not correct to use these types of expressions with other disability groups.

A few people do not like the person-first language, because they feel that the disability is an important part of their identity. Sobsey (1994) reported:

> One physically disabled person [*sic*] told [me] that she is not *a woman with a disability*, she is a *disabled woman*. She feels strongly that her life-long disability is as essential a part of her as her gender or heritage, and she feels that the person-first rule fails to recognize this critical aspect of her identity. People should have the right to reject any labels that they do not like, and forcing an unwanted label on anyone is abusive. (p. 320)

The Person Is Not the Condition

The second basic guideline is often, "the person is not the condition." So, there are no "diabetics," "schizophrenics," or "quadriplegics," but rather "individuals with diabetes, schizophrenia, or quadriplegia." Once again, this type of language communicates that the individual is not the condition or the disability. No one would speak of a group of people diagnosed with cancer as "the cancerous," but we often hear and read the phrase "the mentally ill" or "the deaf," or "the blind." Sometimes, people with disabilities are identified by their use of assistive technology. For example, a server in a restaurant said, "I have three wheelchairs and two white canes." Wheelchairs don't eat, they don't pay restaurant bills, and they don't leave tips. Also, because most people with disabilities are not sick, it is inappropriate to refer to them as patients. For example, Bickenbach (1993) made the observation that "many people with disabilities make no more use of medical services than anyone else" (p. 83).

The disability should not be mentioned if it is not relevant, and it is surprising how often the disability simply is not pertinent. The following is an example of an inappropriate statement: "Dr. Smith, who uses a wheelchair, gave a brilliant lecture." Certainly, it is important to mention the use of a wheelchair when planning accommodations, such as a lowered podium from which to deliver the lecture, or ramps up to the podium. Nonetheless, in the sentence used here, the use of the wheelchair should not be mentioned. When the media include the disability when it is not relevant, they are giving the incorrect impression that the disability is the focus of the individual's life or that everyone should view the person as his or her disability. Indeed, most of the time, it is probably more accurate to say "people" rather than "people with disabilities." No one likes to be referred to, or thought of, as only one aspect of his or her nature. No single label can capture the meaning of a person's entire personality and character.

Avoiding Sensational and Emotional Terms

Sensational and emotional words should be avoided because these types of words are demeaning. The word *survivor* is preferred over *victim*, and it is more correct to say that an individual "experiences" a certain disability rather than that he or she "suffers from" the disability (Lynch & Thomas, 1994). A humorous bumper sticker on a car reads, "I don't suffer from insanity. I enjoy every minute of it." Clearly, the message of the bumper sticker is twofold: (a) avoid the use of emotional terms such as *suffer*; and (b) no one, except for the individual with a disability, can describe the experience. It is better to use the expression *congenital disability* rather than *birth defect*. A person *uses* a wheelchair and is not *confined to* a wheelchair. Words such as *cripple*, *lame*, *dumb* (meaning someone who does not speak), *afflicted*, *stricken*, *maimed*, *invalid*, *infirm*, *misshapen*, or *withered* communicate a condescending attitude. Also, instead of the word *fit*, *seizure* is considered to be more accurate.

According to Michalko (2002), a disability scholar, when a PWD is said to "suffer" a disability, it

> discursively points to and constructs the value of able-bodiedness while devaluing disability. It implies that disability is a life bereft of value, and not only is this idea offensive to those of us who are disabled, but it is also not true. (p. 51)

Disability is difficult, time-consuming, and expensive, and it can be painful. Nonetheless, PWDs do not exist in a continuous state of suffering and misery, uninterrupted by pleasure and satisfactions, and it is clear that this type of language conveys the false idea that a disability automatically results in a low quality of life. Linton (1998) states that sensational language "attributes life, power, and intention to the condition (the disability) that disempowers the person with the disability, rendering him or her helpless and passive" (p. 25).

The History of Certain Words

For the most part, certain words, such as *cripple* or *maimed*, were not consciously used to be demeaning and insulting. Sinason (1992) stated,

> Each worker introducing a new term hopes that the new word brings new hope and a period of historical change. Each time the new word is coined, it is coined honorably.... It is therefore doing a grave disservice to past pioneers to point contemptuously to their chosen term. (p. 40)

Nonetheless, their use has become demeaning, insulting, and often inaccurate. The word *handicap* should be avoided simply because of its history. Many believe that the word derived from the act of begging because beggars had their "cap in their hand." It should be noted that this story has no basis in fact. However, in the past, many individuals with disabilities, in the absence of any other opportunity, begged for a living. Certainly today, when it is stated that anyone has "his or her cap in hand," the unstated message is that the person is perceived as humble or inferior. Indeed, the first disability laws in the United States were enacted in the 1860s, when Civil War veterans with disabilities were seen begging on the streets of American cities. Therefore, it is best to use the word *disability*. Incidentally, the first hospital for children with orthopedic impairments was established in New York City during the Civil War. The name of the hospital was the New York Hospital for the Ruptured and Maimed (Byrom, 2004).

Some disability advocates do use the word *handicap* to describe obstacles and impediments in the environment but never in reference to a condition an individual experiences. *Special* and *exceptional* are words that many people with disabilities dislike because these words invoke a history of segregation. There are many stories of parents being told that their child was going to be placed in a special classroom or a special program. The words *special* and *exceptional* also have a euphemistic quality; they are labels that people with disabilities instantly recognize as meaning *segregated* and *inferior*. They are not innocuous terms, because they imply difference and thus are polarizing. Individuals in *exceptional* or *special* programs "are then stigmatized as those who cannot 'get by' under programs designed to meet basic needs" (Bickenbach, 1993, p. 201). One disability scholar explained the use of the word *special* in this way:

> Labeling education and its recipients special may have been a deliberate attempt to confer legitimacy on the educational practice and to prop up a discarded group. It is also important to consider the unconscious feelings such a strategy may mask. It is my feeling that the nation in general responds to disabled [*sic*] people with great ambivalence. Whatever apathy and disdain is felt is in competition with feelings of empathy, guilt, and identification. (Marks, 1999, p. 158)

An article once appeared in the *Disability Rag*, a publication written by and for PWDs, entitled, "Getting Rid of Special" (Woodward, 1991). The author was clearly opposed to the use of the word *special* to describe PWDs or the services PWDs receive. However, the author understood that, even among PWDs themselves, there is disagreement about the word's use. The author quoted a National Spinal Cord Injury Association advertisement that showed a sign for disabled parking. The advertisement read, "We're asking for a special place in your hearts, not just in your parking lots" (p. 41).

Euphemisms

Euphemisms are insulting because their use implies that the reality of the disability is negative and unfortunate. Much of the language used to speak about the disability experience has been condescending, trivializing, or euphemistic. Expressions such as *physically challenged* or *mentally different* are both condescending and euphemistic, suggesting that disabilities cannot be discussed in an open and candid manner. The use of these expressions also trivializes the disability experience, suggesting that disabilities are only minor inconveniences. Richard Harris, director emeritus of Disability Services at Ball State University in Indiana, reported that a "point of view article in the May 1991 *Paraplegia News* entitled 'Cripplespeak' poked some fun at the newest 'acceptable term,' which is 'people of differing abilities.'" The coiner of this term won $50,000. Additionally, the article expressed mild amusement at Michigan's politically correct term for an individual with a disability: handicapper (Harris, 1992, p. 210).

In a disability rights magazine, written by PWDs, an article appeared almost 30 years ago entitled, "The Problem With Challenge." Of course, when this article was written, there was no ADA. The tone is somewhat angry, but it does show (a) that PWDs feel euphemisms used by PWODs are an effort to make themselves more comfortable with others' disabilities, (b) that PWODs who use the *challenge* euphemism are unaware of the obstacles constructed by society, (c) that some PWDs feel that meeting the challenge of having a disability is their responsibility, and (d) that euphemisms such as *challenge* impede the disability rights movement.

Erik Weihenmayer (2001), who is blind and climbed Mt. Everest, wrote about the use of euphemisms:

> Isn't it interesting . . . that the problem isn't always blindness, but all the false assumptions surrounding blindness, and that includes your own. Once a lady wanted to ask me how long I had been blind, but she was too afraid to use the word *blind*. Maybe she thought that blindness was a kind of demon and just the mere mention of the word might give it the power to rise up and crush my spirit. So instead, she asked, "How long have you been a person of sightlessness?" (p. 84)

People, in their attempts to be positive and complimentary, often inadvertently use insulting qualifying statements such as, "Even though she uses a wheelchair, she is beautiful (or intelligent, or funny, or generous, or hardworking, or honest)" or, "I don't think of you as having a disability." While these types of statements are not intended to be hurtful and condescending, they are both because they clearly communicate the speaker's bias against people with disabilities. (It's like the compliment, "You don't sweat much for a fat girl.") The speaker is acknowledging an exception but, at the same time, holding on to the biases and prejudices held against the larger group: people with disabilities.

Later in this book we will learn that some PWDs find positive aspects in their disabilities, an awareness that, ironically, arises, in part, from the difficulties and obstacles inherent in a disability. This type of response of a PWD should not be confused with PWODs' use of euphemisms.

Defiant Self-Naming, or Gimp Pride

Many PWDs use words to describe themselves and their experience that are not appropriate for PWODs to use. The use of slang, imitation of PWODs, and exaggeration are ways to fight against prejudice and discrimination of the larger culture. This type of terminology is called *in-group language* and often is a challenge to PWODs and a reclamation of the in-group's right to name and describe their identity. Defiant self-naming celebrates and takes pride in disability. Linton (1998) explained: "Cripple, gimp, and freak are used by the disability community. They are personally and politically useful as a means to comment on oppression because they assert our right to name experience" (p. 17). In later chapters, we will learn that PWDs have rarely been allowed to establish a group identity. Many in the gimp culture consider the use of this in-group language to be therapeutic. Nancy Mairs (as cited in Thomson, 1997b) illustrated the power of the self-labeling:

> People . . . wince at the word, "cripple." Perhaps I want them to wince. I want them to see one tough customer, one to whom the fates/gods/viruses have not been kind, but who can face the brutal truth of her existence squarely. As a cripple, I swagger. (p. 284)

But there is a paradox to labels. They can also be a language of empowerment, stated Sue Souter (1993), former U.S. Commissioner of Rehabilitation and former President of the World Institute on Disabilities Services. Souter related that the Deaf Culture does not endorse the term *hearing impaired*, preferring the word *deaf*. They are determined to retain the power to define and label themselves. Nonetheless, most legislation, including the ADA, uses the term *hearing impaired* because it is considered to be a sensitive term. To the Deaf Culture, the term *hearing impaired* is a euphemism imposed by outsiders.

Finally, it should be noted that these guidelines are used in American English and not necessarily used in British English or other languages. For example, one disability scholar (Charlton, 1998) noted:

> The struggle to change language describing disability is particularly interesting in Spanish. The most common expression in Latin America is *minasvalidas,* which translates as "less valid." The term *discapitados* (less capable) is also very common. Pejorative terminology about disabilities abounds in Spanish and, in fact, there is not one politically correct term describing disability in the dictionary. We in the disability rights movement created our own terms, *personas con deshabilidades,* or persons with disabilities. The word *deshabilidades* is not in the dictionary. When people point this out, believing that this means we cannot use the word, we proudly tell them we will not accept the language of the oppressors just because some book perpetuates the stereotypes and myths that we are fighting to break down. (p. 67)

Another example of the use of language to describe PWDs has been provided by Ong (1993): "The Chinese term for disabled is 'canfei,' meaning crippled and useless. It depicts the Chinese view of disability" (p. 9).

Labels That Attempt to Describe All Those Different From the Majority

In this section, look for—

✧ the "catch-all" categories

✧ why "crips can call themselves anything they want"

In an effort to organize and simplify, administrators implement labels to describe people that often become catch-all categories. Catch-all categories have often included *exceptional, multicultural,* and *special.* People included in these categories often are people with disabilities, people who are intellectually gifted, people of differing cultural, racial, linguistic, or ethnic groups, and people of differing sexual orientations (Artiles & Trent, 1994; Pugach & Seidl, 1996). Looking at these various types of people, it becomes clear that they have little in common, with the exception of two factors. First, they all have been targets of prejudice and discrimination, and second, administrators and policymakers often view these different types of people as a single group simply because the regular places and services are not viewed as appropriate for any of these people. It is as if everything, and everybody, that defies easy labeling and categorization is put together into a single undifferentiated category. In essence, these catch-all categories are diagnoses of exclusion in which most of the exclusions are positive and those characteristics or needs that remain are placed in catch-all categories. While it may only be thoughtlessness or an attempt to limit the number of categories, the use of catch-all terms communicates that these people are different from the majority, stating, "We don't know who you are, we only know who you are *not*—mainstream." Ironically, these people may also be different from others in the same catch-all category—perhaps more different from them than from the majority.

Experts in racial, ethnic, and linguistic issues deplore linking racial and ethnic groups with disability groups. Pugach and Seidl (1996) stated this objection: "Unless special educators are willing to view current interpretations of the disability–diversity relationship as problematic in the first place, the richness of cultural diversity will always be transformed into a deficit" (p. 5). These highly educated university professors are stating that disability is a deficit, but cultural diversity is richness. Furthermore, it appears that the only concern with including disability groups with racial and cultural groups is the prejudice by association that racial and cultural groups will experience by being somehow related to disability groups, rather than considering that these two groups (both of which are rich in diversity, and neither of which is a deficit) do not belong together simply because their needs are very different. For example, in public education, what is the commonality, in terms of learning, of a child who does not speak English and a child who speaks English and uses a wheelchair?

In contrast to all of the above, people who have disabilities can speak about their disabilities, often referring to themselves as crips or using other seemingly derogatory terms. Such in-group language reflects their (a) anger at their treatment by people without disabilities, (b) need to choose their own identifiers, and (c) identity of belonging to a group as a sign of solidarity with other people with disabilities. As with all in-group language, it is not appropriate for individuals without disabilities to use these terms.

Many agencies, legislation, and acronyms of organizations use incorrect language because they were created and named before the use of correct language. Therefore, there is the Education for All Handicapped Children Act of 1975, and the ARC, which stands for Association of Retarded Citizens. The correct usage today would be Individuals with Disabilities Education Act of 1990 and the Association for Individuals with Intellectual Disability. (ARC still uses the acronym, but has changed the name of the organization.)

In the chapters on society and disability, we will see more clearly the direct relationship between demeaning language and prejudice and discrimination. After reviewing the history of treatment of people with disabilities, the correct language will not seem awkward, cumbersome, or difficult to use.

SECTION 2

SOCIETY AND DISABILITY

In order to more clearly see the relationship between the differing models of disability and the prejudice and discrimination toward PWDs found in society, a simple (and fun) exercise and two short stories are provided as an introduction.

Exercise

Which of the following statements are *most* true? Which of the following situations have straightforward solutions?

1. Ms. Smith cannot get a job because she is blind. (Biomedical Model)
2. Ms. Smith cannot get a job because prospective employers do not provide written material in Braille. (Environmental and Functional models)
3. Ms. Smith cannot get a job because her civil rights, protected by the Americans With Disabilities Act (ADA), are being violated. (Sociopolitical Model)

The following story, a true story, illustrates prejudice and discrimination among employers in the Boston area. The author is Eric Weihenmayer, best known as the blind man who summited Mt. Everest. Weihenmayer used the fairy tale of "The Three Bears" to illustrate the prejudice, discrimination, and lack of awareness that prevented him from obtaining a dishwasher job during college:

Too big, too small, too fast, too hot, like a twisted version of the three bears—the story repeated itself again and again. I had thought somehow, that with my force of will, with my ingenuity, with my tenacity, I could eventually win people over and get what I wanted out of life. I hadn't realized there were doors that would remain locked in front of me. I wanted so badly to break through, to take a battering ram to them, to bash them into a million splinters, but the doors were locked too securely and their surfaces were impenetrable. I never got a dishwasher job in

Cambridge, but I did choke down an important lesson, that people's perceptions of our limitations are more damaging than the limitations themselves, and it was the hardest lesson I had ever had to swallow. (Weihenmayer, 2001, pp. 127–128)

- Notice his efforts to get a dishwashing job—"my force of will, with my ingenuity, with my tenacity." These personal characteristics helped Weihenmayer to climb Mt. Everest, but they were of no use in the face of prejudice and discrimination.
- Notice that Weihenmayer states that prejudice and discrimination are bigger limitations than his blindness.
- Notice the unpleasant surprise when confronting prejudice and discrimination.
- Notice that Weihenmayer considers encountering prejudice and discrimination the "hardest lesson I had ever had to swallow."

Finally, this last story concerns a hearing mother, Barbara, of two Deaf teenagers. Barbara sent her young children to a residential school; however, after she had completed her American Sign Language training, she first obtained a volunteer position at the school and was eventually hired as the school secretary. In this way, she had daily contact with her children. Throughout her children's childhood, Barbara struggled to give her children a sense of self-confidence. Barbara describes her dawning recognition that prejudice and discrimination against PWDs found in society might limit her children's life opportunities:

"The whole time they were growing up, I said, 'You can do anything you want to do. This [the deafness] doesn't limit you.' Then it started to hit me. It's got nothing to do with them. It's got to do with that hearing person across from them at an interview." (Solomon, 2012, p. 106)

Keeping these two stories in mind as we learn about prejudice and discrimination toward PWDs will help us to better understand the next three chapters.

CHAPTER **3**

PREJUDICE AGAINST PEOPLE WITH DISABILITIES, PART 1

- ✧ What is handicapism (institutional and social)?
- ✧ Whose "problem" is handicapism?
- ✧ What are the costs of handicapism to PWODs?
- ✧ Do Americans believe that every life is worthy of investment?
- ✧ What is the "why bother?" syndrome?
- ✧ Has the ADA and ADAAA made positive differences in the lives of PWDs?
- ✧ Why are PWDs (falsely) considered to be "burdens" and "drains"?
- ✧ Does disability always lead to social inferiority?
- ✧ Is disability considered deviance or diversity?
- ✧ What does "second-class citizenship" mean?
- ✧ How does handicapism parallel racism, and how does it differ from racism?
- ✧ What is the the hierarchy of stigma?

The Salience of the Perceived Defining Nature of the Disability, or "It's Not All About My Legs"

In this section, look for—

✦   the definition of salience and its effects on PWDs

✦   why the PWD is often viewed as only the disability

Salience of the disability simply means that the disability is the most important, or the only, aspect of the individual. Nothing else about the individual is acknowledged or noticed, including race, gender, or sexual orientation. One woman remarked: "People meet the disability before they meet you" (National Public Radio, 1998a). Another PWD stated: "You want to be yourself and the world asks you to be your disability" (National Public Radio, 1998a). Moreover, others assume that the disability is the central identity and self-definition of the person with the disability. The word *salience* means *most noticeable* and, in the case of disability, salience also often means *different from the rest of us*. Ascribing such salience and importance to the disability serves to heighten and exaggerate any differences between those with disabilities and those without disabilities. The individual's other characteristics, such as age, sex, educational level, and personality qualities, are neither acknowledged nor understood. The individual becomes his or her disability. Two feminist disability scholars, Fine and Asch (1988), summarized:

> To date, almost all research on disabled [*sic*] men and women seems simply to assume the irrelevance of gender, race, ethnicity, sexual orientation, or social status. Having a disability presumably eclipses these dimensions of social experience. Even sensitive students of disability . . . have focused on disability as a unitary concept and have taken it to be the "master" status but apparently the exclusive status for disabled [*sic*] people. (p. 3)

Amy Purdy, who was the first contestant with double lower limb amputations on the ABC television program, *Dancing with the Stars,* stated, "I know there will be a lot of focus on my legs. But my hope is that people see me as a dancer like anyone else who is going through this [the televised competition]. My hope is that it's *not* all about my legs" (Oldenburg, 2014, para. 16). Ms. Purdy is acknowledging her disability when she uses the words, "it's not all about," but, at the same time, she wants to be viewed as a dance contestant. Therefore, we can see that PWODs consider the PWDs' disability to be his or her most salient characteristic. In contrast, most PWDs consider their disability to be only one characteristic, and certainly not the most important one. In other words, most PWDs do not think about their disability all the time.

The Inferred Emotional Consequence of the Disability, or Difficult Does Not Mean Tragic

In this section, look for—

- ❖ distressed identification
- ❖ the three factors of which PWODs are often unaware:
  - The disability is a familiar part of the individual's self-concept.
  - The individual has learned how to manage with the disability.
  - The individual feels that there are valuable aspects of the disability.

Often termed *distressed identification*, inferred emotional responses usually refer to the fact that most PWODs automatically assume that an individual's disability must be the worst thing that ever happened to the person, an unending, devastating personal tragedy. Certainly, many disabilities are difficult to manage, and the world is not designed for PWDs, but, nonetheless, *difficult* does not automatically translate to *bad* or *tragic*. Another way in which distressed identification is expressed is the belief that the PWD must be of no worth to him- or herself or anyone else. However, most PWDs view their disability(ies) as a familiar part of their identity and have learned how to manage the disability and feel pride and confidence in this mastery. Moreover, many PWDs feel that there are positive aspects of their disability, and we shall discuss these in Chapter 6.

A woman, in an attempt to inform PWODs, stated, "Putting on my artificial leg is no more distressing to me than you putting on your socks" (DeLoach & Greer, 1981). Naturally, it takes more effort and time to put on a prosthetic limb than socks, but the woman was trying to communicate that it is not an emotionally sad task. In much the same way, a father who contracted polio as a boy and wore leg braces from that time on was not viewed by his children as either tragic or an object of pity. Indeed, when this father died, the mortician asked the six adult children if they wanted the leg braces on their father. The children replied "yes," saying that to bury their father without his leg braces would be like burying their mother without her glasses. The braces were a part of their father and, furthermore, were not viewed as a symbol of sadness. In fact, the children reported that the braces were a reminder of happy times. Their father sat on the bed, morning and evening, to put the braces on and take them off, and each of the six children received a turn sitting on the bed talking one-on-one with their dad.

In Safran's (1998) comprehensive review of the portrayal of disability in film, he concluded that the movie-going public, from the advent of film-making, has considered disabilities to be dramatic and out of the ordinary. Such fascination with disabilities, and a little fear, has sold a lot of theater tickets, making disabilities profitable dramatic and commercial devices.

It is true that (a) most disabilities are difficult (including the prejudice and lack of accommodations) and (b) PWDs are more aware of assistive devices and coping mechanisms used by other PWDs simply because they use them themselves. PWDs know what to look for. This is a lot like someone who wears contact lenses being aware of others who wear contact lenses. Those who wear artificial limbs are usually aware of others who wear prostheses; those who wear hearing aids are more aware of others who use hearing aids, and so on. However, the use of these assistive devices and prostheses is not inherently sad and demeaning to PWDs. Of course, people who use these devices are often aware of the emotional reaction of others, and if they have the capability to conceal the use of these devices, the users usually will do so.

Prejudice, according to Allport (1986), is "an avertive or hostile attitude toward a person who belongs to a group simply because he belongs to that group, and is therefore presumed to have the objectionable qualities ascribed to in that group" (p. 7). Allport defined discrimination as follows:

> Detrimental distinctions of an active source ... exclud[ing] all members of the group in question from certain types of employment, from residential housing, political rights, educational or recreational opportunities, churches, hospitals, or from some other social privileges. Segregation is an institutionalized form of discrimination, enforced legally or by common custom. (pp. 14–15)

We can simplify by stating that *prejudice* is attitudes and beliefs and *discrimination* is behavior. Therefore, it is easier to disguise prejudice, but discrimination is overt (visible) and can be witnessed by others. Prejudice is hard to challenge and confront, but it is possible to counter blatant discrimination. Handicapism is defined as a set of assumptions and practices that promote the differential and unequal treatment of people because of apparent or assumed physical, mental, or behavioral differences (Fleischer & Zames, 2001).

Handicapism Is Socially Sanctioned and Continually Reinforced in American Culture

The following are examples of socially sanctioned handicapism: inaccessible environments; jokes about PWDs that go unchallenged; media outlets that sensationalize PWDs, exaggerate disability, and demonize PWDs; federal laws that are not funded, are underfunded, or place the burden of proof on PWDs; and the facile acceptance of abortion and assisted suicide for PWDs. Much of this handicapism is not recognized as prejudice and discrimination; however, the same types of treatment of any racial or ethnic group, religious group, or sexual orientation group would readily (and justifiably) be acknowledged as prejudice and discrimination.

The clearest and most complete definition of *institutional handicapism* can be found in the Findings section of the ADA (presented in Chapter 2). Handicapism occurs in both the social and physical environment, although handicapism is more visible in the physical environment. For example, the availability of elevators and ramps is easy to see because they are part of the physical environment. Equal social status relationships between PWDs and PWODs are part of the social environment and are more difficult to discern. It is, therefore, easier to counter handicapism in the physical environment than handicapism in the social environment. Both the term *handicapism* and the public awareness of handicapism are relatively recent developments. In contrast, handicapism itself has persisted in most societies of the world for centuries.

If disability is biological inferiority, then society is not obligated to confer rights on inferior groups of people, nor is society to be blamed for its unequal treatment of these people who are biologically inferior. Further, these people who are biologically inferior cannot, and should not, fight or resist the unequal treatment. It is now well understood and acknowledged that the inferior status (and not the innate, inherent inferiority) of racial groups and women was solely the result of prejudice and discrimination of the broader culture. There is nothing inherently, or biologically, inferior about racial minorities or women.

In the past, PWODs have had the power to define who had a disability; define what types of services PWDs received; and control the environment, both physical and social. The power to categorize, label, and define is legally conferred by governments, and, in the case of PWDs, the people who understood the experience best and knew their needs were not allowed a voice in the labels and categories conferred on them. Majority and minority status were once theoretically based on numbers, meaning that the majority was the numerical majority. In practice, however, majority and minority status were based on power and not on numbers. A clear-cut example of this is American slavery. On a single plantation, there often were more slaves than slaveholders. But, majority status was based on power, and the single slaveholder was considered to be the majority. Bickenbach (1993), a Canadian disability scholar, discussed the relationship between the power of the majority to categorize and label the physical realities of disabilities:

> Of course, in the case of persons with disabilities it would have to be agreed that disabilities are not entirely arbitrary social or political constructions by those who have the power to label and categorize people. If this were true, then people in power could simply "re-label" or "re-categorize" people. Disabilities do have physical and mental realities. Disabilities are biological facts. (p. 177)

The Handicapism of Well-Intentioned People

In this section, look for—

✧ ways in which well-intentioned people can be handicapping to PWDs

Well-intentioned people who view themselves as neither prejudiced nor discriminatory often promote handicapism. Most of the time, these people are not aware of their handicapism. Nonetheless, it is handicapism, and handicapism results in the disenfranchisement and marginalization of PWDs. The results of the handicapism of these well-intentioned people conflict with their good intentions. Most of these individuals would be quick to assist someone with a disability and also profess to believe in the equality of PWDs. However, by focusing solely on the disability and its limitations and not viewing the PWD as a unique individual who has strengths, abilities, and skills that far outnumber the limitations of the disabilities, these people are engaging in handicapism. Such a narrow focus often is an unconscious attempt to determine and ascribe biological inferiority to the PWD. Proponents of the contact theory and simulation exercises are well-intentioned people who practice handicapism.

Jenny Morris explained that her family and friends "conspire from the kindest and highest of intentions to ensure that we make the wrong choices" (J. Morris, 1991, p. 35). Furthermore, Morris uses the word "pressures" to describe the effects this has on her. Morris's family and friends want her to be "normal" in spite of the fact that she has a disability. This is an example of unintentional handicapism—behaviors and attitudes arise from kindness, but the results of this encouragement are harmful. If we were to substitute any other minority status, such as race, ethnicity, or gender, we can see that it would be absurd to encourage individuals to be something that they are not. Additionally, the clear message behind these ideas is that it is better to be something else—a PWOD.

In the following excerpt, notice that the PWD is willing to sacrifice competence to avoid prejudice. Medical competence and skill in one's physician may seem to be the single, greatest criterion. Nonetheless, for this individual, who feels that she is required to choose between competence and lack of prejudice, being viewed as a complete person and having a physician who views their relationship as a partnership is more important than medical skill.

> Right now I have a very nice doctor who's like really good in terms of trying to work with me. She's just not as competent as I would like . . . there are some doctors who might be better, but what they do to me emotionally it's not worth it. . . . [I]t always feels like I'm walking a tightrope. . . . I'd love to find somebody that's both a really good doctor and who's not prejudiced against me . . . who can really see me for, for [me]. (Putnam et al., 2003, p. 41)

Most PWDs Identify as Typical, Ordinary People

Carol Gill, a psychologist who is paraplegic, noted that most PWDs identify themselves as typical, ordinary people with the usual life concerns, such as family, career, and community life. Nonetheless, often PWDs are unpleasantly reminded that others may not see them as ordinary or typical people:

Unless they have developed a political or cultural consciousness that central-izes difference, most disabled [*sic*] people identify as typical. Disabled [*sic*] people generally lack preparation to be continually conscious of minority status and its life consequences in the way that growing up in a marginal-ized racial/ethnic community informs community members about racism. Moreover, most disabled [*sic*] people think of themselves as ordinary because impairments recede in importance as they are integrated into daily routines. In our world, abnormal is normal. It can be repeatedly jolting for individu-als who identify as ordinary to be persistently categorized as extraordinary or pathetic by those whom they regard as peers, even intimates. (Gill, 2001, p. 351)

The World Is Designed for PWODs

American society has considered the needs of PWDs to be either unimportant or in-visible. Many options available to PWODs are closed to PWDs. The Deaf Culture has a slogan: "It's our world, too." This slogan expresses the right of all PWDs to full so-cial, economic, educational, vocational, and political integration. It may appear to be obvious, but we can ask, "Why do PWDs feel it necessary to remind PWODs that 'it's our world, too'?" Certainly, the world is inconvenient and physically inaccessible for many PWDs, not as a result of the disability itself but as a result of the absence of ac-commodations. The lack of ramps and elevators, sign language interpreters, and a vast array of other accommodations renders the world an inconvenient place for PWDs.

The Biomedical Model of disability regards the PWD as responsible for adapting to the environment and does not consider PWODs to have any obligation to modify or change. The Biomedical Model probably played a large part in the indifference of the public to provide accommodations. When PWDs claim the world as also belonging to them, they are asserting their right to accommodations. The Deaf Culture pro-vides an easily understood example. Because most hearing people have hands, they have the capability to learn sign language, and, indeed, it would be easier for people who can hear to learn sign language than for most people who are congenitally deaf to learn to speak or to read lips. We saw that on Martha's Vineyard many hearing residents learned sign language. This example illustrates the need for PWODs to make accommodations rather than simply expecting PWDs to adapt to an indiffer-ent social and physical environment. Individuals with disabilities, because of the lack of accommodations and inaccessible environments, must plan their activities in ad-vance, build in extra time, have a back-up plan, and demonstrate an unfailing sense of humor. For example, most PWODs do not need to plan their schedules based on the availability of a public bathroom. For many PWDs, there can be no last-minute or spontaneous changes in plans. Therefore, we can see that the lack of accommoda-tions and inaccessible environments unnecessarily constrict the choices and options available to PWDs.

Often, inaccessible environments and the lack of appropriate technology and personal assistance services result in helplessness; dependence; isolation; and narrow, constricted lives for PWDs. Without accommodations (and civil rights), Americans with disabilities cannot succeed and indeed have difficulty simply surviving. Yet, society often views the dependence and isolation to be the result of the disabilities, when these conditions are, in fact, a result of society's failures. For example, many PWDs report feelings similar to these individuals:

> "When I got my electric cart, my life started all over again." Another said, "I've always had cerebral palsy. But . . . I have before the chair and after the chair. . . . I got this chair and I thought 'Whoa. I can hit the road wherever I want to.' And I have more energy and a lot more fun." (Putnam et al., 2003, p. 42)

Lack of accommodations and an inaccessible environment often eliminate basic rights of citizenship for PWDs.

> This particular discrimination, of course, has had a profound effect on the lives of disabled [*sic*] people. It has a psychological effect, among other things, but it also prevents [PWDs] from participating in society actively, getting jobs, paying taxes. . . . This lack of mobility in many cases even affects the participation in the fundamental democratic process, the right to vote. Without transportation, in many cases, it is impossible even to cast your ballot in election, something which means that, at least in part, disabled [*sic*] people are excluded far more or just as much from the process as black people were by closed polls and poll taxes. (Fleischer & Zames, 2001, p. 69)

Wheelchair athletics has captured the attention of America and has substantially increased the quality of life for these athletes. Nonetheless, before the 1980s, *wheelchair athletes* would have seemed a contradiction in terms. Wheelchair sports resulted from assistive technology. Indeed, there were no wheelchair athletics until the sports wheelchair was invented in the 1980s. Today, sports wheelchairs are so specialized that each sport has its own chair that meets the demands of that particular sport. Some sports wheelchairs have three, four, five, or six wheels. In fact, it was World War II veterans who pushed for better wheelchairs (and other adaptive technology, such as hand controls for cars). As we have seen, World War II veterans with physical disabilities had much better survival rates (than the veterans of previous wars) and longer life spans as a result of the introduction of antibiotics. More important, probably because of the large numbers of veterans with disabilities and the fact that the American nation felt an obligation to acknowledge soldiers' sacrifices, the entire field of assistive technology for PWDs was expanded. Compare the lives of today's wheelchair athletes with individuals with the same types of disabilities who, 100 years ago, lived and died in institutions and back bedrooms.

Accommodations often are provided only after legislation has mandated them. In our discussion of the Americans With Disabilities Act we saw that movie theaters, concert halls, and restaurants became accessible to PWDs only after the ADA made the lack of accessibility illegal. It was not the free market, the profit motive, or humanitarian concerns that opened theaters to Americans with disabilities; it was the force of law and the threat of legal action. In addition to the reluctant provision of accommodations, PWDs are expected to be grateful for such accommodations.

Even more important than physical accessibility is the fact that disability public policy, educational services (including goals and curricula), and rehabilitation services, in the past, were designed and executed by PWODs. As a subordinate group, PWDs have been controlled by PWODs. Without any experience of disability or knowledge of the needs or use of accommodations, PWODs have asserted the right to determine the resources and services that PWDs receive. As PWDs have become more empowered, they have begun to claim the right to determine their own needs, policies, and goals.

For example, Patricia Deegan (1991), in her work describing her recovery from mental illness, described how rehabilitation programs designed by PWODs often impede and handicap the PWD. Deegan stated,

> Too often, rehabilitation programs are structured in such a way as to work against this process of recovery. These programs tend to have rigid guidelines for acceptance. They tend to have linear program designs in which a person must enter at point "A" and move through a series of consecutive steps to arrive at point "B." Failure at any point along the way will require that participants return to entry level. (p. 51)

Brenda Premo, former director of the California Department of Rehabilitation, is legally blind. She tells of this experience:

> One time my mother got called into the principal's office because I wouldn't use big-print books. Instead of just bringing me in and chatting with me, the principal brought my mother in. In the meeting, my mother turned to me and said, "Sweetheart, why don't you want to use big-print books?" I said, "Mom, it's like this; I've got four academic classes and all the teachers assign several chapters to read. In large-print books, chapters are in volumes. So if I have four academic classes and I have to have three volumes each, I need a wagon to take my books home." I told her I needed a magnifier, a $1.50 magnifier, but nobody asked me. (Mackelprang & Salsgiver, 1999, p. 141)

Whose Problem Is Handicapism?

The problem of handicapism or ableism belongs to PWODs, in the same way that racism is the problem of "whiteness." Amundson (2000) explained: "In order to study racism, or any scholarship on racism, we must first study whiteness" (p. 78). Davis (1997a) commented,

> So much of writing about disability has focused on the disabled [*sic*] person as the object of study, just as the study of race has focused on the person of color . . . the "problem" is not the person with the disabilities; the problem is the way that normalcy is constructed to create the "problem" of the disabled [*sic*] person. (p. 9)

Longmore (2003) summarized the long history of handicapism: "What we fear, we often stigmatize and shun" (p. 132). There is a tendency to regard anything that threatens our sense of self as alien.

The Costs of Handicapism for PWODs and Society

Thus far, we have discussed the costs of prejudice and discrimination against PWDs (handicapism) only in terms of PWDs. Indeed, the costs to PWODs, and society in general, are rarely considered. Nonetheless, whether acknowledged or not, there are consequences and costs to the dominant group—PWODs. Society pays for its prejudice against PWDs in three ways: (1) the economic costs; (2) the collective, and individual, fear of acquiring a disability; and (3) the narrow and inaccurate view of the world and human experience that PWODs have when they choose to ignore the disability experience. Perhaps there is an additional cost of prejudice—that of our moral ambivalence. A society (or individual) is morally ambivalent when the society (or individual) publicly *professes* one set of values and *acts* on another set of values. For example, our society professes that all people are created equal; however, as we have seen, PWDs have systematically been treated as second-class citizens. Handicapism is deeply rooted, legitimized, institutionalized, and individually internalized throughout American society. Moreover, society blames the victims, telling PWDs that their disabilities are the cause of the prejudice and discrimination. Believing this premise, many consider handicapism to be an inevitable and unavoidable outcome. In contrast, if we could understand that our prejudices and discrimination (and the resulting lack of accommodations) were both irrational and unjustified, then institutional changes could be made.

Existential Angst

Fear of acquiring a disability is sometimes referred to as the *existential angst of disability*. *Angst* is the German word for *fear*, and existentialism is a school of philosophy that holds that human life is fraught with peril, to which everyone is subject. The human condition, according to existential philosophers, is full of unexpected and unwanted circumstances that have the potential to threaten our well-being. Disability is one of these unexpected circumstances, although existentialists usually worry more about death. For an existentialist, every moment as a person without a disability may be the person's last moment without a disability.

Much of the fear, anxiety, and painful reminders of the possibility of acquiring a disability can be easily dealt with by simply avoiding contact with PWDs. When a PWOD meets a PWD, the PWOD often questions his or her own identity as a person totally in control of life. Rather than deal with unpleasant feelings brought on by seeing a PWD, others can simply stay away or, if necessary, institutionalize PWDs so as not to be subjected to their presence. Of course, PWDs are aware of the effect of their disability, and they use in-group words to describe PWODs, such as TABs (temporarily able-bodied), normies, or ABs (able-bodied). Certainly, the label *TABs* points to the possibility or eventuality of most individuals' acquiring a disability and also plays on the TABs' fear of acquiring disabilities. Lucy Grealy (1997), a teenager with facial disfigurements resulting from sarcoma (cancer), found some satisfaction in her "macabre status." Grealy had a part-time job at a horse stable that provided birthday parties, or pony parties, for children from upper-class families.

> While the eyes of these perfectly formed children swiftly and deftly bored into the deepest part of me, the glances from their parents provided me with an exotic sense of power as I watched them inexpertly pretend not to notice me. After I passed around the swing sets and looped around to pick up the next child waiting near the picnic table littered with cake plates, juice bottles, and party favors, I'd stand confrontationally, like some Dickensian ghost, imagining that my presence served as an uneasy reminder of what might happen. What had happened to me was any parent's nightmare, and I allowed myself to believe that I was dangerous to them. The parents obliged me: they brushed past me, around me, sometimes even smiled at me....They were uncomfortable because of my face. I ignored the deep hurt by allowing the side of me that was desperate for any kind of definition to staunchly act out, if not exactly relish, this macabre status. (p. 19)

Paul Longmore (2003) succinctly captures the relationship between anxiety and stigmatization:

> Disability happens around us more often than we generally recognize or care to notice, and we harbor unspoken anxieties about the possibility of disablement to us, or to someone close to us. What we fear, we often stigmatize and shun. (p. 132)

We have been discussing the concept of existential angst as an individual response. However, *collective neurosis* refers to the anxiety and fear of disability experienced by large groups, especially those in power. Collective neurosis often results in segregation and isolation for PWDs.

If PWODs could see that they, or someone they love, could acquire a disability, they would probably become advocates for providing resources and civil rights for PWDs

(Wendell, 2006). Indeed, one of the pleasures of watching charity telethons is the misguided and inaccurate assumption that the PWDs shown have nothing to do with us. Existential angst separates PWODs from what Wendell termed "their future selves" (p. 266). PWODs never tire of denying the possibility of disability.

Fear of acquiring a disability, or existential angst, is a powerful negative emotion. Ironically, two methods to reduce (not eliminate) existential angst would be (a) accord PWDs their civil rights and necessary accommodations, and (b) allow PWDs full social integration. In other words, the solution to existential angst is to see disability for what it truly is—a societal concern rather than an individual concern. If we choose to view disability as an individual condition, which humans have done for most of history, then we construct disability as a terrible reality. If, however, we choose to view disability as a societal concern, we construct disability as a part of life, which we can negotiate *as a group*. If PWDs were accorded their rights, provided reasonable accommodations, and allowed full equal social status relationships, the prospect of acquiring a disability would probably not be so anxiety-provoking for PWODs.

Spread or Overgeneralization

In this section, look for—

- ✧ the definition of spread and how spread affects PWDs
- ✧ how most PWDs view their disability as a single aspect of their identity
- ✧ how FDR understood the importance of controlling the effects of spread

Beatrice Wright, a pioneer in the psychology of disability, coined the term *spread* to describe the overgeneralization (by observers) of the effects of the disability. Another disability scholar (Livneh, 1982) called this the *negative halo effect*. Both describe the widespread discounting and underrating of *all* of the abilities of the individual with the disability. In simplest forms, it is shouting at the person who is blind because it is thought that he or she cannot hear. Such behavior seems laughable, but generalizing the effects of disability is commonplace and usually more insidious. Most PWDs think of their disability as an attribute, not as a problem. Moreover, the disability is only a single aspect of their identity. In contrast, many PWODs consider the disability to be the central, defining characteristic of the PWD. For example, a Washington, DC, lawyer and Congressional lobbyist stated, "People don't think you're smart if you limp." A woman of small stature (i.e. a women with dwarfism) commented, "Most people associate my maturity with my size." It can be seen that all of these examples overgeneralize the effects of the disability—and no one is disputing that the disability does indeed have limitations—to totally unrelated aspects of the individuals. In addition, all of these overgeneralizations tend to be negative.

There are a few exceptions when the overgeneralizations are thought to be positive and flattering; this is called the "Tiny Tim" syndrome. Tiny Tim, the boy with a disability in Charles Dickens's *A Christmas Carol*, was very sweet and appreciative and wished everybody well. Dickens used the character of Tiny Tim to show by contrast how mean and miserly Scrooge was. Not only was Tiny Tim poor, but he had a disability. Scrooge, however, was wealthy and able-bodied, and he was the villain. Nowadays, the Tiny Tim syndrome is a derisive way to describe the idea that a disability automatically results in a sweet and saintly personality. Often we hear that PWDs are compassionate, wise, or insightful or are heroes or saints. These are examples of the Tiny Tim syndrome.

M. J. Bienvenu (1989) related a joke that communicates the tendency of PWODs to overgeneralize the effects of disability: "A Deaf person is having a difficult time vacuuming the carpet. He goes over the same spot of dirt repeatedly, to no avail. In a fit of frustration, he turns around and notices that the machine is unplugged" (p. 19). Bienvenu then explained why the joke is both uninformed and insulting:

> This is a perfect example of humor that is not part of the Deaf culture. Of course, this would never happen in the first place, because a Deaf person would naturally feel the inactive motor and immediately respond appropriately. . . . The fact that the author does not address Deaf people's keenly developed sense of sight and touch is rather significant. (p. 19)

This joke also illustrates that false and negative stereotypes are readily apparent to PWDs. This joke was published in a book entitled, *Hazards of Deafness* (Holcomb, 1977), certainly not a flattering (or accurate) title. Once again, PWODs think they understand the experience of disability (when they do not); PWODs misinterpret the disability experience in negative and insulting ways, and these types of misinterpretation can lead to false stereotypes—for example, the stereotype that Deaf people are easily frustrated. Deaf people do read this joke and laugh. However, it is not for the reason that the author intended.

Far more pervasive, insidious, and damaging is the "twisted body, twisted soul" concept of spread. This widely held view claims that the disability has somehow negatively affected the individual's personality or character, making the individual permanently bitter, angry, deviant, and hostile. A variation of this idea states that the PWD is angry and bitter, not directly because of the disability but because he or she has failed to "accept" the disability, thus "pathologizing" the PWD. Of course, it is others who are making the judgment of the person's character and then ascribing the causes or sources of these character failings.

Esso Leete (1991) has experienced schizophrenia for more than 20 years. She summarized the experience of being stigmatized by making a list.

You understand stigma firsthand when:

- Your college refuses to readmit you after discharge from the hospital because you now have a history of mental illness.

- You are denied a driver's license because you are naïve enough to answer the questionnaire truthfully.

- A general hospital emergency room physician brusquely explains, after reading in your chart the diagnosis of "residual schizophrenia," that your fever, nausea, and vomiting are "in your head."

- Your friends decide they need to develop other relationships on learning of your past troubles and treatment.

- Stigma is an ugly word, with ugly consequences. (p. 19)

It should be noted that some of this treatment would now be illegal under the ADA.

MONUMENTAL MISTAKE
The FDR Memorial Misses the Essence of the Man

They came humbly and quietly last week in wheelchairs and with leader dogs and a sign-language interpreter, hopeful paraplegic old men, and vigorous middle-age people except for their weakened limbs and dimmed eyes, and glowing youngsters with silence in their ears.

They were a coterie representing 50 million disabled Americans who were invited by the U.S. Park Service to preview the sprawling monument for Franklin Roosevelt to be dedicated May 2. The monument spreads out grandly on 7.5 acres along Washington's Tidal Basin, great blocks of ocher South Dakota granite carved with the soaring phrases of FDR's that brought this nation through economic collapse and war.

But in the $48 million monument there is no depiction of Roosevelt in the wheelchair he used for 24 years, nothing in the gardens and along the pathways to show his disability at a glance for those who remember and for children who never knew the personal struggle that shaped him.

The small vanguard of disabled people left the site saddened, believing to a person that the monument seemed lifeless, lacking the heroic vibrancy of FDR with his radiant smile, head back, steering himself into that destiny he saw beyond all adversity. "The essence of the man is missing," said wheelchair user Mike Deland, chairman of the National Organization on Disability.

And a handful of Gallaudet College students in sign language declared it incomplete history as they had learned it and said they would join a demonstration planned for the dedication day.

Mick Countee sensed the emptiness because after he broke his neck in a

Exhibit 3.1

A well-known example of an individual who had a disability and understood the results of others overgeneralizing his disability was President Franklin Roosevelt. Roosevelt contracted polio at age 39 and never walked again. Before and after the onset of his disability, he pursued a political career. However, after he contracted polio, he and his family went to great lengths to hide the disability (they had the financial resources). The American media, mostly print, cooperated by not photographing Roosevelt while he was in his wheelchair or being carried in someone's arms. All of Roosevelt's assistive devices; architectural accommodations, such as ramps into government buildings; and the personal assistance rendered by his sons or members of the Secret Service were systematically hidden from the public view. Roosevelt and his political advisors thought that the American public and international leaders would not accord respect and trust to Roosevelt if they were reminded of his disability too often (Gallagher, 1985). Yet Roosevelt guided the United States through the Great Depression and World War II, becoming one of the most influential individuals of the

diving accident, while he was a Harvard student, his mother told him, "Son, if Franklin Roosevelt could be President, you can finish your education." Countee, a black [person], not only finished, but also went on to get a law degree from Georgetown and an MBA from Harvard. "Not a day went by," he said last week, "that I did not think of Roosevelt and Roy Campanella." Campanella was the Brooklyn Dodger catcher who was paralyzed in a car accident but never despaired in public.

Jim Dickson, the man organizing the demonstration, stood nearly sightless along the huge monument walls and imagined how a statue of Roosevelt in a wheelchair at the entrance would bring the stone to life. When Dickson was seventeen he was told by his doctor that he had juvenile macular degeneration and would soon be blind. As he walked with his parents out of the doctor's office, his mother told him, "If Franklin Roosevelt, who had polio and was in a wheelchair, could be President, then you can do what you want." He never forgot.

This cry for understanding from the disabled community is being heard. At least 16 Roosevelt family members now seek a design alteration. A demonstration at a New York foundry casting some of the sculptures halted a press conference. Another protest is planned around the office of monument designer Lawrence Halprin in San Francisco.

Former Presidents Bush, Ford, and Carter have urged an additional sculpture to show Roosevelt in a wheelchair, and Bush has sent off a "Dear Bill" note to Clinton in hopes he can encourage a peace before Clinton gives the dedication address. Meanwhile every historian of consequence who has considered the issue has concluded that the monument is a tragic misreading of the spirit of FDR and a grave misstatement of history for the generations to come.

20th century. He was also a great advocate for PWDs, especially for those who had survived polio. Roosevelt's image on the dime is often thought to be the result of his work in easing the economic depression, something akin to, "Brother, can you spare a dime?" In fact, Roosevelt's image on the dime is an allusion to his work in founding the March of Dimes, a fundraiser for polio research and services for people with polio.

Today, some in the Disability Rights Movement consider Roosevelt to have been a "closet crip," someone who hid his disability for his own convenience and advancement. Another view of Roosevelt and his disability is described by Hugh Sidey in the *Time* magazine article (April 28, 1997, p. 4) describing the erection of a monument in Washington, DC, to honor Roosevelt (Exhibit 3.1). Originally, the builders planned to eliminate Roosevelt's wheelchair from the sculpture, but many groups of PWDs protested strongly. The protesters argued that the disability was an inherent part of Roosevelt, and, furthermore, it is no longer necessary to prove that the disability of polio was not, or is not, an obstacle to being President. Indeed, many political analysts, not disability analysts (Evans, 1998), consider Roosevelt's disability to have contributed to his national and world leadership achievements because polio forced Roosevelt, for the first time in his life, to interact with, and attempt to understand, the struggles of the "common man."

Contrast the way in which another famous individual, often in the media, has chosen to deal with his disability. Itzak Perlman, the world-famous violinist, has the same disability as FDR had; both had contracted polio, and neither could walk unassisted. Perlman has pointedly insisted that his television appearances show him walking on to the stage on his crutches. Of course, Perlman has the option to hide or minimize his disability simply by appearing in a seated position playing the violin. Olkin (1999) described a result of this:

> Itzak Perlman . . . said that when he began playing violin professionally all the stories about him described him as a man who had polio and also played the violin. It was only after he became one of the four premier violinists in the world did the stories switch to describing him as a premier violinist who also happened to have had polio. (pp. 88–89)

Roosevelt felt he could not afford to remind the American people of his disability, whereas Perlman has chosen to show his self-identity: a violinist who has had polio. This is not to say that one of these individuals is right and the other wrong. These two examples demonstrate the following:

1. The processes and rationales underlying the choice to disclose or not to disclose; certainly both Roosevelt and Perlman knew, or know, that their orthopaedic disabilities had no functional impairments for the chosen occupations, and yet each knew that the public would react to the disability, and, furthermore, each needed the public to fulfill his occupational aspira-

tions. Roosevelt needed people to vote for him, and Perlman needs people to attend his concerts and buy his CDs.

2. The relationship both Roosevelt and Perlman had, or have, with their public is most often not a personal relationship. A teacher or a physician with a disability meets the individuals with whom he or she works and can, therefore, respond to concerns about the disability on a one-to-one basis; Roosevelt never met or talked to each of the American people on an individual basis, and Perlman meets and speaks with very few of the people who attend his concerts or buy his CDs.

3. The differing results and others' judgments of Perlman and Roosevelt choosing to disclose their disability or to hide their disability; for example, many in the Disability Rights Movement resent the fact that Roosevelt went to such lengths to hide his disability or, more correctly stated, the effects of his disability.

4. The capability of both these men to hide their disability simply because they are both gifted and famous; certainly the inability to walk and the use of crutches or a wheelchair is considered a visible disability. However, the juxtaposition of fame and media has enlarged the definition of "hidden" disability for those few who are gifted and famous. Furthermore, because most people do not have the choice, they are not criticized for choosing not to disclose.

A letter from Ann Landers titled "Angry in Montana," in which a woman in a wheelchair said she did not want to talk to the child in the grocery store about her disability or answer the child's questions, clearly shows Ann Landers's quickness to overgeneralize the effects of the disability. In reply, Landers tells the writer with a disability that she has not accepted her disability and the wheelchair. Never does Landers consider that it is the child, and his or her mother, who are rude, insensitive, and intrusive. This is an example of being a "forced representative." Perhaps the woman in the wheelchair does not have a lot of privacy. For example, maybe a personal care attendant must perform many functions for the woman. Therefore, privacy is precious and important to the woman. Perhaps the woman was in a hurry and did not have time to present a one-woman disability-awareness seminar. Perhaps the woman was in a bad mood after having had a hard day. Everyone, including a PWD, is entitled to have bad moods. Perhaps the woman simply did not like children. Landers does not consider for a moment that there is any explanation for the woman refusing to speak to the child other than her disability. The authors of the following letters written to protest Landers's reply to this woman clearly resent Landers's "twisted body, twisted soul" implication (Exhibit 3.2).

The letters are the rebuttals Ann Landers received, commenting on her response to "Angry in Montana." The first writer criticizes Landers, but the second writer, from Lansing, Michigan, states that, as a wheelchair user, she was disappointed when the

ANN GETS AN EARFUL ON DISABILITY RESPONSE

Dear Ann: You goofed. Your reply to "Angry in Montana" about people with physical disabilities and the curiosity of "innocent" children was totally off the mark. "Montana" is right. It is NOT OK for children to ask questions about a physical disability. Just because it comes from a child's "natural curiosity" does not make it all right.

It is natural for a child to want to do away with a new baby who is getting entirely too much attention, but we won't allow it. We also will not allow jumping on the bed in muddy sneakers or taking Daddy's watch apart. When my grandson displayed a bit of "natural curiosity" and attempted to disengage the brake on my car, you'd better believe I lost no time letting him know it was NOT OK. There is no reason to indulge a child's inquisitiveness just because it is "natural."

Your out-of-the-blue statements that Angry in Montana has not come to terms with his disability and the suggestion that he "lighten up" were insensitive and condescending.

—Disappointed in You

Dear D.I.Y.: I appreciate your comment. Keep reading for others.

Lansing, Mich.: I have been confined to a wheelchair since 1957. When I first went to a restaurant back then, a child of about 4 years old came over and asked why I was in that "funny chair." Before I could respond, his mother snatched him away. The child looked startled and probably got the impression that whatever I had must be contagious. I realize the mother didn't want her child to be rude, but her response only made things worse. Times have changed for the better, thank the good Lord. And thanks, too, for those recently installed ramps that now make almost all buildings wheelchair accessible.

Exhibit 3.2

mother of the curious child "snatched" him away. Perhaps Lansing misperceived the situation and the mother was simply teaching her son rules of courtesy and spoke to her son about "the funny chair" in a more private setting.

Findings of the Americans With Disabilities Act

In this section, look for—

  ✧ the difference between prejudice and discrimination
  ✧ the definition and description of institutionalized discrimination in the Findings of the Americans With Disabilities Act (ADA, 1990)

It should be noted that certain legislation and public policy addressed the needs of PWDs before the passage of the ADA. However, these focused on the *service* needs of PWDs, such as education and rehabilitation, rather than focusing on their *civil rights*. The ADA's main thrust is to guarantee the civil rights of PWDs.

The following is the Findings section of the ADA (1990). It is presented in its entirety here for the following reasons: (1) Reading the Findings section is one of the best ways to understand the rationale and intent of the law. (2) This section of the ADA is perhaps the most concise and precise summary of the history of prejudice and discrimination toward PWDs in the United States.

The Congress finds that:

1. Some 43,000,000 Americans have one or more physical or mental disabilities, and this number is increasing as the population as a whole is growing older.

2. Historically, society has tended to isolate and segregate individuals with disabilities, and, despite some improvements, such forms of discrimination against individuals with disabilities continue to be a serious and pervasive social problem.

3. Discrimination against individuals with disabilities persists in such critical areas as employment, housing, public accommodations, education, transportation, communication, recreation, institutionalization, health services, voting, and access to public services.

4. Unlike individuals who have experienced discrimination on the basis of race, color, sex, national origin, religion, or age, individuals who have experienced discrimination on the basis of disability have often had no legal recourse to redress such discrimination.

5. Individuals with disabilities continually encounter various forms of discrimination, including outright intentional exclusion; the discriminatory effects of architectural, transportation, and communication barriers; overprotective rules and policies; failure to make modifications to existing facilities and practices; exclusionary qualification standards and criteria; segregation; and relegation to lesser services, programs, activities, benefits, jobs, or other opportunities.

6. Census data, national polls, and other studies have documented that people with disabilities, as a group, occupy an inferior status in our society and are severely disadvantaged socially, vocationally, economically, and educationally.

7. Individuals with disabilities are a discrete and insular minority who have been faced with restrictions and limitations, subjected to a history of purposeful unequal treatment, and relegated to a position of political

powerlessness in our society, based on characteristics that are beyond the control of such individuals and resulting from stereotypical assumptions not truly indicative of the individual ability of such individuals to participate in and contribute to society.

8. The nation's proper goals regarding individuals with disabilities are to ensure equality of opportunity, full participation, independent living, and economic self-sufficiency for such individuals.

9. The continuing existence of unfair and unnecessary discrimination and prejudice denies people with disabilities the opportunity to compete on an equal basis and to pursue those opportunities for which our free society is justifiably famous, and costs the United States billions of dollars in unnecessary expenses resulting from dependency and nonproductivity.

Prejudice and Discrimination Against PWDs

The following are a few examples of prejudice and discrimination.

- A 1997 Associated Press article entitled, "Handicapped (*sic*) Used as Guinea Pigs" revealed that Sweden forcibly sterilized 60,000 people with disabilities between the years 1935 and 1976. During the years 1943–1953, hundreds of institutionalized Swedes with intellectual disabilities were fed daily diets of candy to provide scientists the opportunity to prove the cause-and-effect relationship between eating sugar and tooth decay. (*Logan Herald Journal*, 1997, September 10, p. A-7)

- A Louis Harris poll, conducted in 1987, found that the unemployment rate of people with disabilities is the highest of any demographic group in the United States. This same poll showed in 2004 that only 35% of PWDs reported being employed full- or part-time, compared to 78% of those who do not have disabilities (http://nod.org/research_publications/surveys _research/harris).

Medical researchers (Lerner & Belts, 2005) stated that the medical profession is not meeting the needs of PWDs, citing "worrisome" differences between the medical care provided to PWODs and the care provided to PWDs:

Fifteen years since the passage of the ADA, people with physical disabilities still find that both the access to and quality of care provided to them lags significantly behind that for people who do not have such disabilities. Insurance isn't the issue either. Even with health insurance, people with disabilities are often unable to get needed care. In spring 2000, a national survey commissioned by the National Organization on Disability of people age 16 and older with and without disabilities found worrisome disparities. Fully 28%

of insured people with disabilities reported that they need particular therapies, equipment or medications that were not covered by their health plans,
compared to 7% of those without disabilities. Nineteen percent of disabled
persons [*sic*] reported that they needed medical care within the previous year
but didn't get it, compared with 6% of nondisabled people. (p. 20)

It is often questioned if fetuses with disabilities should be allowed to live. Hubbard
(1997) stated, "No one these days openly suggests that certain kinds of people should
be killed; they just should not be born" (p. 198).

The *Why bother?* concept is based on the assumption that the individual's disabilities
are so severe and multiple "that treatment would make no difference or that the extra
expenditures would not be worthwhile or cost-effective" (Lehr & Brinckerhoff, 1996,
p. 10). These authors cited examples in which

[p]arents have been told, directly or indirectly, "What difference would it
make if Barry could see better with glasses? He can't understand what he sees
anyway." "Why bother continuing to work on oral motor development? The
tube feeding is going fine." (pp. 10–11)

Extreme examples of the *Why bother?* syndrome are the "Baby Doe" cases in which
infants with severe disabilities were denied lifesaving medical treatment because of
physicians' predictions about their lack of quality of life. In contrast, infants without
disabilities, or with less severe disabilities, were automatically provided with these
lifesaving treatments.

People with disabilities are far more often the targets of crime, physical abuse, and
sexual abuse (Cole, 1984; Cole & Cole, 1993; Craine, Henson, Colliver, & McLeland,
1988; Sobsey & Doe, 1991; Ulicny, G. W. White, Bradford, & Matthews, 1990; Waxman, 1991). For example, Sobsey (1994) reported that studies from many countries,
such as the United States, the United Kingdom, and Australia, "suggest that child
abuse, beatings, and rape are common occurrences in the lives of many, probably most,
people with developmental disabilities" (p. 260). Sobsey and Mansell (1993) reported
that "[The damaged merchandise myth] provides the offender with a rationalization
not only for the choice of victim but also may alleviate any guilt or inhibition about
exploiting the disabled [*sic*] person" (pp. 289–290).

According to Buss (1999), children with congenital disabilities such as spina bifida,
fibrocystic disease, cleft palate, or Down syndrome are "abandoned" (p. 206) more
often than children born without disabilities. Buss defined abandonment as institutionalization and adoption. Children with congenital disabilities who are not abandoned "are abused at considerably higher rates" (p. 206). Buss offered a hypothesis to
explain this abuse and neglect. Titled the "healthy baby syndrome," this hypothesis
states "that the health status of the child affects the degree of positive maternal behavior" (p. 206).

Until recently, it was legal to forcibly sterilize individuals with certain kinds of disabilities. Indeed, in 1931, there were 30 states in the United States that had compulsory sterilization laws. Individuals who were labeled *insane, feeble-minded, epileptic*, and other diseased and degenerate persons were subjected to sterilization. Many states still have eugenic-sterilization laws today (Hubbard, 1997).

PWDs are also bombarded with negative images of themselves, of which most people without disabilities are unaware. Captain Hook, the Hunchback of Notre Dame, and Mr. Magoo are demeaning and offensive (Bower, 1980; Byrd & Elliott, 1988; Gartner & Joe, 1987; Kriegel, 1982; Longmore, 1985; Safran, 1998; Zola, 1992). Those without disabilities probably are totally unaware of such media or the lifelong effects these can have on the self-concepts of people with disabilities. Those without disabilities might argue, "Don't be so hypersensitive. It's just a children's cartoon." These same individuals, however, would not want their own racial, ethnic, or religious group portrayed with such triviality and condescension.

The Deaf Culture labels society's refusal to accommodate people who are deaf to be communication abuse or communication violence. This communication violence includes refusing to provide education for Deaf children in a language they can understand, American Sign Language (ASL); the inability of many people to communicate with their nonsigning family members; and lack of TTYs (teletypewriters) at public phone booths. One of the most extreme examples of communication violence is the lack of TTYs for 911 emergency phone lines, which has resulted in the deaths of many individuals who are deaf (Jankowski, 1997).

Many individuals with disabilities have not been allowed to participate in the religious life of their community or to practice their faith as a result of attitudinal and physical barriers. Rachel Hurst (1998), European Regional Chairperson of Disability, stated, "Religions too have disempowered disabled [*sic*] people . . . denying them access to the priesthood. . . . The leper is always at the gate of the church—never inside" (p. 15). Dr. Judith Heumann, former Assistant Secretary for the Office of Special Education and Rehabilitative Services, and a polio survivor, spoke about the inaccessibility of Jewish synagogues:

> When the environment is made accessible, people have to start going out and becoming more independent, doing things they never did before. A simple example of this occurred in a synagogue that I attended when I lived in Berkeley. The bema, an area where people go to do readings and worship, was not accessible. One day, I told the rabbi, "The bema is not accessible." Two weeks later it was accessible. The rabbi said, "OK, now it's accessible and you have to come up and do some of the things that other people do." I thought, "Oh my God, I've never been trained!" I didn't even know how to participate because I hadn't learned the things that a person needs to learn in order to participate. (Heumann, 1999, p. 53)

The National Organization on Disability (NOD) has begun a program titled "Accessible Congregations Campaign." To join the campaign, an accessible congregation must commit to the following three principles:

- In our congregation, people with disabilities are valued as individuals, having been created in the image of God.

- Our congregation is endeavoring to remove barriers or architecture, communications, and attitudes that exclude people with disabilities from full and active participation.

- People, with and without disabilities, are encouraged to practice their faith and use their gifts in worship, service, study, and leadership.

Before the passage of the Air Carrier Act of 1986, people in wheelchairs were prohibited from flying, or they were required to bring an attendant—and to pay for the attendant's fare. In addition, before the ADA, most airports did not have wheelchair-accessible restrooms. PWDs are much more worried (than are PWODs) about their future health and well-being. Half are worried about not being able to care for themselves or about being a burden to their families, compared with one-fourth of American PWODs. Americans with disabilities rely on assistive technology, and one-third say they would lose their independence without this technology.

Holzbauer and Berven (1996) reported these experiences:

> In Cologne, Germany, Frank Weber, a wheelchair user, entered a department store to buy a concert ticket. Three neo-Nazis, wearing swastikas, leather jackets, and boots surrounded and began insulting him, saying: "They must have forgotten you in Dachau." (This refers to the practice of 60 years earlier of imprisoning people with disabilities along with Jews, Communists, and Gypsies [sic] in concentration camps)....Another German, Gunther Schirmer, had lost his leg in a car accident in 1979. He had learned to ride a tricycle. One afternoon . . . his wife saw boys harassing her husband, spitting on him and saying repeatedly, "You live off our taxes. You'd have been gassed under Hitler." . . . Shortly after this incident, Gunther Schirmer committed suicide. He wrote to his wife that people with disabilities do not have a chance in this world and that he would now personally "destroy the cripple." (p. 480)

The title of an article (Whitney, 1993) that appeared in the *New York Times*, and that also tells the story of Weber and Schirmer above, illustrates that for many Germans (those with disabilities and their family members), the Holocaust is not forgotten. The title is "Disabled [sic] Germans Fear They'll Be the Next Target." From Fries (1997): "It is hereby prohibited for any person who is diseased, maimed, mutilated, or deformed in any way so as to be an unsightly and disgusting object to expose himself to public view" (from a 1911 City of Chicago Ordinance). According to Imrie (1996), these types of ordinances were still on the books in Columbus, Ohio, and Omaha, Nebraska.

Considering a single issue in this list, we can quickly see that Americans with disabilities did not have the opportunities for entertainment, such as attending movies and eating in restaurants. With the passage of the ADA, it is now illegal for theaters and restaurants to fail to provide accommodations, and it is likely that more PWDs than ever before are availing themselves of entertainment options. Nonetheless, it was not free market forces that opened restaurants and theaters to PWDs; it required the force of law. It is safe to state that most of the rights to which PWDs are now legally entitled would not have been provided if the federal government had not made it illegal to withhold said rights.

Second-Class Citizenship (for Which Americans Must Assume Collective Responsibility)

A list of the ways in which PWDs experience second-class citizenship is in order.

- PWODs are the standard of evaluation, beauty, and good. For example, PWDs are rarely part of norm groups used in standardized testing. Thus, PWODs are both the norm and the ideal to which individuals should strive.
- Their sense of otherness is perpetuated; their sense of "differentness" is exaggerated.
- PWDs are pathologized so that PWODs can legitimize and rationalize their treatment of them.
- They are pressured to hide or minimize their identity as PWDs.
- They have a long history of segregation, isolation, and marginalization. When PWDs are institutionalized, the institutions are administered for the convenience of PWODs. When the public does not see PWDs, their absence is not noticed.
- They are consistently undervalued and demeaned.
- They are denied their dignity.
- They must fight for their rights, while PWODs are, in general, automatically given their rights (e.g., a school entrance for children with disabilities was often conditional rather than automatic).
- They are given secondary, inferior facilities (schools, housing, transportation, public buildings, telecommunications).
- Other minority groups, such as racial and ethnic groups, women, and LGBTs (Lesbians, Gays, Bisexuals, and Transgender Persons), do not recognize their members with disabilities.
- When they are given accommodations (which is their right under federal law), they are expected to be grateful.
- They are underemployed and unemployed (when most express a desire to work). They are also first to be laid off in times of economic distress.

- PWODs create and reinforce unnecessary dependency, including financial disincentives for not working and physically inaccessible facilities.
- They are more likely to be poorer than the general population.
- Their abilities and capabilities are underestimated.
- They are less educated than the general population.
- The physical and psychological experience of PWDs is not acknowledged and shared (Wendell, 2006).
- They are considered to be sexually maladjusted, including neutered, incapable of or uninterested in sex, undersexed, or oversexed.
- The contributions and accomplishments of PWDs are not acknowledged. (Sharon L.'s high school counselor told her that no one would know that Sharon's art was "disabled art." Geerat-Vermeij refused to participate in "Handicapped Science Fairs.")
- Their history is ignored; people, including PWDs, do not have access to this history.

The ADA's "Report Card"

"There has yet to be significant progress in many areas" (Kessler Foundation/NOD, 2010, p. 8).

"There is clearly much work to be done in order to narrow the very substantial gaps that still exist" (Kessler Foundation/NOD, 2010, p. 9).

In this section, look for—

- ◇ the three purposes of these surveys
- ◇ the 13 indicators surveyed
- ◇ three new indicators added in 2010
- ◇ areas in which there is improvement

In 2010, the Kessler Foundation and the National Organization on Disability (NOD) commissioned Harris Interactive to conduct a national survey with the following three objectives: (1) "to assess the quality of life of people with disabilities on a wide range of critical dimensions"; (2) "to measure the differences, or 'gaps', between people with and without disabilities on these indicators"; and (3) "track them over time" (Kessler/NOD, 2010, p. 8). The 2010 report is the most recent NOD report, with five previous surveys conducted in 1986, 1994, 1998, 2000, and 2004. In these first five surveys, 10 indicators or dimensions were surveyed: employment, poverty, education, health care, transportation, socializing, going to restaurants, attendance at religious services, political participation, and satisfaction with life. Three new indicators were

Table 3.1

Changes in Gaps Since Benchmark Year (Percentage Points)

	2010 gaps (%)	Benchmark year gaps* (%)	Change in size of gaps
Employment Works either full- or part-time (age 18–64)	38	50 (1998)	−12
Poverty Annual household income $15,000 or less	19	22	−3
Education Has not graduated from high school	6	24	−18
Health care Did not get needed care on at least one occasion in past year	9	5 (1994)	+4
Transportation Inadequate transportation considered a problem	18	12 (1998)	+6
Socializing Socializes with close friends, relatives, or neighbors at least twice per month	11	11 (2000)	0
Going to restaurants Goes to a restaurant at least twice a month	27	25	+2
Attendance at religious services Goes to church, synagogue, or any other place of worship at least once a month	7	11	−4
Political participation** Voter turnout in the presidential election	0 (2008)	11 (1992)	−11
Satisfaction with life Very satisfied with life in general	27	11	+16

* The benchmark year is 1986 unless otherwise indicated.

** Source: Harris Poll, selected presidential election years.

Note. From *The ADA, 20 Years Later: Survey of Americans With Disabilities* (p. 25), by the Kessler Foundation and the National Organization on Disability, 2010, Rochester, NY: Harris Interactive. Copyright 2010 by Harris Interactive. Available at http://www.2010disabilitysurveys.org/pdfs/surveyresults.pdf

added to the 2010 survey: technology, access to mental health services, and overall financial situation.

These surveys are *relative* rankings, meaning that PWDs are compared to PWODs. In other words, many of the results on these 10 indicators may have improved for PWDs; however, many of them have *improved more* for PWODs, showing that PWDs are falling further behind. These relative measures also take into account large societal changes, such as the economic downturn the U.S. has experienced since 2008, affecting both PWDs and PWODs. The series of six surveys may be considered the "report card" of the ADA. Of course, the first survey, undertaken in 1986, was 4 years before the passage of the ADA, but the remaining five surveys allow disability scholars and demographers to track changes through a 24-year period. The overall conclusion is:

Table 3.2

A Comparison Between People With and Without Disabilities on Key "Indicator" Measures (2010)

	People with disabilities	People without disabilities	Gap in percentage points
Base:	1,000	788	
Variables	%	%	%
Employment			
Works either full- or part-time (18–64)	21	59	38
Poverty[a]			
Annual household income $15,000 or less	34	15	19
Education[a]			
Has not graduated from high school	17	11	6
Health care[a]			
Did not get needed care on at least one occasion in past year	19	10	9
Transportation[a]			
Inadequate transportation considered a problem	34	16	18
Socializing			
Socializes with close friends, relatives, or neighbors at least twice a month	79	90	11
Going to restaurants			
Goes to a restaurant at least twice a month	48	75	27
Attendance at religious services			
Goes to church, synagogue, or any other place of worship at least once a month	50	57	7
Political participation[b]			
Voter turnout in the presidential election	59 (2008)	59	0
Satisfaction with life			
Very satisfied with life in general	34	61	27
Access to mental health services[a]			
Did not get help from mental health professional on at least one occasion in past year	7	3	4
Technology			
Uses a computer or electronic device to access the Internet	85	54	31
Financial situation[a]			
Struggling to get by or living paycheck to paycheck	58	34	24

a These variables are "negative" in that a higher score indicates more of a disadvantage.

b Source: 2008 Harris Poll.

Note. From *The ADA 20 Years Later: Survey of Americans with Disabilities*, p. 22, by Kessler Foundation/ National Organization on Disability, 2010, Rochester, NY: Harris Interactive. Copyright 2010 by Harris Interactive. Available at http://www.2010disabilitysurveys.org/pdfs/surveyresults.pdf

While there has been modest improvement among a few indicators, the general trend of these measures is that twenty years after the passage of the Americans With Disabilities Act (ADA), there has yet to be significant progress in many areas. For instance, although there has been substantial improvement reported in education attainment and political participation since 1986, large gaps still exist between people with and without disabilities in regard to employment, household income, access to transportation, health care, socializing, going to restaurants, and satisfaction with life. In some instances, the spread (gap) has actually gotten worse since the inception of the survey in 1986. (Kessler/NOD, 2010, p. 8)

Table 3.1 shows the change in gaps between PWDs and PWODs from 1986 to 2010. Indicators are listed in bold print. In the first column, the gap found in 2010 is listed; in the second column, the gap in 1986 is listed, and the third column shows the difference between these two gaps. Therefore, a positive sign (+) shows the gap *increased*, and a negative sign (-) shows that the gap *decreased*. According to this table, the gap between PWDs and PWODs decreased in four areas: employment, poverty, education, and political participation.

Table 3.2 shows the results of the 2004 survey. The first column shows results for PWDs, and the second column shows results for PWODs. The third column shows the gap percentage, with larger numbers showing greater gaps, or more disadvantage. The largest gap is Employment, with 38% lower employment for PWDs than for PWODs, and smaller gaps were found in Political Participation and Attendance at Religious Services.

PWDs as "Burdens" or "Drains"

In this section, look for—

  ⬧ the three factors that are considered when determining the economic costs of disabilities
  ⬧ the economic motivation of the eugenics movement
  ⬧ the dollar costs of job accommodations that allow PWDs to work
  ⬧ the effect of financial disincentives on the employment of PWDs
  ⬧ the way in which PWDs have been an industrial reserve army

Throughout history, PWDs have been perceived as burdens or drains on the resources of the community. Disability reformers at the beginning of the 20th century "believed cripples became immoral characters who siphoned off the lifeblood of the economy" (Byrom, 2004, p. 25). Thinking in terms of three factors—(a) the loss of tax dollars from PWDs who do not work; (b) tax dollars spent on government programs for

PWDs, such as special education, vocational rehabilitation, Social Security Disability Insurance (SSDI), and public assistance (welfare); and (c) the increased insurance premiums for all policy holders as a result of the high costs of disability—it can be seen that disability is expensive, and everyone, willingly or unwillingly, bears the cost.

Disability is expensive, both for the individual and for society. It is expensive to live with a disability and, at the same time, maintain a reasonable quality of life. One PWD summarized:

> I think we would all agree that the cost for health and maintaining health for Americans with disabilities is a lot more. It costs a lot more . . . in terms of motorized wheelchairs . . . "accessible technology" or devices to help with activities of daily living. Unless we can get hired at jobs that pay enough for us to be able to afford these particular items, we . . . can't get those items. (Putnam et al., 2003, p. 42)

In a climate of scarce resources, waiting lists, rationing of services, and cost containment, the statement, "A tax dollar spent on you is a tax dollar NOT spent on me" appears to be rational. Read two letters written to Ann Landers (Exhibits 3.3 and 3.4).

A writer, "Roanoke," previously had written complaining that PWDs "lie around sucking up taxpayers' money," and the two letters reprinted here are responses to Roanoke. In the first letter, S.H.J. from Oakland begins the letter by describing the resentful attitudes he or she held toward "freeloaders" and "lazy" people, and then goes on to describe his or her own history of independence and hard work, including 90-hour work weeks. S.H.J. briefly describes some of the effects of his or her disability, such as crying in the supermarket and not being able to stand in a line at the pharmacy. By telling us that he or she cannot do these simple, routine tasks, S.H.J. is proving to us that he or she is truly incapable of holding a job. S.H.J. ends the letter by saying, "There are many honorable, hard-working people who used to earn their own way but can no longer do so because they are mentally ill."

The second writer, from Greensboro, North Carolina, describes his or her disability and then makes the main point, "I don't feel that I am a burden to the taxpayers. I earn my disability check because I worked for 36 years and paid into Social Security for my retirement." Note that Greensboro explained (or defended) receiving SSDI funds by telling (a) the severity of the disability (which he or she almost died from) and that he or she continued to experience pain and other symptoms, (b) he or she paid into the SSDI fund for 36 years, and (c) he or she "contributes to society" by doing volunteer work (with people "more needy," i.e., children and immigrants who do not speak English).

Paul Longmore (2003), a disability scholar and activist, told of Richard Lamm, governor of Colorado and U.S. Senate candidate, who was

> a longtime opponent of lift-equipped buses and special education for severely disabled [sic] children, both of which are not "cost-effective." Lamm talks

Dear Ann: I want to respond to "Roanoke," who said people on disability would rather sit back and suck up the taxpayers' money than work. A few years ago, I was singing that same ignorant tune. I had worked hard since I was 14 years old and had no respect for anyone on welfare. I put myself through college and graduate school and always had jobs that paid well. I thought, "If I can do it, why can't they?" I remember using words such as "lazy" and "freeloaders."

I am now disabled by what they used to call a "nervous breakdown." Those 90-hour work weeks eventually caught up with me. I have learned, to my sorrow, that in spite of all the therapy and medication, I will have to struggle with my emotional fragility the rest of my days. I would give anything to lead a normal life again, but I know this is impossible.

I am unable to fill out a form or stand in line in a pharmacy or a bank without fearing that I will suddenly go to pieces. Yesterday I had a crying spell in the supermarket because I couldn't find the bouillon cubes. Any little frustration can set me off.

There are many honorable, hard-working people who used to earn their own way but can no longer do so because they are now mentally ill. Most of us manage to make it back into the workplace, but many do not, and we must rely on the generosity of the American taxpayer. Please ask your readers not to condemn the entire system because of a few perceived abuses. We really do hate being dependent, but we have no choice.

—S.H.J., Oakland, Calif.

Dear Oakland: I'm sure you have the heartfelt gratitude of all the people for whom you spoke today. Your eloquent plea for compassion touched millions of readers. Thank you for a letter that will make a difference.

Exhibit 3.3

about "hard choices." Hard on whom? And whose choice? Once again, a politician is telling us [PWDs] that our basic needs . . . are too expensive and unimportant. (p. 207)

"In times of economic hardship and tight resources" (p. 207), the needs of PWDs are not considered important enough.

Economic calculations of cost–benefit ratio and cost–value often consider disability as a negative factor, for both society and the individual with the disability. If the lives of PWDs are considered to be of less value than the lives of PWODs, and if the lives of healthy people are considered to be more valuable than the lives of people who are not healthy, the concept of utilitarianism becomes relevant. In utilitarianism, economic resources will not be allocated to PWDs. Hahn (1997) explained:

Dear Ann: I agree with the reader from Oakland who defended people on welfare after "Roanoke" criticized them so harshly. I am not lying around "sucking up taxpayers' money" as Roanoke would have you believe.

I am on disability because of a head injury. I taught school for 36 years and was told not to go back to full-time teaching because the stress would be too much. I also became an epileptic because of my head injury.

When my family went to the hospital at the time of the accident, they were told I would either die or become a vegetable. I was in a coma for weeks. It took me nine months to learn to walk and write again. I saw double for months.

As long as I stay on my medication and avoid stress, life is beautiful. I don't feel that I am a burden to the taxpayers. I earn my disability check because I worked for 36 years and paid into Social Security for my retirement.

I do volunteer work at the public schools and am helping children learn to read. I also work with adults who come from other countries and want to learn English.

I still have some pain and my neurologist says the Fourth of July is still going on in my head, but I am not complaining. I consider myself one of the lucky ones. I hope Roanoke sees this.

—Greensboro, N.C.

Exhibit 3.4

Choice often implies a trade-off between people or goods of greater or less value. Thus, health care practices that yield the most benefit for the largest number of people ordinarily can be expected to provide rewards primarily for the nondisabled segment of the population. (p. 15)

The father of James, a child with Down syndrome, wrote:

Among the many things I fear coming to pass in my children's lifetime, I fear this above all: that children like James will eventually be seen as "luxuries" employers or insurance companies cannot afford, or as "luxuries" the nation or the planet cannot afford. I do not want to see a world in which human life is judged by the kind of cost-benefit analysis that weeds out those least likely to attain self-sufficiency and to provide adequate "returns" on social investments. (Berube, 1996, p. 52)

A woman (C. Vash, 1981) who contracted polio at age 16 spoke of how she felt she was a burden ("drag") on society and the way in which she, unlike PWODs, felt that she must constantly "earn" her right to live.

I felt I had been slated to die but somehow tricked the great scythe wielder and lived . . . to be a damn drag on a number of people. A lot of my achievement trip was feeling I had to earn and re-earn my right to a place on the planet. What looked like ambition was actually paying penance for not having been gracious enough to just die. (p. 10)

Furthermore, people with severe and multiple disabilities not only do not work and produce resources, but they also consume resources. Collectivistic societies throughout history, who believed that the group is more important than individual members, often viewed PWDs as burdens. It was a short leap to segregate PWDs; provide them with a low quality of life and care to save money; forcibly sterilize them; and, in extreme cases, abandon them to die or kill them outright. Most eugenic movements have had economic motivations (H. G. Gallagher, 1990). One scholar (Pelka, 1997) stated, "Eugenicists opposed social programs for people who were poor and disabled [*sic*], believing such programs aided the unworthy in the struggle for survival" (p. 115). Friedlander (1995), in his book, *The Origins of Nazi Genocide: From Euthanasia to the Final Solution*, quoted a German legal scholar in the Nazi era, Karl Binder, who spoke of institutionalized Germans with disabilities and the care they received as "the greatest care of beings who are not only worthless but even manifest negative value" (p. 15). Moreover, more than 200,000 Germans with disabilities were mass murdered, and yet no one was indicted or tried for these murders at the Nuremburg War Crimes Court or any other court of law.

American businesses have, in order to avoid compliance with the ADA and the ADAAA, used the argument of the "undue financial hardship." Other businesses, in order to protect their profits, provided only the minimum accommodations. For example, General Motors, "the corporate giant of the industry" (Fleischer & Zames, 2001, p. 57), found that it was cheaper to add wheelchair lifts to the buses already in use rather than manufacture new flat-floor buses, a technologically superior bus for PWDs. Retrofitting old buses allowed GM to comply with the law but at a cheaper cost. Many cities did not train their bus drivers in the use of these new technologies and did not repair lifts when they broke down. Therefore, it was many years after the passage of transportation accessibility laws that PWDs had full access to so-called public transportation.

There are a myriad of ways in which American business owners profit from exploiting PWDs. To cite a single example, the *New York Times* (Barry, 2014), in a story titled, "The 'Boys' in the Bunkhouse," told of adult male workers with intellectual disabilities who worked in a turkey processing plant "in return for food, lodging, the occasional diversion, and $65 a month. For more than 30 years." A social worker came to investigate, and "a few [workers] led her on a tour past the soiled mattresses, the overloaded electrical outlets, the trash bins collecting the snow melt dripping from the ceiling, their home . . . with mice crawling in their rooms." The men were malnourished and needed medical and dental care. The woman caretaker described these "boys" as "employees who were like family." Turkey processing businesses made bigger profits, and Americans paid lower prices for their turkeys.

This exploitation of American PWDs, publicized in the story, "The Boys in the Bunkhouse," was legal under the Fair Labor Standards Act of 1938, which allowed employers to pay subminimum wages to workers with disabilities. In 2013, the case led to the largest settlement under the Equal Employment Opportunity Act, $240 million in damages.

Perceptions of the Disability That May Be Associated With Prejudice

In this section, look for—

- ◇ the increased stigma directed toward individuals whose disability is perceived as "disfiguring"
- ◇ how there are often no functional limitations to a disfigurement
- ◇ how, in the past, there were only two alternatives for those with disfigurements
- ◇ how most PWDs whose disabilities are disfiguring have even less privacy than most other PWDs

It may be clear that there is a great deal of stigma directed toward individuals whose disabilities are considered to be maiming, deforming, or disfiguring. It is less clear, however, why there is increased prejudice. Disability scholars hypothesize that the anxiety and existential questioning that these types of disabilities evoke in others is at the root of this stigma. On viewing someone with a disfiguring disability, often we are reminded that disability and disfigurements can happen to anyone. Another source of stigma may be the overgeneralization and spread that is accorded to PWDs. Simply stated, when we see someone who looks very different from our expectations, or who is ugly, deformed, or maimed, we might assume that his or her personality and character are also very different or ugly, deformed, or maimed. Jenny Morris (1991) explained,

> Our physical characteristics evoke such strong feelings that people often have to express them in some way. At the same time, they feel able to impose their feelings on us because we are not considered to be autonomous human beings. (p. 29)

Perhaps another reason for violating the PWD's privacy is that the observer mistakenly thinks that the PWD is responsible for the strong feelings that the observer is feeling, when, in reality, the observer is responsible for his or her own feelings and reactions.

Disfigurements illustrate the relationship between the disability itself and the handicapism of society. Most facial disfigurements, for example, have no functional limitations, and yet they are considered to be disabilities and, moreover, one of the most handicapping disabilities. The handicaps and limitations have nothing to do with the disfigurement; rather, these handicaps are the result of society's reaction. As would be expected, there is debate today concerning the lengths to which PWDs should submit to eliminate or reduce disfigurements. Parents of children with Down syndrome struggle with the decision of whether their children should undergo cosmetic plastic surgery. On the one hand, such surgery will not result in any functional restoration, and there are risks involved in any surgery. On the other hand, many parents choose the surgery because they hope that their children will be less stigmatized. An English disability scholar (Marks, 1999) told of a man who had cosmetic surgery that decreased his functioning. "One speaker at the Sheffield MA Programme explained that he had been born with one thumb. This thumb was surgically removed in order to give his hands 'symmetry'" (p. 67).

Individuals with these types of disfiguring disabilities experience even less privacy than do individuals with other types of disabilities. JoAnne Rome was born without a left arm below the elbow, and in the following excerpt, she discussed her lack of privacy.

> I used to believe I owed an explanation to whomever demanded one. I felt fearful, intimidated, ashamed, out of control, and outraged, yet "what happened to your arm?" was not a question that I could choose to answer or not. I was a freak, an outsider, an "other" and the world made it very clear that I owed them an explanation. I was also a little girl who was chased home from school with taunts of "Captain Hook!" ringing in my ears, the object of whispers, stares and laughter. (J. Morris, 1991, p. 28)

We have discussed the various ways in which the reactions of PWODs to an individual with a disability may become part of the PWD's self-concept. People with a disfiguring disability understand that they are not the disfigurement and may be forced to isolate themselves from others to maintain this self-identity. One woman called her facial scars "my mask," therefore making it not part of her self-identity, and felt she could be herself only at home. Molly McIntosh was burned as a child and has scars on her face and the upper part of her body. She stated:

> I have horrible scars on my face. What I mean by that is that people react to them with horror. Forty years ago, when I was in my twenties, and also when I was a child, I so hated the way that I looked. I tried not to think about it but every time I went out in the street I would be reminded about how I looked because of the way people reacted to me. As I walked down the street and someone was coming towards me, they would look and then drop their eyes or move their heads, as if the horror was too much. But then they could

never, ever resist looking again. I used to have bets with myself about the second look. I would promise myself a treat if they didn't look again, but they always did. (J. Morris, 1991, p. 24)

In contrast, in this chapter we discussed Lucy Grealy, who stated, "I *was* my face. I *was* ugliness." Throughout her lifetime, she underwent 30 surgeries that were intended to reconstruct her face. Lucy Grealy eventually committed suicide. The account of a 37-year-old man "whose face is grossly disfigured" (Goffman, 1963, p. 118) and who runs a successful real estate business provides an example of a third way to reduce the discomfort of others. The man states,

> When I have an appointment with a new contact, I try to manage to be standing at a distance and facing the door, so the person entering will have more time to see me and get adjusted to my appearance before we start talking. (p. 118)

Notice how the man carefully manages and positions himself and, at the same time, appears to be acting naturally and casually. Also notice that these strategies are not necessary after the first meeting.

In the past, there were only two ways for individuals with disfiguring disabilities to live. Most simply secluded themselves at home, thereby avoiding a lifetime of being objects of revulsion and rejection. A few chose to display themselves in freak shows and circuses, choosing to use people's horror and fascination as a moneymaker (Bogdan, 1988).

Are Disabilities Viewed as Diversity or as Deviance?

In this section, look for—

- ✧ how difference and diversity are considered to be positive
- ✧ how deviance is considered to be negative
- ✧ how, in reality, difference, diversity, and deviance do not have an inherent value
- ✧ how the label of deviance is based on society's fears, anxieties, and false assumptions
- ✧ how society treats those who are considered to be deviant by morally excluding them
- ✧ the relationship between stigmatization and deviancy
- ✧ why the Biomedical Model of disability has contributed to defining PWDs as deviant

Many differences among people are considered to be desirable, enriching, valuable, and strengthening to the larger group. We often use the positive word *diversity* to describe these valued differences. These types of differences and diversities usually do not have a hierarchical component. In other words, individuals who are diverse or have differences are considered to be equal to everyone else. Inherent in this notion of equality is the lack of a standard of evaluation or a widely accepted concept of a norm. In Chapter 1, we discussed the concept of normalcy as a standard of evaluation and concluded that normalcy was defined and measured, evaluated, or assessed by the group in power.

If there is any hierarchical component applied to people who are different or diverse, these people are most often considered to be superior. Indeed, much of the media today plays on our fascination with people we consider to be unlike ourselves. For example, we like to see and hear about film stars and political figures, mostly because they are different from us. Society considers their differences to be desirable, enriching, and strengthening to the larger group. Such diversity and difference are considered to be positive, and although a relatively small portion of the larger society will ever attain such diversity or difference, we still admire and respect these few people who are different. These differences and diversities often translate into power and authority, which is conferred by society, and most people usually like to align themselves with power and authority.

Deviance, however, is considered to be socially undesirable and weakening to the larger group, and people who are labeled deviant are automatically considered to be inferior. People usually do not aspire to become labeled deviant; indeed, most individuals work very hard to avoid this label. Jenny Morris (1991) explained the way in which these attitudes affected her: "It is very undermining to recognize that people look at me and see an existence, an experience, which they would do everything to avoid for themselves" (p. 15). People who exhibit differences that are labeled deviant are not considered to be assets to the larger group. Indeed, often deviants are thought of as drains or burdens to the group or, at minimum, as not having much to contribute. Society tends to avoid, isolate, reject, and segregate people who are labeled as deviants. Also, deviants are often feared and evoke hostile reactions.

Of course, the accurate definition of deviance is simply *differing from a norm*. Chapter 1 presented two important ideas: (1) Technically, the concepts of deviance, difference, and norms do not have an inherent value component—all of these concepts are neutral; they can be either good or bad. (2) Defining groups in power develops norms. When these two concepts are taken into consideration, it can be seen that deviance can also mean *valuable*, *extraordinary*, *superior*, and *desirable*. In addition, simply because societal norms have been in place for centuries, it is often easy to leap to the conclusion that these norms are both immutable (unchanging) and completely valid and appropriate. When we pause to think about societal norms, without which judgments of differences and deviance would be impossible, we can see that norms and standards do evolve and change, and often these standards and norms are arbitrary because they are based on the fears, anxieties, and false assumptions of the defining group (Schur, 1971, 1979, 1983).

Deviance, therefore, is not within the individual; rather, deviance is a judgment of the dominant, defining segment of society (Gellman, 1959; Goffman, 1963, 1997). Without social comparison, there can be no judgment of deviance. Stated in another way, both deviance and normalcy are defined in relation to each other; thus, sociologists consider deviance-labeling to be an interactionist theory. One sociologist (H.S. Becker, 1963) clearly explained:

> Social groups create deviance by making the rules whose infraction constitutes defiance, and by applying these rules to particular people and labeling them as outsiders. From this point of view, deviance is not a quality of the person . . . but rather a consequence of the application by others of rules and sanctions to an "offender." The deviant is one to whom that label has been successfully applied. (p. 9)

Most, if not all, deviance is forced on the individual. Certainly the individual does not choose to carry this label or to be subjected to the resulting prejudice and discrimination. Often his or her family and marriage partner are labeled *deviant by association*, even when these family members do not exhibit characteristics of deviance. Indeed, most individuals considered by others to be deviant do not think of themselves in this way. Furthermore, occasionally, individuals who are stigmatized in this way are not aware of their forced status of being viewed as deviant. In the last section of this book, we will discuss the importance of "a personal awakening, a discovery that the responsibility for being stigmatized does not lie with oneself" (Davis, 1997b, p. 223).

Many PWODs mistakenly believe that PWDs want to be "normal." Jenny Morris explained:

> One of the most oppressive features of the prejudice which disabled [*sic*] people experience is the assumption that we want to be other than we are, that is, we want to be normal. . . . Do we only have value, even to ourselves, in direct relation to how closely we can imitate 'normal' appearance, function, belief, and behavior? The only way in which it seems we can gain acceptance is to emulate normality. . . . [T]he pressures on us to aspire to be 'normal' are huge—friends and family all conspire from the kindest and highest of intentions to ensure that we make the wrong choice. (p. 35)

Nadine LaSpina, a polio survivor, describes her pride in being an individual with a disability, despite some of the difficulties:

> I'm proud of being Italian. There are things I am ashamed of, like the existence of the Mafia—but these things do not stop me from embracing my

Italian-ness. I love being a woman, but I hate going through menopause. But I wouldn't want a sex-change operation just because of menopause. Certainly the pain and physical limitations of disability are not wonderful, yet that identity is who I am. And I am proud of it. (Fleischer & Zames, 2001, p. 202)

LaSpina's viewpoint echoes Jenny Morris's statement—"I can value my disability, while not denying the difficulties associated with it"—and asserts that PWDs are "thrown on the defensive of trying to prove that our lives are worth living by denying that disability sometimes involves being sick, in pain, or generally experiencing an awful time" (Fleischer & Zames, p. 71).

Disability Should be Considered as Diversity

The disability experience should be viewed as a valued type of diversity with the potential to enrich and strengthen the broader culture. Harriet McBryde Johnson (2003) succinctly captured this idea by stating, "We have something the world needs" (p. 55). Every human is required to understand and accept his or her body. Individuals without disabilities may mistakenly (or wishfully) think that they have complete control over their bodies. PWDs could teach us a great deal about accepting our humanity. Disability can happen to anyone, and it is not the worst thing possible. Life with a disability can be satisfying, rich, and happy. We have a lot to teach the normies.

Kleege (2006), a university professor who was blind, worried about the "Normals" and felt like "they need a lot of help."

There is more than one way to be a human being.... On the surface, it seems a pretty innocuous statement, but in fact, it's quite revolutionary. It forces people to question everything they take for granted as normal. It's a message that needs to be spoken of still.... We say it by forcing our way into their notice, into their world.

I worried about a lot of them so much, the Normals I know. If some of them never became disabled ... it will be a bad business. If they could just let go of the fear, I think. I have the fear, too. I'm afraid of losing my hearing. But I know that if or when it happens, I'll make do somehow. Making do is not such a foreign concept to me. For the Normals, making do is dreadful even to contemplate. What would life be without a leg, without eyesight, without hearing, they worry. Life would be life ... I say. Flawed and limited in some ways, rich and various in others.

I don't enjoy feeling like we [PWDs] exist to offer illuminating insights to the Normals. But in my more generous moments (few and far between as they are), I feel it's something worth doing. They [Normals] need a lot of help. (p. 182)

Hierarchy of Stigma

In this section, look for—

❖ causes—ambiguity and lack of understanding

❖ how the hierarchy of stigma closely parallels the history of American disability law

A "hierarchy of stigma" is associated with the four main categories of disabilities (Deal, 2003). In ascending order, this is the hierarchy of stigma: Individuals with physical disabilities have the least amount of stigma directed toward them; individuals with cognitive disabilities have more stigma; individuals with intellectual disabilities experience even more stigma; and, finally, those with psychiatric disabilities experience the greatest degree of stigma (see Figure 3.1). While there is no disagreement on which disabilities elicit the least stigma, there is some disagreement on which disabilities elicit the greatest degree of stigma. Longmore (2003) stated that there is "a complex interaction among such factors as visibility, severity, mode of functioning, and proximity to the face and head" (p. 146). Esses and Beaufoy (1994) found three "key cognitive elements: stereotypes about various types of disability, symbolic beliefs that PWDs may promote or threaten one's values, and control over the occurrence of the disability" (p. 62). Other researchers (Harper, 1999; Janicki, 1970) found facial disfigurements to be ranked lowest in preference scales, and Corrigan and Penn (1999) consider psychiatric disabilities to be the target of the greatest stigma.

Research has consistently shown that there is a great deal more prejudice and stigma associated with disabilities that have episodic courses. Disabilities such as psychiatric disabilities or chronic illness often have periods of remission offset by flare-ups or symptom exacerbation. In contrast to disabilities with a stable course, such as blindness or deafness, episodic-course disabilities result in ambiguity, and this ambiguity leads to stigma and prejudice. "Do you have a disability or not?" and "Do I have a disability

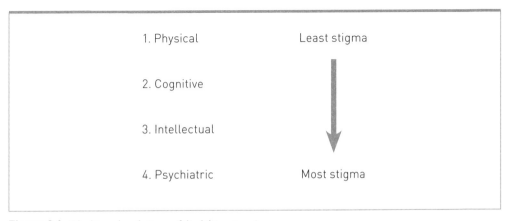

Figure 3.1. *The hierarchy of stigma of disability categories.*

or not?" are questions that are often asked. Once again, in the presence of ambiguity, bad motives are often inferred by others. Nonetheless, the defining characteristics of these disabilities are periods of high functioning interspersed with times of low functioning or no functioning.

An attorney who practices disability law, specializing in psychiatric disabilities, explained the ambiguity of diagnoses on a worldwide, professional basis. Stefan (2001) compared the clear-cut diagnoses of "traditional" disabilities to the ambiguity of diagnoses of psychiatric disabilities. It would be unlikely for the United States to use a different set of categories for cancers than Europe. Traditional diagnoses, such as blindness or paraplegia, are recognized by laypeople and experts alike. These are generally visible, and their existence is usually not subject to dispute.

Disabilities that are not visible to others also appear ambiguous, thus increasing the stigma. In later chapters, we will learn that there is no correlation between degree of impairment and degree of visibility. In other words, invisible disabilities can lead to great functional limitations. To further complicate the picture, there are many disabilities that are both episodic and invisible. Stefan (2001) undertook a national survey. Her findings included the following:

> One of the most striking aspects of the survey responses was the percentage of people who described themselves as disabled but said that other people did not regard them as so, saying things such as, "even the people who know of my psychiatric history do not know what a struggle it is for me to maintain my balance." Another wrote, "Friends and family—they don't understand my illness/disability—they think I am getting away with something—that there is nothing wrong with me. (p. 57)

This hierarchy of stigma has societal implications and implications for individuals with disabilities. The general history of services and benefits to people with disabilities follows the hierarchy of stigma. Those with physical disabilities received services and benefits first; those with cognitive and intellectual disabilities received services next; and those with psychiatric disabilities received services last. Lawmakers and policymakers are subject to society's judgments and evaluations, and it is understandable that the history of disability services closely parallels the hierarchy of stigma toward disability. The hierarchy of stigma, in part, determined which people would be institutionalized and which people would be allowed to live in the community. (Note: Disability rights activists do not use the word *institutionalized*; instead, they use the word *incarcerated*.)

After many years, little has changed (A. Thomas, 2000). Regardless of the legislative process, such as the Americans With Disabilities Act (ADA) and the Disability Rights Movement, the same hierarchy of stigma influences American life. Tringo conducted a study in 1970, and A. Thomas replicated Tringo's study in 2000, finding the same results: Those with physical disabilities experience the least stigma; those with cognitive and intellectual disabilities experience more stigma; and those with psychiatric disabilities experience the most stigma. PWDs also accept this hierarchy. Shakespeare, Gillespie-Sells, and Davies (1996) stated:

> There is a real hierarchy of what is acceptable appearance within the disabled community: what is beautiful, what is ugly. At the top is someone who sits in a wheelchair but looks perfect. I have a friend who has cerebral palsy; she always says cerebral palsy is the dreg. They drool and have a speech impairment, movement problems, that kind of thing. On the high end of the scale is the person with a polio disability because physically they look okay. It's something we have to work on. (p. 71)

Wolbring (2001) suggested that some PWDs advocate eugenics for individuals with other types of disabilities:

> Deaf people, blind people and dwarves may denounce eugenic practices for their own impairment characteristics, but not for others. In resisting the tide of eugenic practices, it is tempting for different groups to see only their own salvation in distancing themselves from others—"Not for me, but them." (p. 46)

Burch (2007) considered the beginnings of Deaf beauty pageants to have been a combination of a reaction to the eugenics movement in the United States and a result of wishing to distance Deaf people from other PWDs:

> Deaf people have long accepted the hierarchy of "handicaps" expressed by early eugenicists and have rejected such negative classifications for only their own population. Deaf leaders and advocates consistently focused on their "normal" intelligence and ability to work—their "able-bodiness"—in public relations campaigns and in expressions to each other. Yet mainstream society commonly perceived deaf people as similar, if not identical, with "defectives" like feebleminded people, undercutting community members' citizenship status. As eugenic ideology intensified during the twentieth century, Deaf activists sought to preserve and protect their society by distancing themselves from other disabled [sic] people and emphasizing their commonality with mainstream, middle-class society. Deaf beauty contests exemplify this strategy. Women's beauty, as projected by the Deaf media and pageants, enforced the notion of normalcy in two ways: sense of commonality with (able-bodied) others, and the sense that beauty specifically suggests healthiness and vitality. The issues of "passing" (as able-bodied), normalcy, and beauty strongly inform the popularity of Deaf beauty pageants. (p. 243)

Those with physical disabilities experience the least degree of stigma and prejudice, probably because these types of disabilities are the easiest to understand. The cause, the onset, the course, and the limitations are easier for most people to comprehend. Simply stated, physical disabilities do not have the degree of ambiguity that other types of disabilities do. Indeed, many people consider physical disabilities to be the only type of disability. The following quotation explains the greater acceptance of people with blindness than of people with other types of disabilities:

> Possibly it is because the unimpaired can easily imagine and sympathize with their plight; unlike mental illness, for example, the state of blindness involves little stigma. Possibly it is because blindness has existed since the beginning of history, so that the blind have had more time to secure a place for themselves as legitimate objects of aid from the state. The very fact that their impairment is less disabling than others gives the blind advantages in political organization. (Berkowitz, 1987, p. 168)

This hierarchy of stigma is a useful model. However, reality is often more complicated than this simple model, and no one model can ever totally represent what a person experiences. For example, many individuals have more than one disability, and it is safe to state that the degree of stigma directed toward these individuals probably is a result of the disability that is most visible or has the greatest number of limitations. Individuals who belong to more than one "minority" group, such as an older Black lesbian with a disability, will experience prejudice, stigma, and discrimination from many sources, and these individuals may not be able to determine the exact source of this evaluation and treatment. Is it racism? Is it ageism? Is it homophobia? Is it sexism? Is it handicapism? Is it all of them? Three of them? Two of them?

Perceived social class is also an important factor. Individuals who are thought to be of a higher social class and who have a disability are perceived more positively than those people with disabilities who are thought to be of a lower social class. Parents of children in wheelchairs often decorate the wheelchair very colorfully to attract children to their child. In much the same way, adults with disabilities know that they will have a greater chance of being accepted if they can present themselves as well educated and of a high social status. Those PWDs who have some sort of ability that is highly valued by society will experience greater acceptance than someone else who does not have a socially valued role or capability but has the same disability. For example, a lawyer spoke in *Time* magazine about her experience with depression and about the kinship she felt with the homeless people on the street, many of whom the lawyer thought had mental illness. The lawyer appeared in a national news magazine precisely because she was a graduate of an Ivy League law school; was employed in a high-paying job; and had experienced institutionalization, medication regimens, and other treatment plans. With whom did the lawyer identify most—the other lawyers or the homeless people on the street? She identified with the homeless people because, according to her perception, they were living the 24-hour-a-day experience of mental illness that she was. She was a lawyer for only 8 to 10 hours a day.

The old joke that a rich person is considered to be eccentric but a poor person who exhibits the same behaviors is considered to be mentally ill reflects the influence that perceived social class exerts on the degree of prejudice and discrimination directed toward the individual. Some of the logic behind the old joke might also refer to the functional definition of disability. Rich people do not have to get up in the morning and go to work; therefore, their mental illness may seem more benign. Rich people not only have fewer functional demands, but they also have more resources with which to hide their mental illness, which, at minimum, would prolong the prediagnosis period. Rich people also have the resources to shield themselves from stress, a known aggravator of mental illness.

The posters of famous and gifted people with disabilities demonstrate the role the perceived social class of the PWD plays in the degree of stigma or prejudice directed toward him or her. Posters of Beethoven and Einstein, with the question, "Did you know he had a disability?" are designed to help people reevaluate their attitudes toward PWDs. As would be expected, the impact of these posters has been difficult to determine, but many PWDs are offended by these posters because they seem to imply that for a PWD to be accepted, he or she must accomplish some superhuman, heroic task, akin to what Beethoven and Einstein did. Certainly, the poster creators needed to use PWDs who were readily identifiable. Celebrities with disabilities today also may present an unrealistic picture of the experience of most PWDs. Nonetheless, most PWDs do not accomplish world-famous acts (nor do most PWODs), and they feel resentful that these posters present only those PWDs who are rich, famous, and extremely gifted. Often, PWDs use the derisive term "super crips" or "overcomers" to describe the famous individuals with disabilities. Furthermore, most PWODs are more comfortable with PWDs who are overcomers.

Society also includes PWDs, and PWDs often are not accepting of other people with disabilities. Coleman (1997) explained: "Moreover, even among stigmatized people, relative comparisons are made, and people are reassured by the fact that there is someone else who is worse off" (p. 218). Some PWDs may feel that they are exceptions to the rule, and they therefore can feel prejudice and discrimination toward other PWDs and yet not consider that this is incongruent. These PWDs consider themselves to have worked harder or somehow done something extraordinary that separates them from other PWDs.

CHAPTER 4

PREJUDICE AGAINST PEOPLE WITH DISABILITIES, PART 2: TODAY IN THE UNITED STATES

✧ the media's portrayal of PWDs

✧ crime and abuse against PWDs

✧ practices that promote prejudice

- simulation exercises
- impression management
- disabled heroes
- assisted suicide
- infanticide of newborns with severe disabilities
- automatic abortion of fetuses with disabilities

✧ four societal responses to disability

- charity
- preferential treatment
- compensation
- civil rights

✧ What is justice?

- everyone receives the same
- everyone receives what he or she has earned
- everyone receives what he or she needs

The Media's Portrayal of People With Disabilities

In this section, look for—

⬧ The mass media has not changed its portrayal of PWDs for hundreds of years.

⬧ The mass media portrays other minorities more accurately and respectfully.

⬧ The depiction of PWDs in media is a type of socially sanctioned discrimination.

⬧ Disability is seen as a symbol (most often for negative characteristics).

The first response to thinking about the portrayal of PWDs in movies, books, and television programs might be as follows: "It's only entertainment, and, besides, nobody thinks that television or movies depict reality. Lighten up." Nonetheless, the ongoing negative and inaccurate depiction of PWDs can lead to a lack of opportunities and civil rights for PWDs. The lives of PWDs are influenced by the way in which the culture represents disability in its media (Hahn, 1988a, 1988b). Many scholars consider the depiction of PWDs in the media to be "hostile fantasies" (Longmore, 2003, p. 134). Furthermore, most consumers of media do not take the time to reflect that these negative portrayals of PWDs say nothing about PWDs but rather are excellent encapsulations of the attitudes PWODs hold of PWDs. Indeed, these distorted images say more about the writers than about PWDs.

Charles Dickens wrote 16 major literary works, of which 14 had a character with a disability (Byrd & Elliott, 1988). Many great novelists used characters with disabilities, and often these PWDs were bitter and self-pitying. Certainly, inaccurate representations of PWDs were found in the media before the introduction of film and television. Therefore, the mass media did not invent prejudice and discrimination against PWDs; the mass media simply made it available to far larger audiences (Norden, 1994).

When movies were first introduced, individuals in racial and ethnic minority groups were portrayed in racist, very simplified, negative, exaggerated, sensationalized, and demeaning ways. These individuals were often the villain, often did not have families or other social statuses, and did not have jobs or professions other than to serve White people. The race of the character was not a secondary characteristic; the character *was* his or her race and little more. Often the minority person served as some type of metaphor or allegory (and so it was unnecessary to endow the person with a personality). Of course, these racist depictions said nothing about racial minority individuals and everything about the White filmmakers. The media now represents racial and ethnic minority individuals in more accurate and complete ways. In contrast, Klobas (1988) concluded that the image of disability represented in film and television has not changed much since the inception of these forms of entertainment.

PWDs are portrayed in exaggerated, sensationalized, and demeaning ways. Women who are blind are often passive and victimized in movies, whereas men who are blind have been endowed with special gifts and wisdom (Safran, 1998). Other PWDs often represent evil, anger, sin, or internal aberration (Byrd & Elliott, 1985; Longmore, 1985; McBrien, 1997). "Captain Hook and Richard III plot and scheme in order to gain vengeance on a world each sees as responsible for his wounds" (Marks, 1999, p. 167).

Disability elicits an emotional response, and writers play on this ignorance and fear to sell tickets and make a profit. The portrayal of disability often heightens comedy or melodrama. J. Morris (1991) summarized:

> Disability is used as a metaphor, as a code for the message that the non-disabled writer wishes to convey. In doing this, the writer draws on the prejudice, ignorance, and fear that generally exist toward disabled [*sic*] people, knowing that to portray a character with a humped back, with a missing leg, with facial scars will evoke certain feelings in the reader or the audience. The disability is used to induce a sense of unease, the more the cultural stereotype is reinforced. (p. 93)

Leonard Kriegel (1987) stated:

> The world of the crippled and disabled [*sic*] is strange and dark, and it is held up to judgment by those who live in fear of it. The cripple [*sic*] is the creature who has been deprived of his ability to create a self. . . . He is the other, if for no other reason than that only by being the other will he be allowed to presume upon the "normals." He must accept definition from outside the boundaries of his own existence. (p. 66)

"Freak shows" and "sideshows," while not very common today, continue to exploit people. In August 2014, a sideshow (or a freak show) at the Boulder County Fair (Colorado) was closed down after the complaints of two parents who objected to the display of "Little Liz, The World's Smallest Woman." The woman is 29 inches tall, and she and her husband "play about 20 events a year with the carnival." The carnival owner was surprised by the reaction of these parents, stating, "I wish there were more sideshows. When people come back from a carnival, they should be able to say, 'I've never seen anything like that.'" Another rationalization of the carnival owner was, "Her sitting on a chair for pictures isn't any different than a guy dressed up as Santa Claus sitting here for pictures. To me, it adds something to life, it's good for them (Liz and her husband) and it doesn't hurt anybody." This short Associated Press (AP) article clearly demonstrates that there is a public who will pay money to view PWDs; carnival owners do not view sideshows as exploitation, but rather see themselves as helping PWDs. Of course, some may think that Little Liz has chosen to display herself and the carnival owner stated, "It doesn't hurt anybody;" but others in the Disability Rights Movement would view Little Liz as impeding other PWDs from winning civil rights and equal social status in the broader American society (*Logan Herald Journal,* 2014, p. A7).

This negative and inaccurate portrayal of PWDs in the media is slowly changing to show PWDs as ordinary people. A *New York Times* article (Navarro, 2007) quoted the actor Robert David Hall, a double amputee who played a coroner on the popular television series *CSI*: "It used to be that if you were disabled and on television, they'd play soft piano behind you. The thing I love about *CSI* is that I'm just Dr. Robbins" (para. 8). The author of the *New York Times* article, Mireya Navarro, suggested three catalysts for these changes. First, the absolute number of PWDs has provided strength in numbers. "The most recent population survey, in 2002, showed the disabled [*sic*] population to be the country's largest minority: 51 million, or 18 percent of all Americans" (para. 21). Second, by providing PWDs with civil rights, there are more PWDs visible in society. Navarro concluded, "With increased access has come visibility. The public image of the disabled [*sic*] is increasingly informed by actual experience of disability rather than the imagined understanding of it" (paras. 26–27). Third, the increasing numbers of actors with disabilities in the Screen Actors Guild have advocated for more stories that include characters with disabilities and, moreover, hiring actors with disabilities to play these characters. Navarro concludes:

> The heart-wrenching movie of the week and fund-raising telethons striving for cures have given way to amputees rock climbing on reality shows like *The Amazing Race* and doing the jive on *Dancing with the Stars*. Sitcoms and crime shows have jumped on the bandwagon, too: An actor who is a paraplegic, for instance, depicts a member of the casino surveillance team on *Las Vegas*. (Navarro, 2007, para. 7)

Effect of the Media on PWDs

Many PWDs, or their families, have spoken about the effect the media has on the individual with a disability when he or she first receives the diagnosis:

> The physical therapist said, "Oh well, it's dwarfism" and she went on about his (her baby son) being a dwarf. She didn't see my reaction was to just fall backwards, because to me dwarfism or being a dwarf was the troll under the bridge in Three Billy Goats Gruff. (Ablon, 1984, p. 351)

Donna Orrin held a master's of social work and provided training for mental health professionals. She wrote of her reaction when she received the diagnosis of bipolar disorder.

> At that time, I was not involved at all in the community mental health [CMH] system; I didn't even know that there was such a thing as CMH. I

hardly knew anyone with mental illness. My education about mental illness consisted of the book, *One Flew Over the Cuckoo's Nest*, which was really bad news. I felt all alone, and I believed there were a lot of really bad things wrong with me. (Mackelprang & Salsgiver, 1999, p. 181)

Rod Michalko (2002) wrote about his experiences watching television and movies, paying particular attention to the characters who were blind:

In my teens, I saw blind people on television and in the movies and sometimes came across a blind character in a book. They were all portrayed as victims of a misfortune. . . . When I saw blind people in the movies or on television and even when I saw the "real" blind ones, I saw incompetence, sadness, and poverty. And I saw misfortune. Whether my perception was accurate or not is irrelevant; that's just what I saw. What I did not see when I saw these blind people is just as significant as what I did see: I did not see me. Still, when I saw them, I experienced a nebulous fear that I later understood was the fear of seeing myself. (p. 24)

PWDs are made the "other" by the media. This is now changing with the introduction of television programs (on the Learning and Discovery channels) that portray the lives and families of people with disabilities in a more realistic way. The mass media has great potential to teach and shape public attitudes about disability and the people who experience them.

Crime, Abuse, and People With Disabilities

In this section, look for—

- ⬦ different thresholds of belief and intervention
- ⬦ mutual forgiving, excusing, or "not knowing" of perpetrators
- ⬦ structured normality of violence against PWDs

The prevalence of violence and crime against PWDs is higher than in the general population. One survey found that noninstitutionalized women with disabilities were twice as likely to experience physical violence as were nondisabled women (Albrecht, Seelman, & Bury, 2001; Chang et al., 2003; McFarlane et al., 2001). Other national surveys have also found physical and sexual abuse of people to be double the national rates for those without disabilities (National Research Council, 1996; Saxton et al., 2006) These statistics do not reveal the full extent of the violence and abuse, because it has also been found that people with disabilities, especially those with severe intellectual disability, experience abuse at a younger age, are abused for longer periods of time, and report larger numbers of perpetrators. Moreover, many PWDs do not report the abuse, or when they do come forward, they are not taken seriously. Michelle McCarthy (1999) summarized: "Among disabled [sic] people there are more girls who are abused than boys, and girls are less often believed than boys" (p. 146). In this study, 32% of the cases of abuse of women with intellectual disability were not taken seriously enough to be reported to service managers, whereas the figure for men with intellectual disability who reported abuse was 7%. McCarthy termed these discrepancies "different thresholds of belief and intervention" (p. 146).

What is abuse of people with disabilities? As with anyone else, it is physical and sexual abuse, robbery, stealing money, abuse of children and pets, and threats of physical harm. However, there are many types of abuse and violence that are specific to people with disabilities, including medication manipulation or withholding; equipment destruction; neglecting to provide needed services, such as feeding or toileting; personal care attendants who come to work drunk or high; rough handling; or deliberately dropping the PWD. A personal care attendant has a great deal of power over his or her employer—access to the individual's home, credit cards, and body. Indeed, many PWDs submit to the abuse because of fear of losing the attendant. One person said, "I just put up with it." A man told of this experience:

> He and I got into the verbal altercation . . . so he thought he put me in my place by throwing me upon the back of the chair, then letting me hang there. I'm on a ventilator. . . . I had already been off for an hour and a half, and I was getting winded. . . . He just kept screaming at me, (forced me) to apologize to him . . . hardly able to breathe, and I'm supposed to apologize to some guy. He really scared the hell out of me. (Saxton et al., 2006, p. 4)

Why is abuse and violence toward PWDs so prevalent? The power differential between the abuser and the victim is very large when the victim has a disability and is therefore unable to avoid the abuse or escape. Some individuals with intellectual disability may not realize that what is being done to them is abuse. The abuser enjoys the feeling of control and power over someone who is weak and often chooses victims who cannot defend themselves. Sobsey's (1994) study revealed that individuals with severe intellectual disabilities were raped far more often than persons with mild intellectual disabilities.

Lack of privacy and the visibility of the disability put PWDs at higher risk (Powers et al., 2002). For example, in hospitals, institutions, and residential schools there are no locks on the bedroom doors. These types of care settings can be closed environments without much oversight or supervision. The large number of strangers with whom PWDs must interact on a daily basis poses more risks; for example, bus drivers know the individual's schedule and where he or she lives. Often, PWDs are subjected to multiple caregivers during the course of the day, and many times, caregivers are alone with PWDs. In or out of an institution, it is easy to isolate a PWD and make it difficult to solicit help.

Institutions and other caregiving settings now require criminal background checks for all their employees and demand full reporting of any abuse, neglect, or violence. In the past, paid attendants in public institutions rarely committed an abusive act just once; most abusers had chronic, long-term patterns of abuse and violence (Zavirsek, 2002). When allegations were investigated, it was often found that many staff members knew of the abuse but chose to ignore or excuse it. If the abuse was discovered, the abuser would leave that particular institution and quickly find work at another care setting to continue his or her pattern of abuse and violence. Fortunately, criminal background checks have greatly decreased abuse and violence in public care settings.

Prejudice and discrimination against PWDs assist perpetrators in avoiding guilt or remorse. Myths such as that PWDs are insensitive to pain, PWDs are less than human, and PWDs are not sexual beings may make it difficult for abusers to feel empathy for their victims. Personal care attendants have often excused their abuse by citing their low wages, the high stress and physical demands of their jobs, and the feeling that they "have a right to something." Unpaid family caregivers often feel even more license to commit abuse and violence against the individual with a disability. This has been called the structured normality of abuse against PWDs.

In one focus group, men with disabilities saw little or no value in reporting abuse to the police, saying, "The cops won't do anything" (Saxton et al., 2006, p. 7). Often, the victim is blamed or, at minimum, not believed. PWDs are told that they need more medication, that they somehow provoked the violence, or that they fabricated the story. Accommodations are not available when PWDs do report crimes. One Deaf woman reported a rape to the police. When she asked for a sign language interpreter, the police replied that finding an interpreter would take too much time and insisted that she write everything. The woman was shaking but nevertheless attempted to write a full account of her rape. The following story shows that, despite reports from the victims, the abuse can continue for decades.

> The *New York Times* broke the story of the Reverend Lawrence C. Murphy, who had admitted to sexually abusing deaf boys at a Catholic boarding school at Wisconsin for 22 years. Victims tried for more than three decades to bring him to justice. They told other priests. They told three archbishops of Milwaukee. They told two police departments and the district attorney. They used sign language, written affidavits, and graphic gestures to show what exactly Father Murphy had done to them. But their reports fell on the deaf ears of the hearing people. (Solomon, 2012, p. 74)

PWDs, especially those with severe disabilities, are not accorded much respect, credibility, or prestige, and, because of this, the legal system is not always quick to prosecute. Even when prosecuted for crimes against PWDs, perpetrators received lighter and shorter sentences than perpetrators of crimes against PWODs. The low social status of PWDs is reflected in the legal system.

Practices That Promote Prejudice and Discrimination

In this section, we will discuss common practices and concerns that relate, for the most part, only to PWDs and not to other types of minorities. All of these *increase* prejudice and discrimination toward PWDs and devalue the lives of PWDs; none of these involve the participation of PWDs themselves, nor do they improve the quality of life of PWDs. All are based on the false perceptions of PWODs. These are

- simulation exercises,
- impression management (being the court jester),
- contact with PWODs,
- "disabled heroes,"
- assisted suicide, and
- automatic abortion of fetuses with disabilities.

Results of These Practices:

- increases prejudice and discrimination
- devalues the lives of PWDs
- does not involve the participation of PWDs,
- does not improve the quality of life of PWDs,
- are based on false perceptions of PWODs
- include life-and-death issues

Simulation Exercises

Simulation exercises are designed to give those without disabilities insight into the experience of disability (Baesler, 1995; Fichten, Compton, & Amsel, 1985). Individuals wear blindfolds to simulate blindness and use wheelchairs and other devices to simulate other types of disabilities, and often students in drug or alcohol abuse counseling classes are required to forgo one type of food or drink for 2 or 3 weeks (often chocolate, coffee, or beer).

However, it is now known that these exercises are useless and they may actually increase prejudice and discrimination toward PWDs (Kiger, 1992; Olkin, 1999; Pfeiffer, 1989; B. A. Wright, 1975). Imagine how a PWOD in the first exercise would feel. For most adults, the idea of being spoon-fed appears demeaning; however, PWDs remind us that PWODs do not feel embarrassed when the stylist cuts their hair.

Allport (1954, 1958, 1986), in his classic work, *The Nature of Prejudice*, discussed the usefulness of role-playing techniques in which a member of the dominant group takes on the role of an individual of a minority group. In Allport's examples, the groups are racial and ethnic groups. Allport explained that the White person is

> required to act out the roles of other people—of employees, of students, of Negro servants, he [sic] learned through such 'psychodrama' what it feels like to be in another's shoes. He [sic] also gains insight regarding his own motives, his anxieties, his projections. (Allport, 1986, p. 491)

Indeed, Allport used the expression "forced empathy" to describe the purpose of these simulations.

Is it possible to simulate a disability? Simulation exercises, regardless of how carefully designed, cannot allow a PWOD to assume the identity of a PWD. The fatigue, pain, and social isolation cannot be simulated (Marks, 1999). John Hockenberry spent more than 10 years with National Public Radio as a reporter, Middle East correspondent, and program host. As you read Hockenberry's description of paralysis, including the uniqueness (like a fingerprint), consider whether the experience of paralysis can be simulated.

> "Paralyzed from the waist down" describes so little of the experiences of a spinal-cord injury that most crips used it as a kind of shorthand joke. In my case, I am paralyzed from the nipples down. When people learn this they are shocked to realize that there is no international checkpoint at the waist. It is an arbitrary demarcation. In actual fact, relatively few people are paralyzed from the waist down. Everyone has their particular line separating sensation from numbness. Each line of separation is invisible to the eye. In some people the aspects of temperature and pressure and muscle control are separate. Some spinal cord-injured people can feel pressure but not temperature in some parts of their body and vice versa. There are people with almost total sensation but with no motor control . . . a partially damaged fiber-optic cable . . . picture, but no sound . . . bad reception. All these metaphors aid understanding, but none is precise. The trace of each paraplegic and quadriplegic's sensory border zone is as unique as a fingerprint. Each person has a different answer to the question: What does paralysis feel like? (Hockenberry, 1995, p. 97)

As discussed before, most PWDs consider their disability to be a valued part of their self-identity, are proud of their mastery of the disability, and have developed many idiosyncratic responses and accommodations. None of these self-defining characteristics can be simulated. Voluntarily giving up coffee, chocolate, or beer may allow an individual to see how difficult such self-control can be, but the experience cannot begin to parallel the experience of recovery from alcohol or drug abuse. Furthermore, how can a PWOD simulate a congenital disability, such as blindness, deafness, or a limb deficiency?

However, it is possible to glimpse some of the prejudice and discrimination PWDs encounter. If a person is required to use a wheelchair for 24 hours, he or she can understand the frustration of inaccessible restrooms, water fountains, and doorways. Nonetheless, the simulator knows that the simulation is of short duration (Sawyer & Clark, 1980).

Most important, simulation exercises reinforce and strengthen prejudice against PWDs because simulations often evoke feelings of dependence, hopelessness, and discouragement in the simulator. People who are blind or deaf or who use a wheelchair are skilled in mastering their environment; people who wear a blindfold or earmuffs or use a wheelchair for a simulation exercise, however, experience 24 hours of frustration, dependence, and hopelessness. Using a wheelchair requires strength and technique, both of which require time to develop. The experience of blindness would be very different if an individual did not know how to read Braille. However, learning Braille is a difficult and time-consuming process. Wandering around the corridors of a university building with a blindfold would probably give the simulator a discouraging and frustrating view of blindness because Braille is used on doors and elevators. (In addition, people who are blind have had orientation and mobility—O&M—training.) Furthermore, the simulator mistakenly may think that he or she now has "expert knowledge" of the disability experience. However, it is not knowledge of disability that has been acquired, but rather the myth that PWDs feel helpless, dependent, and discouraged all the time.

Lifchez and Wade (1982) described simulation exercises and their unexpected results:

> Workshops where one temporarily "tries on" a disability constitute attempts to give . . . an entry into the subjective experience of the disability. Trying on a disability offers . . . a sense of the physical issues involved, but it often backfires, as it can generate so much anxiety. . . . Trying on fails to offer . . . any sense of the way in which the environment affects, feeds, and is sustained by social and cultural prejudices and expectation. (p. 91)

Marks (1999) pointed out shortcomings of simulation exercises:

> Rather than listening to what disabled [*sic*] people are saying, simulation may pander to voyeuristic excitement and give non-disabled people a very distorted and reductive kind of 'empathy,' a cavalier fantasy that an experience has been understood, or an increase in pity for the person with a disability. (p. 134)

Kiger (1992) undertook a review of 60 studies of simulation exercises and found that none had any positive effect on the attitudes of PWODs toward the disability experience. There are other issues in using simulation exercises; one of these issues concerns the response of PWDs to PWODs attempting to "imitate" them. Olkin

(1999), a polio survivor who uses a wheelchair, summarized her feelings about simulation exercises:

> I find it rude for people to "imitate" me as a way of understanding my minority status. It implies that only through direct experience can one come to understand "minority status," as if the word of people with disabilities isn't good enough. For no other minority status do we direct students to use imitation as a means of enlightenment. (p. 330)

Experiential learning is valuable, and most disability scholars advocate the use of such learning methods to help PWODs understand the experience of disability. Indeed, if done correctly, experiential learning activities can decrease the heightened sensitivity and interaction strain PWODs often feel in the presence of PWDs. Beatrice Wright required her university students to undertake a semester-long advocacy project, such as overseeing the accessibility of a public playground or generating a list of public entertainment facilities that are not accessible to PWDs and then developing a plan to facilitate change. Other projects included listing negative, condescending portrayals of PWDs in the media (H. McCarthy, 1993). Olkin (1999) used other types of experiential learning, including having her students use assistive devices, such as TTY telephones, and requiring students to go to the Department of Rehabilitation office and learn how to fill out an application form. (TTY telephones, used by people who are deaf, have a keyboard and a screen. The two callers type to each other.) Both these professor–scholars emphasize that these types of learning activities need to be preceded and followed by the appropriate information and discussion. In an article in *The Disability Rag*, an outspoken magazine written by and for PWDs, the author (who is a polio survivor and whose husband is blind) recounts:

> My daughter Tara had come home from school in tears. It was Disability Simulation Day at Greenwood High [School]. Blindfolded students were being led around by sighted students, others were bumping into walls. The students were terrified of their newly created disabilities. Some had told Tara they thought persons with disabilities had horrible lives; a few thought they might be better off dead. (Brew-Parrish, 2004, para. 8)
>
> I contacted the school's psychology teacher once and tried to get Disability Simulation Day stopped. It was a lost cause. She [the teacher] liked having Disability Simulation Day featured in the local newspaper, and saw no need for me or my husband—or anyone from our local independent living center—to come to her classroom to talk with students. (para. 11)
>
> I am baffled as to why nondisabled people see a need to simulate a disability. Across our nation in February, we celebrate Black History Month. Is it necessary for people with white skin to paint their faces black to better understand this minority? (para. 21)

Some individuals with disabilities advocate the use of simulation exercises but only if a PWD guides the exercise. While the PWD who acts as a guide can offer interpretation and greater understanding of the experience, many PWDs consider all simulation exercises to be useless and demeaning to individuals who experience disability 24 hours a day, 7 days a week.

Impression Management

Most everybody, with or without a disability, engages in some type of impression management. We wear appropriate clothing, are well groomed, speak appropriately, and practice good manners. Especially when interacting with people we do not know very well and we wish to favorably impress, we invest a great deal of time and effort in impression management. First dates and job interviews are classic examples of these types of situations, in that we wish to impress an individual who does not know us very well; furthermore, there is always the possibility that we will be rejected.

PWDs are aware that their disability creates discomfort in others; therefore, impression management for them becomes even more complicated. In fact, many PWDs use disability-specific impression-management techniques in an effort to reduce the tension felt by others. These techniques do not assist the individual's functioning and, in fact, actually may jeopardize his or her functioning. The sole purpose of these impression-management techniques is to reduce discomfort in others. Such impression-management techniques are criticized by many in the Disability Rights Movement because activists believe that the discomfort felt by PWODs is an issue with which PWODs should deal, and that it is not the responsibility of PWDs to become "court jesters" or "Tiny Tims." Some impression-management techniques are so costly to PWDs, in terms of time and physical pain that they decide to abandon these attempts.

In spite of this controversy, many PWDs do actively engage in impression-management techniques to cope with the reactions of others. Some general techniques are the use of humor, the skillful introduction of the topic of the disability, and tactfully correcting PWODs when they make a mistake. Disability-specific techniques include a person who is blind maintaining eye contact with those who are speaking, and turning on the lights at night. Individuals who are deaf have undergone years of speech training to have a more pleasant-sounding voice, and individuals with motor difficulties are subjected to "gait-training" to appear more "normal" to others. Other types of impression management include wearing prostheses for their cosmetic value rather than for their functional use. For anyone, the total impression conveyed is made up of many small, individual elements, and it is this overall impression that is important. Nonetheless, it is safe to state that for many PWDs, impression management is a greater challenge than it is for PWODs.

One of my students who is blind, in a class discussion on impression management, reminded us that it is difficult for a person who is blind to know when it is dark outside, and, therefore, she is not quite sure when to turn the lights on. This student told us that many times visitors had driven to her house, saw her house in total darkness, and drove away, thinking that she was not home. She also said that when she does turn on the lights, it may be days before she remembers to turn them off. Michalko (2002) described impression management as "actions required of the visually impaired . . . that are primarily responses to the sighted person's needs, and have little purpose from a non-visual perspective" (p. 137). "Adapting to the images of the 'sighted world' does not restore sight, it simply acts as demonstration: it demonstrates a blind person's commitment to participating in humanity" (p. 139).

Franklin Roosevelt was a master at impression management. For example, he developed a type of walk in which he used a cane and a man walked on each side of him. (Often these men were his sons.) The three men had devised a carefully rehearsed act, at Roosevelt's request, to talk and laugh as they walked, appearing relaxed. In reality, all three were exerting themselves, carefully shifting Roosevelt's weight with each step and taking turns lifting him. (Roosevelt was lifting his legs with his body muscles because he had no hip muscles.) It was hard work, but it appeared that Roosevelt was walking on his own. Another example of Roosevelt's impression-management techniques was the navy blue cape that he wore. The public mistakenly thought this cape to be part of his "style," much as his cigarette holder was. In reality, it is easier to wear a cape rather than a coat when using a wheelchair; therefore the cape was an accommodation to Roosevelt's disability.

"Disabled Heroes"

Perceived social class, educational level, income, and occupational level do matter. Most of us do not like to admit that we are influenced by an individual's grooming, style of clothing, manners, and speaking ability. Nonetheless, individuals who are believed to be well educated, well mannered, and of high social status are accorded more respect. This holds true for PWDs (although it should be remembered that as a group, PWDs are far more likely to live in poverty, receive inferior educations, and be unemployed or underemployed). PWDs, like anyone else, realize that they will be more readily accepted if they appear in a position of authority and status.

All of us have seen the posters of "disabled heroes," in which individuals who have accomplished extraordinary achievements in science, the arts, athletics, or politics are pictured. Some examples include the physicist Stephen Hawking, American President Franklin Roosevelt, Helen Keller, the composer Beethoven, and Albert Einstein. Their accomplishments are remarkable for anyone, with or without a disability. These posters are intended to reduce the prejudice and discrimination against PWDs, but in reality they perpetuate more prejudice and discrimination simply because they give a false impression of a "typical" PWD and communicate, in a not very subtle way, that anyone can overcome a disability. It is easy to understand why many PWDs resent these disabled heroes.

Furthermore, most PWODs are unaware of the functional limitations of disabilities and therefore are not in a position to evaluate the accomplishments of PWDs. For example, Wendell (2006) made the observation that athletes with amputations or spinal cord injuries do not have as many functional limitations as people with arthritis. Arthritis is a debilitating, painful, pervasive disability that affects many joints in the body, yet it is safe to state that most PWODs would consider a spinal cord injury or an amputation (or congenital limb deficiency) as more limiting than arthritis. However, it would be most unusual to see an athlete with severe arthritis.

These individuals who are considered to be disabled heroes have had remarkable resources available to them, including money, education, family support, innate talents, and intelligence, and, indeed, they are probably more famous for their accomplishments than they were (are) for having a disability. For example, Helen Keller, who was deaf and blind, came from a prominent Southern family, was physically beautiful, and had personal friends such as Alexander Graham Bell, Mark Twain, Eleanor Roosevelt, and Albert Einstein. She graduated from Radcliffe College and occasionally lived on the financial support of admiring millionaires. But, by far, her greatest asset, not available to most people who are deaf and blind, was a companion and teacher who stayed with her for more than 49 years, Anne Sullivan (Herrmann, 1998). It is interesting to note that Keller's family often could not afford to pay Sullivan, but she remained with Helen Keller until her own death. It is also interesting that Helen Keller's parents wrote to the Perkins Institute for the Blind after hearing about the successful education of a young woman, Laura Bridgman, who was deaf and blind. One of Laura Bridgman's teachers at the Perkins Institute was Anne Sullivan, and the Kellers were able to engage Anne Sullivan as the teacher and live-in companion for their daughter, Helen. Laura Bridgman lived most of her life at the Perkins Institute and died there; today there are few people who know who she was, and yet Helen Keller would not have been a celebrity and famous writer if it had not been for Laura Bridgman. (However, Charles Dickens met Laura Bridgman and modeled his fictional character "Little Nell" after her.)

Another example of disabled heroes includes higher functioning PWDs representing lower functioning PWDs. For example, in the case of Down syndrome (DS), higher functioning individuals are often spokespersons for all those with DS. Many families with a DS-member feel like this trivializes their experience and gives a false impression of the difficulties and limitations of DS. Many disabilities are measured and diagnosed using a spectrum or a continuum of functioning, with the diagnoses of those individuals with the greatest deficits and impairments in functioning placed at the low-end of the continuum, and the diagnoses of those individuals with the fewest deficits in functioning placed at the high-end of the continuum. Thus, for a single diagnosis, such as Autism Spectrum Disorder (ASD), there is a wide range of functioning, and it is often individuals on the higher end of the spectrum who are considered to be representatives of all individuals with this particular diagnosis. Indeed, many high-functioning individuals with ASD (which was formerly diagnosed as Asperger's syndrome in the DSM) *celebrate* their ASD. Temple Grandin is the best example of this. Dr. Grandin has written best-selling books about her ASD. Many families and individuals with ASD question if these types of disabled heroes give a false perception, especially when many individuals with ASD are incontinent, do not speak, and often live at home as adults. Such broad-based misperceptions may curtail funding for both services and research on ASD. One mother explained:

> Please don't write about them [high-functioning Asperger's]. They're a handful of noisy people who get a lot of media attention. They're trivializing what autism really is. It's like stealing money from the tin cup of a blind man who you say that it's not an illness; you are getting people who should be making political and social change to think that it's not a problem. (Solomon, 2012, p. 280)

Often the time of the onset of the disability has an impact on the accomplishments of the individual. For example, Christopher Reeve was able to develop his celebrity status before the onset of the disability, and Stephen Hawking received his education before the onset of amyotrophic lateral sclerosis (ALS). (The disability of ALS would not have prevented him from receiving a PhD, but most universities would not have had the accommodations necessary for Hawking, and, therefore, Hawking probably would not have been admitted.) Beethoven became deaf later in life, after he was a famous composer. The lives of these individuals would have been very different if their disabilities had been congenital or acquired early in life.

In the case of learning disabilities, it is difficult to know if these celebrities truly had a disability. Individuals of great achievement, such as Einstein; Edison; the Danish writer of fairy tales, Hans Christian Andersen; the British prime minister Winston Churchill; and the Italian artist Leonardo da Vinci have been reported to have had a learning disability. However, most experts in learning disabilities do not think that any of these individuals had a learning disability. Of course, all of these individuals lived in a time when learning disabilities were not known about or diagnosed. Many of these assumptions are based on these individuals' handwriting, examples of misspelled words, and reports that they had problems in school. Huston (1987) summarized:

> Frequently, in books and articles on dyslexia, writers report a number of notable adults reputed to have had dyslexia. Repetition of these names has become almost a litany. These names are usually just listed in a series in books with rarely any explanation or evidence given why the person is considered to have been dyslexic. The few times any evidence is given it is scanty—often irrelevant or questionable. . . . Often there are more simple explanations for the difficulties these persons are said to have had. (pp. 151–152)

The Drawbacks to Having Disabled Heroes, or Super Crips

Many PWDs use the derisive term "super crip" to label these disabled heroes. Indeed, many in the Disability Rights Movement regard super crips as perpetuating two harmful ideas or prejudices. First, by focusing only on the individual, the efforts and successes of the Disability Rights Movement, the passage of legislation such as the ADA, and the realities of the physical and attitudinal barriers that PWDs confront are ignored. The concept of a super crip concentrates on a remarkable individual and conveniently overlooks the accomplishments of disability advocates who facilitated the creation of the super crip. Once again, by focusing on *individuals*, society can reassure itself that the difficulties that PWDs encounter can be solved by individual effort. Second, posters and other advertisements of disabled heroes subtly plant the idea in the mind of the general public that *all* people with the same type of disability should be able to accomplish at the level of the super crip. However, for the typical PWD (whoever that might be) who does not have all the resources of the super crip, this is impossible. In spite of these realities, in the minds of the public, the super crip now becomes the standard by which *all* PWDs are judged. Covington (1997, as cited in Pelka, 1997) summarized:

> Super crip is usually a character struck down in the prime of life who fights to overcome insurmountable odds to succeed as a meaningful member of society. Through strength of will, perseverance, and hard work, the disabled individual achieves *a normal* life. . . . Too often, the news media treats an individual with disabilities who has attained success in his [*sic*] field or profession as though they [*sic*] were one-of-a-kind. While this one-of-a-kind aspect might make for a better story angle, it perpetuates in the mind of the general public how rare it is for the citizen with disabilities to succeed. (p. 292)

If the public thinks it knows *by name* the few PWDs who have succeeded, then it is also logical, although wrong, to think that most PWDs are failures. Irving Zola, the sociologist, college professor, and disability scholar, was a survivor of polio. He died in 1994 at the age of 59. Zola (1991) described the message and effects of "super crips":

> It is the . . . message that I have recently begun to abhor. It states that if a Franklin Delano Roosevelt or Wilma Rudolph could OVERCOME their handicap [*sic*], so could and should all the disabled [*sic*]. And if we fail, it's *our* problem, *our* personality, *our* weakness. And this further masks what chronic illness is all about. For our lives or even our adaptations do not center around one single activity or physical achievement but around many individual and complex ones. Our daily living is not filled with dramatic accomplishments but with mundane ones. And most of all, our physical difficulties are not temporary ones to be overcome once-and-for-all but ones we must face again and again for the rest of our lives. That's what chronic means! (p. 161)

J. Morris (1991) has stated that PWDs are only allowed two roles—"the pathetic crip and the Super Crip" (p. 100). Each is the opposite of the other; each is an extreme role. Both roles construct the disability as the individual's most salient identity, and neither allows the PWD to be an ordinary person. Neither the "pathetic crip" or the "super crip" is considered to be an individual.

In many ways, Helen Keller was considered to be a super crip by the general public, and decades after her death, she is still remembered as having achieved remarkable accomplishments (for anyone, with or without a disability). Nonetheless, PWDs have raised questions about her contributions to the disability community. Moreover, there are Deaf advocates (Brueggemann & Burch, 2006; Kleege, 2006; Nielsen, 2006) who feel that Keller's notoriety and her personal beliefs harmed the community of Deaf people. Nielsen's article—entitled "Was Helen Keller Deaf?"—shows that Helen Keller did not form any relationships with the Deaf organizations, in spite of the fact that her method of communication, finger spelling, came from the Deaf. Nielsen summarized:

> The newly created American Federation for the Blind (AFB) supplied both an income and a meaningful public life, becoming the center of her and Anne Sullivan Macey's life. Keller's employment with AFB cemented her public identification with the cause of blindness, removing her further from deafness, the Deaf community, and other causes, almost exclusively. (p. 27)

Keller was also an advocate of oralism and did not support the teaching of sign languages, thus hindering the education of Deaf children for decades. Touted as proof of the superiority of oralist teaching methods, Keller was used as a success story by oralist advocates. However, on her lecture tours, newspapers reported that no one in the audience could understand what Keller was saying when she spoke orally. Finally, Keller believed in both eugenics and euthanasia policies for babies and children with severe disabilities. Keller eventually changed her mind and reversed her stance; nonetheless, during the height of her fame, she spoke and wrote publicly in support of policies to prevent the birth of children with disabilities. Much has been written by Deaf advocates about Helen Keller, documenting her beliefs and activities, and it is not surprising that many Deaf advocates view Helen Keller with both suspicion and anger.

It is safe to say that most Americans do not know about the true disabled heroes. These disabled heroes are political activists who fought for the rights of all PWDs. Individuals with disabilities formed organizations such as Disabled in Action; they founded the Independent Living Movement; they fought for housing, transportation, and civil rights for PWDs. Parents of children with disabilities lobbied for a free, public education for their children. Others parked their wheelchairs in front of inaccessible buses, thus bringing public transportation to a halt in many major American cities. (They would have been taken to jail, but the jails were not wheelchair accessible.) Activists have staged sit-ins in front of inaccessible restaurants and hotels. Individuals with disabilities forced the signing of the regulations of federal legislation by staging the longest sit-in (28 days) at a federal building. During this sit-in, phone service was cut off; one of the protesters was Deaf and simply signed through the window to an individual waiting outside, who then relayed the information to the media. Justin Dart is considered to be the father of the ADA. PWDs and their advocacy groups have worked to ensure the civil rights of Americans with disabilities, but most Americans would not recognize their names, and their pictures are not displayed on billboards along the freeway.

Read the book, *Blind Rage: Letters to Helen Keller* by G. Kleege (Washington, DC: Gallaudet University, 2006). On page 1, Kleege introduces herself and gives her reasons for writing the book.

Dear Helen Keller,

Allow me to introduce myself. I am a writer and part-time English professor. I am American, married, middle-aged, middle-class. Like you, I am blind, though not deaf. But the most important thing you need to know about me, and the reason for my letter, is that I grew up hating you. . . . I hated you because you were always held up to me as a role model, and one who set an impossibly high standard of cheerfulness in the face of adversity. "Why can't you be more like Helen Keller?" people always said to me.

I am not alone in this. Many disabled people [*sic*] think you did our cause a lot of harm. Your life story inscribes the idea that disability is a personal tragedy to be overcome through an individual's fortitude and pluck, rather than a set of cultural practices and assumptions, affecting many individuals, that could be changed through collective action. (p. 1)

Ms. Kleege has the unique vantage of a professor of English and a blind person. Because of this, she is able to ask questions about Keller's writings, the play *The Miracle Worker,* and Keller's adaptations to blindness and deafness.

Assisted Suicide

Assisted suicide is based on the Biomedical Model because the disability is the only aspect considered; not the PWD's strengths and resources such as assistive technology, family support, or educational and professional attainment.

Empirical research has shown that medical professionals tend to view severe disability as a tragedy, and, moreover, they are not aware of their misperceptions. Indeed, medical professionals often think they are being compassionate. The opportunity for assisted suicide may become the "duty to die," in a misguided effort to save others expense and the burden of care. Individuals who are newly disabled have not had an opportunity to explore all their options. Assisted suicide of those with severe disabilities, such as quadriplegia, devalues the lives of those who live with quadriplegia.

The Story of Larry McAfee, or There Is a Better Solution

One of the most widely publicized stories of an individual with a disability requesting assisted suicide is that of a 34-year-old man from Georgia, Larry McAfee. In 1989, McAfee was in a motorcycle accident that left him with quadriplegia and on a respirator. At the time of McAfee's injury, he was close to completing an engineering degree at Georgia Tech. After 3 months in a nursing home, he called a lawyer asking for the legal right to commit suicide. McAfee's case went to the Georgia Supreme Court, and the Court upheld McAfee's right to assisted suicide. After the court ruling, McAfee's situation had changed, and he no longer wished to die; therefore, he escaped to a nursing home in Alabama because the Georgia court ruling applied only to the state of Georgia. By 1990, McAfee had become a disability rights activist and testified before the Georgia State Senate, stating, "Medicaid and Medicare policies that do not work in the best interest of the disabled [*sic*] have caused me and those like me to become prisoners of bureaucracy" (Shapiro, 1997, p. 177). Until McAfee's case, Medicare and Medicaid only paid for treatment and services provided in a nursing home.

What changed McAfee's mind? Of course, it is impossible to entirely understand McAfee's situation. Nonetheless, leaving nursing homes and living in a group home that was fully accessible and provided 24-hour personal care attendant service was a beginning. To live in a group home in the community, it was necessary to change the funding requirements of Medicaid and Medicare. Shapiro summarized:

> From a disability rights point of view, the McAfee decision was better understood as the story of how this country fails miserably to care for severely disabled [*sic*] people. Instead of getting help to live on his own, McAfee was sentenced to indifferent nursing homes and hospitals and stripped of basic decision-making about his life. (1997, pp. 171–172)

Second, an individual stepped forward, making it clear that he supported McAfee's right to die, but he insisted that McAfee first consider all of his options. This individual, named Russ Fine, began to acquire assistive technology for McAfee, took him out for rides in a van, and investigated ways in which to circumnavigate Medicaid's funding requirements. A computer engineer in California, Bob Stockwell, saw a television report on McAfee and flew out to Georgia to set up a voice-activated computer that allowed him to turn the lights and television on and off, lock the doors, and regulate the thermostat. Stockwell also set up a computer system with which McAfee could make architectural drawings with a sonar beam directed from a strap on his head. It is interesting that Stockwell knew nothing or very little about disability but he was an expert in computers. After receiving this technology, McAfee no longer wished to die. McAfee used a wheelchair that was powered by his breaths; a respirator was built into the wheelchair. With his customized van and "sip and puff" wheelchair, McAfee had the freedom and independence to go almost anywhere he wanted, whenever he wanted.

Incidentally, the play and subsequent movie, "Whose Life Is It Anyway?" about a young man who was paralyzed and attempted to commit suicide, takes place entirely within a hospital. To the general public this is not an important consideration. However, PWDs, many with the same disability, are dismayed that this man accepted suicide before he had attempted to live independently in the community. This same ill-informed perspective is found in the Clint Eastwood and Hilary Swank movie, "Million Dollar Baby," based on the short stories of F. X. Toole, where the boxing trainer (Eastwood) assists a young woman (Swank) to commit suicide. Therefore, most PWODs assume (falsely) that suicide is justifiable, while most PWDs understand that the character's desire for suicide is premature and totally uninformed.

Support for Assisted Suicide of PWDs

The voluntary self-elimination of PWDs aided by others has received attention in both the media and the American court system. The support for assisted suicide is a result of many factors. These factors are intertwined, often unvoiced, and difficult to assess. The first factor is the false ideas of pity and fear that lead to the inevitable conclusion that, if disability is such a tragedy, then it is simply humane to allow PWDs to die. However, as we have seen, PWODs, as a group, hold an inaccurate view of the disability experience. Lives with disabilities are often automatically considered to be "life unworthy of life." Furthermore, in the few widely publicized cases of assisted suicide for PWDs, no examination of the PWD's quality of life was undertaken. To cite a single example, in Larry McAfee's case, he asked for assistance in committing suicide at the time he was living in a nursing home (rather than at home with a personal care attendant), and he had not received any assistive technology. Indeed, after McAfee received these accommodations, he no longer wanted to die. Furthermore, McAfee was never asked if he wished to undergo counseling or psychotherapy. Shapiro (1997) stated, "To disabled [sic] people, however, Larry McAfee's case was not a simple right-to-die case. Instead, it was a chilling reminder of how a disabled [sic] life was dismissed—by doctors, judges, and the public—as a devalued life" (p. 171).

The second factor is the strong pressure to accord everyone autonomy and personal liberty. However, when a PWOD threatens suicide, an array of services is mobilized to *prevent* the suicide. In contrast, when a PWD asks for assistance in committing suicide, an array of services is mobilized to *facilitate* the suicide. One disability scholar pointed out: "It would be ironic if (at a time when millions of Americans lack adequate health care) the judiciary selected physician-assisted suicide as the one health care right that deserves constitutional status" (Fleischer & Zames, 2001, p. 134).

The third factor, the economic savings to society when PWDs commit suicide, is the most unpleasant, and therefore it is rarely discussed openly. In spite of not being discussed publicly, some disability scholars consider this third argument to be the *only* reason for supporting assisted suicide of PWDs. Two disability scholars, Doris Zames Fleischer and Frieda Zames (2001), explained:

Campaigners for a right-to-die movement in the 1990s Derek Humphry and Mary Clement state that "in the final analysis, economics, not the quest for broadened individual liberties or increased autonomy, will drive assisted suicide to the plateau of accepted practice. (pp. 139–140)

Ed Roberts, considered by many to be the founder of the Independent Living Movement, was a polio survivor who lived for decades by using a respirator. He succinctly stated his judgment of these assisted suicide cases: It's not the respirator. It's the money.

Pitfalls of Assisted Suicide

Disability rights advocates claim that legally supported assisted suicide is simply legalized discrimination against PWDs. Perhaps alluding to the Nazi death trains that transported Jewish people to be murdered, Mark O'Brien, who uses an iron lung to breathe, stated: "We are people who hear the death train. We will not board that train willingly" (Fleischer & Zames, p. 132). Hockenberry (1995) said, "Pray to be normal no matter how impossible that seems is the sentimental message. The alternative is too horrible to contemplate" (p. 204).

O'Brien is an articulate, strong-willed individual. But what of other PWDs? What about those PWDs who are often termed vulnerable? Nat Henoff (1996) considered that the more vulnerable the individual, the more likely it was that he or she would be euthanized:

It's a bitter irony [that a] quintessentially liberal judge [Ninth Circuit Judge Stephen Reinhardt] has opened the door wide not only to assisted suicide but also to euthanasia, because the majority of the resultant dead will be the poor, the disabled, and other vulnerable people. Many of them will persuade themselves to die because they feel nobody thinks their lives are worth preserving. Or that keeping themselves alive will cost too much, thereby burdening their families and companions. (p. 12)

There are a number of empirical research articles that have discovered that PWDs judge their lives to be better than PWODs observing them think they are. For example, in an article entitled, "Health Professionals, Dignity, and Assisted Suicide," Carol Gill (2000) reviewed all the completed empirical studies that compared physicians' view of disability with their patients' view of their disabilities. Results were unequivocal; in all of the studies, doctors were more negative about life with a disability than were the PWDs themselves. One man with quadriplegia explained:

It is extremely easy for a healthy individual to say how they would not live. I am guilty myself. If someone had told me prior to the diagnosis that I would be totally paralyzed, fed by a feeding tube, communicate via computer with a voice synthesizer, and tethered to a ventilator that I would find more meaning in life and living, I am certain that person telling me such a tale was insane. (Longmore, 2003, p. 179)

Abortion of Fetuses With Disabilities

A long-time disability scholar, Paul Longmore, summarized the issue of assisted suicide for PWDs.

> A hidden, but powerful component, of any discussion about disabled people must be brought to the surface and addressed: the usually unacknowledged and unconscious fear and prejudice of many nonhandicapped persons toward people with disabilities. It involves bias against those who look different and function differently. It reflects hostility toward those who require and increasingly demand alternative physical and social arrangements to accommodate them and in some cases need a larger share of societal resources. It stems from the frightened belief that disability inevitably means loss of control, social isolation, loss of an essential part of one's humanity, and the related deep-seated anxiety that could happen to me or to someone close to me. At times, these fears and prejudices burst out in violent words and deeds, but usually, and perhaps even more dangerously, they are masked by an avowed compassion, contempt cloaking itself in paternalism. (Longmore, 2003, p. 150)

Most vulnerable are babies. Individuals who are elderly, women, or of racial and ethnic minorities (or any combination of these identities) and who also have disabilities are also vulnerable. There is a great deal written about euthanasia. For example, euthanasia has been practiced in the Netherlands since 1972, and in 1988, an estimate of euthanasia on newborn babies and infants up to 3 months old was published by the Royal Dutch Society of Medicine. It was reported that 300 babies each year are starved and dehydrated to death or denied lifesaving surgery. Ten babies with disabilities receive lethal injections each year. These babies experience birth trauma or have spina bifida or Down syndrome (Fenigsen, 1997). Peter Singer, the Princeton professor of philosophy, is an outspoken advocate of euthanasia of babies with disabilities, stating: "Killing unwanted infants or allowing them to die has been a normal practice in most societies throughout human history and prehistory" (P. Singer, 1994, p. 159).

One physician is clear in stating that state-supported infanticide, if legalized, would be far more widespread in the United States than in the Netherlands. "The Netherlands? With a homogenous, pretty much law-abiding citizenry, almost all of whom have medical coverage? And America, with many cultures represented, many marginalized people, tens of millions without health care insurance? As bad as it was *there*, in other words, it could be much, much worse *here*" (Fleischer & Zames, 2001, p. 144).

Fenigsen (1997) quoted a Dutch professor's assessment of one of the long-term results of infant euthanasia: "The killing of handicapped children . . . denotes the end, or the beginning of the end, of care for the mentally retarded" (p. 163). In other words, the government will address the "issue" of intellectual disability by eliminating people with this disability, rather than by providing services. Dutch parents of a child with a disability have reported being told, "What? Is that child still alive?" and "How can one love such a child?"

People in these vulnerable categories are well aware that they are more likely to be considered for euthanasia. It is no coincidence that in a 1996 *Washington Post* poll, 70% of Black Americans opposed legalized assisted suicide and 58% of those termed *elderly* opposed legalized suicide. Indeed, members of minority groups with disabilities understand the long history of medical exploitation of people who are poor or institutionalized with either mental illness or intellectual disability, especially children. However, without doubt, it is Black Americans who have experienced the greatest degree of medical exploitation, including forced experimentations and forced sterilizations. Therefore, it is understandable that many racial and ethnic minorities with disabilities view assisted suicide and euthanasia with suspicion and, often, outright hostility. Stefan (2001), a legal scholar whose specialty is psychiatric disabilities, reports the following medical practice and demonstrates that the triple combination of disability, parental race, and perceived poverty resulted in the deaths of infants.

> Researchers at the University of Oklahoma decided to investigate the effects of treatment on the survival rates of infants born with spina bifida. To further their research, they divided infants born at the hospital with spina bifida into two categories, those who would receive treatment and those who would not—obviously without the knowledge or consent of the parents of the children who did not receive treatment. The way the children were divided was based on the researchers' perceptions of the parents' ability to take care of their children, so the children of poor, minority parents did not receive treatment, and the children of more economically stable parents did. Virtually every one of the children who did not receive treatment died. Virtually every one of the children who did receive treatment lived. (p. 155)

When the facts surrounding this "research study" became known, the parents of the dead children sued (*Johnson v. Thompson*, 1992). The court ruled that the parents did not have a case based on race because some of the babies from poor families were White. Additionally, the court ruled that there was no discrimination based on disability because some of the children with spina bifida did receive treatment. Therefore, the parents lost the case. Stefan concluded that this case was "one of the most crushing examples of the way in which the law's obsession with neat categories results in the denial of relief to people who are subject to multiple, intersecting forms of discrimination" (Stefan, 2001, p. 155).

Infanticide of Newborns With Disabilities

Harriet McBryde Johnson (2003) wrote about a visit to Princeton University in an article entitled, "Should I Have Been Killed at Birth: The Case for My Life." The purpose of the visit was to debate a professor, Dr. Peter Singer, who advocates abortion or euthanasia of newborn babies with certain types of disabilities, including the type that Johnson has. In fact, Singer advocates the killing of anyone, at any age, with certain types of severe disabilities. Much of the debate focuses on Singer's attempts to force Johnson to say that her life is miserable because of the disability.

Ascribing "unbearable" and "suffering" to PWDs could be fatal for those with severe and multiple disabilities. Harriet McBryde Johnson (2003), a disability rights lawyer, was born with a muscle-wasting disease. She described herself: "At this stage of my life, I'm Karen Carpenter thin, flesh mostly vanished, a jumble of bones in a floppy bag of skin. . . . Now my right side is two deep canyons. To keep myself upright, I lean forward, rest my rib cage on my lap, plant my elbows beside my knees. Since my backbone found its own natural shape, I've been entirely comfortable in my skin. I am in the first generation to survive to such decrepitude. Because antibiotics were available, we didn't die from the childhood pneumonias that often come with weakened respiratory systems" (p. 52).

Here is Johnson's reaction:

> It's right out of the telethon. I expected something more sophisticated from a professional thinker. I respond: "As a little girl playing on the beach, I was already aware that some people felt sorry for me, that I wasn't frolicking with the same level of frenzy as other children. This annoyed me, and still does." (p. 53)

At the end of the article, Johnson concluded:

> But like the protagonist in a classical drama, Singer has his flaw. It is his unexamined assumption that disabled [sic] people are inherently "worse off," that we "suffer," that we have lesser "prospects of a happy life." Because of this all-too-common prejudice, and his rare courage in taking it to its logical conclusion, catastrophe looms. (p. 54)

Ms. Johnson died in 2008 at age 50.

Four Societal Responses to Disability

In this section, look for—

- ✧ charities
- ✧ preferential treatment

♢ compensation

♢ civil rights

We do not allow PWDs to be ordinary citizens with civil rights and protection under the law when PWODs make them recipients of charity. Most PWDs want to rely on themselves (by working) or on the government (by ensuring civil rights). Indeed, in the 1930s, the slogan of The League of the Physically Handicapped was "We Don't Want Tin Cups. We Want Jobs" (Longmore, 2003, p. 69).

The education of Deaf children illustrates the relationship between civil rights and charity. It was not until 1975, with the passage of the Education for All Handicapped Children Act (later renamed the Individuals with Disabilities Education Act), that the education of Deaf children came under federal supervision. Until 1975, the education of Deaf children was provided in a haphazard way, largely by charities. It is safe to say that most Deaf children received very little education, and most of that was vocational and religious in nature.

> Charity functions to support a society which is based on the unequal distribution of wealth, and where tax concessions offered to donors rather than redistribution of resources maintain an unequal status quo. Charities tend to exist because of socially constructed dependence in a society which fails to address the needs of citizens with disabilities. . . . It does represent a *reparative* intent. Just because an act may emerge as a way of resolving negative unconscious conflict does not mean that this act may not also have valuable outcomes. (Marks, 1999, p. 167)

Many PWDs have had experiences such as this:

> I was in Kansas City, doing Christmas shopping. This old man came up to me and looked at me and said, "Do you need money for Christmas?" I'm a lawyer and I'm working for the government EPA. Nearly every adult with a disability that I knew had a story about being given unsolicited money as donations. As a little kid, absolutely. I would be walking down the street with my mother (and people gave me money). (National Public Radio, 1998a)

Charity Telethons, or "Elephants Running in the Forest"

In the National Public Radio Disability History Project, Inventing the Poster Child (1998a), charity telethons are compared to "elephants running in the forest." This statement is meant to convey the powerful fascination that charity telethons hold for the public. Perhaps this statement also expresses the difficulty, if not impossibility, of asking Americans to examine deeply ingrained assumptions of kindness and charity. Can elephants running in the forest be stopped?

Charity and fundraising exaggerate and sensationalize disability to solicit money.

Exaggeration and sensationalism of the disability can lead to segregation and isolation for PWDs. Many PWDs feel that any money raised is not worth the costs to their self-concept.

Joshua Malinga, of Disabled Peoples International and Disabled Peoples South Africa, stated:

> Charities play a negative social role. They seek to control us. Charities are not interested in empowerment and integration. They support segregation. In fact, once we have integration and equalization of opportunity, these charities will begin to die. Their institutional interests lie with segregation, ours with integration. (Charlton, 1998, p. 92)

Mee (1999), a polio survivor, believed that PWODs view telethons to vicariously "experience" a disability: "I think it is intact people who like to experience the feelings of sorrow and loss and bitterness over and over again—and who always ask injured people about those feelings, to conjure them up and experience them vicariously" (p. 36).

The roots of televised charity telethons lie in the March of Dimes, a charity founded by Franklin Roosevelt, to raise money for polio. As Marks (1999) stated, there are some positive outcomes of charity. Many people with polio, including children, had their hospitalization, treatment, and equipment paid for by the March of Dimes. Additionally, all of the research work of both Sabin and Salk, the discoverers of the polio vaccine, was funded by the March of Dimes. Nonetheless, many polio survivors and their families assert that the American government should have provided public support for both the treatment of polio and the research to eradicate it, rather than depending on sporadic private donations.

Marc Shell (2005) explained:

> "Crippledom" was a good thing for the March of Dimes. It furthered money collection and a cure. It allowed telethon masters to use polios [survivors] as distinctively dehumanized and deformed money collection props. . . . Polios were likewise definitively *commodified*. . . . This exploitative practice . . . seemed to make the public sector both weak and unnecessary. (p. 145)

Commodified means that the poster children were considered to be products, commodities, or objects. It is interesting that one of the greatest politicians of the 20th century, Franklin Roosevelt, who established the National Foundation for Infantile Paralysis and its successor, the March of Dimes, never supported government assistance for polio.

Charity, or benevolence or goodwill, is demeaning and insulting to the recipient and is simply another type of victimization. Certainly the benefactor functions from a position of superiority, and, furthermore, charity is dependent on the goodwill of the benefactor (Alder, B. A. Wright, & Ulicny, 1991). Stated another way, benevolence is dependent on the generosity and kindness of the benefactor. The benefactor may or may not decide to give. Furthermore, the benefactor is free to ration both the amount and the timing of the charity. For example, when money is acquired through charitable fundraising, it is never possible to accurately predict the amount of money that will be available. People may or may not decide to give. On an individual level, if a personal care attendant does not want to feed his employer, the employer (person with the disability) cannot do much about it. Parents of children who require special education often have had to resort to all sorts of fundraising, such as bake sales. Parents whose children do not have disabilities are not required to bake brownies to ensure that their children receive appropriate public education. These children have the automatic right to education. Furthermore, if parents whose children do not have disabilities had to raise funds to pay for their children's public education, they would probably discontinue asking for charity and start advocating for their rights from the government. Often the public considers education for children with disabilities to be a conditional gift, or charity, rather than an automatic right.

Individuals with disabilities have been protesting telethons since the 1970s. In 1976 and 1979, a disability rights group, Disabled in Action, picketed the United Cerebral Palsy Association, calling their telethons "demeaning and paternalistic shows which celebrate and encourage pity" (Pelka, 1997, p. 302). One of the most well-known charities for PWDs is Jerry Lewis's Labor Day marathon television program for raising funds for muscular dystrophy. Since 1991, a group calling themselves Jerry's Orphans has picketed local television stations that carry the program. Incidentally, Jerry's Orphans was founded by two former Muscular Dystrophy Association poster children, Mike Ervin and Cris Matthews.

Because the provision of charity is under the control of the benefactor, often the benefactor thinks that he or she knows what the recipient needs and wants. This is an example of paternalism. Rather than viewing people with disabilities as experts in their own needs, charitable people provide what they think people with disabilities need (even when their ideas are totally wrong). Since the 1970s, many disability advocacy groups require that members of their governing board be PWDs. Two groups were unwilling to change the structure of their boards to allow PWDs to serve. These two were the Muscular Dystrophy Association and the March of Dimes.

The most straightforward example of this is an article that appeared in the September 2, 1990, issue of *Parade* magazine, written by Jerry Lewis, who does not have muscular dystrophy. Lewis wrote, "I know the courage it takes to get on the court with other cripples [*sic*] and play wheelchair basketball." Lewis pretended to write from the point of view of a person with a disability. "I'd like to play basketball like normal, healthy, vital and energetic people. . . . When I sit back and think more rationally, I realize my life is half, so I must learn to do things halfway. I just have to learn to try to be good at being half a person" (Pelka, 1997, p. 301). Torriero (2006) related:

> Led by a former muscular dystrophy poster boy from Chicago, the activists scored what they call their "big triumph" last November as protesters in wheelchairs ambushed Lewis in an appearance at the Harold Washington Library Center in Chicago. . . . Despite the protestors' urgings, the telethon has not changed its ways and has not promoted accessibility for the disabled [*sic*], better housing and employment possibilities, activists say. (para. 3)

Lewis's conclusion about the protesters: "I paid for the wheelchairs." This is a clear-cut example of paternalism because Lewis is implying that the protestors have no right to criticize any aspect of the telethon because Lewis paid for benefits.

Also, if the person is to receive help, he or she must submit to the benefactor's definition of him or her, almost to the point of "playing the part." Essentially, the benefactor has inordinate power over the charity receiver. An adult survivor of polio stated:

> Those telethons featuring a semi-maniacal Jerry Lewis are responded to by men and women who think they are *charitable*. Those well-meaning Shriners interviewed at halftime during the East–West football games they sponsor— let me remind you of the game's motto: "Strong legs run so that weak legs can walk"—do not believe that they have tampered with our reality. (Kriegel, 1982, p. 62)

Children who grew up believing that they needed charity were often programmed with learned helplessness. The message of charity, especially to a child, is "someone has to *give* this to you because you are not capable of *earning* it." Indeed, many adults in the Disability Rights Movement feel resentment about the harmful effects of having been recipients of charity as children. They feel that they have paid a very high price for every dollar received.

Charity is polarizing—it is very clear who is the giver and who is the receiver. Generous people give to poor, pitiful, downtrodden, and unfortunate people. We have seen that, as a result of the increasing rates of disability, many Americans are, and will be, in the ranks of persons with disabilities. Defenders of charity will state, "No one, with or without a disability, is completely independent, and everyone needs help at one time or another." This is true, but people with disabilities are *continuously* in the position of accepting charity. Also, PWODs are more often the recipients of invisible and anonymous charity that maintains their dignity and privacy and does not require expressions of gratitude. Poster children, telethons, and neighborhood fund drives are considered by many in the Disability Rights Movement to be modern-day freak shows.

Charity to people with disabilities has had a pervasive and insidious effect on our society. It is impossible to establish equal social status relationships, in the workplace or in social situations, when one group is always the benefactor and the other group is always the beneficiary. J. Morris (1991) stated,

> Charities need to present disability in such a way as to encourage people to part with their money. The portrayal of a strong disabled [*sic*] person going about his or her life, and enjoying it, is not going to bring in any money. (p. 108)

If the media portray people with disabilities as objects of charity, these individuals will have difficulty in establishing intimate, familial relationships with people who do not have disabilities. Scott-Parker (as cited in J. Morris, 1991) viewed charities as objectifying PWDs. She stated,

> As a study of advertising and disabled put it, charities tend to commission [advertising campaigns] as though they owned their particular 'model' of disabled [*sic*] person, in much the same way that Ford owns Fiesta cars. The charity is assumed to have a similar expert authority, enhanced by unimpeachable motives, and can therefore present its product to the market in any way it sees fit. (J. Morris, 1991, p. 109)

Charities are businesses. A few charities are big businesses, and many professional, salaried people live off charity in that their jobs, their salaries, and their professional identities are dependent on (1) the existence of pitiful, unfortunate people and (2) the generosity of others.

Charity given to one group and not to other groups can create factions within the disability community. Factionalizing the disability community can undermine efforts of advocating for civil rights and raising public awareness. The most clear-cut example of this is televised telethons that raise huge amounts of money for a single type of disability. One writer has termed this *brand awareness* in terms of types of disabilities (Campbell, as cited in J. Morris, 1991, p. 110). Anne Finger (1993) observed:

> But each individual charity must compete with other charities for the "charitable dollar." Thus, charity advertising aims at simultaneously creating an image of 'its' disease or impairment and of that particular charity as the custodian/savior/earthly representative of all those with that dreaded impairment. (p. 29)

Furthermore, benefactors probably do not fully value the objects of their charity. There are no expectations of the recipients other than to be appropriately grateful. Liachowitz (1988) summarized: "Thus, the many handicapped [*sic*] people whose physical disorder is permanent remain in a position of indebtedness—a position that probably accounts for at least some portion of their socially conferred devaluation" (p. 11).

Also, the clear message of much charitable fundraising is that the disability must be eradicated. Rarely is any consideration given to improving the quality of life for those who have the disability. Occasionally, some large-scale charity drives pay for research that supports prenatal testing that likely will result in abortions. One mother told of her son Robbie being asked to be in the March of Dimes charity drives:

> "I'm sorry," I explain, "but I don't feel comfortable telling my son that he is doing this to prevent other children like him. We're trying to help him understand where he fits into a world that is often more confused than he is about his problem. I can't put him out there as something to 'prevent.' This poster thing also seems to use these kids to collect money, yet you tell me none of it goes toward addressing their problems now. That feels sort of dishonest."
>
> I realize that I have given away potential "celebrity" status for Robbie by declining their invitation. I have also risked being labeled an ungrateful parent. But I think I have been true to what I really want for him. Free lunches and pictures in the newspaper are not going to help push his wheelchair into a community that sees him as something that should not have happened. (Toombs, Barnard, & Carson, 1995, pp. 32–33)

The argument can also be made that it is the benefactor who needs the charity more than the beneficiary. Recipients of charity must be grateful for whatever they can get. (Often benefactors are irritated if the recipients are not appropriately and sufficiently grateful.) This simply reinforces the power relationship between those with disabilities and those without disabilities. Being charitable comes from a position of superiority, and gratitude comes from a position of inferiority. Charity can objectify the recipients. Society needs objects of charity. The objectifying of people with disabilities is clearly seen in the poster children. (There are never "poster adults" because adults have the ability to fight the objectification, and the public's sympathy would not be as aroused as it is for sweet, innocent, lovable children. However, according to Shapiro, 1993, some adults resent having been poster children.) Everybody feels good when they give to "Jerry's kids." Charity allows the benefactor to defend his or her privileges to himself or herself and to the public (Allport, 1986). However, on closer scrutiny, people with disabilities want the rights and responsibilities of citizens, not charity. It is no coincidence that Labor Day (the same day that the Jerry Lewis muscular dystrophy telethon is held) was chosen for the "Onarollathon." The Onarollathon, sponsored by Disability Talk Radio, raised funds for the Literacy Volunteers of America, an organization that helps adults learn to read. Radio host Greg Smith, who has muscular dystrophy, stated,

> I know in my heart that our community, people with disabilities, care about important social issues, beyond those that directly impact us. We are a part of a powerful civil rights movement that can create positive change, which is why we are joining forces to help advance another great cause. On this

particular weekend when people with disabilities are depicted as hopeless objects of pity, we want to deliver the message that we are important builders of this society.

In 2011, the Muscular Dystrophy Association (MDA) decided to end the Jerry Lewis Labor Day telethons. These telethons had a 61-year history and, throughout this long history, had earned a total of $2 billion, 600 million. Do the ends justify the means? Do the millions of dollars raised justify the results for PWDs? Most PWDs would say no.

Preferential Treatment

Like charity, preferential treatment is demeaning and insulting to the individual it is designed to help. Like charity, preferential treatment is also often thought to be a positive response. Preferential treatment for people with disabilities can include such things as showing hiring preferences and promotion preferences, lowering standards, granting admission to schools solely on the basis of disability, and applying differing standards.

The ADA does not mandate preferential treatment for people with disabilities. It does not require the hiring, promotion, or admission of unqualified people, nor does the ADA mandate quotas in jobs or schools. The ADA *does* mandate accommodations and provision of opportunities to compete for qualified people with disabilities.

Proponents of preferential treatment accurately point out that there is not equal competition in acquiring jobs and education, and, therefore, preferential treatment is necessary to "level the playing field." Advocates of preferential treatment for groups who have experienced inequities remind us that historically there have been groups of individuals who have received preferential treatment, such as White Anglo-Saxons without disabilities. However, opponents assert that there are better ways to provide equal opportunity and it is unreasonable to correct an inequitable system by simply substituting another group with which to provide preferential treatment.

Preferential treatment and charity are thought, perhaps at an unconscious level, to be an appropriate compensation, or redress, for the well-documented history of prejudice and discrimination experienced by people with disabilities. However, past discrimination can never be fully redressed or compensated. Most people with disabilities do not want, or need, preferential treatment; furthermore, the *public perception* of preferential treatment may further undermine the position of people with disabilities. If the public thinks that people receive freebies and perks simply because they are members of a designated group, resentment and factional rivalry will result. The perception of preferential treatment often results in cries of reverse discrimination. Furthermore, there are those who would say, "I am not personally responsible for the prejudice and discrimination experienced by people with disabilities, so why should I have to make amends?"

Preferential treatment communicates, in an unsubtle way, that PWDs are not capable of competing with others who do not have disabilities. The individual is being told that he or she is inferior and does not have the ability to be successful on his or her own merit. Preferential treatment for people with disabilities is a fairly common occurrence and, in the long run, usually does not have positive results for the individual. Eventually, standards are upheld; honest feedback is given, and the individual must, at a later date, be judged according to widely accepted standards. For example, someone who is admitted to medical school because he or she is a member of a certain group (disability, gender, or racial or ethnic group) must graduate from medical school. Simply thinking in terms of the individual does this individual little good, and perhaps much harm, to have standards lowered so that he or she be allowed to enter medical school only to be "flunked out" later.

Preferential treatment of a person with a disability often results in excusing the individual from widely held standards or expectations. Such indulgence and exemption from standards are seen in ideas such as, "Children with disabilities should not be disciplined" or, at minimum, "Parents of children with disabilities should be less strict than other parents." Even as adults, PWDs may be sheltered or protected from life's demands, such as working or managing the disability.

In the next chapter, we will discuss the high rates of substance abuse among PWDs, and we will learn that one of the factors is the enabling behavior of PWODs who, out of pity or something else, assist PWDs in obtaining drugs or knowingly choose to ignore the PWD's substance abuse. Such enabling is another form of preferential treatment based on the premise that PWDs should not be held to standards. Preferential treatment of PWDs does not lead to positive results for the PWDs or for society as a whole.

Compensation and Benefits

Compensation to PWDs includes pensions; insurance benefits, such as workers' compensation and Social Security Disability Insurance (SSDI); and private insurance benefits. Implicit in the assumption of compensation is the idea that no further expectations are required of the individual, and, because he or she has documented or proved that he or she has a disability, the individual will receive a monthly check. The idea that the individual has somehow earned the right to benefits is also part of the rationale behind compensating PWDs. The Supplemental Security Income (SSI) program, created in 1972, is another form of compensation to PWDs, but it is not based on the premise that the individual has worked and thus "paid into the system." Instead, SSI is a sort of safety net for people who have failed to qualify for SSDI because they have not worked. SSI also has a "needs test" that requires the applicant to prove financial need. However, SSDI, workers' compensation insurance, private insurance funds, and military veterans' benefits for disability all consider that the individual has contributed to the system and therefore is eligible for benefits. Most compensation schemes do not include individuals with congenital disabilities, simply because it is thought that these people never had the opportunity to contribute. Of course, these congenital disabilities must be sufficiently severe that the individual is unable to work.

The public purse pays individuals who have acquired disabilities through participating in socially valued activities, such as work or war, and for whom there is no possibility of returning to work. Often, in-kind benefits, such as Medicare and Medicaid, or subsidized housing are included in the benefits. For some PWDs, affordable medical care and medications and vouchers "documenting" a disability may be complicated, but after the disability has been proved, the compensator (government, military, or private insurance company) pays the PWD. Society then feels that it has fulfilled its responsibility to PWDs, and the PWD knows that he or she has contributed to some sort of scheme, which has provided the benefits and therefore does not consider the benefits to be charity. Some have conceptualized the relationship between compensator and compensatee as, "We'll send you a check if you keep out of our sight" and "I get a check every month simply because I have a label (disability)." There is some truth to this.

First, compensation schemes often have built-in financial disincentives that make it difficult for the individual to return to work even if accommodations for the disability are provided. Simply stated, the PWD, if he or she were to become employed, would lose the financial benefits. Therefore, there is no economic advantage to accepting minimum wage jobs, especially for individuals who have high costs associated with the management of the disability or individuals who have many dependents. Thus, the PWD is caught in a double bind: He or she cannot "afford" to work and, furthermore, is stereotyped as lazy and unmotivated. Policymakers are working to dismantle this system of disincentives, developing strategies that will allow PWDs to work and still guarantee their benefits, especially their medical benefits. The government has the difficult task of providing for those who truly need assistance and, at the same time, not sabotaging a work-based society.

Second, there are those people who "milk the system." This means that these individuals are capable of working, but they prefer to receive benefits. The most extreme examples of these types of people are seen on television newsmagazine programs where private detectives with video cameras "catch" people with severe back injuries, which supposedly prevent them from working, performing all sorts of recreational activities, such as skiing, painting the house, or hang gliding. Naturally, the public is outraged that there are people who would take advantage of the system. (Television viewers choose to watch these types of programs that may present a one-sided and distorted view of disability issues.) However, most experts consider individuals who fake disabilities (malingerers) to be relatively rare.

Another shortcoming of compensation systems is the difficulty in the determination or diagnosis of a disability. Some applicants are skilled in seeking out those physicians who have a reputation for defining disability very broadly, and insurance companies and government agencies seek to offset this strategy by requesting second opinions from physicians who have reputations for rarely giving disability diagnoses. The determination-of-disability process can become both complicated and adversarial.

The system of public disability insurance has developed in a patchwork manner because (1) most public insurance programs, with the exception of programs for federal employees, are administered by the states, and there is wide variation in both the definition of disability and in the amounts of compensation from state to state, and (2) the desire to care for those who truly need assistance often conflicts with the need to keep as many individuals in the labor market as possible.

Liachowitz (1988) recounted that during the American Revolutionary War of 1776, both soldiers and sailors who were judged to be "invalids" were required to stay on active duty if they were "found to be capable of doing guard or garrison duty . . . or doing any other duty on board the navy or any department thereof, shall be liable to be so employed" (p. 25). Also, invalid sailors and soldiers were required to teach various subjects to young soldiers and sailors. Early in American history, military veterans with disabilities were encouraged (or required) to return to work because the military had broadly defined work to include noncombat jobs and because the military recognized the value of these invalid sailors and soldiers. Ironically, the word *invalid* means *without value*. Implicit in this requirement was the assumption that these veterans were capable of making valuable contributions.

Civil Rights for PWDs

The three responses to PWDs of (1) charity, (2) preferential treatment, and (3) compensation are all based on the inherent inferiority of the individual. That is to say, for an individual to receive charity, preferential treatment, or compensation, he or she must first be declared inferior, subordinate, and needy. Of course, most would be quick to add that the inferiority of the individual is the result of a process of nature (the onset of the disability) for which the individual is not personally responsible. In spite of this, inferiority is the basis of the entitlement.

Furthermore, each of these three responses is viewed as a corrective, virtuous, and benevolent action of the larger society. Rarely do proponents of these types of programs consider that self-empowerment, self-determination, and dignity are not possible for PWDs in these types of systems. In addition, much of the discussion of any response toward Americans with disabilities very quickly arrives at the money question. Costs of workplace and transportation accommodations, costs of care and treatment, and all the other costs can be, and are, calculated. In contrast, the national discussion preceding the passage of the Civil Rights Act of 1964 rarely, if ever, mentioned money or costs. For example, the Civil Rights Act assisted in the desegregation of public schools (building on *Brown v. Board of Education*). Such desegregation must have been expensive, yet there was little, if any, discussion of putting a dollar figure on the right of American children, regardless of their skin color, to integrated education.

Civil rights for Americans are not accorded on the basis of monetary cost, although the ADA does take into consideration the costs to employers of accommodations. Civil rights for PWDs, as outlined in the ADA and the Amendments of 2008, are accorded on the basis of American citizenship. Ensuring, by the power of the law, that all important benefits and opportunities of citizenship are extended to PWDs shifts the responsibility for disability issues from the individual to the American nation. The "problem" of disability, as the ADA states clearly and at length, is society's prejudicial attitudes and actions. Therefore, the solution for the disability problem is the responsibility of the American nation, and the first step is the passage of national legislation. Parallel with the rationale behind the Civil Rights Act of 1964, the intent of the ADA is to eradicate prejudice, discrimination, segregation, and reduced opportunities for PWDs.

Civil rights for anyone are individually empowering because these rights are an automatic entitlement and are legally protected. The individual does not have to depend on the goodwill of others to receive benefits. The ADA, or any other legislation, cannot redress past injustices. However, the ADA stated that the status quo (in 1990) was not going to continue, meaning a certain group of American citizens had been intentionally excluded from employment, education, housing, transportation, public buildings, and telecommunications. Further, this disenfranchisement was the collective responsibility of the American people, both for allowing it and for stopping it. Centuries of discrimination and prejudice cannot be redressed, but discrimination and prejudice against PWDs can be stopped.

What Is Justice?

In this section, look for—

- ✧ why standardization is important if everyone is to receive the same treatment
- ✧ why the standard of evaluation has been White, middle-class males without disabilities
- ✧ the argument that accommodations cannot be provided for PWDs because everyone else does not receive these accommodations
- ✧ the definition of a *meritocracy*
- ✧ the relationship between Social Darwinism and meritocracies
- ✧ why a "disability-blind" society is not necessarily good
- ✧ how a society determines which needs are legitimate and which needs are not
- ✧ the concept of *equal outcome*

Basically, there are three types of justice: (1) everyone receives equal treatment, (2) everyone receives what he or she has earned, and (3) everyone receives what he or she needs.

Everyone Receives Equal Treatment

The "everyone receives equal treatment" philosophy of justice is based on accurate standards and guidelines that are upheld for everyone. The word *equal is* used in this case to mean *the same*. Standardization is important if everyone is to receive equal treatment. For a long time, the standard of evaluation in the United States, according to many authors, was the White, middle-class male without disabilities. Naturally, not everyone who applied for entrance to schools, jobs, or anything else met all these criteria. In fact, it is debatable whether the numerical majority ever comprised individuals who met all these criteria. Despite this, the rationale was not that everyone or even the majority of people were White, middle-class males without disabilities, but that everyone should *compete* with this group. Therefore, testing and evaluation procedures were validated on norm groups composed of individuals who met the criteria (White, middle-class males without disabilities). Application, admission, promotion, tenure, and termination policies were developed with this standard-of-evaluation group in mind. Administrative policies could be clear, straightforward, and without exception. Another advantage was the applicability of the standards and rules to *everyone*. All of these examples are termed *institutional policies*, and until recently, these institutional policies were not often questioned or challenged. The idea of equal treatment for everybody appeared to be justice. This type of justice chooses equal opportunity but also understands that there will not be equal outcomes. For example, everybody is free to apply to Harvard, but not all applicants are accepted.

When teachers or employers argue that they cannot provide certain accommodations for PWDs because they "cannot provide the same thing for everybody else," they are invoking the "everyone receives equal treatment" view of justice. Of course, not all students need (or want) their textbooks in Braille. But, if we follow the "everyone receives equal, meaning same, treatment" logic, then the student who is blind cannot have Braille textbooks because the other students do not have Braille textbooks. Ed Roberts, founder of the Independent Living Movement and a polio survivor, was repeatedly refused high school graduation because he had not taken two courses: physical education (PE) and Driver's Ed. Roberts was quadriplegic. Roberts's experience provides an absurd example of holding everyone to the standards.

The polio epidemics provided many examples of school teachers who believed in this type of justice where everyone receives identical resources and equal treatment:

> There were many teachers who did not know how to work with students with disabilities, had no desire to learn, and openly displayed their displeasure. For example, Jennifer Williams' second-grade teacher "just couldn't relate to a child with a handicap [*sic*]." This teacher was always hard on the young girl and refused to believe she was any different. As Williams remembers, "She would always say things like, 'They're doing it, so you have to do it too. You know we can't play favorites.'"

Wanda Peterson's sixth-grade teacher would talk about her in front of the class. The teacher would declare, without naming Peterson, "Some people in this room think they are so great because they aren't supposed to run in P.E." The teacher also made her move her desk away from everyone else's. . . . The attitudes and actions of teachers could make all the difference in the class. Those who were supportive helped polio survivors to fit in as best they could and to excel where they were able. The worst helped make school a living hell. (Wilson, 1990, pp. 187–188)

Everyone Receives What He or She Has Earned

In the view of justice that everyone receives what he or she has earned, everything is earned, including rewards and penalties. This type of society is called a *meritocracy*. Some people are clearly "superior" because of intelligence, motivation, skills, or other personal characteristics, and they should be able to enjoy more freedom, more justice, and more rights. Conversely, some people are "inferior" because they lack the requisite personal characteristics to earn their rewards. Further, regardless of the situation in which either of these two types of people (superior or inferior) are placed, the inferior will fail and the superior will rise to the top.

Much of the rationale for this view of justice is derived from Darwinism and Social Darwinism, both of which were based on survival of the fittest. Social Darwinism was also based on success of the fittest. Any attempts at distributive justice (reallocation of rights and resources) will fail because, as stated before, some people are inferior and some people are superior. If we give the inferior people rights or welfare assistance, they would not know what to do with them and they would end up squandering both. Thus, the inequities in the system are deserved. The superior people do not have to feel guilty about their privileges or feel sorry about the plight of the inferior people. The inferior people should not be jealous of the rights and privileges of the superior people, because they could have the same rights and privileges if they would only exert the effort. Social inequities are irrelevant to government policy.

Under this type of justice, PWDs are thought to have acquired their disabilities through their own bad luck. Disabilities are seen as deviance and inferiority because this type of justice assumes that the world is a predictable and moral place. If superior people consider their superiority to be justly earned, then they also consider others' inferiority to be justly deserved. Sanctimonious pity is enough for PWDs, and in some societies, such as Nazi Germany, PWDs, because of their (perceived) lack of merit, were efficiently murdered.

Naturally, when outlined in such a straightforward way, this type of justice makes us uncomfortable, violating our values of compassion and equal opportunity for all. Further, a meritocracy depends on accurate definition and measurement of merit. The most astute authorities cannot agree on what merit is. Inferiority must also be defined, and, in the case of PWDs, much (if not all) of the inferiority is the result of society's handicapping, prejudice, and discrimination.

Everyone Receives What He or She Needs

The view of justice that everyone receives what he or she needs takes individual differences into consideration and also believes that by allowing individuals rights and opportunities, the group as a whole benefits. Of the three types of justice discussed here, the ADA is based on the premise that justice is ensuring that everybody has what he or she needs. The long list of court litigation of ADA issues demonstrates that this type of justice can be complicated and difficult to enact. How does a society determine which needs are legitimate and which needs are not?

Such a view of justice may appear contrary to those who argue that the United States should be "disability-blind" (or "color-blind" or "gender-blind"). Inherent in this view is the idea that there are some groups that have stronger claims for resources, including PWDs. This can result in many groups making claims for resources and accommodations. Where do we stop? But, if we accept that there are biological and functional realities to the experience of disability, then accommodations are both necessary and legitimate. It is expensive to live with a disability. PWDs do require more resources to maintain a reasonable quality of life. Furthermore, as we have learned in this chapter, if society gives PWDs their civil rights and necessary accommodations, society will benefit economically. In addition, and perhaps more important, there are benefits to having a diverse society.

PWDs do have differences from people who do not have disabilities, although the differences are not as great as most PWODs consider them to be. Stefan (2001), a legal scholar, demonstrated that physical differences are relevant and important, and, further, individuals with these differences (such as disabilities) have the right to government resources. Stefan argued that women and men in the United States have had different rights and resources provided to them based on their gender differences, and this has never been considered as inequality:

> Women get pregnant, give birth, live longer, and are, on average, shorter and lighter. These differences, although relevant in a variety of ways, do not necessarily justify disadvantageous treatment, even when no comparison appears available. Thus, gross underfunding of breast cancer research was denounced as discrimination against women without showing that more research was being funded for breast cancer in men. (p. 113)

Stefan argued that Americans with disabilities have legitimate rights to government resources as a result of the needs of their disabilities; further, these rights should not be considered preferential treatment.

This view of justice is linked with the *equal outcome* concept, meaning that if everyone were to receive what he or she needs from infancy, all types of people would succeed in gaining the rewards of society. Everyone would be earning the same reward, at the same standards, but with differing accommodations. All types of people would graduate from Harvard, become movie stars, and become President of the United States.

CHAPTER 5

EXPERIENCING PREJUDICE AND DISCRIMINATION (HANDICAPISM)

What are the effects for PWDs of the following behaviors and attitudes?

- ✧ stereotyping
- ✧ role entrapment
- ✧ pity
- ✧ lowered expectations
- ✧ lack of privacy
- ✧ hypervisibility and over-observation
- ✧ solo status
- ✧ token status
- ✧ infantilization, paternalism, and "motherese"
- ✧ objectification
- ✧ being viewed as animals
- ✧ unnecessary dependence
- ✧ marginality
- ✧ lack of equal social status relationships

Stereotyping

In this section, look for—

- ⬩ the difference between a category and a stereotype
- ⬩ how PWDs can internalize society's false stereotypes
- ⬩ how seemingly positive stereotypes about PWDs are handicapping
- ⬩ the three factors that serve to maintain and reinforce false stereotypes

To be viewed as a person with a disability is to be both categorized and stereotyped. The person is no longer viewed as an individual. Stereotyping is defined as "an exaggerated belief associated with a category. Its function is to justify (rationalize) our conduct in relation to that category" (Allport, 1986, p. 191). Most stereotypes about PWDs are unsupported by fact. For example, we saw in Chapter 2 that PWODs have a tendency to sensationalize the disability and to impute emotional reactions to disabilities that PWDs simply do not experience. Some examples of stereotypes that are unsupported by fact include the ideas that blindness is a dark pit and that PWDs do not have "normal" sexual feelings. It would, therefore, appear logical that PWDs would not adopt these stereotypes as self-identifiers. However, especially in the past, some of the stereotypes held by PWODs have been so pervasive and widespread that PWDs (and their families) have internalized these false stereotypes. Reread the story of Gunther Schirmer in Chapter 3. Tragically, Schirmer had taken society's prejudice and discrimination as his self-concept. Speaking of himself, he said he would "destroy the cripple." Schirmer committed suicide.

A stereotype is not a category; it is a *belief* about a category. Therefore, it is not prejudicial to recognize someone as having a disability. It is prejudicial to assume that this one category (or any other one category) is the sole determinant of the individual's attitudes and behaviors. Categorization of people is sometimes necessary, although not as often as we think. The tendencies to over-categorize and to stereotype people in categories are the result of our need to simplify a vast array of different types of people and their individual characteristics and identities.

Stereotypes are usually negative and categorize people in subordinate positions. Of course, there is the *possibility* of positive stereotypes. For example, consider this stereotype: PWDs are compassionate and wise because their suffering has given them sensitivity and insight. On the surface, this appears to be a positive statement. However, this stereotype is false, and it is also negative. In much the same way as unintentional handicapism, positive stereotypes may not be malicious in *intent*, but their *results* are harmful to PWDs. All types of stereotyping (even those we think are positive) are detrimental for the following reasons: (1) stereotypes do not portray people in the category as individuals, (2) stereotypes are polarizing because they make a clear demarcation between those in the category and those not in the category, and (3) stereotypes of any kind lead to behaviors and actions that limit and reduce the opportunities of people in that category. Using our example of the false stereotype of PWDs as compassionate, we can see that many professions requiring assertive, competitive, win-at-all-costs behaviors (such as being a courtroom attorney) would automatically be ruled out for a PWD because PWDs are thought to be too nice and compassionate. In Chapter 4, we learned that our culture, especially the media, reinforces and builds on our stereotypes. In short, stereotypes are socially supported.

Positive stereotypes are often difficult to recognize as false and limiting beliefs. Irving Zola, in the National Public Radio Disability History Project (1998b), remarked that the most troubling stereotypes about PWDs were positive ones. Zola spoke of two such positive stereotypes: (1) being brave and courageous in the face of adversity and (2) being endowed with special gifts and qualities. Jenny Morris, the Englishwoman who is paraplegic, described her difficulty in recognizing positive statements as stereotypes:

> During the years following my accident, I have on countless occasions been told by both strangers and acquaintances how "wonderful" they think I am. It took a while to realize why this kind of remark provoked such anger in me. After all, those who say it seem to think that they are praising me for struggling against the difficulties which a physical disability brings. When I eventually unpeeled the layers of patronizing nonsense I realized that at the heart of such remarks lay the judgment that being disabled must be awful, indeed, intolerable. It is very undermining to recognize that people look at me and see an existence, an experience, which they would do everything to avoid for themselves. (J. Morris, 1991, p. 15)

Professionals also fall prey to stereotypes. In his autobiography, Henry Kisor, who became deaf at age 3, discussed standardized testing and diagnostic procedures and concluded that these professional tools are based on false stereotypes. For example, Kisor was offended by the mandatory psychological counseling that people who are deaf are required to undergo before they are allowed to receive speech therapy. Kisor submitted to the psychological counseling and therefore did receive speech training, but decades later, he found it insulting that "deaf experts" had automatically assumed that he needed counseling. Kisor termed his practice of mandatory psychological counseling as "official stereotyping" (Kisor, 1990). Requiring psychological counseling before an individual can be given speech therapy is also an example of pathologization of disability. Certainly, the false assumption underlying is that many Deaf people often experience psychological and mental problems.

Stereotypes are not harmless, because job, housing, educational, and social decisions are based on stereotypes. Also, since policy-makers and legislators are exposed to the same media as everyone else, legislation is based on deeply held assumptions that are often stereotypes. Stereotypes circumscribe opportunities for individuals and handicap society as a whole. Stereotypes are resistant to the truth, probably as a result of these three factors: (1) constant reinforcement by the media, (2) the human need to simplify and organize people, and (3) the prejudice and discrimination that allow those in power to benefit and profit from the subordinate status of stereotyped groups.

More than 30 years ago, an article appeared in a scholarly rehabilitation journal that strongly argued that there is no one personality type associated with a certain disability (Shontz, 1977). For example, there is no "rheumatoid arthritis personality" or "paraplegia and quadriplegia personality." Well-written and comprehensive, much of the value of Shontz's article lies in its extensive listing of scholarly writings that have stereotyped individuals according to the type of disability they experience. As long ago as 1977, the listing of the stereotypes was amazingly long. For example, the list of personality attributes ascribed to patients with arthritis is lengthy. They have been said to have weak egos; to repress hostility; and to be compliant and subservient, potentially psychotic, depressed, dependent, conscientious, masochistic, emotionally labile, compulsive, introverted, conservative, perfectionistic, moody, nervous, worried, tense, overly concerned about personal appearance, and prone to express psychopathology in physical symptoms (Shontz, 1977, p. 339).

Shontz (1977) summarized much of the scholarly writing on various types of disabilities (in addition to rheumatoid arthritis) and concluded that "the recent literature provides no support for the hypothesis that particular disabilities are associated with particular personality characteristics or for the hypothesis that disability is a sufficient cause of maladjustment" (pp. 340–341). The Deaf have had many stereotypical psychological characteristics applied to them. Lane, Hoffmeister, and Bahan (1996) reviewed the scientific literature on the "psychology of the deaf" (there is no such thing as the "psychology of the deaf"), reading more than 350 journal articles and books. Lane et al. then developed a list of these characteristics and divided them into four columns: (1) social, (2) cognitive, (3) behavioral, and (4) emotional. There are 67 adjectives on the list. Lane and colleagues summarized:

> In general, people who are deaf are characterized as socially isolated, intellectually weak, behaviorally impulsive, and emotionally immature. The list of traits attributed to the Deaf is inconsistent: they are both *aggressive* and *submissive; naive, shrewd, detached, passionate, explosive, shy, stubborn and submissive, suspicious* and *trusting.* However, the list is consistently negative; nearly all of the traits ascribed, even many in pairs of opposites, are unfavorable. Clearly we must suspect that the "psychology of the deaf" consists of hearing people's stereotypes about others who are deaf. (p. 349)

None of these stereotypes have been confirmed. Further, these examples demonstrate that stereotyping can occur in very sophisticated and scholarly settings. The perpetuation of these stereotypes was labeled as education, science, scholarship, and research. In the not-too-distant past, university students memorized these disability stereotypes for exams. The better the students learned these stereotypes, the more successful they were in their "education." Physicians and psychologists, who are the products of their professional education, approach their patients with disabilities with these false stereotypes in mind. Furthermore, the continuing education and upgrading of skills required to maintain the licensure and certification of most clinicians is often accomplished through reading professional and scholarly journals. And, as we have seen, many of the professional journals have simply maintained and reinforced these false stereotypes of individuals with disabilities. The stereotypes held by physicians, psychologists, and other clinicians have negative consequences for their patients with disabilities. For example, individuals who are deaf experience longer lengths of stay in psychiatric hospitals than people who are not deaf; there is inappropriate placement of people who are deaf in institutions that care for individuals with intellectual disability; and they face psychiatric misdiagnosis. Lane and colleagues (1996) attributed much of this to negative stereotypes of the Deaf.

Reread the description of the "arthritis personality" and ask yourself if you would like to go out on a date with this type of individual (not an individual with arthritis, but someone who has a weak ego; represses hostility; and is potentially psychotic, depressed, emotionally labile, moody, nervous, tense, and worried). Of course you would not—it would be the date from hell. People with arthritis are not like this, but if these stereotypes persist, it will be difficult for people with arthritis (or any other disability) to enjoy equal social status relationships.

For the individual who is the target of these stereotypes, it is often easier to accept the stereotypes than to fight them. We have learned that the "disability role" is a normative role, meaning that there are rules and expectations that describe how an individual should act. The individual knows that these stereotypes are untrue, and, indeed, much of the humor of the Disability Rights Movement makes fun of these stereotypes. Nonetheless, when the PWD acts according to these expectations and stereotypes, he or she is rewarded, and when the PWD violates the expectations of PWODs, often PWODs withhold the rewards and even punish the individual. Therefore, often it is simply easier for PWDs to accept the stereotype than to fight it. For those who have invisible disabilities and therefore have the option of disclosure, they may choose to keep the disability hidden. However, those with visible disabilities may react to stereotyping by attempting to downplay or minimize the disability or to conceal its effects. Many PWDs have consciously developed strategies to comply with these stereotypes.

Before the advent of disability rights groups, an individual with a disability understood that if he or she decided to fight the stereotypes, it would be a difficult (and probably losing) battle because these stereotypes have developed over centuries and have been subscribed to by millions of people. Because of this, the individual may decide to focus his or her attention and energy elsewhere and simply comply with the stereotype. Also, it should be remembered that PWDs were often isolated and that these societal stereotypes were often held by family members of the PWD. Therefore, the PWD had few places of refuge where he or she could escape the stereotyping. In addition, because PWDs have heard these stereotypes so often and from prestigious and authoritative sources, they may accept these stereotypes as truth. This situation was especially common for individuals with congenital disabilities or disabilities acquired early in life because young children unquestioningly accept the attitudes and viewpoints of the adults around them. PWDs who have experienced institutionalization are isolated from the broader culture and have no way to disprove these stereotypes; as a result, these PWDs internalize society's stereotypes, and these false assumptions become a part of their self-concept. Society has effectively taught them to feel inferior.

Pity

In this section, look for—

- ✧ how pity can be fatal
- ✧ pity's four (negative) components:
    1. an outsider's judgment of a PWD's life
    2. the idea that disability is a tragic catastrophe
    3. pity derived from a position of superiority
    4. lack of respect for the individual
- ✧ how pity reinforces the power structure between PWODs and PWDs

The concept of pity was discussed in the section on charity and charity telethons in Chapter 4; nonetheless, pity merits attention here. Pity, like charity and paternalism, appears to be a positive and beneficent behavior; therefore, the demeaning and exploitative results of pity are difficult for PWODs to understand. Those without disabilities, who rarely experience being pitied, struggle with the idea that pity has resulted in a lack of opportunities for PWDs; social isolation and institutionalization of PWDs; reduced social and legislative change; and most important, the deaths of many PWDs. Remember, Jerry Lewis has stated that he would rather be dead than disabled (Barnartt, Schriner, & Scotch, 2001). Pity also makes it difficult for PWDs to achieve self-respect when pervasive, generalized pity communicates that they are only worthy of recognition for being (perceived as) inferior.

At its extreme, pity requires PWDs to defend and justify their lives. Furthermore, pity forces PWDs to prove their quality of life. These are unnecessary burdens PWODs place on PWDs (and then expect PWDs to be grateful for the pity!). Dr.

Peter Singer, a professor of philosophy at Princeton University, has written books and lectures on his ideas that some PWDs, especially those with severe and multiple disabilities, should be killed. An individual who debated Singer at Princeton summarized his views:

> In the lecture hall that afternoon, Singer lays it all out. The "illogic" of allowing abortion but not infanticide, of allowing withdrawal of life support but not active killing. Applying the basic assumptions of preference utilitarianism, he spins out his bone-chilling argument for letting parents kill disabled [*sic*] babies and replace them with nondisabled babies who have a greater chance of happiness. (H. M. Johnson, 2003, p. 53)

Most PWDs separate their disability from the prejudice and discrimination of society. Michalko (2002) explained: "No one aspires to . . . be a disabled person. Being a person who is not welcome, who is feared, pitied, and looked upon as a type that no one would aspire to be is often difficult to bear" (p. 1).

Mark O'Brien lived in an iron lung, was a journalist, was a member of a group called Not Dead Yet, and was the subject of the 1997 Academy Award-winning documentary "Breathing Lessons." O'Brien, cited in Fleischer and Zames (2001), wrote:

> It is tempting to pity a man in an iron lung. But pity has become a lethal weapon. On January 8, [1997], the Supreme Court heard arguments in favor of killing people like me—out of pity—to end our suffering. An iron lung has been my second skin since the 1955 polio epidemic. For forty years, people have said, "That poor thing—how he must suffer. He's terminally ill, you know." I'm not "suffering," "terminal," or even "ill." Don't waste your pity on me. I want to live. Every year, practitioners of mercy death kill thousands of people against our will—out of pity. If the Supreme Court declares mercy death legal, that's like declaring open season on people with disabilities. We're not contagious or dangerous. And we aren't affiliated with any political party. We are people who hear the death train. We will not board that train willingly. (p. 132)

Pity makes it possible for PWODs to morally exclude PWDs without feeling guilty. PWODs often feel that their pity constitutes an interest in the lives of PWDs when, in fact, pity categorizes, distances, and polarizes PWDs. Furthermore, pity makes it clear that PWODs are superior and PWDs are inferior. Pity makes it possible for society to refuse a fair share of the nation's resources for PWDs because, after all, society gives generously to charities. It is a small step from pity to exclusion, discrediting, and segregation. Pity is often invisible and indirect, and most often is considered to be a positive, beneficent attitude, yet pity erects many barriers for PWDs.

Role Entrapment

In this section, look for—

- ✧ the definition of role entrapment
- ✧ why the individual may choose to accept the role entrapment
- ✧ the Bulova Syndrome and the "five Fs"
- ✧ how the inferior education given to PWDs may contribute to their occupational role entrapment

Role entrapment occurs when the group in power, in this case PWODs, defines those roles minority individuals can and cannot assume. Role entrapment can be social or occupational and usually includes only inferior and undesirable roles. Often occupational role entrapment has been termed "occupational stereotyping." Individuals who are ethnic and racial minorities have long been aware of role entrapment; for example, years ago, Black American men were expected to do certain jobs. Role entrapment is not self-imposed unless the minority individual comes to internalize the majority's view of himself or herself. Once again, as in categorization and stereotyping, the person is not viewed as an individual, and his or her strengths and abilities are never considered. It is a matter of "Your kind of people do [or do not] do these type of things."

As with stereotyping, often the PWD simply accepts the role entrapment rather than fight it. Since it is the group in power that makes the rules, they reward those minority people who know their place, keep their aspirations and achievements at a modest level, and refrain from testing the limits of acceptance (Yuker, 1988). Individuals who attempt to assume roles that are not endorsed by the majority are called "uppity" and told that "they don't know their place." The entrapment may be more powerful for PWDs than for racial and ethnic groups because society often feels that they have provided many benefits to PWDs (charity, special services, etc.) and consider these attempts to escape role entrapment to be lack of gratitude. According to this viewpoint, PWDs should accept their inferior quality of life with gratitude and equanimity. Davis (1997b) summed up this view: "[You PWDs should] accept our [PWODs'] construction of your life or give up your access to equal citizenship" (p. 167).

Social role entrapment occurs when PWDs are told that they should associate with their own kind. Social relationships in which one individual has a disability and the other does not have a disability are often automatically assumed to be asymmetrical. The most extreme example of social role entrapment is segregation and institutionalization.

Occupational role entrapment for PWDs has been so widespread as to gain derisive nicknames. The "Bulova Syndrome" refers to the tendency to place men in wheelchairs in watch repair. While the Bulova Watch Company should not be faulted because they were hiring PWDs when very few companies were, the Bulova Syndrome refers to a time when people with a certain disability (usually paraplegia) were often automatically assigned a life's occupation. As a side note, it was the combination of the Bulova Watch Company, the Bulova School of Watchmaking, and the Bulova family who were the first and primary financial supporters of the organization of wheelchair sports (Berger, 2009).

Today, the nickname for role entrapment for PWDs, especially those with intellectual disabilities, is "the five Fs": food, filth, flowers, filing, and folding. *Food* is work in fast-food restaurants; *filth* is janitorial and housekeeping work; *flowers* refers to work in yard maintenance and landscaping; *filing* is simple office work; and *folding* refers to work in laundry facilities. Men who were deaf were often placed in printing jobs because their disability was viewed as an asset because they could not hear the loud machinery. Women who were deaf and not homemakers were often placed in textile mills, and in the late 1960s, girls in residential schools who were deaf were trained for keypunch work or to be seamstresses; men who were blind often trained for photographic darkroom work (Sinick, 1969). At the Perkins School for the Blind, girls were trained to be typists or Dictaphone users, and boys were trained to be piano tuners (Holcomb, 1990). It is not an exaggeration to state that, first, most individuals with physical disabilities were placed in lower-level jobs requiring manual skills, and, second, much of this role entrapment was a result of the false stereotype that individuals with physical disabilities were intellectually incapable of managerial or professional-level jobs. (This is another example of spread.) Further, most of these jobs were low paying. For example, men who were deaf were rarely the managers of printing companies; they were allowed only to run the machinery and produce the printing products.

As stated earlier, in the past, occupational role entrapment was often termed *occupational stereotyping,* and there is some indication that the tendency of professionals to relegate an individual to a job on the sole basis of his or her disability is decreasing. It should be noted that Hahn (1997) strongly asserted that relegating PWDs to lower-paid jobs has little to do with the disability itself; rather, it is the result of a capitalist system that needs workers willing to work for low wages for employers to maintain high profits (refer to the *New York Times* story, "The Boys in the Bunkhouse"; Barry, 2014). Simply stated, according to Hahn, keeping PWDs in low-level jobs maintains the social order.

Occupational role entrapment began early in life for PWDs. The little education that children with disabilities received emphasized manual skills and vocational training. There were no career days at schools for children with disabilities, nor were there individual career or college planning sessions with the school counselor for these children. The type of disability determined the child's career. Sharon L., the medical social worker we met in Chapter 3, clearly remembers the day that the school counselor told her she should become a professional artist. The counselor told Sharon that (1) she was good at art, (2) she would not have to be around people, and (3) no one would recognize her art as "disabled art." Probably the reason why this one day in Sharon's high school career is so indelibly etched in her memory is that she was surprised by the role entrapment that the counselor was attempting to enforce. Also, as we will see in the chapter on the individual's adjustment to disability (Chapter 9), stigma recognition is often shocking to the PWD. In many situations, PWDs are not aware of the stigma that others hold toward their disability. For example, what did the counselor mean by "disabled art," other than to imply that such art would be inferior to "nondisabled art"? Even individuals like Sharon, who have had their disabilities for many years, are unpleasantly surprised when confronted with prejudice, discrimination, and stigma. Disability scholars have labeled this experience "stigma recognition." As a teenager, Sharon was unaware that some school officials thought she would be forced to choose a profession that would not require interaction with people; after all, she had been attending high school, church, and community activities all her life. The high school counselor, probably out of good intentions, tried to guide Sharon to art. (This is an example of the handicapism of well-intentioned people.) There is nothing wrong with being an artist. The error lies in (1) someone else choosing Sharon's life work, and (2) choosing a profession based on how others *might* react to the disability.

When considering the situation of PWDs, we can indulge in the circular argument: Did the inferior education of children with disabilities lead to occupational role entrapment? Or, did the occupational role entrapment lead to inferior education for children with disabilities? The answer to each question is "yes." An extreme example of the practice of preparing children with disabilities for a life of occupational entrapment is presented in Margret A. Winzer's (1993) work, *Education, Urbanization, and the Deaf Community: A Case Study of Toronto, 1870–1900.* Winzer makes two points: (1) "The Ontario institution tried to reproduce the factory conditions as a means of socializing its students and disciplining them to the rigidity and monotony of modern industrial labor" (p. 127); and (2) "these efforts were a mistake. . . . [T]hey limited the opportunities for deaf workers and made them easily expendable as technology changed" (p. 127). It does not sound like school was much fun for these children.

David Wright, a South African who was deaf and who worked as a university professor of literature in England, wrote an autobiography. He related his lifelong response to the role entrapment perpetuated in schools for children who are deaf:

> Since then, I have had an aversion to doing anything with my hands. To this day, I cannot draw, or tie up a parcel properly, if it comes to that. . . . But, for a long time, dating from my attendance at this school, if it was a school, I refused on principle to learn, or was deliberately bad at manipulatory skills like carpentry, painting, and so on. Schools of this type, where the teacher was usually untrained—they probably do not exist nowadays—took the line of least resistance and while teaching their deaf pupils a little speech and lip-reading, concentrated on instruction in handicrafts. This seemed to me, even then, to be equating deafness with stupidity; and I resented it. So much so that I took cleverness with the hands to be a badge of deafness, and I would not wear that badge. Instead of being taught to use my head, because I was deaf, I was being fobbed off with handicrafts. (D. Wright, 1994, p. 40)

The concept of *helping your own kind* probably arose from the assumption that PWDs could best understand other PWDs. Also, the need to counter the paternalism of PWODs who worked with PWDs probably activated the desire for PWDs to be taught by other PWDs. However, we have learned that PWDs can, and do, hold false prejudicial views about individuals with other types of disabilities. Further, it would be impossible to match each individual with a counselor or teacher who has the same type of disability. This is to say nothing about limiting the career opportunities for PWDs. In addition, the *help your own kind* philosophy is blatantly holding disability to be the most salient characteristic of the individual.

Lowered Expectations, or "Let's Give Those Poor Disabled People a Break"

In this section, look for—

- ✧ how lowered expectations can result in fewer opportunities for PWDs
- ✧ overprotection and sheltering and their results
- ✧ the difference between providing accommodations and lowering standards
- ✧ misguided acts of perceived kindness

Related to both stereotyping and role entrapment of PWDs are inappropriate pessimism and the practice of automatically lowering expectations. Such a relaxing of standards communicates that PWDs should be excused or indulged and, furthermore, that PWDs are not considered capable of being judged against high standards. PWDs often report that they have been told, "You did pretty well for a (deaf person, a blind person, a PWD)," and, subsequently, they felt insulted and demeaned. Deaf children were often told, "You're deaf, don't shoot too high" (Solomon, 2012, p. 57).

When widely held standards and expectations are lowered for PWDs, the credibility and competence of the PWDs are questioned. However, when PWDs do succeed, many PWODs are genuinely surprised, which is also insulting and demeaning. Praising a PWD for minor accomplishments is another way in which lowered expectations are expressed.

The provision of accommodations for the disability is often confused with lowering standards. Brenda Premo, who for 4 years was the director of the California Department of Rehabilitation, and who is legally blind, described this difference when she stated:

> I really appreciated the teachers in high school who would accommodate me but who had high expectations. They would ask me, "What can I do that

would make this better for you?" but they wouldn't let me slide at all academically. There was a math teacher, an old gruff guy. He would accommodate me, but I had to achieve and I had to earn my grade. I always got B's from him but I respected him so much more than some other teachers who always gave me easy A's. The same thing happened in college. I always appreciated the teachers who expected the most out of me and I worked my hardest in their classes. I got the most out of them. (Mackelprang & Salsgiver, 1999, p. 142)

Behaviors and attitudes that (1) do not allow the PWD to be an equal partner, (2) communicate the message that he or she is not capable, and (3) reduce the range of opportunities open to the individual are harmful. Lowered expectations, which at first glance may appear to be kindness and generosity, harm the individual because he or she does not receive helpful and honest feedback. And, without honest feedback, an individual is kept in an inferior and dependent position. Praising the individual for small achievements (when the individual is capable of much more) is insulting and demeaning for the individual. Robert Scott (1969), in his book, *The Making of Blind Men: A Study of Adult Socialization*, observed one additional result from lowered expectations: The individual begins to believe that the disability (in this case, blindness) is the cause of his or her incompetence.

Clients are rewarded by trivial things and praised for performing tasks in a mediocre fashion. This superficial and overgenerous reward system makes it impossible for most clients to assess their accomplishments accurately. Eventually, since anything they do is praised as outstanding, many of them come to believe that the underlying assumption must be that the blindness makes them incompetent. (p. 85)

PWDs are aware when standards are relaxed for them, which implicitly states, "You're never expected to be any good." Those who have lowered expectations of PWDs often do not allow PWDs opportunities for achievement. One woman with a disability described this experience when she said, "Even if you can, no one will let you." Often, overprotection and sheltering of the PWD are other forms of lowered expectations. The PWOD falsely assumes that he or she is not reducing the PWD's independence and achievement; the PWOD thinks he or she is protecting the PWD. Lowered expectations often result in failure to inform PWDs of available opportunities and the standards and requirements for gaining these opportunities. Frequently, educational opportunities, job openings, and social occasions are not considered relevant, because PWODs are quick to judge such opportunities to be unobtainable and unrealistic for the individual with a disability. Lowered expectations often lead to lack of challenge and achievement for PWDs. The following are examples of PWDs refusing the lowered expectations that are often thrust on them:

Erik Weihenmayer (2001), the blind man who climbed Mt. Everest, appeared on a popular daytime talk show. Weihenmayer wrote about his appearance:

> Throughout the rest of the segment, I squirmed in my seat. I should have been proud to be picked out as being "amazing and inspirational," but strangely, I felt more embarrassed and even a little sick. I was no more accomplished (than the other blind guests). I was simply a blind person who planned to climb a mountain and nothing more. But people sensationalize the lives of blind people when, often, all they did was exhibit a semblance of normalcy. I have been receiving these accolades my whole life: give someone directions to my house—incredible. Make eye contact in a conversation—amazing. Each of us on the panel was being honored for our heroic tables, but the recognition spoke more loudly of low expectations than of accomplishment. (p. 167)

Chuck Close (1993), an artist who became paralyzed, wrote of the importance of selling one of his paintings to the Museum of Modern Art, which he considered to be the "Good Housekeeping seal of approval" in the art world:

> After I got back to work, I didn't want all of a sudden to become known as the "handicapped artist." People around me were very reluctant at first to let me do interviews; they were very protective of me. I'd had a successful fifteen, twenty year-long career as an artist. Now all of a sudden not to be seen as an artist anymore, but as a "handicapped" artist was a risk. Would people think differently about what I had made? So that was the real fear. It was very important that the very first large painting I made when I got out of the hospital was bought by the Museum of Modern Art . . . not only important to me, but important to the art world, because it was sort of a Good Housekeeping seal of approval. The Museum of Modern Art is not in the business of buying handicapped art, you know, just to make someone feel better. (p. 24)

R. W. Harris (1992), a coordinator of a university program designed to provide services for students with disabilities, summarized the effects of lowered expectations:

> Misguided acts of perceived kindness are a much harder construct to deal with than even overt negative discrimination. One of the reasons for this is generally neither party understands the pernicious effects of this behavior. It may be years before the person with the disability realizes that he/she has been victimized by inadequate preparation and a lack of necessary independence." (p. 208)

Failing to discipline children with disabilities, and providing "mercy graduations" for schoolchildren with disabilities are examples of the lowered expectations of PWDs from PWODs. Lowering expectations, excusing, indulging, and tolerating poor performance from PWDs are all forms of discrimination.

Lack of Privacy

In this section, look for—

- ✧ reasons why PWDs experience less privacy than others
- ✧ explanations of why the "dehumanization" of assistive technology is appealing to many PWDs

Most PWDs experience less privacy and anonymity than do PWODs. Goffman (1963), speaking of a stigmatized person, described this lack of privacy: "To be present among normals nakedly exposes him [*sic*] to invasions of privacy" (p. 212). Some of this lack of privacy may result from the disability itself. Individuals who are deaf and use sign language interpreters, and individuals with visual impairments who often require readers or scribes are examples of loss of privacy that are a result of the disability itself. Personal care attendants dress PWDs, assist them in using the bathroom and using suppositories and catheters, and assist with menstrual needs. These types of losses in privacy are unavoidable. Such a continuous, daily loss of privacy, in areas of life that are considered to be the most personal, is difficult for most PWODs to understand.

Sue Suter (1993), former U.S. Commissioner of Rehabilitation and President of the World Institute on Disability Services, described the loss of privacy that many PWDs experience when the services of a paid personal care attendant are necessary. Suter related the following anecdote of a PWD advocating before a state legislature: "One consumer, named Terry Gutterman, made the issue understandable to legislators by simply asking them to 'Imagine giving the keys to your house to 14 different people in a single year.'"

Higgins (1992b), in his book, *Outsiders in a Hearing World*, interviewed a married couple who uses sign language. He explained: "When one deaf couple dines in a restaurant, they imagine that they have drawn a curtain between themselves and the hearing people who stare at them" (and mimic their signing) (p. 128). PWDs who must sustain this loss of privacy often regard privacy and anonymity as precious resources to be carefully defended. Individuals who use sign language must occasionally guard against others "overseeing" (not overhearing) them.

Hospitalization, institutionalization, and resident schooling of PWDs all greatly decrease the PWD's opportunity for privacy. Living with large groups of people the individual has not chosen to live with, day after day, allows little chance for either private time or private space. Chubon and Moore (1982) studied individuals in a large rehabilitation center for spinal cord injuries. They observed that many people spent large amounts of time in bed with the blankets pulled over their heads. When they interviewed these individuals, they learned these patients were attempting to gain some seclusion and privacy. Chubon and Moore termed this behavior "cocooning."

Often, PWDs interpret and define privacy differently than PWODs. Beisser (1989), who contracted polio after graduating from medical school, was paralyzed from the neck down and placed in an iron lung. Dr. Beisser related that hospital caregivers asked permission before they touched his head. In contrast, caregivers poked, prodded, handled, and displayed the rest of his body without asking permission or giving prior warning. Beisser realized that everyone was very respectful of his head. Assistive technology, such as voice-activated computers and TDD (telecommunications device for the deaf) telephones, offers a measure of privacy to PWDs and thus eliminates the need for a family member or a personal care attendant to perform certain types of functions. Ironically, the very "dehumanization" of technology is appealing to PWDs. Technology, in contrast to people, always maintains confidentiality, does not get sick, and does not refuse to assist when irritated or in a bad mood, thus allowing the user more independence. Technology can, and does, break down and crash, but technology is far more reliable than most people. Technology provides both independence and privacy to PWDs.

Hypervisibility and Over-Observation

In this section, look for—

- ✧ the definitions of hypervisibility and over-observation
- ✧ the power relationship between the individual who is staring and the individual who is being stared at
- ✧ the effects of hypervisibility
- ✧ having unintended meanings attributed to PWDs' actions
- ✧ why most PWODs think their intrusive staring and asking inappropriate questions are invisible to PWDs
- ✧ why some PWODs think that PWDs should be grateful for over-observation

Individuals with visible disabilities also enjoy less privacy and anonymity and experience more hypervisibility and over-observation. Kenneth Fries (1997) compiled a book of essays, poetry, and fiction written by PWDs, titling the book, *Staring Back*. There is a clear message in the fact that all the writers and artists, with their differing life histories and various types of disabilities, shared one experience in common: being stared at. Such hypervisibility is exhausting—emotionally, mentally, and physically. A woman who acquired a spinal cord injury at age 36 stated, "When I was first in a wheelchair, I was terrified that people were going to stare at me" (Mackelprang

& Salsgiver, 1999, p. 100). In American Sign Language, the sign for the word *stare* communicates both the intrusiveness and hostility felt by the Deaf. The sign is "the fingertips of both hands almost poking into one's own face" (Walker, 1986, p. 100). A student of mine, a middle-aged former professor who is blind, was stopped by a young student at the doorway of my classroom. The student said, "I've been watching you walk down the street and seeing how many times you mess up." From a distance, my student's white cane made him hypervisible. Most people who do not have visible disabilities are not stopped by strangers and asked questions or told they had "messed up." Thomson (1997c) perceptively noted the power differential between the person who is staring ("the spectator") and the person who is being stared at ("the spectacle"), stating, "One role is to look, judge, and act while the other role is to be gazed upon, measured, and passive" (p. 300). Read the letter from the mother of an infant with a disability (see Exhibit 5.1).

Parents of infants and children with visible disabilities report that they are often asked (by strangers): "Is this baby yours?" Little People (LP) are often the subject of aston-

---

Dear Ann Landers: I gave birth to my first child last April. "Crystal" was 12 weeks premature and weighed less than 2 pounds. We were afraid that she would die or have severe handicaps, but we were blessed with good fortune as her only remaining requirement is the extra oxygen she receives through a nasal tube worn 24 hours a day.

Her doctors told us, "Don't let her alter your lifestyle." We took their advice and take Crystal everywhere. She's been to the mall, five restaurants, a small boat harbor, and the county fair.

Because the nasal tube makes her look different, I have received a lot of unsolicited and rude comments. People ask, "What's wrong with her? Was she born that way? What's her problem?" I do not wish to discuss my daughter's medical condition with strangers, and considering the handicaps she might have had, my husband and I feel there's nothing wrong with Crystal at all.

Ann, please alert the boneheads out there that if they see a child who is "different," to coo over the baby the way they would a "normal" child. The parents already know their child looks different, and they love the child anyway. The anguish they have already gone through doesn't need to be rehashed to satisfy a stranger's curiosity. A kind word would make a world of difference.

—Grateful Mom in Buffalo, NY

Dear Buffalo Mom: Thank you for speaking up about an intensely personal matter. You have performed a valuable service by sharing your problem with millions of readers today. Many of them will see themselves and be reminded of your letter when they see a child who is "different."

Exhibit 5.1

ished fascination and lack of privacy. Martha Undercoffer, an LP, has devised a method to deal with staring and insensitive, obtrusive questions. She has a business card which she gives to the offender. The front of the card reads: "Yes, I noticed your behavior towards me." On the back, the card reads: "I realize that you probably mean no harm by your actions and/or comments. However, realize they did cause harm and were not appreciated." Ms. Undercoffer said this about over-observation: "For some reason, the public seems to think we don't notice their treatment of us" (Solomon, 2012, p. 145).

For everyone, there are times when we wish to remain in the background or totally anonymous. For someone with a visible disability or someone who uses some sort of assistive technology (such as a hearing aid or wheelchair), remaining in the background is not possible. A woman with a disability explained: "Having a visible disability means always being noticed, standing out, being different, *everywhere you go*." Indeed, she terms her disability "a blinking neon sign" (Olkin, 1999, pp. 80–81). Following is an example when anonymity would be desirable. A professor in a large class of 300 students states that attendance will not be taken and therefore will not affect students' grades. Almost every student can skip class, realizing that the professor has no way of knowing who is attending and who is not. However, anonymity is not possible for the one student enrolled in the class who uses a wheelchair, or the one student who uses a sign language interpreter, or the one Black American student.

For someone who is subjected to hypervisibility, life can become an unending public performance in which he or she is expected to exhibit positive behaviors and attitudes. One woman quantified what "unending" means when she used the phrase, "every few hours":

> Every few hours I run up against people who feel free to remind me that I'm their inferior and that I should conform to whatever they've decided "people like me" are supposed to be like. . . . We should drop everything to satisfy other people's curiosity about us, and we should do it in a manner that is pleasant and convenient for them even if it is physically impossible for us. . . . Every few hours I run up against people who are so convinced that this is true that they are mystified that I'm not grateful for the experience. (Montgomery, 2006, para. 12)

In Chapter 4, we discussed that disability is a normative experience, meaning that there are rules, usually unwritten but strongly held, about how PWDs should behave. Coupled with these rules of disability is the general lack of knowledge about disabilities. Nonetheless, PWDs are aware that they are being scrutinized and often judged. The individual in the wheelchair who falls asleep during an important meeting is thought to be rude simply because it never enters the minds of others that this PWD must take large doses of medication to control muscle spasms, which make him or her sleepy. With hypervisibility, everything the PWD does takes on added meaning, and this added meaning is often the result of negative inferences. Public performance, with the subsequent judgment of others, is stressful and anxiety-provoking. The individual is not allowed to relax and "just hang out." Some individuals can escape hypervisibility by returning home or someplace where there are a lot of other people who look like them. These people have a place where they can blend in. Often, PWDs do not have this haven or sanctuary. Frequently, the PWD feels alienated and different from even his or her own family. Many PWDs cannot shed their hypervisibility and simply be a person, not for an evening, not for a weekend, not for the holidays.

Much of the attention directed toward PWDs is well-intentioned and not planned to annoy or inconvenience anyone. Unintended or not, attention that is not wanted or attention that is directed solely toward the disability, rather than the person, is both irritating and inconvenient. Intrusive and insulting questions that would never be asked of PWODs are often asked of PWDs. Murphy, Scheer, Murphy, and Mack (1988) described hypervisibility in this way: "noticed by everyone and acknowledged by nobody" (p. 239). Stated differently, PWDs are subjected to staring and intrusive questions; but at the same time, PWDs are not considered to be individuals with identities other than the disability. Therefore, PWDs are "acknowledged by nobody" because they are often not involved in ordinary social situations. Read the letter to Ann Landers in Exhibit 5.2.

Two circumstances may account for the different responses of Grateful Mom in Buffalo, New York, and S. R. in Meraux, Louisiana. Grateful Mom was dealing with adults who were strangers, while S. R. was responding to children who may have been friends of her own children, people with whom she had a relationship. It is probably safe to say that the curiosity and fascination of complete strangers has more potential to insult and irritate PWDs than the interest of people with whom they are acquainted. Second, PWDs often report that children are more honest and forthright in their interest than are adults, who often display subtle (and sometimes not so subtle) hypocrisy about the disability. Furthermore, children have not yet acquired the stereotypes and myths about disabilities; therefore, their questions are free of demeaning, preconceived ideas. Susan Wendell (2006) summarized the experience of being an object of curiosity: "Visibly disabled [sic] women report that curiosity about medical diagnoses, physical appearance and the sexual and other intimate aspects of disability is more common than willingness to listen and to understand the experience of disability" (p. 267).

Such intrusions of privacy also affect the partners and family members of PWDs. Most people on family outings do not enjoy being approached by strangers and being forced to deal with others' misinformed and negative attitudes toward disability. Lefley (1991) summarized: "Generalization of stigma to families is an additional source of psychological risk" (p. 127). In an empirical research study that focused on the brothers and sisters of a child with a disability entitled, "Experiences of Siblings of Children with Physical Disabilities," the authors summarized one of the findings: "The siblings [of a child with a disability] took the view that the behaviour of strangers was certainly open to improvement. They thought that people should be better informed, should

Dear Ann Landers: I was interested in the letter from "Upfront in Vermont," who taught children to ask questions rather than just state people are different. As a person who has had a disability since birth, I was especially pleased that you printed it. Growing up, I was hurt far more by people who gawked and made comments among themselves than by those who asked me questions.

My right arm ends just below the elbow, and when I see children looking at it curiously, or if they ask what happened, I explain that God makes each of us different. Some people have brown hair, some blond; some people are tall, some are short; some people have two hands, some may have only one. But each of us is special in our way. Sometimes, the children touch my arm or want to know how I can drive with one hand. I never take offense to their questions. I simply hope they learn that we can all be and do whatever we want. It's about ability, not disability.

Some parents are embarrassed when their child asks a question, but I believe children should feel free to ask questions so long as they do so politely. How else are they to learn? I was worried that my daughter would be upset by other children's reactions to my arm. Now, at age 6, she answers questions, saying, "That is how God made her and my mom can do anything."

—S. R., Meraux, LA

Dear S.R.: What a wonderfully positive attitude! Some people would see the cup as half empty, but in your case, it is overflowing. Thanks for writing.

Exhibit 5.2

behave more 'naturally,' show more respect, and certainly refrain from staring" (Cate & Loots, 2000, p. 403). Lee Martin (2000) wrote about his childhood with his father, who had lost both hands in a farm machine accident and wore hooks: "I had never gotten used to the attention those hooks drew, the furtive glances from people trying not to be rude, the out-and-out stares from others who were so surprised to see the prostheses they couldn't begin to mask their curiosity" (p. 114). It is interesting that, throughout the years, Martin never became accustomed to the stares directed at his father.

Wilson (1990) read many first-person accounts of individuals who had survived polio, and noted the difficulty that polio survivors experienced because of hypervisibility and staring. Wilson focused on the emotional reactions of the polio survivor.

Going out in public for the first time was a big step psychologically and emotionally and one every polio survivor needed to talk about if he or she was to have a social life, or go to school or work. For example, Jan Little remembers that in her community, "being in a wheelchair carried a fair amount of shame." After her parents took her to a local concert, one of their neighbors chastised them for "taking a child like that out in public." Arnold Beisser remembers that it was a "major step" to go out in public after having been isolated for years in a hospital. On one of Hugh Gallagher's initial forays into the outside world a young girl "crossed herself as we passed." Gallagher was shocked, especially when "she said a prayer that she wouldn't be like me." (p. 179)

In another book about individuals with polio, a man, Leroy, enjoyed photography as a hobby and continued with his hobby while at Warm Springs Rehabilitation Hospital in Georgia:

> There was Leroy who must spend the rest of his life flat on his back. Sometimes the curious ones would make so bold as to stand directly above him. Without a word, they would stand and stare.
>
> Photography has long been Leroy's hobby and he decided that a splendid opportunity has come to get unusual shots. Slightly concealed in his clothing so that no one would suspect, he planted his candid camera. Now let the curious ones come!
>
> Slowly as before, they approached his cot. Now they stood beside him. Now they were bending over to *really* get a look. Eyes were opened wide. The jaw had dropped a bit. Then *click* went the camera. And bewildered, nonplussed onlookers fled speedily away.
>
> What a collection Leroy must have now. (Lee, 1948)

A Black American male with a disability commented on the additive effects of his gender, his race, and his disability:

> I've gotten used to the stares. . . . it's like—and especially if it's a young African American male in a wheelchair. I can almost read their minds. Gang member. Drug dealer. It's all negative. It's always negative. (Putnam et al., 2003, p. 43)

Often, PWDs do not want to be ignored; however, instead of asking intrusive, personal questions, it is more appropriate to engage in simple small talk. Sports, weather, current events, and other innocuous subjects are good starting places for developing a relationship or chatting with any individual we do not know. As one PWD summarized, "At least PWDs in circuses and freak shows got paid."

Solo Status

In this section, look for—

✧ the definition of solo status

✧ what it means to:
  • be a forced representative
  • be in an unending public performance
  • have no role models

Related to lack of privacy and hypervisibility is solo status. Solo status is when an individual is the only person with a particular visible characteristic; in many settings, there may be only one PWD. Solo status often constrains PWDs to become forced representatives. Regardless of whether an individual has the desire or inclination, he or she now becomes the spokesperson for the disability group. At any time or place, the individual is expected to speak for individuals who have the same disability or to present extemporaneous educational and entertaining lectures. Being solo, for whatever reason—gender (the only woman), race (the only Black American), nationality (the only American), profession (the only professor)—adds another duty to the individual's list of jobs. Whenever a committee needs (1) a woman, (2) a Black American, (3) an American, or (4) a professor, there will be no question who will be asked! Goffman (1963) explained: "A new career is likely to be thrust upon him, that of representing his category" (p. 26). At the committee meeting, the members will turn to the solo and ask, "How do women (Black Americans, Americans, professors, or PWDs) feel about this issue?" It is automatically assumed that the forced representative will know. If this occurs frequently, it can be burdensome for the PWD (Olkin, 1999). When an individual states, "I am not the poster boy (or girl)" for whatever disability the individual has, he or she is refusing the forced representative role.

In addition to being a forced representative and feeling isolated, the solo may be viewed as his or her category rather than as an individual. The solo is often viewed as "the disabled," "the deaf," and so on. Everything the solo does and says takes on unintended meaning simply because the solo has, in the eyes of others, become the group he or she is thought to represent. Olkin (1999) explained: "One's failings or mistakes also can be misinterpreted as representative of the group. Thus, the person with a visible disability is always an ambassador from the disability community on assignment to the able-bodied (AB) world" (p. 82). Ironically, occasionally solos do not subscribe to the identity that the larger group has given them. Once again, it is not the *actual* identity or characteristics of the individual that determines his or her treatment, but the *perceived* identity.

Often solos do not have access to informal communication networks, such as office gossip; they have no role models or mentors. Informal communication, role models, and colleagues are all sources of professional development and emotional support. Much of the helpful (and interesting) information at school and work is derived from informal sources. In addition, professional development can be facilitated by coworkers and mentors who can "clue the new person in." However, the one individual who is perceived as different, the solo, the PWD, will be accorded all his or her rights under the ADA but often will not be viewed as a peer by coworkers. The solo may sit alone at lunches and on coffee breaks and will not be "in" on the office gossip.

Harilyn Rousso (1993), a woman with cerebral palsy, tells of the importance of role models in her book, *Disabled, Female, and Proud!*:

> When I was about twenty-two, I had an unexpected, important experience. I worked one summer for a prominent woman economist who happened to have cerebral palsy. I can't tell you my surprise when I met her at the job interview. It was a bit like looking at myself in the mirror. Betty had a powerful effect on me. I was impressed that a woman with cerebral palsy, not a very socially acceptable disability in our culture, could become so successful in her career, particularly in a "man's field," anti-trust economics. I was even more impressed that she was married. . . . It never occurred to me that I had any alternative, that I could have *both* a career and a romantic life. Betty's lifestyle, her successful marriage to an interesting, dynamic man made me question for the first time the negative assumptions that I had made about my social potential. (p. 2)

As can be seen, meeting and working with this economist occurred at an age, 22 years old, when Ms. Rousso could take advantage of an expanded view of both work and romantic options available to her. We can also see that Ms. Rousso identified with her employer because she states, "It was a bit like looking at myself in a mirror."

Poster Children

The invention of poster children (or poster boys and girls) began with polio. As you recall, polio was first called "infantile paralysis" because most of those who contracted the disease (until the epidemics of the 20th century) were children or infants (H. Gallagher, 1985; Shell, 2005; Wilson, 1990). Polio was also the beginning of a new type of charity—"handicapitalism," the antecedents of the modern telethons. Handicapitalism is the large-scale solicitation of funds for both the treatment and the eradication of a certain disability or disease, using celebrities and the modern media. President Franklin Roosevelt was the celebrity for polio, while today there are many celebrities who choose to solicit charity for different types of disabilities. Poster children and polio seemed to be a natural combination: Here was a disability that struck randomly and predominantly affected innocent children who in no way could be considered at fault for their disability. Poster children and handicapitalism also seemed a natural combination. Innocent children who were paralyzed elicited a great deal of sympathy and pity (far more than adults with the same disability). Of course, the most important element of charity telethons is pity. One PWD stated, "The larger the lump in the throat, the larger the check." Another definition of a poster boy or poster girl is someone who is seen only as a disability and not as an individual.

Token Status

In this section, look for—

- ⟡ the definition of token status
- ⟡ why tokens are not acknowledged for their achievements and talents

Token status refers to being viewed as having received rewards and privileges as a result of membership in a certain category. When we discussed the ADA in Chapter 2, we learned that this law does not mandate hiring for jobs or entrance into schools of anyone with a disability who is not qualified. In spite of this, many PWODs think that PWDs have special privileges or exemptions from qualifications. On a personal level, being perceived as a token is both demeaning and frustrating. On a national level, these misperceptions can affect both legislation and policy. It would make no economic sense to hire someone who is not qualified, even if he or she belongs to a minority group or has a disability. Further, the law does not mandate that companies hire, or schools admit, individuals from any particular group. The law does require that application and hiring processes be open to all.

As would be expected, when an individual is considered to be a token (for membership in any type of group), years of hard work, preparation, study, and sacrifice are disregarded and ignored. The individual is thought to have received his or her position because he or she is a member of some disadvantaged group. Further, the token's talents, abilities, skills, intelligence, and work habits are also unacknowledged. Thus, the token fully understands that if he or she were not a member of this some "disadvantaged" group, his or her accomplishments would be recognized and acknowledged as *individual* achievements. Certainly, the token realizes that it is his or her membership in the group that results in being perceived as a token. It is clear that being viewed as a token is the result of the mistaken stereotypes of the token's associates.

Paternalism

In this section, look for—

- ⟡ why the practice of paternalism is common when serving PWDs
- ⟡ when paternalism is justified
- ⟡ when paternalism is not justified
- ⟡ what "limited paternalism" and "paternalism by permission" mean

✧ the principle of informed choice
✧ the principle of self-determination

Paternalism has been defined as "acting upon one's own idea of what is best for another person without consulting that other person" (Marchewka, cited in G. R. Anderson, 1987, p. 177). Sissela Bok (1979) defined paternalism as "to guide and even coerce people in order to protect them and serve their best interests, as a father might his children. He must keep them out of harm's way, by force if necessary" (p. 215). Both these definitions emphasize that the individuals for whom this guidance, protection, and service are provided are, at best, not consulted, and, at worse, coerced. Therefore, an individual's autonomy has been violated. However, the concept of a father implies someone who (1) has the best interests of the child in mind and would not want to harm his child, and (2) is more knowledgeable and qualified than his child. The "child," or patient or client is considered to be vulnerable and in need of guidance. It is not difficult to determine that paternalism is a product of the Biomedical Model of disability. As you will remember, the Biomedical Model relies on the expert knowledge of physicians and other health care providers.

Of course, there are situations in which paternalism is both appropriate and desirable, and therefore society provides the power and resources for paternalism to be enforced. For individuals with severe intellectual disability who do not have the ability to understand the nature, extent, and ramifications of important decisions, paternalism is desirable. Indeed, Anderson (1987) stated:

> Some might argue that because of cognitive impairment, the incompetent or severely mentally retarded [sic] have no right to the truth as they have no "true liberty." This leads to a logical difficulty: if people have no liberty, it is not possible to abridge that liberty, and therefore it is not paternalistic to choose for them; in fact it is not possible to be paternalistic. (pp. 183–184)

Paternalism is justified when it is thought that the individual may make decisions that would cause harm to himself or herself. (The parent–child example already mentioned applies here as well.) Often, professionals ask the question, "How serious are the potential consequences of the individual's making his or her own decisions?" However, many PWDs feel that paternalism has been overused.

The unethical use of paternalism is readily apparent when decisions are made for individuals who have the capability to make their own decisions. A woman who has experienced schizophrenia for 20 years related her experiences with paternalism: "You are given insulin coma therapy and ECT [electroconvulsive therapy] without being consulted or informed because your psychiatrist and your family assume you are too ill to understand" (Leete, 1991, p. 19). Ruth Moore has a degenerating physical disability. She worries that as her condition deteriorates, physicians may make paternalistic decisions about the quality of her life. Further, she knows that physicians have the power to enforce their decisions, regardless of how wrong or patronizing:

> The neurosurgeon told me that he was only interested in quality of life and that in no way would he be looking to prolong my life if he didn't feel the quality would be acceptable. However, neither he nor anyone else has asked me what criteria I would use in judging what was an acceptable quality of life. I am very worried that if I get admitted unconscious or without the power of speech, he will make a decision based on his judgment and his criteria about what is an acceptable quality of life. (J. Morris, 1991, p. 62)

Here is another example of paternalism: "Upon retirement, the head of the Spastic Society of Britain was asked if he could envision the day when a person with spasticity would head that charity. 'That'd be like putting dogs and cats in charge of the Humane Society,' he quipped" (Pelka, 1997, p. 3; quoted from the November/December 1993 issue of *Mouth: The Voice of Disability Rights*). Incidentally, this short story also illustrates other concepts that we have discussed in this book: (1) the use of improper language ("The Spastic Society"), (2) comparing PWDs to animals, (3) the use of humor to stereotype and devalue PWDs, and (4) the harm that so-called "charities" perpetuate on people they claim to help. Not so quickly discernible is the unintentional misuse of paternalism for individuals who are not capable of making decisions (and for whom society therefore deems paternalism to be appropriate), but these important decisions are based on false stereotypes, inaccurate information about the PWD, or both. We have seen that highly trained professionals hold many false stereotypes of PWDs, and in those cases where paternalism is both necessary and desirable, it is important to ensure that these judgments and choices, made on the behalf of another person, are based on accurate and complete knowledge of the individual. Many disability rights advocates have argued that an individual's worst behavior, regardless of how infrequently that behavior occurred, determined the individual's placement and treatment plans.

Thus, there are types of abuse of paternalism. The first, and most clear-cut, is enforcing paternalism when the individual can make decisions for himself or herself. The second, and less obvious, is enforcing paternalism when the individual cannot make decisions, but unintentionally basing decisions on inaccurate information, false stereotypes, or both. Indeed, unjustified paternalism has resulted in restrictive and humiliating treatment for PWDs.

Why have PWDs been subjected to so much paternalism? First, the normative role of a PWD demands dependency, compliance, and passive acceptance of treatment, benefits, and rehabilitation. The power is in the hands of the physicians and counselors who, if they choose, could withhold treatment and benefits if a PWD questions or challenges their decisions. Second, the overgeneralization or perceived spread concerning the effects of the disability often contributes to the mistaken idea that a PWD does not have the mental capacity to make decisions on his or her own behalf. Third, the (unnecessary) need to protect and shelter the PWD may lead some service providers to withhold information from the PWD. Fourth, simply as a result of the nature of the living and treatment environments, many PWDs experience daily, lifelong contact with care providers. These types of settings, rather than any characteristic or need of the client, promote and encourage the paternalism. Fifth, some service providers may be paternalistic simply for the convenience and ease of the institution, hospital, or agency. These service providers often feel that "things just go more smoothly when the client or patient does what he or she is told to do." (This last example may not be true paternalism, because paternalism implies beneficence or consideration of the individual's best interests.)

Overall, the greatest motivation for paternalism is kindness. There is a fine line between paternalism and beneficence, both on an individual level and on a societal level. We have seen the way in which misguided acts of kindness may be interpreted as paternalism. Nonetheless, it is important to judge the behavior by its results. For example, charity, especially telethons, is considered paternalism by PWDs. Hahn (2005) clarified the relationship between paternalism and charity and the long-term results: "Because of historical traditions that had defined disabled [*sic*] people as the 'deserving poor,' the disability movement was enmeshed in a legacy of charity. Most nondisabled observers claimed that they were sympathetic to disabled [*sic*] people, even if they did not actively support their objectives. Paternalism implies that benefits for disabled [*sic*] people are motivated by private philanthropy instead of government decision making" (p. 7). Hahn concludes that paternalism and charity prevented opportunities for PWDs and "a healthy debate concerning disability policies" (p. 7). Several disability reformers, such as Samuel Gridley Howe, Alexander Graham Bell, and Helen Keller, are considered by many to have actually limited the opportunities and civil rights for PWDs. On an individual level, it is somewhat easier to understand how the need to be helpful and kind can result in paternalism.

Two other movements, both supported by federal legislation, designed to minimize paternalism are (1) informed choice, in which the client is given all available information about the disability, the various treatment plans and options, and their consequences, and (2) self-determination, in which the individual has the right to make decisions about his or her treatment, living arrangements, job placement, and social networks. Often, self-determination is called empowerment. Both of these movements acknowledge that the individual is the expert in his or her own needs and desires.

Indeed, PWDs have had to *fight* for their rights, whereas *most* others are automatically *given* their rights. The right to control their own lives has often been denied (needlessly) to PWDs.

Infantilization

In this section, look for—

- ✧ the definition of infantilization
- ✧ the definition of "motherese"
- ✧ which types of people are subjected to motherese

PWDs have often been viewed as "eternal children," in need of control, management, and spiritual guidance (Imrie, 1996). Wolfensberger (1981) explained:

> Adults [with disabilities] may be cast into the roles of eternal children by being encouraged to play children's games and to follow children's school schedules rather than adult work schedules; by children's decoration and children's clothing; by funding of services for adults coming from departments charged with serving children; and by such names as "day care center" for day programs for adults. (p. 205)

Thus, it can be seen that infantilization is practiced both on an individual level and on an institutional level.

Sharon L., a medical social worker with a congenital bone disease that has resulted in her small stature, stated, "It is difficult to cross that border from childhood to adulthood." Sharon has developed presentation strategies to offset the tendency of others to, as she states, "associate my maturity with my size." For example, when she speaks on the telephone, her voice sounds like the voice of a child; therefore, she uses "big words" so as to sound like an adult. Charities have often used poster kids, and, indeed, some celebrities have demonstrated a tendency not only to infantilize people with a certain type of disability, but also to claim a paternalistic relationship. For example, Jerry Lewis terms individuals with muscular dystrophy (MD) as "Jerry's Kids." It is safe to say that most people with MD do not consider themselves either to be children or to belong to Jerry Lewis.

One woman with a disability talked about her difficulty in crossing the border from childhood to adulthood:

> With one extremely painful exception, as long as I was in the protective custody of family life or college, scheduled and lived without exercising my rights as an adult citizen, the forces of society were kindly and unruffling. It was after college, business schools and innumerable stretches as a volunteer worker on community projects that I was often bogged down by the medieval prejudices and superstitions of the business world. Looking for a job was like standing before a firing squad. Employers were shocked that I had the gall to apply for a job. (Goffman, 1963, p. 34)

PWDs are often spoken to in a speech pattern that has been labeled "motherese" (Gouvier, Coon, Todd, & Fuller, 1994). Other authors label this type of speech pattern as "child-directed speech" (Warren-Leubecker & Bohannon, 1989). Motherese "involves exaggerated prosodic inflections and other characteristics such as the use of diminutives in naming (e.g., Bobby rather than Bob) and shortened phrase and sentence length . . . greater redundancy and higher usage of questions and concrete referents" (Gouvier et al., 1994, p. 264). *Prosodic* refers to singsong speech. Gouvier and his colleagues surreptitiously audiotaped conversations of bookstore employees giving directions to customers in wheelchairs and to customers who had no visible disability. Employees speaking to customers in wheelchairs used more words, more repetition, and more questions than when these employees were speaking to customers without a visible disability. Incidentally, none of these fake customers had a disability of any kind (they simply used the wheelchair for the purpose of the experiment), and all were university students. Furthermore, each student played both roles; he or she would use the wheelchair one time and then on another day walk into the bookstore. These students reported that when they used the wheelchair, they sensed "a reverse discrimination in which people actually seemed 'nicer' to them than when they approached in the walking condition" (p. 267). Gouvier and his colleagues concluded:

> This study offers clear behavioral validation that people do speak differently to individuals with disabilities, and that some of these differences parallel those observed in the way people speak to their infant children, pets, and other individuals of lower social standing. (p. 266)

We can hear motherese spoken when a nurse asks someone, "How are we feeling today?" or "Did we eat all our dinner?" Terms of endearment such as "honey" or "sweetheart" used when addressing adult strangers are another indication of motherese. PWDs are often addressed in this insulting and degrading manner. Indeed, adults in institutions were and are often deprived of some small pleasure as a form of punishment. "If you don't do your physical therapy, you won't get dessert" and "If you don't take your medication, you won't be allowed to watch television." These are all examples of motherese. J. Morris (1991) related a story of motherese that was clearly abusive:

> Mary Lawson felt that she must be nice to the people who were helping her with the most intimate tasks otherwise they would refuse to do them, or do them in such a way that caused her pain and humiliation. "I want them to help me so I've got to somehow make them like me." One night she was being lifted into bed by two care assistants when she noticed that her shoes were still on. When she said, "Could you take my shoes off?" the care assistant responded by telling her to say "please." As Mary said, "I don't know whether

the humiliation and anger I felt at saying "please" was worth the benefit of having my shoes taken off." (p. 32)

Incidentally, personal care attendants are employees of the individual with the disability, and most of us do not tell our bosses to say "please" when they ask us to do our job.

PWDs are subjected to intrusive touching by strangers. In our society, adults usually do not touch other adults they do not know. Other than a handshake, in which both individuals must cooperate, a stranger touching another adult is usually considered to be intrusive. PWDs are patted on the head and hugged, and their assistive devices (such as wheelchairs) are moved. All of these behaviors are viewed as intrusive and infantilizing by PWDs.

There is a complex relationship between infantilization, paternalism, dependence, and the Biomedical Model of disability. PWDs are often thought to be sexually neutered and to not be capable of working and making contributions to society; both of these characteristics we usually attribute to children. Furthermore, PWDs are expected to comply with the rules made by PWODs, again a characteristic of childhood in that a child is expected to obey his or her elders and superiors.

Ludwig and Adams (1968) undertook a study in a large rehabilitation center to assess the relationship between patient dependency and subordination and the patient rehabilitation success rate. The authors stated:

> The role of a patient has been likened to that of children by many. . . . What is held in common, of course, among these . . . social positions is the lack of independence, the necessity of accepting a subordinate position and submitting to others. (p. 227)

Their study, which included 406 PWDs,

> hypothesized that persons whose normal role relationships and social position contained elements of dependency or subordination would be more inclined to successfully perform such a role and complete treatment. Persons in dependent age status, females, Negroes, the unemployed . . . were found more likely to complete recommended services, thus supporting the general hypothesis. (p. 235)

This study was completed more than 45 years ago. Nonetheless, the straightforward and clearly stated hypothesis (and the entire purpose of the study) sought to demonstrate that childlike patients were more successful in their rehabilitation. Hypothesizing that PWDs who were women, Black Americans, or unemployed would be more submissive clearly shows that these types of individuals, with or without disabilities, also are not accorded full adult status in our society. Moreover, it appears these researchers were unaware of their blatant prejudice, discrimination, and racism.

Viewing PWDs as Objects

In this section, look for—

◇ the history and purpose of freak shows
◇ present-day freak shows

The long history of freak shows and circuses in which PWDs were put on display for the entertainment of others provides a clear definition of the objectification of PWDs. Nervous curiosity and fascination with people who are viewed not as being human, but rather as objects, continues today. However, the media, such as movies and television, have replaced most of the freak shows and circuses. It was thought that there were moral lessons to be learned by viewing these "freaks," and, indeed, these individuals who were put on display were thought to be symbols of evil, disease, and sin. Pelka (1997) described these "sideshows":

> The Catholic Church, during the Middle Ages in Europe, sponsored travel-ing exhibitions of disabled [*sic*] people, while families exhibited their dis-abled [*sic*] members for a fee or sold them to royalty at court. By Victorian times, these forms of "entertainment" had evolved into carnival sideshows or "dime museums," where the public paid to see "armless and legless wonders," "giants," "dwarfs," "seal boys," "living skeletons," and "pinheads." Such exhib-its were particularly popular in small-town America. (p. 127)

Ironically, many, if not most, of these individuals experienced no functional limita-tions. It was simply their appearance that made them "freaks."

Circuses and freak shows were often viewed by PWDs as sources of income when there were not many opportunities for employment and integration with the general population (Thomson, 1996). Furthermore, these PWDs who worked in circuses and freak shows felt a sense of acceptance and understanding by living, working, and trav-eling with other people who knew what it meant to be labeled a freak. There was a dark and brutal side to these traveling circuses, and many PWDs were abused and ex-ploited simply because the operators of these circuses and freak shows knew very well that there were few places to which the PWD could escape (Bogdan, 1988). Clearly, these PWDs were exploited and objectified for the entertainment of avid audiences with the express purpose of making money for others.

Deborah Marks (1999) read many first-person narratives of PWDs who worked as freaks in circuses and sideshows and came to the conclusion that many of these PWDs felt that their jobs helped them to "exact revenge." These PWDs derived some sort of satisfaction and power from creating discomfort in their audience,

> ultimately consoling themselves with the thought that they were exacting some revenge on a hostile, insensitive world of ignorant suckers by exploit-

ing their vulgarity and credulity, and rather effortlessly taking their money. At the same time, we should not be surprised by another state of mind, perhaps coexisting and competing with cynicism. In the narratives of freaks who retrospectively interpreted their lives in terms of the progress of their careers, we see evidence of the effort to give coherence and meaning to life by seeing it in terms of volition and unfolding purpose rather than oppression and victimization. (Marks, 1999, p. 32)

The efforts to raise awareness and funds for the education of PWDs often included prestigious authorities, such as physicians and teachers, displaying a PWD and showing the audience what the PWD could do. Basically, these types of demonstrations consisted of a teacher putting a PWD "through his or her paces." Thus, physicians and teachers used PWDs as objects, albeit under the guise of advancing education and medical science. Helen Keller, an honors graduate of Radcliffe College, performed in vaudeville twice a day for 4 years, much to Helen's mother's disappointment, who had claimed that her daughter would "go on stage over my dead body" (Herrmann, 1998). After the act, the audience was allowed to ask Ms. Keller questions. Ms. Keller said that she enjoyed acting in vaudeville, but it also solved her financial problems. Before her vaudeville days, and after, Ms. Keller relied on the charity of millionaire philanthropists and income from lecturing. She did view herself as a spectacle. She wrote of herself and her fellow actors, "for the sake of many for whom fate is unkind. . . . I can conceive that in time the spectacle might have grown stale" (Herrmann, 1998, p. 223).

Paul Higgins, a disability scholar, forthrightly depicts telethons and other charitable fundraising activities as modern-day freak shows. Higgins (1992a) explained, "Fund raisers still exhibit disabled [sic] people for 'profit.' Audiences marvel at the accomplishments of the disabled [sic] people who are presented to tug at our heartstrings—and our purse strings" (p. 94). Another example of objectification is the story of Charlie, a deaf child who came home one day and said that for sports, he had been asked to be the goalpost (Solomon, 2012, p. 65).

Today, PWDs feel viewed as objects when they state, "I was *something* to stare at," or "I was interesting to people, and that's dehumanizing." A woman who was born with spina bifida described an unforgettable experience of objectification:

> I was barely human. One time, as a 14-year-old, I was paraded in front of a whole class of doctors so they could see my "abnormal gait." I was wearing only my panties. They would never have done that to a nondisabled girl but it was OK to parade me almost naked. The crazy thing is, it wasn't until years later that I realized they had dehumanized me. (Mackelprang & Salsgiver, 1999, p. 39)

Two ideas are immediately apparent from reading this adult's memory of the treatment she received as a teenager. First, the woman has become aware that the doctors could have had the same quality of training and demonstration while, at the same time, according the girl some measure of respect and dignity (i.e., allowing her to wear more clothing). Second, rather than being overly sensitive and hyper-vigilant for any evidence of prejudice and discrimination, the 14-year-old willingly complied with the doctors' requests and, amazingly, only comes to an awareness of this disrespectful treatment years later. Mee (1999) reported the same experience:

> Dr. Blount, proud of his work, kept inviting me back to Milwaukee whenever he brought together a group of doctors from around the world, to put me on the stage in the medical theater. I would arrive early, strip, and put on a little loincloth, like a diaper. This, in itself, was a disagreeable experience. I was, in any case, an embarrassable adolescent boy. But to be reduced to an object, as these days, finally, everybody knows, is profoundly diminishing. In fact, I was reduced to something even less than an object: I was a specimen. (p. 175)

Solomon (2012) related an extreme example of objectification, a widespread practice called "dwarf tossing." A dwarf is put into a harness and a person of average height, often drunk, hurls him as far as possible onto a padded surface. A 2005 Securities and Exchange Commission investigation into excessive and inappropriate gifts to securities traders found dwarf tossing among the festivities featured at a lavish $160,000 stag party financed by Fidelity Investments for one of its star performers. Another example is "dwarf bowling," where a dwarf is placed on a skateboard and is rolled down a bowling alley to knock over a set of pins.

The perpetrators of crime against PWDs and sexual abuse of PWDs often defend themselves by stating that they did not view their victims as people. Reading David Hevey's (1997) essay, *The Enfreakment of Photography*, we learn that modern-day photography has exploited PWDs. A line from the first paragraph states, "I ask the reader to join me on a journey into oppressive disability imagery" (p. 332). PWDs report that they feel objectified when PWODs, including their own families, "put them on a pedestal." While these PWODs might think they are showing admiration or providing a positive experience for the individual with the disability, it is both distancing and objectifying.

Viewing PWDs as Animals

In this section, look for—

- ✧ ways in which society views PWDs as less than human
- ✧ the four dimensions of ascribing humanness to PWDs, according to Bogdan and Taylor (1987)

You will remember that in Chapter 1 when we discussed the concept of normalcy we read the following statement of Wolfensberger (1972): "Normalcy is often confused with humanity" (p. 205). Implied in this statement is the corresponding idea that disability is not associated with humanity. Davis (1997b) stated, "To have a disability is to be an animal" (p. 20). A brief listing of the derisive names applied to PWDs illustrates Wolfensberger's statement: Joseph Merrick, the 19th century Englishman with neurofibromatosis, was called the "Elephant Man"; a woman who was born without several fingers on each hand is called "Lobster Claws"; freak shows exhibited "Jo-Jo, the Dog-faced Boy" and "Lionel, the Lion-faced Man"; Samuel D. Parks, a dwarf without legs, was billed as "Hopp, the Frog Boy"; a native of New Guinea, Prince Randian, had no arms or legs and was billed as the "Snake Man" and the "Caterpillar Man" (Pelka, 1997); and a man with intellectual disability is called "Monkey Boy." Mackelprang and Salsgiver (1999) proposed that "disabilities suggest to people humankind's imperfections and dissimilarities to God while illuminating humankind's relationship to the imperfect animal kingdom" (pp. 37–38). In 1998 in Utah, a manager of a large grocery store referred to and addressed an employee who bagged groceries (and who had an intellectual disability) as "Monkey Boy." When the bagger was out in the parking lot gathering up shopping carts, the manager would use the loudspeaker to call the bagger back into the store, addressing him as "Monkey Boy." The bagger's parents sued the grocery store chain (Mims, 1998).

People who used sign language were called "ape-like." A teacher at the Pennsylvania School for the Deaf observed in 1873 that sign language was "being decried, denounced, and ridiculed . . . as a set of monkey-like grimaces and antics" (Pettingill, 1873, cited in Baynton, 1997b). Furthermore, the ability to speak was often "the constituting force of humanity" (Nelson & Berens, 1997, p. 52), and, therefore, people who were deaf and did not speak were not considered to be human "in the relentlessly aural world of early modern England . . . [where] civilization was possible only through *spoken* [italics added] language" (Nelson & Berens, 1997, p. 52). St. Augustine denied church membership to individuals who were deaf, including the right to communion or the other sacraments, based on the assumption that they could not confess their sins.

Rée (1999) emphasized that it was not only novels and plays that have declared Deaf people to be less than human, but also scholarly works of science, philosophy, and anthropology:

> Such stories and parables about the inhumanity, irrationality, stupidity and depravity of the dumb (mute) are numerous and quite well attested, and for centuries they have been circulated as if they were plain and unassailable facts. And yet, the accounts cannot possibly be true, not even metaphorically and approximately. . . . There are numerous fictions about mutism, but they are to be found not in works of imaginative literature, but in the archives of natural history and philosophical anthropology. (p. 93)

Commenting on the experiences of Joseph Merrick, Darke (1993) made the observation that English Victorian society dehumanized and objectified PWDs "rather than representing abnormality/disability as human and valid in itself" (p. 340). Darke remarked that PWDs were thought of as "potential exhibits in what was a cross between a zoo and a museum" (p. 339). What are typically viewed in a museum? Objects. What are typically viewed in a zoo? Animals. Goffman (1963), speaking about all types of stigmatized people, stated, "[They] are not quite human" (p. 3).

A famous Deaf actor, Bernard Bragg, provided another example of PWDs being viewed as less than human, perhaps on a subconscious level. Bragg was approached by a producer of documentaries who wished to make a film on language and asked Bragg to write and star in a segment on sign language. On asking about the other segments of the proposed film and learning that the other parts of the film would present communication among whales and chimpanzees, Bragg refused to participate. The film producer was surprised and perplexed, not understanding how insulting such associations are (Bragg, 1989).

It is well known that people who live in institutions are often not thought to be fully human by their caregivers (Livneh, 1980). Criminals often choose PWDs as their targets because they often do not think of PWDs as human, and, therefore, these criminals do not experience guilt and remorse for their crimes. Also, the myth that PWDs are insensitive or indifferent to pain increases the likelihood that they will be abused. Other examples of not viewing PWDs as fully human include scientists and researchers who have, in the past, used PWDs as research subjects. Of course, it is not unethical to use people as research subjects; however, PWDs have often been used in unethical medical experiments simply because PWODs would have refused to participate (and had the power to enforce that refusal). For instance, in the 1960s in Sweden, individuals with intellectual disability were fed high-sugar diets to establish a causal link between sugar and tooth decay. The headlines of the news stories that reported these experiments included the words *guinea pigs* and *laboratory rats* to describe the subjects of these studies.

Wolfensberger and Tullman (1982) described ways in which society views children with disabilities as animals:

> If a group of children is [unconsciously] viewed as animals, then they may be segregated in a special class that is given an animal name—often even the name of animals that are seen as expressive of the devalued children's identity. Thus, a class for retarded [*sic*] children may be called "The Turtles." The animal kingdom may serve as an analogue for or source of service measures for that group of people. (pp. 134–135)

Technology and neonatal medical science have added another dimension to the question of ascribing humanity to PWDs. Such questions of humanity now apply to unborn babies. Now that it is possible, in some cases, to determine the presence of severe and multiple disabilities in unborn children, should these babies be born?

Unnecessary Dependence

In this section, look for—

◇ how PWDs define dependence differently
◇ how PWODs often misinterpret adaptive coping responses of PWDs to be dependence
◇ how PWODs often promote unnecessary dependence for PWDs

The idea of independence and dependence is probably defined a little differently by everyone. In other words, independence and dependence are very idiosyncratically defined. Nonetheless, we can broadly state that independence means having control over one's life and one's decisions, which includes (a) control of the resources necessary to care for oneself; (b) the choice of affiliation with other people, in families, in friendships, and in colleague groups; and (c) the freedom to make choices for oneself. For anyone, with or without a disability, the resources necessary to care for oneself include economic empowerment (which usually means a job); in addition, for PWDs, included in the resources necessary to care for oneself may be medical care, complete information about the disability, assistive technology, personal care attendants, and the services of other types of caregivers. Physical independence is relatively easy to describe and define; emotional independence is more difficult to define. However, Anne Finger (1990) observed that some types of physical dependence are acceptable to PWODs, while others are not. She uses the examples of using a car (acceptable to PWODs) and using a wheelchair (unacceptable to PWODs). A second set of examples includes going to a hairstylist for a haircut (acceptable to PWODs) and having an attendant wash your face (not acceptable to PWODs). For instance, what one person describes as emotional independence, another might describe as loneliness and isolation.

Of course, no one, with or without a disability, is completely independent. Everyone depends on someone else to some extent; however, most of us would agree that the greater the degree of independence an individual experiences, the more options he or she enjoys. Indeed, independence is considered to be one of the *sine qua non* of quality of life. It is safe to state that our "value system distrusts and devalues dependence in other people and vulnerability in general" (Wendell, 2006, p. 261). PWDs are often viewed as both dependent and vulnerable.

PWDs often define and interpret dependence and independence differently. Whereas independence is valued and needless dependence is avoided, PWDs do not "glorify independence" (B. A. Wright, 1960). Control and consent are important components of independence. Indeed, what is thought to be independence, for many PWDs, is neither possible nor a great need. A professional artist who requires the services of a personal care attendant explained:

> My attendant is an extension of my body. It takes a very emotionally strong as well as spiritually strong person to understand that and not resent it. If I don't direct the person, then I'm dependent on that person. Then I'm not autonomous and ultimately it's harder on the attendant. I made it very clear that I'm not making decisions for *them*, only for myself. (Panzarino, 1993, p. 111)

Notice the way in which Panzarino redefined the concept of autonomy (or independence). Most people who have had no experience with personal care attendants would assume that being fed, bathed, and dressed by a paid attendant would make an individual feel dependent and helpless. In contrast, when Ms. Panzarino is directing the attendant, she feels autonomous and in control. Notice also that she is aware that when she does not remain independent and directive, it makes the attendant's job harder. Ms. Panzarino also explains that it is possible for an individual to become overly dependent on an attendant.

Leonard Kriegel, in his book, *Falling Into Life* (1991), details how learning to fall was a turning point in the recovery of his independence. When he was 11 years old, Kriegel contracted polio and his legs were paralyzed. To learn how to walk in his braces, it was necessary to learn how to fall properly and to get back on his feet. The physical therapists taught these skills to all the patients, but Kriegel would not allow himself to fall, explaining:

> The prospect of letting go was precisely what terrified me. That the other boys in the ward had no trouble falling added to my shame and terror. I knew there was virtually no chance of injury when I fell, but the knowledge simply made me more ashamed of a cowardice that was as monumental as it was unexplainable. (pp. 10–11)

For Kriegel, falling down meant a loss of independence and succumbing to failure. When he does learn to fall, he writes in almost biblical language of how learning to deliberately and autonomously sacrifice his independence by falling is the beginning of learning how to control his body:

> I dropped. I did not crash. I dropped. I did not collapse. I dropped. I did not plummet. I felt myself enveloped by a curiously gentle moment in my life. In that sliver of time before I was kissed by the mat, I could sense my shame and fear drain from my soul, and I knew that my sense of my own cowardice would soon follow. In falling, I had given myself a new life, a new start. (p. 8)

Kriegel, at age 11, had redefined independence.

In the American culture, independence is both highly valued and narrowly defined. Naturally, PWDs value independence and autonomy and also know that they have a right to independence. They simply redefine these concepts. Also, they manipulate both their personal environment and the disability to achieve independence. However, PWDs cannot manipulate all of the physical environment or the attitudes of PWODs. Obviously, for some PWDs, there are activities they will not be able to do, regardless of how much they "try harder" (Phillips, 1991). PWODs may unwittingly curtail the independence of PWDs in an attempt to be helpful. For example, encouraging the use of prostheses that serve no functional purpose, but instead are uncomfortable and confining, diminishes the independence of the PWD.

Often PWODs misinterpret assertive and independent behaviors of PWDs. For example, the use of certain assistive devices to conserve energy (an individual using a wheelchair or scooter when he or she is capable of walking but wants to conserve his or her energy for something more important), the side effects of medication (falling asleep in public places), and all sorts of strategies to complete activities of daily living (such as keeping the clean dishes in the refrigerator) are sometimes viewed, erroneously, by PWODs as maladaptive and dependent behaviors. When PWDs ask for accommodations or assistance, for example, they are often seen as being dependent and passive. Does it make sense for a very highly paid corporate attorney to spend 2 and a half hours in the morning dressing himself or herself and finishing exhausted, or should a personal care attendant be hired? Obviously, the attorney is capable of dressing himself or herself, but how rational is the decision to do as much for oneself as possible in this particular case? At other times, when PWDs resist or refuse assistance, they are seen as rude and ungrateful. Unwanted assistance may be viewed by PWDs as attempts to control them. Certainly, because PWODs have so little understanding of the experience of disability, it is difficult for them to judge the degree of independence a PWD has.

Society can, and does, impose unnecessary dependence on PWDs. Certainly, the Biomedical Model of disability has never encouraged PWDs to be active, assertive, or independent (Zola, 1972). Medical and human service bureaucracies are often dehumanizing, expecting passive compliance from patients and clients. The services provided are intended to assist the individual; however, the expectations of passive compliance promote needless dependence and prevent the individual from making his or her own choices and decisions. Residential schooling, institutionalization, and prolonged hospitalization also contribute to promoting needless dependence. Decision making is a skill that individuals learn in small incremental steps. For example, children in kindergarten make their daily clothing choices, and young adults choose marriage partners and careers. In between kindergarten and young adulthood, there are many choices and decisions appropriate to the individual's age. For individuals who have lived in institutions and have not been allowed to make decisions of when they will sleep, when they will eat, or what they will eat, typical adult independence can seem overwhelming.

Society institutionalizes dependence for PWDs. By giving children with disabilities inferior education, by making policies and regulations that incorporate financial disincentives that make it difficult for PWDs to go to work, and by refusing to provide accommodations, society has institutionalized unnecessary dependence for PWDs.

The unwillingness to provide accommodations (as mandated by the ADA) can be recognized in thoughtless comments such as, "Don't these people lip read?" It can be seen in a sign with a picture of a wheelchair that states, "Ring for assistance" or in signs that direct wheelchair users to use the delivery entrance. Another example of reluctance to provide accommodations is reflected in efforts to determine if PWDs will attend specific events. As we have already learned, it is both irrelevant and illegal to provide physical accessibility *only* after it has been determined that PWDs will need them. Certainly, it is clear from these examples that the independence of PWDs has been needlessly limited, and it is surprising that most individuals would consider these examples to be adequate accommodations for PWDs. Imrie (1996) summarized: "Mobility [is] liberty for the human body" (p. 18). Facilities, both public and private, that are accessible to PWODs and are necessary for day-to-day living are unavailable to PWDs. This is an example of institutionalizing needless dependence for PWDs.

A blind English–Spanish court interpreter for the New York State Supreme Court told how difficult it was to ask for accommodations when she was new on the job. (She had threatened a lawsuit to be considered for the job and was therefore unwilling to appear demanding.)

> Having Braille indicators on the elevators would have made my life easier, but I didn't ask for them because I felt I shouldn't make any special demands. Now, eight years later, I feel a lot more comfortable asking for what I need, but I feel silly demanding changes in the elevator at this point, when I have been using them as they are for so long. I guess asking for help is not yet as easy for me as I would like it to be. But it is an issue that all of us as disabled [*sic*] people need to keep struggling with—to make sure we get what we need. (Crespo, 1993, p. 98)

Until the last 50 years, the greatest limitations faced by Deaf individuals were illiteracy and lack of language (not a *spoken* language, but a *signed* language). It is clear that these limitations were not caused by deafness, but rather society's *management and treatment* of Deaf people. The oralist movement insisted that Deaf children learn to speak vocally and lip read. The difficulty, if not impossibility, of teaching Deaf children to speak orally and lip read is explained below.

> Imagine you were born in a glass cage. There are people on the outside mouthing Japanese at you, but you don't know Japanese. How would you ever learn to lipread the language? (Fox, 2007, p. 28)

Without a language, it is impossible to communicate, receive, and discuss abstract ideas, and the intellectual development of even the brightest Deaf child can be permanently arrested (Fox, 2007). The misguided and paternalistic oralist movement led to the origins of the Deaf Culture. Unnecessary dependence, and other issues, resulted from PWODs trying to help. Forbidding children to use sign language does not turn Deaf children toward speech, but away from language—both spoken and signed.

Dependence is also fostered by the false stereotype that PWDs can never contribute. According to this stereotype, all assistance and contribution is one-way—all given to the PWD, with the PWD never being acknowledged as a benefactor or a contributor. Looking back to Chapter 4 and the example of Greg Smith and his Onarollathon fundraiser for Literacy Volunteers of America, we can see that PWDs, like everyone else, like to contribute to the community and to their families. Smith planned his fundraiser to coincide with the Labor Day Jerry Lewis telethon to make a strong point that PWDs participate in community service.

Marginality

Everyone wants to know where he or she belongs in the world. The concept of marginality was originally discussed in relation to members of racial and ethnic minority groups (Stonequist, 1937). The condition of marginality occurs when an individual, because of his or her membership in a devalued group (sometimes referred to as *defining status*), is not allowed to participate fully in the life of the community according to his or her interests and abilities. Stonequist posited that because racial and ethnic minority individuals were barred from full participation in the life of society, these individuals were caught between two groups—the dominant, powerful majority group and their own minority group. Gist and Dworkin (1972) described a marginal person as "one who lives in two worlds, in both of which he [*sic*] is more or less a stranger" (p. 10).

A mother of an older child with Down syndrome always says to people, "Invest in inclusion, but keep one foot firmly planted in the DS community. This is where your kid's ultimate friendships are going to come from (Solomon, 2012, p. 175). Another mother with children with ASD succinctly summarized, "Nobody liked my kids. They weren't likeable, but if somebody had acted like they were, maybe that would have helped" (Solomon, 2012, p. 240).

The solution to remedying the condition of marginality seems simple—the individual should choose his or her identity in one of the two groups. This is not possible, because the power of definition is held by the dominant group. In other words, it does not matter how the individual defines himself or herself, because the individual's position is determined by how the dominant group defines him or her. Therefore, the defining characteristic must be visible. The theory of marginality holds that (a) the majority group will not allow the minority individual entrance, stating that the individual has no legitimate claim to this status, and (b) the minority individual does not want to identify with his or her minority group because of the subordinate status. Therefore, the individual belongs to neither group and lacks a strong identification with any one group. Minority group individuals know far more about the majority group than the reverse. To survive, minority group members, including PWDs, must know about the majority culture. In contrast, majority group members often have little interest in or need to know about the minority group. Indeed, PWODs, unless they have had a family member with a disability, usually have not been interested in learning about the experiences and perspectives of PWDs.

Some aspects of marginality can be applied to individuals with disabilities, while others cannot. Charles Mee, a survivor of polio, wrote of one of his first realizations of his own marginality. He described marginality perfectly: "This world seemed too foreign to me, and at the same time so familiar" (p. 131). Notice how, as a teenager, the only way in which he can describe this realization is to compare his situation with that of a racial minority.

> I spent many hours in the living room, watching Ed Sullivan's *Toast of the Town* and Sid Caesar's *Your Show of Shows* and *Ozzie and Harriet* and *I Love Lucy*.
>
> These shows, and their commercials, made me dizzy with their vision of a world so wholesome, intact, healthy, vigorous, upbeat, smooth-skinned, smiling, sleek, plump; with all the unattainable girls in swimming suits, each one of them incredibly sexy even as they were evidently not thinking about sex or anything other than purity, purity of soap and purity of complexion and purity of thought, the purity of a perfect Ipana toothpaste smile; clean people, good people, winning people, with their milk shakes and hamburgers and French fries, bobby sox and swirling skirts and snug sweaters, their pep and vigor. This world seemed too foreign to me, and at the same time so familiar: actually, in many confusing ways, this vision of the close-knit, happy family, secure in the possession of the basic consumer durables, described my life. But at the same time, in some way I couldn't put my finger on, I knew this was not my world at all. I thought: Oh, I think I know how *Negroes* feel. I thought: These people on television could be from the moon. (Mee, 1999, p. 131)

In 1948, a disability scholar (Barker, cited in Goffman, 1997) stated that PWDs "live on a social-psychological frontier constantly facing new situations" (p. 215). Disability scholars use words such as "marginality" and "frontier" to describe the experience and identity of PWDs. An individual who is deaf and blind communicated his sense of marginality when he stated, "I see myself within the world, against the world, but not really part of the world" (Petty, 1979, p. 10).

In his classic text, *Stigma: Notes on a Spoiled Identity,* Goffman (1948) related the following example of marginalization, told by a newly blinded man:

I was expected to join this world (the blind world). To give up my profession and to earn my living making mops. I was to spend the rest of my life making mops with other blind people, eating with other blind people, dancing with other blind people. I became nauseated with fear, as the picture grew in my mind. Never had I come upon such destructive segregation. (p. 37)

In the case of visible disabilities, the PWD is often denied membership in the dominant culture. However, the concept of marginality includes the necessity of two cultures, between which the PWD can be caught. Until recently, there was no disability culture with which a PWD could identify. Indeed, much of the literature on the marginality of racial and ethnic minority individuals speaks about the loss of minority cultures because individuals have decided to take on the identity of the dominant group or, at minimum, to have their children and grandchildren take on this identity. Again, until very recently, there has been no disability culture to lose or to retain. Nonetheless, many PWDs do feel caught. For example, the title of Higgins's (1992b) book, *Outsiders in a Hearing World*, clearly communicates the alienation of the Deaf.

The term *status inconsistency* describes the experience of the person who is marginal. Status inconsistency refers to the ambivalence, self-hatred, and heightened sensitivity to insults and threats that the marginal person experiences. Rather than viewing these individuals as bicultural, adaptable, and flexible, social scientists and scholars viewed them as being "pulled in two directions" or having internalized the negative views of the dominant group toward their own group. Thus, the dominant group has effectively taught minority individuals to feel inferior.

Margins and frontiers (or borders) sound like physical places, but in sociological and psychological references, margins and frontiers are most often used as metaphors. However, when we read the autobiographical accounts of PWDs, there are often references to "I lived in another country" (R. M. Cohen, 2004; Murphy, 1987). Robert Murphy, a professor of anthropology at Columbia University, became paralyzed as a result of a tumor of the spinal cord, from which he eventually died. Murphy used his academic field of anthropology to understand and describe his experience of disability. He describes the feeling of marginality as going on a long trip (or sojourn) and leaving his native culture:

Just as an anthropologist gets a better perspective on his culture through long and deep study of a radically different one, my extended sojourn in disability has given me, like it or not, a measure of my estrangement far beyond the yield of any trip. I now stand somewhat apart from American culture, making me in many ways a stranger. And with this estrangement has come a greater urge to penetrate the veneer of cultural differences and reach an understanding of the underlying unity of all human experience. (pp. 102–103)

When Anne Finger (1990), a polio survivor, attended her first support group with other polio survivors, she said, "It was as if I was living all my life in a foreign country, speaking a language which was not mine." Until that first support meeting, which she attended when she was an adult, we are left to conclude that Finger felt that everyone around her was speaking a foreign language. Nonetheless, there may be some status inconsistency because Finger said, "I wanted to be able to embrace this community. And I wanted to be able to walk away from it, too. I want to be able to return to the world in which I more or less passed for able" (pp. 16–17).

Simpson and Yinger (1985), two sociologists, stated:

> Other authors emphasize the personal instability that they believe is likely to characterize persons who lack a strong feeling of identification with one group. Minority-group members who feel torn between association with the group in which they are categorically placed by prejudice and their feelings of identification with the dominant society may lack some of the security that comes from stable and acceptable group relationships. (p. 124)

Whether the psychopathology, psychological strain, personality disorganization, ambivalence, and lack of identity (none of which is a positive trait) must always be present in the marginal person is somewhat unclear. The scientific theory of the marginal person may have added to the prejudice and discrimination against minority individuals (see Stonequist, 1937, 1961).

Most PWODs experience a certain level of acceptance and respect and are allowed to function within a relatively wide comfort zone. Physical accessibility of the environment also contributes to the privileges of PWODs. According to I. Young (1990), marginalization is the "most dangerous" (p. 54) form of discrimination for PWDs because marginalization removes PWDs from social life, and inferior education and lack of accommodations remove PWDs from economic life. Further, marginal people, including PWDs, must submit to "the invasive authority of social service providers and other public and private administrators who enforce the rules with which the marginal must comply, and otherwise exercise power over the conditions of their lives" (p. 54).

Sociologists describe individuals who experience status inconsistency as people who have acquired many of the achievements and statuses of the dominant group but, nonetheless, are still identified as being a member of a minority group. Therefore, PWDs with high occupational positions, high incomes, high levels of education, and prestige are aware that, notwithstanding these accomplishments, they are readily perceived as members of a devalued group. Therefore, when these PWDs are among strangers, the strangers have no way (usually) of knowing the *achieved status* (the education, money, prestige), but only see the PWD's *ascribed status* (as a PWD).

In summary, PWDs must negotiate a relationship with a world that ignores, devalues, and rejects them. Further, the PWD may be open to attack from both sides—from PWODs and PWDs. If the PWD tries to pass as not having a disability, other PWDs may think of him or her as a "closet crip." If the PWD appears to be overly eager to please PWODs and "grateful for any crumbs" (Pelka, 1997, p. 305), other PWDs may call him or her a "Tiny Tim."

Equal Social Status Relationships

In this section, look for—

- ✧ differing levels of social distance
- ✧ the way in which dating is, for PWDs, Mount Everest

Friendships, family relationships, and loving and sexual relationships are quality-of-life issues. Most people seek out and develop these types of equal social status associations. However, the segregation, isolation, and institutionalization of PWDs have created physical distance between PWDs and PWODs, which in turn has created social distance. Moreover, the stereotyping, role entrapment, lowered expectations, solo status, infantilization, paternalism, objectification, and unnecessary dependence that PWDs experience work together to make equal social status relationships difficult to initiate and maintain.

Social distance is defined by sociologists as "the degree of intimacy which group norms allow between any two individuals" (Poole, 1927, p. 115). Theories of social distance were originally developed to describe relationships between individuals of differing racial, ethnic, cultural, and religious groups. Bogardus (1928) devised a numerical scale that listed six degrees of social distance. These include allowing members of a certain group (6) to visit my country, (5) to gain citizenship in my country, (4) to gain employment in my occupation, (3) to live on my street as neighbors, (2) to join my club as personal friends, and (1) to have close kinship by marriage. This order, from least intimate to most intimate, describes the degree of social relationship desired or allowed.

Other measures of social distance include the progressive steps of speaking with an acquaintance, speaking with a work colleague, having a member of a family marry this type of individual, and marrying this type of individual oneself. While these measures of social distance may be somewhat outdated (and were originally developed for racial and ethnic minority relationships), there are several ways in which they apply to PWDs. As we have discussed, perceived characteristics of PWDs, such as intelligence, social class, and level of education, influence the judgment of others. Those PWDs who are thought to be of higher social class, with more education, will probably experience less social distance than PWDs who are thought to not possess these characteristics. Therefore, there is an interplay of both the disability status and other types of desired characteristics.

However, it is safe to state that most PWDs experience more difficulty in establishing all types of equal social status relationships (DeLoach, 1994; Fisher & Galler, 1988). The widely held idea that PWDs are not able to contribute and must always be passive recipients contributes to this difficulty. On an impersonal level, we have seen how the idea that PWDs are incapable of making contributions has led to their high underemployment and unemployment rates. In spite of this widely held myth, PWDs have made important contributions as workers during labor shortages and world wars. On a personal level, this false idea has led to the unquestioned assumptions that PWDs must overachieve to be considered equal. Often, others, including professionals, automatically assume that a child with a disability is an unwanted burden to his or her parents, never considering that a child with a disability is more likely a source of joy to the parents.

Intimate, loving relationships are even more difficult (than friendships or workplace colleagues) for PWDs to achieve as a result of two widespread ideas: (a) PWDs are not interested in or capable of intimate and loving relationships, and (b) an intimate relationship between a PWD and a PWOD must be asymmetrical, or unbalanced, with the PWOD holding the position of power.

Many PWODs think that the onset of a disability means the end of all sexuality for the individual. For those with congenital disabilities, it is often thought that the individual will experience neither sexuality nor intimate, loving relationships. Romance is assigned the lowest value. The sexuality of PWDs is often misunderstood. At times, PWDs, such as those with intellectual disability or mental illness, are viewed as sexually dangerous and threatening; at other times, PWDs are seen as sexually unattractive, and at still other times, PWDs are viewed as uninterested or incapable. None of these views are true, but all these ideas consider PWDs to have some sort of sexual maladjustment.

Intimate relationships between a PWD and a PWOD are viewed as asymmetrical and stressful because the PWD is often thought to be a burden. Several scholars have written on the perceptions of PWODs who choose to marry a PWD or to engage in any long-term relationship with a PWD. Asch and Fine (1997) reported that others view the PWOD "as a saint or a loser" or someone who was forced into a "default position" (p. 247). Toombs (1995), a professor of English with multiple sclerosis, related that many people have said to her, "How *lucky* you are to have your husband" (p. 16). Unbalanced relationships of any kind, in which one individual is seen as the contributor and the other as the passive recipient, are stressful for both partners. The contributor (saint) might become resentful, and the recipient (burden) may feel insecure, fearing that his or her partner will leave.

PWDs have often internalized this view of relationships and have made comments such as, "There is a tendency for PWDs to feel grateful when someone loves them or pays attention to them." Another PWD says, "We are perceived as burdens" (Nordqvist, 1980). Abby Kovalsky stated, "I joined a dating service a year and a half ago. All I hear from the agency is that anyone who reads my profile and then sees my photo is basically not willing to meet someone with my disability" (Mackelprang & Salsgiver, 1999, p. 17). Equally distancing is the perception (held by PWODs) that

PWDs are either "saints" or "heroes." One woman with a disability stated, "I have a lot of people who respect me, but I have no friends."

Naturally, there are difficulties related to the disability itself when initiating and establishing relationships between PWDs and PWODs (Perduta-Fulginiti, 1996). M. J. Scheer (1993) quoted a man:

> On the romantic side, women have a tendency to move away from me. . . . It's like "see ya later." I mean, it's easy to find someone to say, "Okay, let's go out," but when it comes to the romantic side of it, they're not quite sure what to do, what to expect. Too, it's hard to approach someone when you're in a wheelchair, as opposed to the way it was before. I mean, what do you say? Can I buy you a drink, and, by the way, would you help me with mine? (p. 9)

Ironically, research shows that married people enjoy better health, probably as a result of eating better; having emotional support; and having someone to monitor one's health, including such behaviors as regular exercise, seat belt use, and undergoing routine medical examinations.

SECTION 3

THE INDIVIDUAL AND DISABILITY

To most readers, this section, which deals with the way in which the PWD and his or her family responds to a disability, is the most interesting. Nonetheless, before we can really understand the experience of the PWD, it was important to gain some insight into the topics of the first two sections of this book. The definition of the disability and the way in which society has chosen to deal with both disability and the individuals who experience disabilities direct the daily life of PWDs (or direct if they are allowed to live). Also, often the individual accepts societal viewpoints and definitions as self-definitions.

Most PWODs have little understanding of the day-to-day lives of PWDs, and, even worse, what little understanding they do have is often flawed, negative, and uninformed. In 2014, the film *The Theory of Everything* depicted the life of "the most brilliant celebrated astrophysicist, Dr. Stephen Hawking." Dr. Hawking was diagnosed with a degenerating motor neuron disease when he was a young adult. Termed a "British biographical romantic film," it is based upon the book written by Hawking's former wife, Jane Hawking. Jane Hawking's book, *Travelling to Infinity: My Life with Stephen* (2007), described many examples of day-to-day life with a husband who is quadriplegic, requiring help with all the basic functions of life, most of which were not included in the film. Juxtaposed with the very public glamor, awards, and international fame was the private struggle to gain accommodations and services from the government, and the daily grind of caring for someone who is quadriplegic. At the end of the book, Jane summarizes:

If, however, as once I did when being interviewed for the *Guardian* [a newspaper], I allowed myself to show any dissatisfaction with the trite, old clichés about the rewards of living with a genius—those oft-repeated truisms which dwelt on fame and fortune as if illness and disability were not fundamental factors in our lives—I would be accused of disloyalty to Stephen. But as I saw it, if I continued to perpetuate the myth of cheerful self-sufficiency without even mentioning the hardships, I would be cheating the many disabled people who were probably suffering all the heartache, the anxieties, the privations, the stress and strains. . . . I could no longer truthfully offer the carefree, smiling façade, giving the erroneous impression that our lives were contented and easy, marred only by a little local inconvenience. . . . I described how we fluctuated between the glittering peaks of brilliant success and the black sloughs of critical illness and despair, with very little ground between. (p. 447)

This third section includes many candid, unflinching first-person accounts of disability.

CHAPTER 6
THE INDIVIDUAL'S RESPONSE TO DISABILITY

✧ Why would many PWDs choose *not* to eliminate their disability if they could?

✧ Is there a real difference between the terms *acceptance of disability* and *response to disability*?

✧ How does an individual's ethnic, racial, cultural, or linguistic identification influence his or her response to a disability?

✧ When discussing an individual's response to a disability, why is it important to consider the individual's environment?

✧ Of the three types of response to disability—affective, cognitive, and behavioral—which is the most difficult to measure?

✧ Why is the PWD's subjective judgment of his or her disability often more important than the objective medical diagnosis?

✧ What is the difference between coping strategies and defense mechanisms?

✧ What are the advantages of the stage theory of adaptation and response?

✧ What are the three types of denial?

✧ Why is denial often considered to be therapeutic?

✧ How is transcendence defined?

✧ Why is transcendence in conflict with the Biomedical Model of disability?

✧ What are some cautions in implementing the stage theory?

The three major divisions of this book are (1) the definition of disability, (2) society and disability, and (3) the individual and disability. These convenient, easily understood demarcations are a starting point to learning about disability. However, these divisions are not actually experienced by anyone, nor do they represent reality. For instance, it is important to learn about the various definitions of disability—what a disability is and what a disability is not. So far we have learned that there are four definitions of disability: clinical, legal, cultural, and personal. This final section of the book will discuss the personal definitions of disability. However, definitions of disability are closely tied to society's perception of disability, and, furthermore, the individual's experience with a disability involves both the definition of disability and society's response to his or her disability. These interrelationships are complex and idiosyncratic (specific to each individual). No one with a disability thinks of his or her disability in these three divisions; indeed, to the individual there can be no neat, three-division paradigm to the disability experience. Nonetheless, it does make sense to discuss some basic issues to gain a preliminary understanding, but with the knowledge that these basic issues are only a starting point and that some aspects of the disability experience apply only to specific individuals. Disability happens to one person at a time.

Perhaps the title of this chapter should be "The Individual's Response to *Acquired Disability*" because an individual with a congenital disability, or a disability acquired during infancy, has incorporated the disability into his or her identity. Individuals with congenital disabilities have no memory of not having the disability. Nonetheless, there are adjustment demands for these individuals—not to a new identity, but to stigma recognition. Often, children with disabilities do not know until they enter school that their disabilities are perceived as inferiority and deviance. These children understand that (1) they have a disability and (2) their disability requires management, treatment, and accommodations, but they may not have experienced prejudice and discrimination. Therefore, a child with a disability must learn to adjust to and negotiate a prejudiced and discriminating environment.

Jacob, a boy who is deaf, asked his hearing mother, "Are you deaf?" She said that she was not. He asked, "Am I deaf?" She said he was. Then he signed, "I wish you were deaf" (Solomon, 2012, p. 76). Notice that Jacob does not say that he wished he could hear; he simply wanted his mother to be like him. At age 5, Jacob has not encountered (or understood) the stigma of being deaf.

For these reasons, this section of the book will use many first-person narratives in which PWDs tell us what they have experienced and learned. Can the disability experience be understood by someone who has not lived it? Probably not, but PWODs can begin to learn about disability. However, most PWDs have not written about their experiences, and, thus, their experiences with disability are unrecorded (Couser, 1997; Frank, 1991, 1995; Hawkins, 1993). Some of these narratives have found publishers because the authors are seen as super crips or disabled heroes, people with extraordinary resources or celebrity. Indeed, most of those who have written about the disability experience have been White, upper-class, highly educated individuals. Also, on the one hand, first-person accounts carry the weight of someone who has lived the experience, giving us an immediate and direct look at disability (Kleinman, 1988; Mairs, 1997a). On the other hand, every disability account must, of necessity, speak about individual circumstances. Nonetheless, there are some universal aspects of the disability experience, and furthermore, we can learn from the idiosyncratic aspects of these narratives (see Appendix 6.A for a listing of published narratives).

View From the Outside Versus Life on the Inside

In this section, look for—

✧ how PWODs assume that all PWDs would eliminate their disability if they could

✧ how most PWDs

- consider their disability to be an integral part of their identity
- are proud of their mastery of the disability
- consider their disability to have positive options

✧ how PWODs assume that the onset, acquisition, or diagnosis of every disability is always distressful to the individual

Myths Held by PWODs

Outsiders (meaning those who do not have a disability) often think they understand how PWDs feel about their disability. Naturally, such conceptions are based on an outsider's point of view; it is difficult to imagine the life of someone else. Moreover, rarely do PWODs question their own assumptions. We learned in Section 2 that most PWODs sensationalize and misunderstand disability, thinking that all disabilities are an unending source of tragedy and grief for the individual. One misconception, widely and strongly held, is that if the PWD were offered a way to eliminate the disability, he or she would enthusiastically accept it. Rarely do PWODs consider the possibility that the disability is an integral part of the PWD's self-identity or that the PWD might be proud of the mastery and control that he or she has gained over the disability.

Many of the first-person accounts of disability reveal that the individual would *not* choose to eliminate the disability (Davis, 1995). The most straightforward example is that of cochlear implants for individuals who are deaf. Cochlear implants are comprised of electrodes that are surgically placed in the inner ear to stimulate the nerve cells along a pathway to the auditory region of the brain. Designed to improve the individual's speech perception and oral communication, the cochlear implant has not been unanimously accepted by the Deaf community. First, it should be stated that not all cochlear implants are successful. But, even more important, the Deaf Culture feels that, as one scholar wrote,

> in America, the recognition of the status of the Deaf community, fueled by the civil rights movement, is leading to greater acceptance of people who are deaf. The interest of the child who is deaf and his [*sic*] parents may best be served by accepting that he is Deaf, with an elaborate culture and linguistic heritage that can enrich his parents' life as well as his own. We should heed the advice of the teenager who was deaf who, when reprimanded by her mother for not wearing the processor of her cochlear prosthesis, hurled back bitterly: "I'm deaf. Let me be deaf." (H. Lane, 1992, p. 238)

In learning about how the individual experiences his or her disability, it seems appropriate to begin by making the point that most PWDs consider their disability to be an integral part of their identity—not their sole identity, or even the most important part of the identity, but an important part. Therefore, it follows that PWDs would not eliminate the disability if they could. Cochlear implants, very much favored by people who are not deaf, including parents of children who are deaf and physicians, are sometimes refused by the Deaf.

Other first-person accounts describe PWDs who think of their disability as part of their identity and have no wish to eliminate it. In Rousso's book, *Disabled, Female, and Proud!* (1993), Rousso interviewed Barbara Cole-Appel, a woman who became paralyzed from an automobile accident. Cole-Appel told of a friend who asked her if she would rather win a $30 million lottery or regain the use of her legs, if either were possible. Cole-Appel responded:

> I decided that I would rather have the $30 million because losing the use of my legs has not inhibited me other than walking, as far as I'm concerned. Not being able to walk is something I have learned to live with. It's no longer something that I have to be able to do in order to feel complete. (p. 41)

Disability also involves impairment, sometimes the loss of valued activities, and sometimes pain; it often makes time demands on the individual and most often includes the prejudice and discrimination of the larger society. Nonetheless, the onset, acquisition, or diagnosis of a disability is not automatically distressing to everyone. Shontz (1991) summarized:

> Though many efforts have been made to correlate disability with overall personality maladjustment, no systematic evidence has yet been published to show that reactions involving psychiatric disturbance occur any more frequently with a truly representative sample of people with disabilities than within the general population. . . . The personality resources of an individual

may be strengthened, not weakened, when the stresses that disability imposes are successfully managed. (p. 108)

We have seen in Section 2 that the tendency of PWODs to view all disability as devastating and overwhelming tragedy has resulted in abortion, murder, and institutionalization of PWDs.

Acceptance of Disability or Response to Disability

In this section, look for—

- ✧ four reasons why *response* to disability is now the preferred term:
    1. It is not the disability itself, but the meaning the individual ascribes to it.
    2. There are many other types of acceptance, not simply psychological acceptance.
    3. The word *response* does not pathologize the disability experience.
    4. The individual copes with and responds to a disability throughout his or her life.

Disability scholars have used the terms *adjustment, adaptation,* or *acceptance* of disability to describe the end result of coping with a disability and successfully integrating the disability into the individual's life and identity. In the early stages of scholarship, adjustment to disability was conceptualized as a series of stages through which the individual passed, ending with acceptance of the disability. The current model of coping with a disability uses the term *response.* The word *response* is more accurate because it communicates more fully that (1) it is not disability itself, but the meaning that the individual ascribes to the disability that will determine the response to the disability; (2) there are many types of responses or adjustments to disability in addition to the psychological adjustment, including occupational and social adjustment or response; (3) the words *adjustment, adaptation,* and *acceptance* pathologize the experience of a disability, meaning a disability is automatically assumed to be an undesirable state (we would not say that a person adjusts to being a woman or a person of color); and (4) the individual, including those individuals with stable disabilities, copes with disability and makes adjustments throughout his or her lifetime, and, therefore, *acceptance* is not a one-time event. In this chapter, the expressions *response* and *reaction* and *adjustment, adaptation, and acceptance* will be used but with the awareness that *response* and *reaction* are more accurate terms.

In this section, we shall discuss the individual's response to disability in terms of the American culture. At times, references will be made to other cultures because an individual's cultural, linguistic, or ethnic identity affects the way in which the individual views and treats the disability. Further, behavioral manifestations of responding to a disability can only be interpreted with knowledge of the individual's cultural identity. What is considered to be acceptance of disability in one culture may not apply in another culture. Moreover, we have learned that disability itself is culturally defined, and, further, symptom recognition is also culturally and socially determined. For example, a man with a large family to provide for and who works at a physically demanding job may not recognize his chronic back pain as a disability. In this case, the individual's economic situation does not allow him or her to recognize (much less respond to) subjective discomfort. Also, the individual's perception of etiology is shaped by his or her cultural identification. For example, someone from a culture that is deterministic and fatalistic may feel that his or her automobile accident was meant to happen and not the result of anything that individual did or did not do. In contrast, an individual who identifies with the American culture may view the same automobile accident as his or her fault and thus engage in self-blame (Bordieri, 1993).

Carolyn Vash (1981), another disability scholar, introduced the concept of *transcendence*, which is a step beyond acceptance or adjustment to disability. Transcendence of a disability is a combination of refusing to idealize normality (lack of disability), adopting a spiritual or philosophical orientation to the disability, and "embracing the experience" (p. 135). Inherent in the concept of transcendence are the questions, "What can I learn from this disability?" and, "What positive options are available?" The disability is seen as a catalyst for the individual to grow and develop, with the individual feeling that he or she is a better person for having experienced a disability. According to Vash, when an individual has achieved transcendence, he or she views the disability as a tool, an asset, and an opportunity.

Consideration of the Individual's Environment

Reacting to a disability is not only a response to a physical, intellectual, cognitive, or psychiatric impairment; it also includes other factors in the individual's environment. Factors such as economic security, educational level, family support, and availability of treatment influence the disability experience. Therefore, Shontz (1975) argued that clinicians and researchers should consider the individual's environmental resources, rather than simply focusing on the psychodynamics of the PWD.

The factors that have not been fully addressed in the individual's response to the disability concern the degree of prejudice; discrimination toward the type and severity of disability; and whether the individual is also subject to prejudice or discrimination because of other perceived identities, such as belonging to other cultural, ethnic, or racial groups, being a woman, being older, or having a different sexual orientation. The degree of stigma and prejudice the individual experiences will influence his or her response to the disability. For example, people who do not have a heterosexual orientation and who also have a disability have a humorous way to describe their doubly stigmatized status: "I want to come out of the closet, but the doorway isn't wide enough for my wheelchair."

In addition to the PWD's social environment, the physical environment must also be considered. Certainly living in one's home is preferable to living in a residential facility. In the following excerpt, men and women with TBIs who lived in a residential facility were referred to as "lifers."

> I know Billy, Candy, Darrel, Michelle, and maybe Philip they're—they're lifers, they'll never get out of here you know, so they have to deal with someone telling them what to do for the rest of their lives and they, a lot of them, don't have an outside source that would speak for them. (Nichols & Kosciulek, 2014, p. 26)

Notice that many PWODs in residential facilities often do not have family or friends who could act as advocates and monitor the quality of care and services.

What Is a Good Response to a Disability?

In this section, look for—

✦ the three categories of response to disability: cognitive, behavioral, affective

✦ which response is easiest to define and measure

There is a vast range in the definitions of disability; there is great variability in the severity or degree of disability; and PWDs have many environmental factors and varying types of psychological and emotional coping abilities. Added to this combination of disability variables are the differing levels of stigma directed toward specific disabilities. In Chapter 4 we learned about the hierarchy of stigma toward disabilities. The clinical picture of an individual's adjustment to a psychiatric disability would not be complete without recognizing that psychiatric disabilities are the most stigmatizing disabilities in our society. Having stated the great variability of the experience of disability, it is nonetheless possible to list some general attributes, behaviors, and manifestations of a positive response to disability.

Generally speaking, response to a disability can be divided into three categories: cognitive, behavioral, and affective. *Cognitive* means how one chooses to view (or to think about) the disability. A positive or good cognitive response to disability includes redefining reality rather than ignoring it or denying it. *Behavioral* responses to disability include active mastery of the disability; compliance with treatment regimens; seeking out social support; returning to work; and, for many PWDs, actively fighting against the stigma and prejudice of society. *Affective* response means how the individual feels about the disability and how he or she manages emotions. Of course, the individual does not view his or her coping responses as neatly divided into these three categories. A behavioral response to disability is relatively easy to operationally define and measure. Cognitive and affective responses are more difficult to measure. These types of assessments are made either by interviewing the PWD or family members or via paper-and-pencil psychological instruments. Of course, extreme and severe affective (emotional) responses such as total denial of the disability, externalized anger and aggression, abuse of alcohol or drugs, family conflict and dissolution, and openly expressed self-blame are readily observable. However, most affective responses are less extreme and, therefore, are less obvious and more difficult to measure and assess.

The literature on the individual's response to disability describes an individual with a positive response as someone who is flexible, demonstrates active mastery, rallies social support, and is capable of tolerating a degree of ambiguity. On acquiring a disability, normality (which is the absence of ambiguity, and what is familiar to the individual) is gone. For most people, the experience of acquiring a disability, especially a severe disability or multiple disabilities, is a novel situation, one with which he or she has not had any experience. One of the first responses of a PWD is a desire to return to normality—that is to say, the individual's idiosyncratic conception of normality. A positive response does not view normality as the absence or cure of the disability; it conceptualizes normality as the reinstatement of the individual's identity, family, social system, home, status, income, professional identity, and sexuality (after the medical stabilization of the disability). The extent to which the individual is able to regain these aspects of his or her life will determine his or her response to the disability. An individual who is considered to have a positive response is judged to have a realistic view of the disability—is aware of the limitations but not exaggerating them (Yoshida, 1993).

As would be expected, it is easier to judge or assess the behavioral manifestations of response to disability than the affective or cognitive responses. Behavioral responses can be observed, measured, and quantified. In contrast, clinicians must rely on the self-report of the PWD to obtain some understanding of affective or cognitive responses. Behavioral responses such as complying with treatment and rehabilitation regimens, increasing activity levels, seeking out social support, and returning to work are relatively easy to operationally define and measure. The degree of emotional stress, physical pain, hope, and optimism for the future, however, are difficult to define and measure. Nonetheless, it is these subjective responses to disability that influence the individual's help-seeking behaviors and response to the disability.

What Is a Poor Response to a Disability?

In this section, look for—

♦ the indicators of a poor response to disability

♦ the difference between coping skills and defense mechanisms

An individual may perceive his or her disability as (1) loss of status, (2) loss of social support, (3) loss of functioning, and (4) loss of control, with the thought that he or she will be isolated, dependent, and a burden on others. Further, in the American culture, the PWD may feel that he or she has somehow violated his or her duty to *not* acquire a disability.

Other studies of individuals with various types of disability have described poor response to disability as including unnecessary dependence on others, social isolation resulting from shame about the disability, feelings of helplessness, negative body image and self-esteem, anger and aggression toward others, longstanding feelings of dissatisfaction, high levels of stress, hypersensitivity to criticism, passivity, developmental immaturity, exhibiting an external locus of control, hypermorality, internalized anger and depression, holding unrealistic hopes of a cure, relying on defense mechanisms such as rigidity, holding on to the past, emotional lability (widely fluctuating moods), resignation (giving up), and humorlessness. Coupled with these poor responses is the lack of a realistic plan for dealing with the disability.

Coping strategies are different from defense mechanisms. Coping strategies are considered to be goal-directed, positive steps, such as rallying social support, obtaining treatment and rehabilitation, redefining life goals, and seeking information. In contrast, defense mechanisms are an effort to avoid anxiety and reality, and, most often, the individual is not aware that he or she is using them. Examples of defense mechanisms are regression (preoccupation with the past when the individual did not have the disability, or returning to a less mature pattern of behavior), projection (attributing one's own feelings to someone else), displacement (blaming others), withdrawal (socially isolated and unable to form therapeutic alliances with service providers), denial (at certain stages in the adjustment period, denial is considered to be therapeutic), and depersonalization (detachment from self). Professional caregivers *reinforce* coping strategies but *challenge* the use of defense mechanisms.

The Stage Model of Adaptation to Disability

In this section, look for—

- ✧ how not all disabilities have a traumatic, acute onset or diagnosis
- ✧ how, for most disabilities, the individual is not able to engage in anticipatory adjustment
- ✧ how *difficult* does not always mean *tragic*
- ✧ how the stage model does not apply to deteriorating conditions
- ✧ how it is helpful to have some broad guidelines in predicting the course and outcome of the adjustment or response process

The stage theory of adaptation, or response, to disability provides some helpful guidelines in understanding and predicting the course and outcome of the individual's response process. This process is a gradual assimilation of an altered identity and is a continuous, ongoing process, not a one-time event (Livneh, 1986a, 1986b). Arnold Beisser (1989), the physician who contracted polio on his way to report for military duty, termed his response to the effects of polio to be like a marriage because he and his disability were in a long-term but ever-changing relationship. Fred Davis studied 14 young patients with polio and their families in Baltimore, Maryland, in the 1950s. Davis's study clearly showed how slowly the families and the individuals with polio adjusted to the idea of residual disability and a lengthy rehabilitation. Most of the families had expected a fairly short time in rehabilitation with no resulting disability (Wilson, 1990). Parents of a baby who was diagnosed with dwarfism reported that each time they attended support meetings they came home and took Pepto Bismol.

> Paul said, "Why don't you come over to our house after the meeting. We're going to have dessert in the evening." I remember sitting on the couch. These people had all their furniture cut down. Well, we had the best time. We got up ready to go and when we stood, that's when it hit me. Because when we were sitting, everyone was the same. But when we stood up, these people were down below my waist. Our heads were spinning and our stomachs were churning and we went home. We ended up being involved, and going to other meetings that they had because we felt that it was important for Joey to have that exposure at that time, if he was indeed a dwarf, which is a permanent condition. These people were real people in different professions and a lot of members were a big help during that time. But we used to have to take Pepto Bismol when we got home, because even though we'd had a good time; it was the reality of it all. And I think that's what's good. I think that's good for parents, to be hit with the reality. You find you're enjoying it, but when you go home, you suffer the effects of that reality—that my child is not going to grow. He's really going to stay small. (Ablon, 1989, p. 357)

Interestingly, the parental adjustment after the birth of a baby with achondroplasia (dwarfism) might continue for generations since Little People tend to marry other Little People and these couples may have children who are Little People.

Responding to a disability is a continuous process and a reorientation of personal priorities and relationships. Not all disabilities have a sudden, acute, traumatic onset. For example, disabilities such as diabetes and lupus have an insidious onset, and therefore it is more accurate to speak of the time of diagnosis rather than the time of onset. Moving through these stages requires goal-directed changes in attitude and behavior, but this does not imply that the onset or diagnosis of every disability is thought to be tragic. The stage theory is based on theories of adaptation to loss, especially Kübler-Ross's (1969) theories of acceptance of one's death. The value of these theories to individuals (and their families) facing loss and death cannot be underestimated. However, there are two differences in the stage theory for death and loss and the stage theory of adaptation to disability. First, in many losses, or with regard to one's impending death, there is a period of anticipatory adjustment that allows the individual to both behaviorally and emotionally prepare for the loss before the loss actually happens. Such an anticipatory period rarely occurs for a PWD. (Exceptions to this would include situations such as individuals who have time to prepare for a therapeutic amputation.) Second, in losses such as divorce or death, the individual experiencing the loss usually does not experience prejudice, stigma, and discrimination from society, and, therefore, these stage theories do not consider the added stress of prejudice and discrimination. Indeed, many PWDs report that their greatest difficulty is not in dealing with the disability, but in confronting prejudice and discrimination. However, the stage theory of adaptation or response to disability remains silent on the prejudice and discrimination of society.

The stage theory of adaptation or response to disability probably does not apply as well to individuals who have gradually deteriorating conditions, especially elderly individuals. For example, people who experience the onset and diagnosis of a chronic, degenerating disability, such as arthritis or old-age deafness, typically do not go through the initial shock stage, nor would such individuals tend to experience long-term depression or mourning. These stages are neither inevitable nor universal (Olkin, 1999).

The Stages of Response in Disability

In this section, look for—

- ✧ shock
- ✧ defensive retreat
- ✧ depression or mourning
- ✧ personal questioning
- ✧ adaptation, change, and integration

Shock or Initial Impact

Robert Perkins, in his book, *Talking to Angels: A Life Spent in High Latitudes* (1996), described the shock of the diagnosis and onset of his mental illness:

> In the spring of 1968, I was nineteen and a freshman at Harvard College. I was soon to leave school, without even passing "GO" or finishing the year, to start a journey. A journey I have yet to complete. . . . To have the wind knocked out of you, hard, at nineteen. To give you the feeling of it, I'd hit you

on the side of the head, when you were not expecting it, with a flat board or a piece or rubber tubing. The shock of the thing! (pp. 5, 15)

In this stage, the individual's thinking is often disorganized, and he or she may feel overwhelmed and confused. Rereading Perkins's description, we can see the total unexpectedness and the devastating impact. First, he relates the abruptness of the onset as not being able to pass "GO." Then he describes the devastating impact in physical terms: being hit on the side of the head. Individuals in this stage of initial shock often feel that more is happening to them than they can understand or absorb. They are unable to think or feel. The combination of the suddenness of the onset and the significant changes often leads to shock.

An artist, Chuck Close (1993), described the sudden and thorough onset of his paralysis:

I was at Gracie Mansion in New York giving an award to someone. I suddenly had a tremendous pain in my chest that went through my back and my arms. I thought it was a heart attack. I went across the street to Doctors Hospital where, within a very a short time, I was totally paralyzed from the neck down. It was several days before they figured out what had happened, which was that an occluded or collapsed spinal artery had cut off the flow of blood to my spine and knocked out nerves all over my body. Virtually everything from the shoulders down was affected. (p. 17)

Another individual (Frese, 1997) describes the onset of schizophrenia:

I cannot tell you how difficult it is for a person to accept the fact that he or she is schizophrenic. Since the time when we were very young we have all been conditioned to accept that if something is crazy or insane, its worth to us is automatically dismissed. . . . The nature of this disorder is that it affects the chemistry that controls your cognitive processes. It affects your belief system. . . . It is exceedingly difficult for you to admit to yourself that the mind does not function properly. It fools you. (pp. 145–146)

From Frese's excerpt, we can see that society's prejudices and myths exerted a powerful influence on his reaction to his disability and on his self-esteem. The onset of Close's and Frese's disabilities was sudden and unpredictable, and the functional limitations were great. It is interesting to compare the cause of Frese's schizophrenia ("the chemistry that controls your cognitive processes") with the cause of Close's paralysis ("an occluded or collapsed spinal artery"). Although the causes of both disabilities are physical, it is only in Frese's account that prejudice and discrimination are mentioned.

It is not only the diagnosis and onset of a disability that precedes this type of shock. For some individuals, it is a particular point in the treatment or rehabilitation process that has idiosyncratic, shocking meaning. For example, one individual with a progressive neurological disease stated, "Going into the wheelchair was awful!" Another individual stated, "Going into the assisted living center was the worst day of my life. I will never forget it."

Jack Hofsiss experienced the shock of a "life that has been unalterably changed and played around with" when he returned home from the hospital. Hofsiss was paralyzed after a diving accident in a swimming pool.

> Still, in no way was I prepared for returning home. The hardest part is those first two or three months after you get back home. When you're in the hospital, the anonymity of the space allows you to keep at a distance the fact that your life has been unalterably changed and played around with. But when you get home, you're surrounded by all the things of daily life before the accident: Then you walk into the kitchen to get yourself a cup of coffee or a glass of milk. No longer. That's where the serious adjusting takes place. (Hofsiss & Laffey, 1993, p. 81)

Defensive Retreat or Denial

As the word *defensive* implies, this stage is often considered to be a therapeutic, adaptive strategy on the part of the PWD. Denial can take three basic forms: (1) denial of the presence of the disability, (2) denial of the implications of the disability, or (3) denial of the permanence of the disability. Denial allows the individual to maintain his or her self-identity (K. G. Langer, 1994; Stewart, 1994). An individual who denies the implications of the disability may think, "I'm the same as I always was" or may think, "I'll soon be walking" or, "I don't need to change any of my plans" or, "Everything will be like it was before." The individual understands that he or she has the disability but minimizes and downplays the effects of the disability and often tries to live in his or her predisability world. For example, Franklin Roosevelt denied the implications of his disability because he maintained that some day he would be able to walk. When an individual denies the permanence of the disability, he or she may feel that the disability will disappear, or, "Soon, I'll be my old self again." Denial of the presence of the disability is rare; denial of the implications or the permanence of the disability is more common. Families of PWDs frequently engage in denial when they view the disability as not changing the PWD's life or when they insist that the PWD will "return to normal." For example, a wife asks physicians, "When will he walk out of here?" (M. Dunn, 1996). Chuck Close (1993), the artist who became paralyzed, remembered the medical stabilization process as "calm and not as scary" as the day when the permanence of his paralysis became apparent:

> But my recollection was that it [medical stabilization] was quite calm and not as scary as when the deadening reality of the kind of day-in and day-out existence of not being able to move really set in. On the tenth, eleventh,

twelfth day you haven't moved a muscle from shoulders on down, and people are rolling you and over and back, attaching tubes and things, *that's* when you think, "Oh, it's never going to get any better than this." That's when it really gets scary. (p. 17)

For individuals with amputations, the stage of denial is often complicated and compounded by phantom limb pain.

A freelance journalist, Miles O'Brien, required the amputation of most of his left arm when a heavy case of photographic equipment fell on his left forearm. In the following excerpts he describes the way in which an injury progressed to an amputation, his phantom limb pain, and the idiosyncratic way in which he denied the amputation:

What began as a fairly bad bruise evolved into something life-threatening: acute compartment syndrome, which blocks blood flow. When I got to a doctor in Manila, (in the Philippines) he recognized the problem and sent me in for emergency surgery. He tried to save the arm, but it was too late. It was a life-or-limb decision. But, when the anesthesia receded and I rejoined the world of the living, I was convinced that the doctor had saved it.

. . . while my arm may be missing physically, it is there, just as it always has been, in my mind's eye. I can feel every digit. I can even feel the watch that was always strapped to my left wrist. . . . Doctors don't really know how to treat pain in a part of the body that is no longer there.

. . . I didn't let anyone know what had happened to me for more than a week. Maybe I could just heal a little, then sneak back home. You know, denial. . . . But, there was also a practical problem: As a freelancer, I eat what I kill. I had spent a lot of money on travel and on hiring local help. I had to deliver the work or take a huge loss. So I wrote my scripts, and when friends and family checked in, I acted as if all was well. (M. O'Brien, 2014, p. 36)

Defensive retreat or denial can prevent what is called *emotional flooding* and allows the individual to gradually assimilate both the permanence and the full implications of the disability. Individuals in this stage, in an attempt to guard against the trauma, may refuse to accept information, insist that there has been a mistake, or seek out other service providers. Richard Cohen, who was diagnosed with multiple sclerosis at age 25, expressed denial in this way: "My radar screen was blank, not even plugged in and turned on" (2004, p. 13). Deegan (1991), in *Recovery: The Lived Experience of Rehabilitation*, described denial:

Needless to say, we didn't believe our doctors and social workers. In fact, we adamantly denied and raged against these bleak prophesies for our lives. We felt it was all just a mistake, a bad dream, a temporary set-back in our lives. We just knew that in a week or two, things would get back to normal again.

We felt our teenage world was still there, just waiting for us to return to it. Our denial was an important stage in our recovery. It was a normal reaction to an overwhelming situation. It was our way of surviving those first awful months. (p. 48)

The individual in denial does not have any motivation (or understanding) to learn to live with the disability. For this reason, denial, or defensive retreat, is considered to be therapeutic if it does not continue too long. Service providers often counter denial with the concept of "dosage of information" (Naugle, 1991). Dosage of information refers to carefully determining exactly how much information can be tolerated. Timing of information is also important. Naugle summarized:

Equally important is the concept of dosage. If the individual is overwhelmed with information, that material is less likely to be accepted. Failure to recognize and accommodate an individual's tolerance level for distressing information may have the effect of interfering with participation in any treatment regimen. Smaller "doses" of information allow the individual to assimilate that information at a more controlled, self-determined rate. (p. 147)

Often, there is a rhythm of adaptation in which the individual, and his or her family, are allowed some necessary respite through the use of denial.

Toombs (1995), a professor of English with multiple sclerosis, clearly describes the way in which she uses denial as a tool:

Now that my disease is actively progressive, I must face this fear more often. . . . There are thoughts that come unbidden in the night to reawaken my deepest anxieties. There is no way for me to look at them in the face and remain intact. I must push them back. Back into the recesses of my consciousness. It is an act of will. I must think only of the new. Of this day. Of this moment. Of what I have. Of what I can do. Of what gives me joy. Please, let me think only of this. Sufficient unto the day is the evil thereof. (p. 22)

Of course, in Freudian terms the clinical diagnosis of denial includes the element that the individual is unaware that he or she is engaging in denial, and we can see that Toombs very deliberately and consciously uses denial to filter out unacceptable information. One of the ways in which Toombs supplements the protective factors of denial is to focus on positive aspects of her life. She is allowing only those interpretations of reality that are within her adaptive capabilities.

Barnard (1995) uses a slightly different type of denial, in which negative information is ignored. By conceptualizing negative information as related to only a *part* of himself, his self-esteem remains intact:

Negative information is filtered out to the extent that it is trivial, or short-term in its implications. More significant information, with greater potential impact on the person, is brought into awareness. Or information that reflects badly on the self may be identified with a particular *part* of the self, but be prevented from influencing one's self-concept in a global fashion. This part of the self can then be interpreted as distance from one's "core" or "essential" nature, further minimizing the impact of negative information on self-esteem. (pp. 45–46)

Richard Cohen (2004) wrote about his therapeutic uses of denial that continued for years. Cohen referred to his denial as "a child-like response" (p. 33) and stated that "[s]erious sickness is a large reality sandwich for a skinny young man to swallow" (p. 19).

For months I had lived in the house of denial. Now, in one moment, it had given way. It had been a flimsy structure, built on wishful thinking, but it had sheltered me from the weight of a reality that I could not bear to confront. Ignorance had been my ally; I had not even asked many questions of the doctors. Silence was an odd tactic for a journalist who, by trade, is all questions all the time. But I did not want to know too many facts. Facts would lead to truth and truth had been unacceptable. I was facing facts now. I had to admit to myself that I had MS.

Years would pass, however, before I easily and openly acknowledged my illness. Knowledge came slowly, too. (R. M. Cohen, 2004, p. 22)

Denial can be used repeatedly, as the following excerpt demonstrates:

When I got up at last . . . and had learned to walk again, one day I took a hand glass and went to a long mirror to look at myself, and I went alone. I didn't want anyone . . . to know how I felt when I saw myself for the first time. The person in the mirror *couldn't* be me. I felt inside like a healthy, ordinary, lucky person. Over and over I forgot what I saw in the mirror. (Goffman, 1963, p. 7)

Denial, if continued too long, can be counterproductive and impede the response to the disability. Louis Sternburg contracted polio and was in an iron lung.

Louis Sternburg asked his physician when he was going to walk out of the respiratory center. After a long, painful pause, the doctor told him that not only would he never walk again, he would also probably never breathe again without assistance. Sternburg heard himself scream, "You sonofabitch, you're lying!" (Wilson, 1990, p. 94)

Until relatively recently, PWDs were often encouraged by both caregivers and their families to deny the disability and to never discuss it. After medical stabilization, they were encouraged to "get on with their lives" as though they had no disability. Furthermore, they were advised not to dwell on "what might have been." They were encouraged to focus their energies on their physical rehabilitation and to repress or deny their feelings and emotions about their experiences. There was sometimes a hidden cost in terms of both physical and psychological well-being (Wilson, 1990, pp. 200–201). Marc Shell (2005) stated, "My own father did not speak with me directly about my having had polio" (p. 84). Veterans of World War II and the Korean War who returned home with disabilities were given medical care and physical therapy, but no one questioned the lack of psychological rehabilitation. These soldiers were told to forget about their disabilities.

Depression or Mourning

Denial is often considered to be past-oriented, in that the individual is trying to retain his or her former identity. Depression is considered to be future-oriented because the individual now struggles with questions of an uncertain future and an uncertain identity. Often, the PWD feels that "my family would be better off without me." In this stage, the PWD often does not have the energy or motivation to invest in a rehabilitation program. The individual often withdraws from others and has trouble sleeping, eating, and concentrating.

A man with a spinal cord injury described the grieving process:

> If someone is stuck in the grieving process . . . it's like an adjustment to a death. The only thing is, for an injury or disability, it's not as easy to adjust as with a death because with a death, the person's no longer there. With a disability, you have a constant reminder. So, sometimes it takes even longer to grieve and adjust. A lot of people turn to alcohol and drugs, which is a way of going through denial. As long as you're smashed, you can forget about your disability. (Scherer, 1993, p. 115)

It is often typical for the PWD to experience cycles of loss of hope, apathy, and deep depression. Also associated with depression are feelings of guilt and self-blame. As the grief subsides, the individual is able to acknowledge that he or she feels better. Grieving is experienced by family members. One mother described her grief over a daughter with "so much potential" who was diagnosed with a mental illness:

> The problems with my daughter were like a black hole inside of me into which everything else had been drawn. My grief and pain were so intense sometimes that I barely got through the day. It felt like a mourning process as if I were dealing with the loss of the daughter I had loved for 18 years and for whom there was so much potential. (Marsh, 1992, p. 10)

The Difference Between Grieving a Disability and Society's "Requirement to Mourn"

Grieving a disability, by the PWD and his or her family, is a valid reaction toward a disability, and, like the other stages in responding to a disability, grieving can be an important step to self-mastery. Grieving is an idiosyncratic acknowledgment of specific losses, including future plans and goals. However, the "requirement to mourn" (B. A. Wright, 1983) is imposed by society to maintain the superiority of PWODs. After all, if PWODs believe (mistakenly) that disability is always a tragic misfortune, then it makes sense to expect PWDs to live in a constant state of suffering and grief. The combination of the false perceptions of disability as tragedy and constant grieving serves to make lack of disability (or normality) appear valuable, desirable, and superior. Jenny Morris (1991) expressed her views on society's "requirement to mourn": "Not all of us view our disability as the unmitigated disaster and diminishment that seems expected of us" (p. 187).

Grieving and loss are also culturally defined. To cite a single example, researchers of societies that consider men superior to women have found that a congenital disability of a male infant is considered a greater loss than the birth of a female with the same disability. Also, in these types of societies, the probability of marriage for a man with a disability is greater than for a woman with the same type and severity of disability. This greater opportunity for marriage results from the fact that the woman with a disability is considered to be doubly disadvantaged—by her gender and the disability—while the man is thought to have only a single disadvantage, the disability (Westbrook, Legge, & Pennay, 1993).

Self-blame—or some other type of responsibility attribution in which the individual holds himself or herself to have acquired the disability through irresponsibility, negligence, or carelessness—has been found to hinder the acceptance process. Further, there is a strong societal insistence on determining causality, accountability, and blame for disability. As we have seen, society wants an explanation of the cause of the disability and, even more important, to be reassured that the disability is not some random event that might someday affect them. If PWODs can believe that the PWD caused his or her own disability (and that they would never be so foolish or negligent to cause themselves a disability), they can remain confident that they are exempt from disability. Therefore, perhaps the PWD may overcome feelings of self-blame, but his or her family and friends might consider the PWD to be guilty of self-inflicting a disability. Blame for the disability serves two purposes: (1) it relieves everyone else of responsibility for the disability because the "individual did this to himself or herself," and (2) it allows others to believe (falsely) that disability will never happen to them. Establishing blame, especially blaming the PWD, perpetuates the myth that the body can be controlled completely. Carolyn Vash (1981) talked about the power that blame can assume:

> Accidents, in which an official designation of responsibility is made, are simply the most obvious case. To believe that a permanent disability resulted

from a momentary, foolish act of one's own may strongly affect reaction to the disability itself—at least until the feelings of self-blame are resolved. Blaming someone else may have an even stronger impact. Keith, who lost a leg when the motorcycle he was riding collided with a truck, became consumed with hatred toward the truck driver, especially after the courts found him not at fault. Fred, shot in the spine accidentally by his younger brother, believes both of their lives would have been better if their parents had permitted him to express the anger he felt. (p. 11)

We have also seen that the perceived onset of the disability determines, in part, the degree of stigma directed toward the individual. Looking at the examples of Keith and Fred, we can speculate that if their disabilities had been the result of war injuries, perhaps both the societal stigma and their own self-blame and anger would have been reduced.

Arthur Frank (1991) discussed the relationship between his disability and randomness: "As soon as cancer happened to me, it ceased to be random." Frank continues that although he understood that many people are diagnosed with cancer, "I could not resist asking, 'Why me?' As a bodily process, cancer 'just happened to me.' The explanations I like best are fairly medical" (p. 87). Commenting on Frank's assessment of the cause of his cancer, Michalko (2002) explained:

> Medicine does have its charm. Its explanations of phenomena such as cancer are far more attractive than those to be found in religious ideas involving the omission or commission of acts, which lead to guilt and self-blame. Medicine's neutral physiological depiction of cancer leads us away from such self-blame to the more comforting, "just happened." There is nothing that we did or did not do that causes cancer; it "just happens." (p. 35)

In contrast, if there is any self-blame in congenital disabilities, it is typically the parents who experience such feelings. Wilson (1990), who reviewed dozens of first-person accounts of polio survivors, found that the parents of these survivors often felt guilty for not protecting their children from the virus. These parents endlessly replayed the events leading up to their children's illness, trying to determine where and how their children were exposed. Charles Mee (1999) was a teenager on a family car trip from Chicago to visit his older sister at the University of Colorado when he became ill with the polio virus. In an effort to pinpoint the location in which he contracted polio, Mee tried to remember every public restroom he used on the trip.

Leonard Kriegel also contracted polio as a child. When his mother visited him in the hospital for the first time, Kriegel saw how frightened she looked and watched her "make her frightened way across the room. I yelled, 'Momma, I'm sorry.' She had the unconscious grace to cry. And I cried with her, relieved that I had won forgiveness" (Kriegel, 1991, pp. 13–14).

The individual with a congenital disability is often relieved of asking and answering the question, "Why me?" Rod Michalko (2002) was born with a type of degenerating blindness. He concluded:

> I have nothing to do with the onset of my blindness since I have no role to play in the configuration of my genetic makeup. My blindness is caused by flawed genes and not by a flawed self or any other kind of self for that matter. (p. 33)

Regression

Closely tied to the stage of depression, regression occurs when the PWD simply gives up or regresses to an earlier, less mature stage of life. Deegan (1991) described regression in herself and a fellow resident:

> Our denial gave way to despair and anguish. We both gave up. Giving up was the solution for us. It numbed the pain of our despair because we stopped asking, "Why? and How will I go on?". . . . Giving up meant that for 14 years he sat in the day rooms of institutions gazing at soap operas, watching others live their lives. For months I sat in a chair in my family's living room, smoking cigarettes and waiting until it was 8:00 p.m. so that I could go back to bed. At this time, even the simplest of tasks were overwhelming. I remember being asked to come in to the kitchen to help knead some bread dough. I got up, went in to the kitchen and looked at the dough for what seemed to be an eternity. Then I walked back to my chair and wept. The task seemed overwhelming to me. (p. 49)

Richard Cohen (2004) described his experience with regression after he heard his diagnosis on the telephone: "After the phone was returned to the cradle, immediately I wished I could be also [returned to the cradle]. This would be a great time to be an infant again, to be picked up and rocked" (p. 18).

Another type of regression occurs when the individual romanticizes and idealizes "normality" or his or her premorbid identity. A lot like reminiscing about the "good old days," which may or may not have been so good, the individual nostalgically idealizes the memories of himself or herself without a disability. Charles Mee, the writer who contracted polio as a teenager, deeply resented his father's regression. Mee (1999) wrote:

> For the rest of his life after I had polio, my father carried a picture of me in his wallet that he had taken at the halftime of a football game. I was sitting on the grass with my teammates while the coach talked to us. My father had come around to the side of the group, and as I turned to look at him, he took the picture: an adolescent boy in the vigor of youth, a strong jaw and neck, a

crewcut, massive shoulders with the football pads. . . . I always took the fact that he carried that picture with him as a sign of disappointment in me, and it filled me with rage. . . . The photograph was still on a table not far from his bed when he died at the age of ninety-four. (p. 170)

Personal Questioning, Anger, or Both

In the personal questioning or anger stage, the individual may ask, "Why did God allow this to happen to me?" The onset of a disability seems unfair. Anger is often a combination of feelings of helplessness, frustration, fear, and irritability. Other types of personal questioning may take the form of the PWD replaying the accident or pre-diagnosis period in his or her mind in an attempt to find ways in which the disability could have been avoided. In trying to find the reason or meaning, which are not the same as the cause, the individual may lose trust in the world and in his or her value systems. For some individuals, this type of questioning is both lonely and futile. The responsibility or cause of the disability often becomes self-blame for the individual; for some individuals, holding themselves responsible for the disability is the price they pay for maintaining their belief that the world is not a random and unpredictable place.

If carried on for too long, compulsive, obsessive questioning and search for cause and meaning can delay the treatment and rehabilitation process. Helping the individual to understand the difference between the cause (responsibility) for the disability and the meaning and purpose can be therapeutic. Often, the individual's religious, spiritual, or philosophical belief systems can be implemented to help the individual clarify his or her beliefs about the purposes of his or her disability.

Mee (1999), a survivor of polio, had the following conversation with a Jesuit priest:

> [Mee said,] "I've lost my faith. I no longer believe in God."
>
> "I see," the priest said. And then he made a mistake. Instead of honoring my thoughts and feelings—instead of gently exploring the anger that had taken me to this place I was in—he decided to bully me, to intimidate me back into the church with his superior reasoning. (p. 202)

Mee told what the priest did wrong, which was not honoring his thoughts and feelings, and also stated what the priest should have done, which was to gently explore the anger. Wilson (1990), citing Mee (1977), related the way in which Mee learned to keep his anger hidden,

> keeping up the outward appearance of a "well-balanced, emotionally stable all-American boy." The façade, however, was maintained by "sheer will," for underneath was a seething cauldron of repressed emotion in which the "damaged" and "wounded" boy repressed the urge "to kill." (p. 84)

Family members may feel angry that their loved one has a disability, and they may question and challenge God about the unfairness of the disability. In a published case study of a girl with a disability who had five adult siblings, the authors reported:

> Two of the five siblings expressed anger at God. One sister said, "When you see her lying in pain, you get angry at God, it's not fair. Sometimes I get cross at K because she died." It was exhausting emotionally. Because we thought how much more does she have to endure? It seemed so cruel. (Rodger & Tooth, 2004, p. 63)

A man with a spinal cord injury spoke of "anger that just sits there and grows." He said,

> I wish I'd had counseling regularly . . . on a fairly regular basis. I'm not sure what would've come out of it, but if you see someone enough, eventually you're going to say something. Try to bring things out, some of the anger, and things like that. That was something that was never done, and that anger just sits in there and grows. (Scherer, 1993, p. 160)

Erik Weihenmayer (2001) became increasingly blind during his adolescence. He also became more and more angry. In this excerpt, Weihenmayer described the way in which he focused his anger at his assistive technology (the cane) and his orientation and mobility instructor, Mrs. Mundy; ironically, both the cane and the instructor would eventually expand his world. However, in recalling his teenage anger, Weihenmayer understood what the cane and Mrs. Mundy represented:

> Until this point, my anger flowed at the world like water from a sprinkler, spraying in too many directions to be dangerous, but in my brief meeting with Mrs. Mundy, I had found a target, a perfect candidate on whom to focus the force of my rage. I hated my cane almost as much as I was learning to hate Mrs. Mundy. In my mind they both represented the vast gulf that existed between me and everyone else. No matter how hard I tried, I'd never be able to bridge that insurmountable expanse. (p. 49)

Overwhelming feelings that worthwhile goals may no longer be possible are common. Anger can be directed toward others. Tuttle (1984) related this example:

> I went to my club for lunch and sat opposite a woman whom I had known slightly for a long time, and who, in my opinion, had made very little use of her life. Her presence filled me with such anger and jealousy because she was keeping her sight while I was losing mine, that I could barely speak civilly to her. (p. 178)

One individual found spiritual growth in dealing with his anger: "I needed to grow in working with my anger. And this experience of being disabled has made me face and go through, and get angry, learn how to use my own anger. . . . Definitely spiritual" (B. Boswell, Knight, & Hamer, 2001, p. 21).

Integration and Acceptance

The individual reaches the integration and acceptance stage when he or she (1) understands and accepts the reality and implications of the disability, (2) establishes new values and goals that do not conflict with the disability, and (3) explores and uses his or her strengths and abilities. Often, integration and growth necessitate changes in the environment such as assistive technology, changes in role functioning, and assuming responsibility for the management of the disability. Weihenmayer (2001) discussed his initial acceptance of his blindness:

> Ironically, as I relinquished my grip on sight, I sank into bitter relief. I had not a clue how I would survive as a blind person, how I would cook a meal, walk around, read a book, but trying to live as a sighted person was becoming more painful than blindness could ever be, and the uncertainty of what each tomorrow would bring was almost more terrifying. I knew nothing about blindness. I had no action plan. While I couldn't see well enough to . . . see an equation on the blackboard, I also couldn't accept myself as being blind. But one thing I knew: compared to this in-between world, total blindness couldn't be any worse, or any more terrifying. (p. 47)

Patricia Deegan (1991), who has a mental illness, spoke of her acceptance of her disability in much the same way as Weihenmayer:

> In fact, our recovery is marked by an ever-deepening acceptance of our limitations. But, rather than being an occasion for despair, we find that our personal limitations are the ground from which spring our own unique possibilities. This is the paradox of recovery, that is, in accepting what we cannot do or be, we begin to discover who we can be and what we can do. (p. 50)

Transcendence

In this section, look for—

- ✧ the way in which the concept of transcendence is in direct conflict with the Biomedical Model of disability
- ✧ dimensions of transcendence
- ✧ finding meaning and purpose in the disability

- ✧ reevaluating goals and identities
- ✧ discovering personal strengths
- ✧ finding positive aspects of the disability
- ✧ taking pride in the mastery of the disability
- ✧ seeking out new experiences
- ✧ assisting other PWDs

Carolyn Vash (1981) has termed the final stage *transcendence*, in which the individual feels that the disability is an opportunity for growth and learning. This stage is never complete; life continues to make demands and challenges of everyone. Reed (1991) defined transcendence as follows:

> There is a universal human desire for transcendence and connectedness. Transcendence is defined as a level of awareness that exceeds ordinary, physical boundaries and limitations, yet allows the individual to achieve new perspectives and experiences. Awareness of self-transcendence refers to the developmental maturity whereby there is an expansion of self-boundaries and an orientation toward broadened life perspectives and purposes. (p. 64)

PWDs, on reaching this stage, often begin advocacy and support work with other PWDs and their families. Further, they view their advocacy, service, and political activity as a means of bringing meaning and purpose to their own disability experience. PWDs and their families often feel increased empathy for others, saying that their own disability experience taught them important life lessons and gave their lives purpose and meaning.

In the past, such an integration and growth perspective toward a disability was thought to be some sort of denial, detachment, or inability to accept the realities of a disability. As we read these first-person accounts, we shall see that these individuals have achieved transcendence *because* of their disability and not *in spite of* their disability. These individuals manage their disability, develop and implement highly effective coping abilities, and experience positive outcomes and increased empowerment. They have incorporated the disability into their self-perception and consider the disability to be a source of potential.

Through reading the first-person accounts of PWDs and considering the various dimensions of transcendence, it will become clear that much of transcendence is in direct conflict with the Biomedical Model of disability and the societal view that disability is an unending tragedy and a mark of inferiority. In these false conceptualizations of disability (typically held by PWODs), all disabilities should be eliminated (if the means were available), and all PWDs must want a cure. We can readily see results of such faulty thinking. If PWDs are truly miserable and helpless (and, without doubt, it is expensive to provide a reasonable quality of life for PWDs), then elimination of disability through abortion and assisted suicide seems more reasonable and, perhaps, humane.

Transcendence of disability is a more holistic view (in contrast to the Biomedical Model) and considers the individual and his or her strengths and assets; considers the religious, spiritual, or philosophical identity of the individual; and considers the provision of civil rights and accommodations. In Chapter 9, we shall answer the question, "What do PWDs want?" Much of that discussion will parallel these ideas of transcendence. However, this chapter is focusing on the *individual's* response to disability, whereas Chapter 9 will discuss PWDs as a *group*. Nonetheless, many of these concepts are parallel, for both individuals and groups. In Chapter 9 it can be seen that by accommodating PWDs and incorporating their views, history, and experiences into the wider cultural life of the nation, PWODs will benefit greatly.

Finding Meaning and Purpose in the Disability

Many PWDs state that *because* of their disability, they have richer, more satisfying lives. Their disabilities have transformed their lives, giving them a broader view of life. One woman ascribed religious and spiritual purposes to her disability:

> My reactions came as a result of believing that this is probably not a freak accident that I became a quadriplegic. But, it has some purpose of the world I live in, and that I am not just here . . . because there's some reason or purpose that God intended to fulfill through a disability. (B. Boswell et al., 2001, p. 23)

Some PWDs state they have formed lasting and deep friendships, have become more compassionate toward others, and have a clearer view of what is really important in life. Michael Weisskopf (2006, October 2) was a journalist who lost his right hand while covering the war in Iraq (see p. 256). Weisskopf's experiences, and his skillful retelling, emphasize that he feels that he has gained more than he has lost.

In the book, *A Life in Science* (M. White & Gribbin, 1993), the authors described Stephen Hawking's disability, the assistive technology that has allowed Hawking to continue working, and the fact that his disability "seemed to act as a spur, focusing his intellect and his energy."

> Many would argue that his liberation from the routine chores of life has enabled him to make greater progress than if he were able-bodied. In 1963, Hawking, just 21 years old, working in Cambridge on his Ph.D. in physics, was told that he had two and a half years to live as a result of ALS, a degenerative motor neuron disease that causes atrophy of muscles throughout the body. Inexplicably, however, Hawking continues to thrive beyond any reasonable expectation. With a voice synthesizer, provided after his 1985 tracheotomy resulting from his bout with pneumonia, and a small personal computer mounted on his wheelchair, his ability to lecture and to collaborate

with other physicists, as well as to publish books and articles, have not been compromised. For Hawking, the knowledge that he had a severe disability seemed to act as a spur, focusing his intellect and his energy on his study of cosmology:"Before my condition had been diagnosed, I had been very bored with life. There had not seemed to be anything worth doing. But shortly after I came out of hospital, I dreamt that I was going to be executed. I suddenly realized that there were a lot of worthwhile things I could do if I were re-prieved." (M. White & Gribbin, 1993, p. viii)

Survivors of polio often "believed that their disability made a substantive improve-ment in their lives" (Wilson, 1990, p. 14). In the book, *Living with Polio: The Epidemic and Its Survivors*, Wilson read dozens of first-person accounts of individuals who had contracted polio. Two accounts illustrate the way in which polio changed the direc-tion of the lives of these individuals:

> In high school in rural southern Wisconsin, Jan Little participated in forensics and debate, which didn't require standing and walking. "Roger and Bill, my debate partners, managed to carry me up and down stairways in schools all over southeastern Wisconsin and only dropped me a little one time." (p. 186)
>
> Robert Owen recalls that before polio struck when he was twelve, he was constantly in trouble, and fought to and from school. In addition to fighting, he also "loved to play football and things like that." He remembers that prior to polio, he "had only read about three books in my whole life." After he re-turned to school, following a year of rehabilitation, he focused on his studies. Owen is convinced that if he hadn't had polio, he probably would not have become a physician. (p. 202)

Andrew Solomon (2012), after years of interviewing many PWDs and their fami-lies, described transcendence when he summarized: "[A disability is] surprising, iso-lating, mystifying, petrifying. One of the most startling patterns that emerged during my research was that many people come to value abnormalities that are ostensibly undesirable" (p. 405). Note, the author (interviewer) is "startled." He might have be-gun his research with the preconceived false idea that most disabilities are tragic losses.

Others have discussed the way in which their disability reoriented them to different interests and goals. The director of the movie, *The Elephant Man*, Jack Hofsiss, became quadriplegic in a diving accident in a swimming pool. The accident occurred after *The Elephant Man* was made, and Hofsiss saw a connection between his disability and his work on the movie.

> It's odd, but I'm beginning to see a greater unity in my life. I came to terms with the worst experience of my life, which was this accident, and the best experience of my life, which was the pure, sweet sense of satisfaction that *The*

Elephant Man gave me—the sweetness of working on that piece of material and being responsible for a large number of people knowing about that man and what he was like and how much we had to learn from him. (Hofsiss & Laffey, 1993, pp. 86–87)

Another individual begins his assessment of his disability with the exact words of Jack Hofsiss, "It's odd." Randy Souders (1993) views his disability (and the necessary recovery process) as rescuing him from a life in a "mediocre position in a mediocre little ad agency":

It's odd. If I had a crystal ball to see what would have happened had I not had the injury, I don't see myself having done what I've done at all. I would probably have a mediocre position in a mediocre little ad agency and be like the rest of society—up to my ears in debt, just trying to get by—and frustrated that I didn't go for something that would have truly inspired me all along. . . . I don't know that I would have dedicated myself to art. Art was a vital part of my recovery from my injury. I found myself in a situation of being the same person in a new body, one that didn't work, along with the loss of self-esteem and self-confidence and all the things that come along with a traumatic injury. Once I realized that I still had a chance at being creative and of value through my artwork, I just really focused in on that. It was a real part of my recovery. (p. 153)

Perhaps the most well-known individual with a disability was President Franklin D. Roosevelt. Roosevelt contracted polio at age 39 and never walked again. In 2006, Jonathon Alter published a book about FDR entitled, *The Defining Moment: FDR's Hundred Days and the Triumph of Hope*. Widmer (2006), in his review of this book, stated, "Roosevelt reinvented the American presidency through bold policy innovations, brilliant speeches and broadcasts and a person connected with the American people which has not been equaled since." How was FDR able to accomplish all this? According to Widmer, Alter views the way in which Roosevelt "embodied hope to a people consumed by despair." Widmer continues:

[Alter] gave much of the credit for this ineffable confidence to Roosevelt's earlier struggle with a disability relatively few Americans were aware he had. Through his agonizing triumph over polio and the bond he discovered with fellow sufferers, Roosevelt discovered "traits that would prove instrumental to the presidency"—a theatrical bonhomie, mental suppleness and an empathy . . . that had not characterized his early career" (p. 15).

In other words, historians credit Roosevelt's great political successes to the lessons he learned in responding to polio.

Reevaluating Goals and Priorities

The disability and the resulting recovery process can provide the opportunity for individuals to consider their strengths and needs and allow them the time and space to redefine who they are. Some PWDs have reported that they found the goodness in themselves and in others (McColl et al., 2000). Another individual explained: "I found that by being alone—it just sort of sorted itself. It's about looking at yourself—need to put things in balance—I had to re-evaluate my whole life" (Faull et al., 2004, p. 134). Two authors summarized the way in which better perspectives and priorities can be developed: "A catastrophic event [such as a disability] generally results in disintegration of existing patterns, which in turn offers the opportunity for constructive reintegration" (Marsh & Lefley, 1996, p. 3).

A senior correspondent for *Time* magazine, Michael Weisskopf, was reporting from Bagdad in 2003. One night, while riding in a Humvee with three soldiers, a grenade was thrown and, without thinking, Weisskopf picked it up. In the process, he saved four lives, including his own, and lost most of his right arm. In 2006 (*Time*, 2006, October 2), he wrote an article entitled, "How I Lost My Hand but Found Myself." In the following paragraphs, Weisskopf explains both the process of achieving transcendence and the ultimate result:

> As I tossed and turned in the early hours of Independence Day, the simple truth of the psychologist's words hit me. It was true: I was mad at myself . . . and it was that anger that was preventing me from savoring the achievement of a lifetime: saving my own skin and that of three others. My failure to get rid of the grenade before it exploded was only the first in a long list of wrongs I would have to pardon before I could finally put the ordeal behind me.
>
> I had gone to Iraq for adventure and glory, discounting the interests of family and friends.
>
> I had blithely ridden into danger with little to gain journalistically.
>
> I had focused more on the loss of my hand than on the higher importance of preserving life. (p. 37)

One woman with a mental illness felt that the recovery process was instrumental in changing her priorities. Note that she refers to her self-image several times in this short excerpt:

> The illness itself has not had any good effects, but the process of getting healthier has, especially on my spirituality, my self-image, my character, and personal qualities. Now I have a greater sense of serenity, self-liking, wonder at the world, and caring for myself and others. (Marsh & Lefley, 1996, p. 10)

A psychologist (D. S. Dunn, 1996) interviewed 138 individuals who had experienced amputations, asking each of them if they had found a "silver lining" in their disability. Dunn categorized their responses into five categories, one of which was "Redefined event/Reappraised life." One respondent stated, "All good has come out of it. I found God through it. It has given me purpose. It makes me special." Another stated, "I think I've become a much better person—more humble, more considerate and less selfish. I now know that I am not perfect." A third respondent said, "I was very much a 'wallflower' and since I can no longer blend in, I've become more outgoing." Each of these respondents speaks of having developed positive personality attributes.

A woman of an adult son with a mental illness speaks of her son's willpower and her own "stubbornness," which, if not the result of the disability, certainly strengthened their ability to deal with mental illness.

> My son has great willpower. He has graduated from college, also got his master's degree and has been working as a chemist for the past two years. My son has been hospitalized six times (four of which were court commitments) and he has been homeless. Through my stubbornness we rescued him from the streets. He is now so well and enjoying life. It gives me gratification that I never gave up hope. (Marsh & Lefley, 1996)

A polio survivor told of her awareness of and compassion for others:

> But now, far away from the hospital experience, I can evaluate what I have learned. For it wasn't only suffering: it was learning through suffering. I know my awareness of people has deepened and increased, that those who are close to me can count on me to turn all mind and heart and attention to their problem. I could not have learned *that* dashing all over a tennis court. (Goffman, 1963, p. 11)

Disability can also allow individuals to appraise their life situations and make improvements and other types of changes. An Englishwoman wrote about the positive changes she made and the irony of having others view her disability as a negative experience:

> I feel that most of the people I know think my life has gotten immeasurably worse since I had the diagnosis of multiple sclerosis. In fact, it's better. I'm not denying the difficulties, but being told that I had this illness made me rethink what I was doing. I was able to get out of a very repressive relationship and to live with my mother and my daughter—which is wonderful, it's what I've always wanted. And not having to go to work every day is also wonderful, it's so liberating. The writing that I am doing now, I would never have done if I hadn't been told that I had MS. And yet, if I told my able-bodied friends that my life has improved they would think I was mad [insane], which makes me feel sad. (J. Morris, 1991, p. 38)

Other individuals have described the use of humor. Nick Vujicic was a 23-year-old Australian who was born without arms or legs. In a speech in Laguna Beach, California, in July 2006 (Basheda, 2006), his sense of humor was evident; nonetheless, Vujicic was clear in stating, "I'm not here to say I understand your pain" (p. 1). His parents formed a church in Australia, and the membership of the church mourned when he was born. Vujicic remembers reading a Bible scripture in Sunday School that said that all people were created in the image of God. His response was, "Yeah, right" (p. 1). When people ask what happened to him, he uses a one-word reply: "CIGARETTES!" At the end of the speech, Vujicic remarks, "If you run fast, I'm gonna get someone to throw me at you" (p. 7).

In New Zealand, researchers described the use of humor, especially making fun of oneself, by PWDs:

> Notably the ability to laugh at oneself and with others about experiences and situations [was important]. A dominant characteristic of humor described was that it was "in-house" or "black," and in some way at the expense of the teller. Stories often told of catastrophic experiences [in] which humor was used to make more bearable and acceptable an aspect of normal life. Humor such as this was seen to indicate an ability to view oneself from the outside and to see oneself in the context of a wider picture. Moreover, it [humor] was considered to reflect the New Zealand cultural norm of understatement, together with an awareness of life which is precious and enjoyable. (Faull et al., 2004, p. 137)

Humor can also defuse and desensationalize disability:

> On several occasions the siblings mentioned humor as a coping mechanism within the family context. Jokes about "spastics" and "epilepsy" became avenues for tension release within the safe bounds of home, where everyone had a shared understanding of the funny and the serious sides of the jokes. One sibling talked about epileptic jokes and said, ". . . We all just laughed, it was part of our lives. We could laugh, it wasn't that it was too shocking or cruel." (Rodger & Tooth, 2004, p. 61)

It should be noted that the humor is "in-group" humor, told by PWDs themselves and with audiences who know the PWD and understand the disability. None of this humor would be appropriate for PWODs to use.

Discovering Strengths

The PWD, by understanding his or her needs, values, and strengths, can decide on goals and the accommodations and compensations needed (Estroff, 1995). By conceptualizing, initiating action plans, and maintaining motivation, the PWD is able to move forward. The disability can also offer strengths and assets. For example, the golfer Casey Martin stated that his disability has been an asset because, "I have expertise in adapting to change" (H. McCarthy, 2003, p. 203). Erik Weihenmayer (2001) seems to believe that an easy life is not exciting, challenging, or rewarding:

> After sixteen years of blindness, one thing I've learned is that life is never meant to be easy; exciting, challenging, rewarding from time to time, but never easy. Ironically, when I finally accepted this reality, that's when life got easy. (p. 282)

One mother described the way in which raising her son "made us who we are":

> If I could cure David, I would for David. But, I think we have grown so much as a result of having to deal with this. We've had so much purpose. I'd never have believed 23 years ago when he was born that I could come to such a point, but I have. For David, I'd cure it (the disability) in an instant; but for us, I wouldn't exchange these experiences for anything. They've made us who we are, and who we are is so much better than who we would have been otherwise. (Solomon, 2012, p. 219)

In a Canadian study conducted with individuals with traumatic-onset disabilities, two individuals stated that they felt physically invincible since the acquisition of their disability:

> One said that he felt invincible because he had seen what his body could survive, and the other said that she thought she would live longer than she might have predicted before the accident, because of changes to her lifestyle. (McColl et al., 2000, p. 561)

Another individual stated, "I do believe that I am as good as all those wobblies who walk around on two legs" (Faull et al., 2004, p. 136).

Many PWDs have ascribed sacred meaning to their disability and consider their spirituality to be a strength that results in "a feeling of well-being that God knew their needs and empowered them to cope in difficult times" (J. Kaye & Raghavan, 2002, pp. 237–238). Indeed, a number of researchers have found spirituality to be a primary resource among PWDs. Fitzgerald (1997) summarized that spirituality is

> . . . both a grand project and an everyday task, referring simultaneously to a process of coming to terms with both the finite and the infinite—the losses and limitations that accompany a disability and the possibilities for a meaningful life and relationship with the world and a higher power. Such a spiritual understanding would overcome the negative themes in traditional

theology, such as the notion of disability as punishment, as a tribute to the power of God, as a defect or imperfection, as glorification of suffering or as the object of charity. (p. 407)

A woman with a congenital limb deficiency discusses her spirituality and its relationship to her disability. At first she accepts society's prejudicial views as a self-identifier and abuses alcohol.

> Being disabled is a deep wound, a source of pain. But like all wounds, it is also a gift. As Eastern wisdom has always known, it is hard to tell good luck from bad luck. . . . Having one arm is an endless koan. It is what it is, which is unknowable, and it attracts a lot of ideas, stories, and images. Caught up in the negative story, I felt ashamed, incomplete, and not okay. I drank to die. Later on, caught up in a more positive story, I felt pride and a sense of identity. . . . In a way, I have gone back to the innocence of a baby. When little babies encounter my arm—the arm that ends just below the elbow—it is seen as just another interesting shape to explore and put into their mouths. There is nothing scary or creepy or taboo about it . . . Not labeling what appears as either a deficit or an asset, perfect or imperfect, beautiful or ugly, but wondering openly without conclusion, without trying to get somewhere else. In such open being there is freedom and possibility for the new, even in the midst of what we call imperfection or limitation. I don't mean that the injustices or painful circumstances disappear, but they no longer bind us in the way they did. (Tollifson, 1997, p. 111)

A *koan* in Zen Buddhism is a paradox that is used to meditate on to gain enlightenment.

Assisting Other PWDs

Many PWDs volunteer in peer-support groups or become active in advocacy and disability rights groups. Some may choose to become professional providers of services to other PWDs and their families. A mother of a man with a psychiatric disability described her son:

> Well, he is the most kind, wonderful human being—probably because of all he has been through. He volunteers at our local crisis unit. Patients will go in because he is there. Other families request him to speak to their mentally ill loved one. Because of Clozapine [an anti-psychotic medication], he is in an MSW [master's of social work] program at our university, and he wants to work with severely mentally ill patients when he graduates. Our mental health center said they want him to work there. (Marsh & Lefley, 1996, p. 6)

An individual who was 1 and one half years post-injury with a traumatic brain injury (TBI) gave a detailed description of the way he helped "newbies" with TBI:

> I help anyone who walks through that door. I try to make them feel at home, you know, and I know what it's like, and I went through it when I first got here. I'm a peer to them, I'm just another client—so they'll listen to me. I can calm them down. I can sit down, I can talk to them, I can help them out—I've had a year and a half to practice, you know—so everyone who walks comes, I'll help them any way I can. (Nichols & Kosciulek, 2014, p. 26)

Notice how being "just another client" gives this individual the ability to help others. Imagine how reassuring and helpful it is for the newbies to have someone sit and talk with them.

A Vietnam veteran and a U.S. senator, Max Cleland is also a triple amputee. In his autobiography, *Strong at Broken Places*, he describes the way in which he acquired his disabilities in 1968: "Then I saw the grenade. It was where the chopper had lifted off. It must be mine, I thought. I bent down to pick up the grenade. A blinding explosion threw me backwards." Cleland served in the Georgia State Senate and wrote the state law for disability accessibility to public buildings. Today, he sits on the Senate Armed Services Committee. Max Cleland's advocacy for PWDs is at a high level with a great deal of national visibility; nonetheless, it was his disabilities that led him to a career in politics and public service.

Advantages of the Stage Theory

In this section, look for—

- ⬦ how the theory facilitates the selection of the most suitable forms of treatment
- ⬦ how the theory emphasizes the need for both short-term treatment and long-term support
- ⬦ how the theory allows the PWD to understand his or her own feelings and reactions
- ⬦ how common variables can be tailored to the individual PWD
- ⬦ how the theory helps to validate and normalize the PWD's intense and often contradictory emotions
- ⬦ how the theory recognizes that adjustment or response is a process and not a one-time event

Educating the PWD and his or her family about these stages helps to normalize and universalize the experience of adaptation or response. When the PWD and his or her family learn that other individuals experience the same types of feelings, the PWD will not feel as isolated. It is strengthening to an individual to know that others understand his or her experience. The individual feels validated and is able to put his or her feelings in context. Proponents of the stage theory maintain that these types of responses of PWDs (and their families) are neither pathological nor dysfunctional. These stages can be steps to self-mastery. Occasionally, however, if the responses are prolonged or associated with major impairment, then interventions can be implemented.

The stage theory also assists service providers in understanding the process of response or adaptation and, in so doing, helps service providers to choose the best treatment goals (Livneh, 1986b). Tailoring concrete short-term goals compatible with the stage of adaptation or response can provide a task-oriented approach that does not overwhelm the individual. Conceptualizing the adaptation or response to a disability as a process can also assist service providers in encouraging and supporting the individual to progress to the next stage while not permitting coping mechanisms of one stage to become long-term habits. Caregivers cannot counter maladaptive responses and behaviors unless they understand the demands of each stage. Case management, in which many different professionals provide services to a single individual, is facilitated when there is agreement and understanding concerning the stage in which the PWD is operating. This agreement among members of the treatment team will ensure that all treatment will be coordinated. Furthermore, educating and supporting PWDs and their families can assist in maintaining family equilibrium and help families to avoid making major life changes until they are further along in the process.

Understanding the stages of adaptation or response assists family members in their efforts to support the PWD. For example, family members can be educated about the importance of noncritical acceptance of the PWD's denial. Family members learn that confronting or arguing with the PWD is counterproductive. Another example concerns the individual who is in the anger stage. Often, this anger is expressed toward the most accessible people—family members or care providers. Helping family and caregivers to understand that the anger of the PWD is an attempt to regain balance and control will reduce their stress and help to eliminate compassion fatigue and burnout. Therefore, if caregivers and family members understand the stages of adaptation, it is less likely that the PWD will become socially isolated. The stage theory promotes hope and optimism and provides a starting point for assisting the PWD. Deegan (1991) stated, "Hope is contagious" (p. 53).

Often professional caregivers minimize or purposely avoid certain stages of the adaptation or response process. For example, some professionals are not comfortable with individuals who are experiencing the anger stage (L. D. Clanton, Rude, & Taylor, 1992). By understanding the stage theory and developing an awareness of their own responses to certain stages, professional caregivers can develop alternative treatment strategies, such as referring PWDs to other caregivers.

Assisting PWDs to understand the stages of adaptation or response can allow them to draw on their strengths and capabilities at each stage (Livneh & Antonak, 1990).

Of course, such an understanding is more than an intellectual understanding; it is a deep, therapeutic conceptualization of a long-term process. Often, PWDs join support groups with individuals who have experienced the same disability. Because group members may be at different stages in the adaptation or response process, members often learn from the experiences of others. These self-help groups can do much to promote and maintain hope. Further, group members know that others understand their experiences.

Cautions in Implementing the Stage Theory

In this section, look for—

- ⬩ some stage theories that are specific to the disability, such as therapeutic amputations
- ⬩ how, in some disabilities, the stages progress not in a linear fashion but in a curvilinear fashion
- ⬩ how each stage encompasses a wide variety of behavioral characteristics
- ⬩ how the stage theory does not consider the prejudice and discrimination of others and how these affect the adaptation or response process
- ⬩ how individuals can recycle through the stages, repeat a stage, or skip a stage
- ⬩ how disability is not a single event but a process

The stage theory of adaptation or response to disability faces some criticism, even to the point of terming the stage theory "social oppression" (Kendall & Buys, 1998, p. 17). The idea that *every* PWD, and his or her family, regardless of the type or severity of disability, experiences a predictable, orderly, sequential, linear, hierarchical progression through these stages has never been suggested by the proponents of the theory. Nor has the wide variability in behavioral characteristics of each stage been disputed. One critique does, however, have merit. Kendall and Buys argued, "Stage models of adjustment also normalize responses such as denial and distress following acquired disability, which may lead rehabilitation workers to expect, or even encourage, such responses" (p. 17). Nonetheless, proponents of the stage model have noted the following:

> The process of adaptation is not irreversible. Individuals who experience a chronic illness or sustain a permanent disability may regress to an earlier phase or skip one or more phases of psychosocial adaptation. Phases of adaptation comprise nondiscrete and categorically overlapping reactions. These

reactions may fluctuate and blend with one another, providing for the experience of more than one reaction at a time. Attempts to specify the duration of each phase, or of the entire adaptation response, are futile at best. (Livneh & Antonak, 1997, p. 19)

Therefore, it is difficult to understand the criticism that rehabilitation workers, and other care providers, might encourage certain responses such as denial or distress. The stage theory provides *only* guidelines and acknowledges that PWDs do not proceed through these stages in a one-time-only, sequential, time-dated process. PWDs whose disability has been medically stabilized may recycle through these stages as the demands and stresses of developmental tasks and other life transitions arise.

The stage theory does propose a linear process, but it also acknowledges that, for some disabilities, the adaptation or response process is a curvilinear process. Many individuals with chronic, degenerating disabilities and chronic illnesses are thought to experience a curvilinear response, with a positive response in the beginning (when the symptoms and pain are not very great), a negative response in middle age (when the symptoms and pain increase), and a positive response in older age (when the individual has few functional demands).

There are a few disabilities for which the stage theory has been specifically adapted. For instance, the stage theory has been applied to individuals with amputations and congenital limb deficiencies. Individuals who undergo a surgical (therapeutic) amputation experience four phases: (1) realization that the loss of a limb is imminent; (2) early postoperative hospitalization; (3) in-hospital rehabilitation, in which the individual receives such treatments as the fitting of a prosthesis; and (4) home rehabilitation, in which the individual returns to his or her normal life (Bradway, Malone, Racy, Leal, & Poole, 1984).

The stage theory advocates viewing the person as someone with resources and capabilities. By acknowledging various stages, PWDs can understand their own feelings and the feelings of family members better. For example, clients (with or without disabilities) tend to terminate counseling or psychotherapy when they feel they are not getting better. Recognizing and understanding that "you might feel worse before you feel better" may help clients to continue in counseling. Caregivers (both professional and family members) will be less likely to withdraw support if they understand that some of the typical stages a PWD experiences are often unpleasant. Rereading Patricia Deegan's *Recovery*, we can see that her family members never withdrew their support and encouragement, in spite of the fact that she sat on the couch all day. Arnold Beisser, the physician who contracted polio, described his relationship with his disability as like a marriage, especially when he realized that there was no final and complete stage to accepting his disability.

The argument that the stage theory promotes the idea that a disability is an undesirable state (pathologizing disability) has not been validated by research or by anecdotal evidence. Powers (1993) explained:

The topic of disability-related grief is also associated with sensitivity and controversy when considered in relation to current positive perspectives of disability. Theories that postulate the existence of grief or chronic sorrow in response to a disability are sometimes regarded as promulgating the notion that disability is an inherently tragic event with an enduring negative impact on families. Yet . . . it can be through the validation and processing of grief that many family members shift their perspectives of disability from tragedy to challenge and opportunity. (p. 120)

An excellent summarization on the need for counseling support (and the dangers of not providing it) is provided by a PWD who said:

People in this condition need mental rehabilitation more than anything else. Because that is 90 percent of physical rehabilitation. [Rehabilitation doesn't] want to face that because it's too expensive. So you adapt. You develop coping mechanisms and some of them, like drinking, are not good ones. If way back then they had given us good coping mechanisms, a lot of problems could have been prevented. (Scherer, 1993, pp. 159–160)

FIRST-PERSON NARRATIVES OF PEOPLE WITH DISABILITIES

Ballin, A. (1930). *The deaf mute howls.* Los Angeles, CA: Grafton.

Beisser, A. R. (1989). *Flying without wings: Personal reflections on being disabled.* New York, NY: Doubleday.

Black, K. (1996). *In the shadow of polio: A personal and social history.* White Plains, NY: Addison Wesley Longman.

Brookes, T. (1995). *Catching my breath: An asthmatic explores his illness.* New York, NY: Vintage.

Callahan, J. (1989). *Don't worry, he won't get far on foot.* New York, NY: Random House.

Cohen, L. H. (1994). *Train go sorry: Inside a Deaf world.* Boston, MA: Houghton Mifflin.

Cohen, R. M. (2004). *Blindsided: Lifting a life above illness: A reluctant memoir.* New York, NY: HarperCollins.

Fries, K. (Ed.). (1997). *Staring back: The disability experience from the inside out.* New York, NY: Plume.

Gallagher, H. G. (1985). *FDR's splendid deception.* New York, NY: Dodd and Mead.

Hannaford, S. (1985). *Living outside inside: A disabled woman's experience towards a social and political perspective.* Berkeley, CA: Canterbury Press.

Hockenberry, J. (1995). *Moving violations: War zones, wheelchairs, and declarations of independence.* New York, NY: Hyperion.

Hull, J. M. (1991). *Touching the rock: The experience of blindness.* New York, NY: Pantheon.

Keller, H. (1903). *The story of my life.* New York, NY: Doubleday.

Kisor, H. (1990). *What's that pig outdoors? A memoir of deafness.* New York, NY: Hill and Wang.

Mee, C. L. (1999). *A nearly normal life: A memoir.* Boston, MA: Little, Brown.

Merker, H. (1994). *Listening.* New York, NY: HarperCollins.

Murphy, R. (1987). *The body silent.* New York, NY: Henry Holt.

Perkins, R. (1996). *Talking to angels: A life spent in high latitudes.* Boston, MA: Beacon.

Price, R. (1994). *A whole new life: An illness and a healing.* New York, NY: Atheneum.

Rousso, H. (1993). *Disabled, female, and proud: Stories of ten women with disabilities.* Westport, CT: Bergin & Garvey.

Schaller, S. (1991). *A man without words.* New York: Summit.

Scott, R. (1969). *The making of blind men: A study of adult socialization.* New York, NY: Russell Sage Foundation.

Sidransky, R. (1990). *In silence: Growing up hearing in a deaf world.* New York, NY: St. Martin's Press.

Sienkiewicz-Mercer, R., & Kaplan, S. B. (1989). *I raise my eyes to say yes.* Boston, MA: Houghton Mifflin.

Vermeij, G. (1997). *Privileged hands: A scientific life.* New York, NY: Freeman.

Weihenmayer, E. (2001). *Touch the top of the world: A blind man's journey to climb farther than the eye can see.* New York, NY: Dutton.

White, M., & Gribbin, J. (1993). *Steven Hawking: A life in science.* New York, NY: Penguin.

Wright, D. (1994). *Deafness: An autobiography.* New York, NY: Mandarin.

Zola, I. K. (1982). *Missing pieces: A chronicle of living with a disability.* Philadelphia, PA: Temple University.

CHAPTER **7**

THE ONSET AND DIAGNOSIS OF THE DISABILITY

- ✧ Why is psychoeducation often therapeutic?
- ✧ Do you agree that parental response to a baby with a congenital disability is often not validated by society?
- ✧ What are low-incidence disabilities?
- ✧ What are some of the atypical experiences of children with disabilities?
- ✧ What is prelingual deafness?
- ✧ Why do many in the Deaf Culture advocate residential schooling for children who are deaf?
- ✧ Do cochlear implants make deafness an elective disability?
- ✧ For individuals with acquired disabilities, why do their prejudices often become self-identifiers?
- ✧ Explain this statement: Many disabilities and chronic illnesses of children are low-incidence disabilities.
- ✧ Why is the time of onset of schizophrenia so disabling?
- ✧ Why is the role of women traditionally one of "caring for vulnerable people"?
- ✧ Why have few rehabilitation services been provided for elderly people with disabilities?
- ✧ Why is old age itself often considered to be a disability?
- ✧ Why do elderly people often respond positively to the onset of the disability?

✧ In what ways is the acquisition of a disability thought to be timelier, both socially and chronologically?

✧ What are the differences between insidious-onset disabilities and acute-onset disabilities?

Factors That Affect the Impact of the Onset of Disability

In this section, look for—

✧ the three broad categories of variables that affect the individual's adaptation or response to disability
  1. factors in the disability
  2. factors in the environment
  3. factors in the individual

Carolyn Vash (1981), a disability scholar, constructed a model that assists in understanding the factors or variables that affect an individual's response to a disability. The broad categories are (1) factors in the disability itself, (2) factors in the environment, and (3) factors in the individual. Factors in the environment include the degree of family support and acceptance, the availability of self-help and mutual support groups, the assistive technology that is available, the quality of professional services rendered, and the individual's income level. As can be seen, most of these factors in the environment are tangible, measurable elements.

In contrast, factors in the individual are often difficult to measure. These factors include the individual's previous experience with PWDs, the individual's premorbid (before the onset of the disability) coping skills (Affleck, Tennen, Pfeifer, & Fifield, 1987), problem-solving and decision-making abilities, challenge orientation, level of emotional control, cognitive appraisal skills, levels of self-esteem and self-confidence, and the individual's religious, spiritual, or philosophical belief system. Reviewing this list of factors, it can be seen that all of these pose difficulties in measurement and clinical assessment. However, the individual's marital status (PWDs who are married or have a partner usually respond better to a disability), the individual's level of education (PWDs who are highly educated usually respond better to a disability), and the individual's work history and transferability of skills (PWDs who have a long and varied work history usually respond better to a disability) are factors that can be more easily measured and assessed.

This chapter will focus on the onset of the disability itself. Exhibit 7.1 lists all of these factors. Each factor will be discussed in some detail in this chapter, focusing on time of onset. The next chapter will go into more detail about type of onset and the

FACTORS IN THE DISABILITY THAT INFLUENCE AN INDIVIDUAL'S RESPONSE TO DISABILITY

Time of onset

Type of onset

Functions impaired

Severity of disability

Visibility of the disability

Degree, if any, of disfigurement

The course of the disability—stable, progressive, episodic

Prognosis of the disability

Treatment required

Exhibit 7.1

rest of the factors. Remember, as we discussed previously, this model is an oversimplification of reality. For example, many PWDs have more than one disability, and, furthermore, it is not the disability itself that influences the way in which the individual views the disability; it is the meaning the individual ascribes to the disability. Therefore, each disability is an idiosyncratic experience; moreover, there is no one personality type associated with a particular disability. Nonetheless, there are some general guidelines in understanding specific types of disabilities. Indeed, knowledge and understanding of specific disabilities and their impact on individuals is one of the main functions of mutual support and self-help groups. In these types of groups, individuals with the same disability (and their families) meet together to discuss all of the factors listed in Exhibit 7.1. This is what is termed *psychoeducation,* and psychoeducation alone—just learning about the disability itself from others who have experienced the same disability—is therapeutic. Psychoeducation can do much to eliminate anxiety and ambiguity and create a feeling of universality, or the feeling that "someone else is experiencing the same thing I am." Exhibit 7.1 contains a list of all 10 factors. Two factors will be discussed in this chapter.

Time of Onset

In this section, look for—

- ✧ time of onset—congenital or acquired
- ✧ some aspects of congenital disabilities:

- often involve treatment considerations of the parents and siblings of the PWD
- the individual has no memory of not having a disability
- there is no premorbid functioning with which the individual compares himself or herself
- the parents must make treatment and habilitation choices
- individuals with congenital disabilities often have atypical childhood experiences
- society attributes less stigma to congenital disabilities (than to acquired disabilities)

Basically, the time of onset of a disability is divided into two categories: congenital and acquired. Congenital disabilities are, by definition, those disabilities that exist at or before birth as a result of hereditary or environmental factors. Some disabilities are *only* congenital, such as Down syndrome, muscular dystrophy, cerebral palsy, spina bifida, and achondroplasia (dwarfism). Other disabilities, such as blindness, deafness, and intellectual disability, can be either congenital or acquired later in life. You will remember that we learned in Chapter 3 that the type of onset of the disability influences the degree of stigma directed toward the individual. Generally speaking, congenital disabilities elicit less prejudice and stigma than do acquired disabilities. (This lack of stigma may be a result of the fact that individuals are usually not held responsible for the cause of a disability with which they are born.) Of course, disabilities acquired for "noble purposes," such as war, are viewed with less stigma than congenital disabilities. Also, keep in mind that we are discussing perceived onset because, in many cases, others do not actually know if the disability is congenital or acquired.

Generally, the earlier the age of onset, the better the response and adjustment. While this is not always true, it has been found that, for example, children with congenital limb deficiencies adjust better than children with acquired amputations, and children whose diabetes is diagnosed early adapt better than those who are diagnosed with diabetes later in life. This may be a result of several factors: (1) children's cognitive and affective resiliency and flexibility, (2) the fact that there are no premorbid identity or functional losses, (3) children have not internalized society's prejudices and discriminations about disability, and (4) children have not fully developed their body image. Children can be resilient and accepting of disability, able to learn medical self-management techniques and other adaptive strategies that are appropriate to their developmental level. For example, using a dialysis machine or hearing aids or putting on a prosthesis, for most children, is not a distressing and emotionally fraught experience. For these children, the adaptive strategies are part of daily living. Also, these children have no non-disability identity. Geri Jewell, a comedienne, explained, "It's not like I wake up every morning and say, 'Oh my goodness, I have cerebral palsy!'

I was born like this." Many individuals with congenital disabilities state: "For me, abnormal is normal!" Finally, it is safe to say that the older the individual is when he or she acquires the disability, the more he or she acquires the prejudices, stereotypes, and attitudes of the tragic, limited view of life with a disability. Of course, there are some exceptions to this. For example, individuals who have a family member with a disability would have a more accurate view of life with a disability. In addition, a child with a disability will not confront, on a daily basis, all the prejudices and discrimination against disabilities until he or she enters school.

Brenda Premo, born with a degenerating type of blindness, described what she considered to be the advantages of a congenital disability:

> The fact that I was born with my visual disability has had advantages. I have what my eye doctor calls "compensating skills." My brain has compensated and fills in the pictures of what I cannot see with my eyes. For example, I remember where steps are if I have been on them before. I see the steps because the brain is filling in what the eyes can't see. Sometimes I make mistakes, so I have to be careful, but my brain gives me the picture. It's easier for me than for someone who is blinded later in life. (Mackelprang & Salsgiver, 1999, p. 140)

Ruth Tollifson (1997) was born without her right hand and half of her right arm. From this excerpt we can see that Tollifson had an unusual reaction to her congenital disability:

> I remember the first time I actually looked closely at my arm, without looking away. I was twenty-five years old at the time, in therapy, sobering up from a near-suicidal nosedive into substance abuse. It was a terrifying moment. I was drenched in sweat, literally. But amazingly enough, I found that the arm I was seeing was not some loathsome, ridiculous, scary object I had imagined, but something else entirely, a world I had never seen before. (p. 106)

A student of mine related in a class discussion the difference (for him) between congenital blindness and acquired blindness. My student was born blind and attended the Utah School for the Deaf and Blind and is, therefore, trained in orientation and mobility (O&M) and knows Braille very well. He was asked to speak to an older woman who was slowly losing her sight. The woman had had a highly successful career as a nurse and hospital administrator, which her degenerating vision required her to give up. While both the woman and my student were blind, my student felt that he could offer little help because he had no idea of what it is like to lose one's vision. With most disabilities there is a great deal of difference between congenital onset and an acquired onset, making the experience of the same disability very dissimilar.

Parents of Children With Congenital Disabilities

In this section, look for—

✧ how knowledge or perception of the cause of the disability is important in determining how the family deals with the disability

We have learned in Chapter 1 that of the 62.2 million American children under the age of 15 in 2010, 8.4% had a disability, and 5.2% had a severe disability. Therefore, more than one half of all children with disabilities had severe disabilities (Brault, 2012).

When a baby is born with a congenital disability, it is the parents who respond and adjust to the disability. Often, the parents grieve over the loss of the baby that they had imagined, the baby without a disability. At the same time that parents are grieving for the "loss of one baby," they must care for and provide treatment for the "baby that remains" (Powers, 1993, p. 121). Furthermore, although the onset and diagnosis of the disability occurred at the time of birth (or before), the symptoms, manifestations, or medical crises that occur later may create additional losses for the parents. Often, the unpredictability of the course of the disability, or even the prospect of the baby's death, makes the response and adjustment process difficult and unpredictable for parents and siblings. As we learned in Chapter 1, there are more congenital disabilities than ever before because of the advances in neonatal medicine. Many adults with disabilities report that the doctors, and their parents, did not expect them to live (when they were infants) and, moreover, doctors were not quite sure of the type of medical treatment to provide for them. Some parents with infants with congenital disabilities are told by medical professionals that a definitive diagnosis can only be made after an autopsy. In other words, only upon the individual's death will a diagnosis become possible. The importance of a diagnosis, not only for treatment and prognosis, is clearly described below. Note that the diagnosis becomes a part of a PWD's self-identity, and when a definitive diagnosis is not possible, a part of an individual's self-identity is missing.

> Jerome Groopman [physician and author] wrote in *The New Yorker*, "The name of the illness becomes part of the identity of the sufferer." The sadness of a poor prognosis is vastly easier than the chaos of no prognosis. Once the course is clear, most people can accept it. Since knowledge is power, syndromes associated with dire prospects are borne more nobly than those of which little can be understood. Identity is a function of certitude. (Solomon, 2012, p. 366)

Without a diagnosis, it is difficult to determine prognosis. In addition, many adolescents who had congenital disabilities or acquired disabilities early in life were not provided with either sex education or career counseling and exploration services be-cause no one thought these children would survive to adulthood. Therefore, both sex education and career counseling were considered to be irrelevant for these teenagers. However, many did (and do) survive to adulthood.

As we discussed in Chapter 6, there is a stage theory of adaptation or response to disability. The stage theory holds that there are predictable, normal stages of respond-ing; however, this theory is most often thought of in terms of the individual who is ex-periencing the disability. In the case of congenital disabilities, the parents and siblings (and perhaps grandparents) progress through these stages. Parental adaptation or re-sponse to a congenital disability in their baby is often not validated or even "normed" by society. That is to say, others, such as relatives or neighbors, may not understand the grief, anger, or questioning experienced by the parents (Harper, 1999; G. H. S. Singer & Irvin, 1989; G. H. S. Singer, Powers, & Olson, 1996). Reread the letter from "Grateful Mom in Buffalo" in Chapter 5 for an example.

Parental guilt plays a role in the adjustment or adaptation response. You will re-member that in Chapter 6 we learned that many PWDs engage in self-blame and guilt for the onset of the disability. With congenital disabilities, it is the parents who attri-bute the cause of the disability to something they did or did not do. Often, parents, especially mothers, feel responsible for the disability. One father did not assist his wife in caring for their newborn baby with a disability because he held his wife responsible for the baby's disability (Nixon, 1993). Genetically based disabilities elicit guilt in both the mother and the father. Friends and neighbors may ask what the mother did or did not do during the pregnancy, thus unintentionally blaming the mother for the disabil-ity. Parents also blame themselves when they are not able to help the child. The role of a parent is to protect the helpless infant, and when a baby is born with a disability, the parents may feel that they failed to protect the child from harm.

Often, parents feel directly or indirectly blamed by medical professionals, either for the cause of their child's disability or for the management of their child's disability. We also learned that self-blame is the price some individuals pay for devising an etiol-ogy for the disability. Rather than viewing the infant's disability as a random event, parents blame themselves and thus alleviate the stress of an unknown etiology. Parents can blame each other and, in so doing, place stress on the marital relationship with comments such as, "This came from your side of the family." Older brothers and sisters often think that they did (or did not do) something to cause the disability. According to the National Public Radio (1998c) Disability History Project, often, extended fam-ily members look at the newborn with a congenital disability and say, "This should have been caught." Parents who know about the disability before the birth and choose not to have an abortion may be seen as irresponsible and selfish. Because of the com-bination of the capability to test for several types of disability before the birth of the child and the belief, held by some, that disability should be avoided at all costs, the parents may be blamed for refusing an abortion. In addition, the "super-parent" ideals of doing everything possible for the child or of being 100% responsible for the child often lead to parental guilt when these unrealistic and self-imposed expectations cannot be met.

Families who have an infant with a congenital disability must deal with all the typical family demands and at the same time begin to negotiate a host of disability-related concerns. Parents must learn about the disability itself and must also learn to deal with a complex medical system. These parents are faced with a staggering amount of technical and medical information. Reread the excerpt in Chapter 6 that tells of the parents, who, on returning from peer support groups meetings, took Pepto Bismol. Further, some of the information and treatment recommendations are contradictory. For the first time, for many families, they are required to contact and elicit the assistance of governmental agencies. Simply moving through the medical and legal service systems can be bewildering. The parents are faced with these changes and tasks while experiencing the shock and grief many experience at the birth of a child with a disability (Head, Head, & Head, 1985; Rolland, 1994). In addition, many of their familiar social supports may have disappeared. Often, parents reported that they dream of their children doing activities that their disabilities will not allow them to do, such as dancing, speaking, or reading books. Friends and relatives often distance themselves from the parents who have a child with a disability; therefore, exactly when the parents need support, stability, and instrumental assistance, they slowly begin to understand that their familial and social networks are no longer there (Santelli, Turnbull, Lerner, & Marquis, 1993). Often, both parents are sleep deprived, the mother has just finished a physically stressful pregnancy, or both. In addition, there may be older siblings that require care and support in their adjustment process (Graliker, Fishler, & Koch, 1962; Keydel, 1988). Sometimes one of the parents (usually the mother) must quit his or her job to provide care to the infant, further straining the family's financial status. Many parents feel overwhelmed.

One mother told of her experience:

> There are heavy demands for a highly functional, two-parent family that is financially stable. However, many families that have children with disabilities do not enjoy these advantages. The increasing number of single parents (most often, mothers) and the mobility of the U.S. population make it far more common for the family of a child with a congenital disability to be a single mother without extended family nearby.

In Solomon's (2012) book, *Far From the Tree,* there are many examples of parents making successful adjustments to a birth of a baby with severe and multiple disabilities. Nonetheless, many of these parents also experienced overwhelming grief. One father spoke of his daughter, Maisie: "Just once or twice I've thought it might be better for all of us if Maisie died. I can never tell how much that's sympathy for Maisie's frustration and pain, and how much it's something selfish" (Solomon, 2012, p. 364). A mother who gave birth to a second son with severe and multiple disabilities, Sam, considered suicide for herself and both her sons. A few months after Sam's diagnosis, the mother, Sara, hit rock bottom: "I sat on the kitchen floor trying to convince myself to take the boys with me to the garage and turn on the car and let all of us go on the carbon monoxide" (Solomon, 2012, p. 363).

Another mother (Miller, 1988) did not feel that she experienced the typical stages of adjustment:

> I had read many times about the grief surrounding the birth of a child with defects [*sic*], but the literature had not seemed to apply to me. My life certainly included denial, anger, bargaining, depression, and acceptance. But for me these were not milestones on a timeline, but were aspects of every day, sometimes every hour. Furthermore, there was little grief attached to the "expected baby." The grief was tied up with the whole mental picture I had for myself, my family, and our future. Feeling I had failed myself, Kurt [her husband], Beth [the baby], the family, and even society itself, what I really had lost was my whole sense of self-esteem. (p. 145)

Baby Beth's mother seems to be caught up with both grief and self-blame.

Another mother related:

> Later, the words which have already reverberated in my head are pronounced by the neurologist: cerebral palsy. As he reviews the findings, a door slowly shuts. While there will be no miracle, neither will Robbie die soon. As we leave the clinic carrying our reprieved son, the ghost of Robbie-might-have-been begins to drift away. (Curry, 1995, p. 26)

Note the way in which the mother expresses her growing awareness of her baby's disability: a door slowly closing and a ghost drifting away.

Grief over a disability is closely related to the individual's and his or her family's perception of loss and of normality. With the birth of a child with a congenital disability, many families may believe that their high standards can no longer be maintained. According to Rolland (1994):

> Families with strong beliefs in high achievement and perfectionism tend to equate normality with the optimal, to define normality or successful family functioning in terms of ideal or problem-free circumstances. Families that define normality in this way are prone to apply (disability) standards that are inappropriate because the kind of control they are accustomed to is impossible in this situation. . . . The fact that life cycle goals may take longer or need revision may require some modification in beliefs about what is normal and healthy. Sustaining hope, particularly in situations of long-term adversity, demands an ability to embrace a flexible and broad definition of normality. (p. 135)

However, the birth of a child with a congenital disability often results in a great deal of family cohesion, strong family bonds, and a high level of competence. The stress and demands of a baby with a disability can provide the opportunity for the family to change and grow in constructive ways. As old friends and extended family members drift away, new social networks are formed, often with families of children with congenital disabilities.

Parents often must make decisions concerning medical care, living arrangements, and the type of education for their child with a disability, all of which have long-range ramifications for both the child and the family (Greenberg, 1980). For many community services, such as schools, children with severe congenital disabilities are "peripheral" to their basic mission (Sailor, Kleinhammer-Tramill, Skrtic, & Oas, 1996, p. 329), or insurance policies may not pay for noninstitutional care, or the prevailing professional opinion advocates a certain type of treatment or education. Faced with an array of needs—a complicated structure of services and payment requirements—parents must make decisions. Occasionally, as would be expected, the children of these parents grow up and later question or resent the decisions made by their parent(s).

In previous chapters, we have learned about several types of treatment, care, and education decisions that parents must make for their young children with disabilities. These include: the type of education for children who are deaf, oralism or ASL (American Sign Language); cochlear implants for children who are deaf; limb lengthening for children who are Little People; facial plastic surgery for children with Down syndrome; a series of corrective surgeries; and residential school or community schools. Parents, of course, make what they consider to be the best decisions after consultation with other parents and professionals.

Today, there are elderly parents with middle-aged children who have been in institutions for decades. These parents feel themselves unjustly maligned when they are asked why they allowed their children to "be put into an institution." These parents remind us that when their children were born, there were no special education classes in the neighborhood schools, no home nursing care, no respite care, nor the array of community and home services available today. Moreover, if the disability was or is a low-incidence disability, such as deaf–blindness, there were (and are) still fewer services. For example, if the parents lived in a rural area and their child had a severe disability, the physician may have had no experience in treating people with this disability. In sum, these parents felt they had no choice.

Couser (1997) stated, "The prevailing norms of the modern American family presume the absence of a disability" (p. 252). For example, most television comedies or dramas that feature families do not show families that have a member with a disability. Television programs portray families with LGBT (Lesbian, Gay, Bisexual, or Transgendered) parents, biracial families, and single-parent families. This makes sense because these types of families are representative of typical American life and viewers can relate to these imaginary TV families. Nonetheless, there are few, if any, families on television who have a member with a disability.

Westbrook and Legge (1993) conducted a study in Australia that provides a glimpse of the difference in familial coping with children with disabilities. Westbrook and Legge sought to learn the perceptions and attitudes of families toward children with disabilities because, as they stated, "The family's perception of the cause and meaning of the disability is communicated to the child and also influences the experiences which are provided for the child and the life roles that he or she is expected to achieve" (p. 176). The researchers studied six communities in Australia, labeling two of the communities *individualistic* and four of the communities *collectivistic*. The collectivistic communities were the Arab, Chinese, Greek, and Italian groups, and the individualistic communities were Anglo-Australian and German groups. Westbrook and Legge found the following:

> In all four collectivistic communities, there were significant differences [when compared with the individualistic communities] in believing that it is a greater tragedy to have a son with a disability and that it is desirable to conceal the existence of a child with a disability. However, they considered that such a child places less strain on the parents' marriage than do Anglo-Australians. Giving birth to a disabled [*sic*] child was considered more shameful in the Greek and Chinese communities. In these and the Arabic communities there was a stronger belief that disability in a family reduces relatives' marital chances. (p. 183)
>
> There was significantly less expectation within the Italian, Greek, Arabic, and Chinese communities that children with disabilities would attend school, accompany their families on social outings, or behave like other children. (p. 182)

This is a single study, and as the authors themselves concluded, there are few studies that seek to examine cultural differences in family attitudes toward children with disabilities. Nonetheless, the questions they asked merit consideration because questions such as these underscore the importance of considering the family's cultural values before automatically assuming that the family responds to the child with a disability in the same way that Euro-American, middle-class families do. Clearly, not all families are Euro-American and middle-class (D. Brown, 1997).

Atypical Childhood Experiences

In this section, look for—

- ✧ how the atypical childhood experiences of individuals with congenital disabilities may include the following:
  - prolonged hospitalizations

- early socialization into the role of patient
- overprotection
- relaxation of discipline
- a large number of adults with whom to relate
- abuse, neglect, and abandonment

Individuals with some types of congenital disabilities often have atypical childhood experiences. Repeated hospitalizations; frequent surgeries and other types of medical treatments; and, occasionally, residential schooling are experiences that children with certain types of congenital disabilities (and disabilities acquired early in life) undergo. Thus, the infant or young child is completely socialized into the role of patient. These are not the typical childhood experiences; however, as the child is experiencing many of them, he or she is often not aware that his or her life is unusual. Nonetheless, most adults with congenital disabilities view their childhoods, in retrospect, as unique and different from the experiences of most children.

One adult described the prolonged and frequent hospitalizations during his child-hood: "I was in the hospital so much, my parents were my best friends." Naturally, as a small child, he would not have known that his lack of friends of his same age was unusual. Another adult whose mother had a mental illness and spent years in residential care facilities succinctly stated, "I grew up running up and down the hall of mental hospitals." Children without disabilities usually have very little contact with physicians. In contrast, children with disabilities are thoroughly socialized into the world of medical professionals.

One of the most commonly reported experiences of children with congenital disabilities is the overprotection of their mothers. Linda Pelletier, a woman with cerebral palsy, told of two experiences of overprotection. The first is somewhat humorous.

> One of the complications of this birth trauma was that I was more suscep-
> tible to respiratory infection. . . . [my mother] was afraid to allow me to go
> outdoors for fear of my getting a chill. . . . One of my most vivid recollections
> is going to see fireworks on the Fourth of July. I was sitting in a car with the
> windows rolled up, wearing ski pants, thermal underwear, and a winter coat.
> I became nauseous and almost fainted before the fireworks were even over.
> (Pelletier, 1988, p. 55)

In contrast, Ms. Pelletier labels her mother's overprotectiveness as destructive in the second description.

> My mother's overprotection was also a destructive element in my develop-
> ment. She assumed complete care of all of my physical needs. This meant that
> I was lifted in and out of bed, onto the toilet, and in and out of our car. I was
> bathed, dressed, groomed and fed without my lifting a finger to help myself. I

realize now that it would have been extremely difficult for her to sit by passively and watch me struggle to perform these basic activities of daily living.
Although my mother meant well by catering to me in this way, it retarded
my physical development because I was never given the opportunity to work
on doing these essential tasks. Such a relationship caused me to be completely
dependent upon my parents. (Pelletier, 1988, p. 58)

Often, children with congenital disabilities are not disciplined, or standards of behavior are lowered for them. Parents, caregivers, and teachers often tolerate inappropriate behavior, explaining they don't "have the heart" to discipline children with
disabilities. Remember, this is related to the concept of sympathy and pity for PWDs
or "let's give these poor PWDs a break" that we discussed earlier in Chapter 5. Read
the following statement in which a young child begins to suspect that he is sick when
the discipline is relaxed: "I know I'm very sick . . . because everyone treats me differently. Before I became ill, my parents never let me get away with bad behavior. Now,
I can even hit my little sister without being punished" (Whitt, 1984, p. 77).

Overprotection and relaxation of discipline can result in a lack of mastery, competence, and self-confidence and can often isolate the child. Those behaviors and attitudes, begun in earliest infancy, often continue until the individual reaches adulthood.
Thus, often children with congenital disabilities are needlessly handicapped. One of
my students is blind. In a class discussion, this student told of a friend of hers who is
also blind. The woman, who was born blind, was never allowed in the backyard or the
basement of her home. She simply had no concept of these areas of her house, or of any
house. Often, the overprotection of children who are congenitally blind is discovered
when they begin school. Occasionally, these children cannot do the most basic tasks
because family members have relieved these children of responsibilities such as dressing themselves or placing a telephone call.

Many adults who were born with congenital disabilities have expressed gratitude
and some degree of amazement that their parents were able to demand services and
accommodations for them. Parents demanded that their children be allowed to attend public school, often when they themselves did not have much education, and
family members required that the child with the disability accomplish as much as
possible. These adult PWDs credit much of their success to their parents and families. Erik Weihenmayer climbed Mt. Everest, and he is blind. He related an experience in which his mother insisted that he, as a young child, be permitted to enter
school.

I don't know how my mother found the strength to oppose the world. Maybe
it's simply a mother's primal instinct to nurture and defend her child. She was
as unprepared as the administrators sitting across from us. Somehow, though,
she believed in me. I was just a little boy with my ink-smudged nose pressed
against the page. I had nothing yet to prove myself, so how she saw strength,

opportunity, and promise, while other people saw problems, obstacles, and limits, I'll never know for sure. (Weihenmayer, 2001, p. 14)

A story of the way in which a child, Max, with severe and multiple disabilities escaped overprotection occurred because another child with disabilities was able to convince Max's mother that Max was more than okay and that he was "having the time of his life." Max went off to a special summer camp for the first time when he was 9 years old, and Susanna (Max's mother) phoned the camp. Finally, one of the other campers took the call and offered some friendly advice, "Mrs. Singer, Max is having the time of his life. My parents always go away when I'm at camp; maybe you should consider doing that" (Solomon, 2012, p. 373). Mrs. Singer probably had phoned repeatedly and heard the same message from adult camp leaders, but it was another child who was able to make Mrs. Singer understand.

One clear-cut exception is the case of children with learning disabilities (LD) or attention-deficit disorder (usually boys) who are overpunished. Parents, relatives, and teachers attribute the inability of these children to focus, to sit still, to control impulses, to complete tasks on time, and to respond to multiple requests at one time as defiance and willful lack of cooperation. Because of the misunderstanding of others, or because of lack of a diagnosis, these children with LD are subjected to a great deal of punishment and negative feedback. Indeed, many experts on LD attribute the high rate of these children dropping out of school to their wish to escape the punishment and humiliation from their teachers and peers.

Abuse and Neglect of Children With Congenital Disabilities

Parental depression, caregiver stress, or both can lead to abuse or neglect of the infant or child with a congenital disability. Stressors that are thought to lead to abuse and neglect include "(1) regular loss of sleep because of caregiving demands, (2) the child's severe medical problems, (3) the child's severe behavior problems, (4) the child's unusual appearance, and (5) adversity in the family combined with caregiving responsibilities" (G. H. S. Singer, 1996, p. 25). The more support the parents have in providing care for an infant, the smaller the probability of abuse and neglect occurring. Such support includes linking parents with self-help groups in which they can meet with other parents who have a child with the same type of disability, providing respite care, providing in-home health care for complicated medical procedures, providing financial subsidies, and offering supportive counseling. Two generations ago, all these types of support were usually provided by extended family members. With the changing demographics of America, such as divorce and geographic mobility, these types of support are now provided by professional caregivers.

A Large Number of Adults With Whom to Relate

Simply because the world of medical care is populated by adults, many children with congenital disabilities are in the care of a large number of different adults. Children probably do not form long-term relationships with many of these caregivers, because (1) there are too many of these caregivers, (2) these relationships are often transient in nature, (3) the caregivers must obey hospital and agency rules, and (4) most caregivers are motivated by pay. A secretary at a residential school for children who are deaf reported,

> They have so many people to relate to. They go to bed with one houseparent and wake up with another one, and then numerous adults engage them all day long, they must deal with various administrators and different security officers throughout their lives here. . . . (Evans & Falk, 1986, p. 100)

There are risks for children who are exposed to a great many adults, including (1) the lack of ability to develop healthy reciprocal, empathic feelings (attachment bonds) and (2) vulnerability to physical and sexual abuse. Rutter (1989) found that young children in institutions and hospitals typically encounter 50 to 80 caregivers before reaching school age.

In the PBS (1988) video, *A Paralyzing Fear*, a woman told of a night in the hospital when she was a little girl with polio. The little girl was crying because she was homesick and missed her family. The nurse came in and told the girl that if she did not stop crying, the nurse would unplug her respirator. The little girl stopped crying that night, but she wept, as an adult, when she recounted the experience. When an adult is exposed to many different caregivers, he or she usually has the ability to question and challenge the treatment or the lack of treatment. However, children with disabilities are powerless and must submit to adults. Indeed, many adults report that it is only in retrospect that they understand the power that adult caregivers wielded over them when they were children.

The child who lives at home and attends community schools has daily reminders that, because of his or her disability, he or she is different from other children. Medical treatments, assistive devices, and doctors' appointments serve to remind the child that he or she is different. If the course of the disability is episodic, life threatening, or both, medical treatments can be unexpected emergencies that require aggressive treatment. At these points, the child understands that hospitalization or treatment is more important than school attendance.

Children with disabilities can be at risk for emotional maladaptation, including behavioral problems, low self-esteem, and poor resolution of developmental tasks (Breslau, 1982; Breslau & Marshall, 1985; Heller, Rafman, Zvagulis, & Pless, 1985). These researchers found that (1) central nervous system involvement in the disability (i.e., intellectual disability) was associated with greater psychosocial problems, and (2) the family's coping responses affect the child's response.

Nonetheless, most parents learn to adapt to their child's disability and raise their child to think of himself or herself as being just like anyone else, with the exception of the disability. Many parents and other family members come to accept and celebrate the child and his or her disability.

Prelingual Deafness

In this section look for—

◇ the characteristics of prelingual deafness
  • The individual does not have speech abilities.
  • The individual does not have a memory of sound or language.

◇ differences between a child who is deaf being born to hearing parents and a child who is deaf being born to parents who are deaf

Time of onset is an important factor in deafness; however, time of onset is thought of as neither congenital or acquired, but rather as prelingual deafness or postlingual deafness. Prelingual deafness refers to deafness acquired before the development of speech, and postlingual deafness refers to deafness acquired after the development of speech. (Of course, prelingual deafness can also be congenital deafness.) An example of an individual with prelingual deafness is Helen Keller. She was not born deaf or blind, but at the age of 19 months, she developed what was then called "brain fever." Most physicians today think that the baby Helen Keller had either scarlet fever or meningitis. After her recovery, she was both deaf and blind with few, if any, memories of vision or hearing.

The earlier in life a child acquires deafness, the more likely he or she is to identify with the Deaf Culture. Gershon (as cited in Edwards, 1997) used the term *permanent exile* to describe all people who are deaf because they are exiled from the hearing world, and he used the term *immigrant* to describe individuals who become deaf later in life. These individuals are immigrants to the Deaf Culture because "they never lose their hearing accent." Those who grow up deaf are natives of the Deaf Culture (Edwards, 1997, p. 42).

Individuals with prelingual deafness have no memory of sound, of language, or of being able to hear and to speak. Congenital deafness also involves another element that most congenital disabilities do not—whether or not the parents are also deaf. Lane, Hoffmeister, and Bahan (1996) describe the reaction of parents who are deaf to the birth of a child who is deaf:

> In general . . . many members of the DEAF-WORLD would prefer to have a Deaf child to having a hearing child, those whose happiness at the advent of a Deaf child is tinged with sadness (after all, that child will face many extra challenges) commonly overcome their reservations quickly. If you belong to a hearing culture, you may find such Deaf preferences hard to understand. (pp. 24–25)

It is difficult to understand the Deaf Culture without knowledge of the tragic and horrific history of the oralist movement and residential schools.

Lane et al. explained why parents who are deaf often want children who are deaf:

> The birth of a Deaf baby in a Deaf household signifies that the Deaf heritage of the family will be secure. Deaf families with many Deaf members are commonly proud of their genealogy.
>
> In other words, when a Deaf infant of Deaf parents is diagnosed as Deaf, the joy of the parents reflects the fact that most Deaf parents, like parents generally, look forward to having children who are a reflection of themselves.... Deaf parents bring their Deaf baby home to a nurturing environment in which communication is naturally dependent on visual, not aural (hearing) cues. Almost all use the signed language of the DEAF-WORLD to interact with their child. Their home is already functioning as an environment conducive to using vision as the main means of learning and communication.... Like the hearing child born to a well-functioning hearing family, the Deaf infant in a Deaf family ... is immediately exposed to a world suited to maximizing his or her social, emotional, psychological, cognitive, and linguistic development. (pp. 25–26)

Some couples, in which both partners are deaf, have undergone genetic testing when they are expecting a baby to ascertain the "risk" of having a hearing infant (Mackelprang & Salsgiver, 1999). Deaf parents of a baby who is deaf realize that their baby's physician and other medical care providers view the deafness as a negative situation and as a condition that must be ameliorated as quickly as possible. Many parents who are deaf appreciate the concern of the physician but resist the physician's attempts to pathologize the deafness of their baby or to subject the baby to hearing aids and other prostheses. Obviously the physicians often view disability from the Biomedical Model, and Deaf parents of children who are deaf view it from the Environmental Model.

Deaf children with Deaf Parents ("Deaf of Deaf) learn sign language immediately after birth, and, therefore, ASL is their first language, and these children are considered "native" signers. Deaf of Deaf, when compared to Deaf children with hearing parents, typically achieve fluent written English and score higher in academic areas and social skills, such as independence, reliability, and willingness to communicate with strangers. However, most children who are deaf, whether the time of onset is congenital, prelingual, or postlingual, are children of hearing parents. Indeed, 80% of all babies who are born deaf are born to hearing parents; further, the diagnosis of deafness usually occurs months or years after birth. Most often, the child is isolated within his or her own family because of the lack of communication. Both the parents and the child are frustrated.

People who are deaf, like most PWDs, have been handicapped by medical and educational professionals who have advocated treatment and education that have not been in the best interests of the Deaf. Nonetheless, the Deaf have been subjected to more professional misjudgment, paternalism, and control than any other disability group.

For example, for years, most educators of the Deaf (who usually were not deaf themselves) advocated the oralism method, in which children were not allowed to use sign language and instead were required to speak. (Alexander Graham Bell, the inventor of the telephone, was the most famous advocate of oralism.) Oralism was impossible for many, and, for most children who were deaf, it provided years of frustration and failure, especially because these children were not allowed to learn and use sign language. In some schools, children were required to sit on their hands or had their hands tied so they could not use their hands to sign. Lip reading was taught, in spite of the fact that lip reading is not very accurate. Training or educating children who were deaf in oralism and lip reading was an attempt to reduce discomfort in people without disabilities and force the Deaf to fit into a hearing world, without making any demands on the hearing world. In so doing, children who were deaf were deprived of a language and a culture. Today, the Deaf Culture actively fights against these types of attempts by hearing physicians and educators to "make deaf people fit in."

The debate over cochlear implants often makes deafness appear to be an "elective disability." Sweden is the only country with a law requiring parents considering cochlear implants to consult with a member of the Deaf community before making this decision. In this way, the parents learn about living with deafness before consenting to the surgery. Although the technology of the implants has improved and the acceptance of the implants by Deaf families has increased, there are still those who refuse them. This illustrates the difficulties in viewing Deafness as a culture rather than as a disability group. Societies go to great lengths to preserve languages and cultures and understand the great loss when languages die. Cochlear implants have the potential to greatly reduce the use of sign languages. As we have learned, the Deaf Culture has sought to refuse the pathology, inferiority, and handicapping attitudes of PWODs. However, does society have an obligation to pay for accommodations and specialized education when deafness can be ameliorated? Tucker (1998) explained the dilemma facing the Deaf Culture:

> The primary argument against deliberately seeking to produce deaf children is that it violates the child's own autonomy and narrows the scope of her choices when she grows up; in other words, it violates her right to an "open future." Insisting that children who are deaf be raised in a Deaf cultural community denies those children the right to choose for themselves to accept or reject the larger hearing world.
>
> When most deafness becomes correctable, which for many people has already occurred and for others may well happen in the near future, an individual who chooses not to correct his or her deafness (or the deafness of his or her child) will lack the moral right to demand that others pay for costly accommodations to compensate for the lack of hearing of that individual. In this age of budget crises and cries for tax reform, when there is talk of, and some action with respect to, the need to cut funding for welfare, Medicaid,

Social Security, federally supported food banks, and other social welfare programs, it is unrealistic, at best, to expect society to fund expenditures that
could be eliminated. (p. 8)

Oliver Sacks, the neurologist and author, conducted a study that showed that sign
language, when learned as a native language, is a language comparable to any spoken
language. Andrew Solomon, in his 2012 book, *Far From the Tree*, summarized the results of this study:

A Deaf person with a left-hemisphere lesion after a stroke will retain the
ability to understand or produce gesture, but lose the ability to understand
or produce Sign, much as a hearing person with a left-hemisphere lesion
will lose the ability to speak and understand language, but will still understand and produce facial expressions. Neuroimaging shows that while
people who acquire Sign early have almost all of it in the language regions,
people who Sign in adulthood tend to use the visual part of their brain
more. (pp. 52–53)

Congenital Blindness or Blindness Acquired in Infancy

In this section, look for—

✧ Individuals with congenital blindness:
- have no visual experience with concepts such as color,
  shape, distance, or proportion
- are not able to learn by observation

People who are born blind or become blind early in life have no visual experiences
with concepts such as colors, distance, depth, or proportion. Falvo (1991) explained:

[Individuals who have congenital blindness] because of their lack of visual
experience in their environment, such as the observation of tasks or behavior
of others . . . must learn by other means concepts that sighted individuals
often take for granted. This adaptive learning of tasks then becomes a natural
part of their developmental process so that the adjustment to visual limitations is incorporated into their self-perception and daily activities as a normal
part of growing up. Individuals who lose their vision later in life have the
advantage of being able to draw on visual experiences in the environment as
a frame of reference for physical concepts, but they may find it more difficult
to accept their blindness than those who have never had vision. (p. 255)

Residential Schools

In this section, look for—

- ♦ why mainstreaming children in the community school is not always better than placing the child in a residential school
- ♦ why, for children in residential schools, "school is family"
- ♦ the negative aspects of residential schools, which can include:
  - poor quality of education
  - bureaucracy and regulations leading to regimentation
  - abuse and molestation
  - lack of social skills
  - children not being socialized into their parents' world

Some children, especially those who are blind, deaf, or both, attend residential schools. Up until the 1960s, residential schooling was the only educational option for children who were deaf, blind, or both; indeed, before the 1960s, 80% of all children in the United States who were deaf attended residential schools (Lane, Hoffmeister, & Bahan, 1996). Residential schools offered education from preschool through high school and sometimes adult education. Since the 1960s, mainstreaming or inclusion into community schools has been facilitated by (a) providing sign language interpreters, (b) using "itinerant" teachers (teachers who teach at several different schools), and (c) providing self-contained classrooms for children who are deaf. Nonetheless, most children with severe hearing loss attend residential schools.

Thus, at an early age, children who attend residential schools are separated from their families, and many of these children are "homesick" for the school when they are at home for the holidays. In essence, school is their family. Residential education offers these children communication skills and socialization. Children in these types of schools, because everyone is deaf, blind, or both, participate in all school activities, including student body offices, athletics, and debate (opportunities they probably would not be afforded if they were mainstreamed in a community school). Other advantages of residential schooling include the availability of role models—teachers who are deaf, other students, and alumni of the school. Indeed, many individuals with congenital deafness or blindness have reported that their parents had very low educational and vocational expectations of them. It was the role models at residential schools who encouraged these individuals to fulfill their potential. Individuals in the Deaf Culture have campaigned against the closing of residential schools for Deaf children.

Dr. Geerat Vermeij, an evolutionary biologist, paleontologist, and professor at the University of California, Davis, has been blind since infancy. Dr. Vermeij argued for mainstreaming in local schools but also advocated that the child receive a solid foundation in learning certain skills in a separate classroom before being allowed to attend class with sighted children.

> The ideal situation, it seems to me, is for a blind child to attend a local school. At first, full attention should be devoted to learning the essential skills—Braille, independent travel, getting to know one's physical and social surroundings—in a class wholly dedicated to that purpose. Gradually, blind children should be eased into class with their sighted peers, with time being set aside to hone and expand the fundamental skills of blindness. Whatever the right solution is for any particular child, the goal of providing the necessary techniques as well as the self-confidence and social adaptations to live and compete successfully in sighted society must remain clearly fixed at center stage. (Vermeij, 1997, p. 36)

Mainstreaming children in community school is not always better than residential schooling. In a community school, the quality of education and accommodations for the disability may not be very good, and a child may simply attend school rather than receive an education. In the case of children who are deaf, sign language interpreters often have poor skills and, even more frequently, are not trained in the subject matter they are interpreting (such as chemistry). In addition, many children need to ride a bus for as long as 2 hours each way to attend a community school, thus consuming a large part of each school day. Also, there are no interpreters for casual, social encounters with hearing classmates. Therefore, the educational placement of children with deafness or blindness is complicated. Added to the complexity is the lack of coordination between medical services and educational services. For example, physicians who treat babies who are deaf often are not trained in or aware of available educational programs. Further, parents may receive conflicting advice from medical caregivers and educational professionals.

As would be expected, the quality of residential schools varies. Some of the negative aspects include the following:

- The quality of education at some schools was or is very poor; indeed, some schools concentrate on vocational education, especially in the manual trades. For example, in the past, the majority of graduates of residential schools for the Deaf did not continue on to college. (This is also a result of lack of accommodations at colleges and universities.)
- The bureaucracy, rules, and regulations often lead to regimentation. One graduate of a residential school spoke of the "damned bells" (Evans & Falk, 1986). This individual was referring to the fact that every minute of the day was controlled by the bells, and a set, unchanging, monotonous schedule was enforced. This organization of every detail of daily life can inhibit children's sense of self-mastery, independence, individuality, creativity, and initiative.

- Any bureaucracy may respond more to the administrators' needs and convenience than to the needs of the students. For example, one book I read had a schedule of a residential school for the Deaf. The children were allowed to go home for Thanksgiving only for the Thursday and Friday of Thanksgiving.

- Families assume that they are placing their children in a safe, secure environment when, in reality, abuse of children may occur in residential schools. Indeed, one houseparent stated, "You have to break deaf kids when they're young." This houseparent whipped the children with a large leather belt when they "misbehaved" (Evans & Falk, 1986, p. 100). These beatings were administered for relatively minor infractions. Another type of abuse is discussed in this statement: "A top administrator estimates that one-third of all students were 'abused and molested' children" (Evans & Falk, 1986, p. 99).

- Children may become dependent because all their basic needs of life are met. Indeed, there is a risk of "learned helplessness," or overcompliance, when the child is required to yield self-mastery, or never learned self-mastery in the first place.

- Children educated in residential schools usually experience less privacy and may have difficulty in adjusting to being alone; they also may be unprepared to take risks. Indeed, those in the Disability Rights Movement speak of the "dignity of risk," whereby an individual is allowed, and encouraged, to take risks, even with the possibility of failure. The dignity of risk is better than overprotection.

- The assumption that children can practice social behaviors in a supportive learning environment is not always true. Wolfensberger and Tullman (1991) argued that residential schools can be "culture-alien," and thus, residential education can contribute to a child's lack of social skills and ability to live outside the school. Wolfensberger noted,

  > The skills, habits, and relationships that are prerequisites for a meaningful life in open society are difficult to acquire in settings that are culture-alien, that lack familiar cues, reduce opportunity, suggest or impose alien or devalued roles, and so on. (p. 207)

- Barnes, Mercer, and Shakespeare (1999) summarized the "mortification of self" as described at length in Goffman's 1963 book, *Asylums*:

  > The process starts with the "mortification of the self." From the moment of entry into the institution, the patient is subjected to a series of "degradation rituals" designed to produce docility and submissiveness. The old self is removed and a standardized, institutionalized alternative is provided. A process of stripping, washing, and re-clothing removes almost all remembrances of their former life and produces a new identity. Permission is required to undertake even ordinary activities. The institution then engages in a "reorganization of the self" by supplying a

new patient identity with appropriate social props such as standardized clothing and set routines. A "privilege system" is operated to reward appropriate behavior and punish wrongdoing so that inmates identify with the "organization's goals and fate." (Barnes, Mercer, & Shakespeare, 1999, p. 45)

Goffman's description makes residential schools for children who are blind, deaf, or both sound like prison or the Marines!

- Regardless of how excellent the education, a residential school is not a home. Children educated in residential schools are often not socialized into their parents' world, including such aspects as siblings; extended family; racial, ethnic, and cultural identification; and religion.

Who decides the identity of a child who is deaf? Most babies who are deaf are born to hearing parents who typically have no knowledge or understanding of deafness, American Sign Language, or the Deaf Culture. Deaf adults who know all about deafness are strangers to their hearing family (Gulati, 2003).

It should be noted that we are not discussing institutions, such as those institutions that care for individuals with severe intellectual disability or individuals with severe mental illness. These types of institutions typically do not offer education as residential schools do.

The Cost of Residential Schools to PWODs

By failing to provide quality accommodations and adequate education in the community schools to children with disabilities, society pays for this segregation. First, our tolerance for diversity and difference is, unnecessarily, reduced. Second, society reinforces the existential angst and fear of acquiring a disability. In other words, if, as children, everyone were educated and socialized with children with disabilities, PWODs would understand the experience of disability more realistically and not fear it. Wendell (2006) clearly explained: "The public world is the world of strength, the positive [valued] body, performance and production, the able-bodied and youth. Wellness, illness, rest, recovery, pain, and death and the negative [devalued] body are private, hidden, and often neglected" (p. 266).

Although Wendell was not speaking of residential schools, she made the point that by not acknowledging or trying to understand the disability experience (by relegating PWDs to a "private, hidden" world), PWODs harm themselves.

Acquired Disabilities

In this section, look for—

- ✧ aspects of acquired disabilities
- ✧ the distinction between diagnosis and onset

◈ how the PWD may have internalized prejudices about disability
◈ how the individual may have a well-defined social role and status
◈ how, often, there is a literal overnight change

When we discussed congenital disabilities, we read that Geri Jewell said, "It's not like I wake up every morning and say, 'Oh my goodness, I have cerebral palsy!' I was born like this." Christopher Reeve, the actor who had a spinal cord injury, said in a television interview that on awakening every morning, he is surprised to find that he has quadriplegia. Obviously, the individual's disability identity, or lack of disability identity, differs in those with congenital disabilities and those with acquired disabilities.

It is important to make a distinction between onset and diagnosis. In many disabilities, the onset and the diagnosis occur at the same time; however, in some congenital and acquired disabilities the time of the onset and the time of the diagnosis are different. For example, deafness can be congenital, yet it often is not diagnosed until the infant is older; therefore, the time of onset (birth) and time of diagnosis are different. (Before the advent of universal newborn screening, the average age of diagnosing congenital deafness was 15 months.) In the case of some types of acquired disabilities, such as diabetes, macular degeneration, and schizophrenia, the time of onset is unknown (the onset is considered to be *insidious*) and it is the time of diagnosis that is referenced (although, in these types of disabilities, the genetic predisposition to develop these disabilities is present at birth). Nonetheless, for many disabilities, such as spinal cord injuries, traumatic brain injuries, and amputations, the time of onset and time of diagnosis are the same. In these types of disabilities, the onset is considered to be *acute*.

Acquired Disabilities and Prejudice and Discrimination

An individual who acquires a disability later in life has often internalized prejudices and discrimination about the disability. For an individual who has not had much experience with or knowledge of PWDs, he or she has been subjected to the prejudicial stereotypes and inaccurate views of disability. PWDs are often thought to be victims of tragic circumstances, socially isolated, without any quality of life and with few choices. Kevin Shirley, who acquired a traumatic brain injury at age 30, remarked, "Before I became disabled, I used to feel sorry for disabled [*sic*] people. I would feel sorry for them and do what I could to avoid them" (Mackelprang & Salsgiver, 1999, p. 205). If an individual has internalized these inaccurate assumptions and prejudices and then acquires a disability himself or herself, these prejudices, stereotypes, and attitudes now become *self-perceptions* (Glueckauf & Quittner, 1984).

Karen Pendleton acquired a spinal cord injury at age 36. In the following excerpt, she explains how little she knew about disability, even after she sustained her spinal cord injury:

It seems weird now, but it took me a while to become really accepting of others with disabilities. A really good eye-opener for me was a college course I took on the psychological aspects of disability. I took the class thinking I would know everything and get an easy A. But I really learned a lot in the class about other disabilities. Since then, I've learned a lot from other people with disabilities. I'm much more accepting of people with disabilities and of myself with a disability. (Mackelprang & Salsgiver, 1999, p. 99)

Lifelong attitudes and beliefs can be difficult to change, and, furthermore, most individuals never consider the possibility that one day they might have a disability, or they consider the possibility to be very remote. As we have stated before, disability is the only open minority group, meaning that anyone can join at any time. Nonetheless, most people deny the possibility that they might acquire (or discover) a disability, and, moreover, most people unquestioningly accept the widely held stereotypes of what life must be with a disability. Then, in some cases, overnight, these prejudices become self-perceptions. In contrast, prejudices and stereotyped attitudes toward racial, ethnic, and cultural groups, religious groups, sexual orientation groups, or political groups are not likely to become self-perceptions, because, in all likelihood, prejudiced individuals will never become a member of one of these groups.

An Acquired Disability Often Requires a Change of Identity

While not all acquired disabilities are considered to have a traumatic onset, such as the result of an accident, injury, or violence, most acquired disabilities are unpredictable and occur without warning. Because of this lack of warning, the individual has not been allowed to engage in anticipatory preparation. Many of life's transition points can be anticipated, including the natural results of aging, widowhood, retirement, and the death of one's parents. Instrumental preparations include financial arrangements, such as retirement plans and insurance policies. Perhaps even more helpful are the emotional preparations for life's transitions. Many life transitions require a change in self-identity, and changes in self-identity are stressful. Transitions include a new beginning and a simultaneous ending. In addition, many life transitions are viewed as universal (they happen to everybody sooner or later). However, the onset of a disability is not thought of as *happening*, especially in the earlier years of life.

An acquired disability may seem like the loss of identity, status, and independence. Individuals who acquire a disability in midlife often have earned a place of status and prestige in the community and are people with well-developed self-concepts. Individuals in midlife often feel that this will be a period of life to enjoy. Because of this well-established identity, the disability can seem to be an overwhelming loss. Karen Pendleton, who acquired a spinal cord injury at age 36, spoke about her change in identity. Notice the way in which she speaks of herself before the onset of the disability in the third person and how she buried the old Karen. The word *buried* communicates the total change in identity—she is implying that the old Karen is dead: "Over time, I figured out that old Karen was no more. It's like I had to bury her and get to know the Karen that was left here. I found that I like the new Karen a lot better than the old one! . . . Now all I have left is me" (Mackelprang & Salsgiver, 1999, p. 98). We can see that Ms. Pendleton feels that she has sustained a loss, but she views it as a positive loss.

In 1976, Robert Murphy was diagnosed with a spinal cord tumor when he was 52 years old. A professor of anthropology at Columbia University, Murphy wrote a book entitled, *The Body Silent in America* (1987). Murphy was an articulate man who was trained in foreign cultures. He described receiving the diagnosis of his disability as entering a country stranger and more foreign than any country in Africa or the Amazon.

Robert Murphy's sentiment is similar to the journalist Richard Cohen, who described his diagnosis period as a "journey into a strange land. That place would be exotic and rude" (R. M. Cohen, 2004, p. 17). Cohen said that he had had no training, education, or experience in dealing with the onset of a disability; nothing in his earlier life had prepared him for a disability. He felt that the label "winner" had been replaced with the label "damaged goods" (p. 27).

The acquisition and onset of a disability can alter an individual's sense of the future and, in some instances, the individual's sense of the past. Deegan, who was diagnosed with schizophrenia, explained:

> We experienced time as a betrayer. Time did not heal us. Our pasts deserted us, and we could not return to who we had been. Our futures appeared to us to be barren, lifeless places in which no dream could be planted and grow into a reality. As for the present, it was a numbing succession of meaningless days and nights in a world in which we had no place, no use, and no reason to be. (Deegan, 1991, p. 49)

The reaction to the diagnosis or the onset differs. Some individuals dealing with a diagnosis feel that they have an entirely new identity, whereas others consider themselves to be the same person as before (with the exception of the disability). In the following excerpt, the 24-year-old who woke up one morning with polio felt that she was a stranger to herself:

> Something happened and I became a stranger. I was a greater stranger to myself than anyone. Even my dreams did not know me. They did not know what they ought to let me do—and when I went to dances or parties in (my dreams), there was always an odd provision or limitation—not spoken of or mentioned, but there just the same. I suddenly had the very confusing and mental and emotional conflict of a lady leading a double life. It was unreal and it puzzled me, and I could not help dwelling on it. (Goffman, 1963, p. 35)

Other PWDs state that they did not experience a radical shift in identity on the acquisition or onset of their disability. Michalko (2002) is clear: "You are who you always were. You haven't changed" (p. 7). Jenny Morris has a spinal cord injury and described her initial terror and the way in which she decided on her identity:

> At the time, lying there in hospital, my terror was not about the disability as such, but that I might have destroyed the structure of my life. However, this terror did not last long. I resolved that the structure I had built would remain unchanged. All that had happened was that I would now be doing things from a sitting position. I needed to sort things out in order to be able to do this. (J. Morris, 1991, p. 4)

Family and friends also react to an acquired disability. These associates often change the way in which they view the PWD, feeling that he or she has sustained a loss of identity and belonging. However, the PWD often knows that he or she is the same person as before the acquisition of the disability, but he or she is also aware of the ways in which others do not relate to him or her (Crewe, 1997).

The Developmental Stage of Acquisition

In this section, look for—

- ◇ developmental stages
- ◇ required age-appropriate mastery of tasks
- ◇ how development theories are silent on the topic of disability
- ◇ how PWDs must negotiate the development tasks of each stage in addition to managing the disability

Developmental stages are usually defined as predictable phases that require certain responses from the individual. Basically, a child develops from requiring full support to being an adult with complete autonomy, with the individual mastering the tasks of each stage before moving on to the next stage. In other words, certain achievements are expected at each stage; indeed, there are age-appropriate tasks (or demands) that must be mastered. Each level of growth and development requires readjustment. Further, psychologists theorize that the successful, or unsuccessful, completion of these developmental tasks has a lifelong impact on the individual. Of course, these developmental stages do not proceed exactly on schedule for any individual; nonetheless, developmental stages provide a framework in which to view the phases of life.

The beginning, or successful completion, of a developmental stage is often marked with a rite of passage. We celebrate, hold observances, wear specific clothes (such as graduation robes and wedding dresses), receive gifts, host parties, give speeches, participate in religious ceremonies, send out announcements, send flowers, eat good food, and in general go to great lengths and expense to move an individual from one social status to another. These rites of passage ensure that society changes its perception of the individual and that the individual changes perceptions of himself or herself. Rites of passage are one way in which society enforces its cultural beliefs; to be specific, rites of passage communicate that these social statuses are both positive and significant (Turner, 1979). There are no rites of passage when an individual acquires a disability, probably because disability is seen as tragic and out of the ordinary (J. F. Smart, 2012a). Society has not endowed disability with a social category or identity. In spite of this lack of rites, many PWDs divide their lives into two categories: before the disability and after the disability. Marc Shell (2005) reviewed dozens of first-person accounts of polio and discovered that some polio survivors divided their lives into two parts—before polio and after polio—while others conceptualized the polio experience as a type of graduation.

> A few polio-authors present themselves as having two lives—BP and AP—before polio and after polio. For others, the moment of poliomyelitic "rebirth" is marked off as if the individual had graduated from something like a university or a "school." (Shell, 2005, p. 22)

There is little, if any, social role guidance for the disability experience (Agich, 1995), and there is no valued social category for disability. The absence of role guidance (and role models) exaggerates the difficulties of receiving a diagnosis. One 24-year-old woman explained:

> But suddenly, I woke up one morning and found that I could not stand. I had had polio and polio was as simple as that. I was like a very young child who had been dropped into a big, black hole. . . . The education, the lectures, and the parental training which I had received for twenty-four years didn't seem to make me the person who could do anything for me now. (Goffman, 1963, p. 35)

Before we begin our discussion of these developmental stages and their corresponding tasks, it should be noted that psychologists, such as Erikson (1963) and Havighurst (1951), devised their theories without much attention or awareness of disability issues. Nonetheless, individuals with disabilities must negotiate all the developmental stages that PWODs are required to negotiate. In addition, PWDs must respond to and manage the disability and society's prejudices and discrimination.

The acquisition of a disability, at any age or developmental stage of life, may signal the loss of universal and normative tasks. It may be necessary to alter, delay, or give up the developmental tasks of the next stage. Children with disabilities often see their older siblings successfully (and happily) negotiating developmental stages and expect that they, too, will have these experiences. Therefore, each developmental stage reached by siblings without disabilities can result in grieving for the child with a disability and for the entire family. In spite of this, it is becoming more and more common to allow children and young adults opportunities and experiences that were previously considered beyond their capabilities.

Infancy and Preschool Children

In infancy, the most important developmental task is that of establishing trust with the world. According to Erikson (1968), this trust is established primarily through the infant's relationship with the mother or other primary caregiver. For the infant with a disability, this may be difficult if he or she is hospitalized for long periods and is cared for by a host of different professionals (Bendell, 1984). In this situation, caregivers change with every 8-hour shift, and a trusting relationship with the mother is difficult to develop. Even when the infant with a disability is cared for at home, the parents may be depressed, withdrawn, exhausted, and resentful and, therefore, find it difficult to care for and relate to their baby. Of course, this type of parental withdrawal does not always occur.

A preschool child masters his or her environment by (a) learning sex roles (e.g., little children know whether they are a boy or a girl), (b) gaining some independence from the mother (feeding and dressing himself or herself), and (c) learning to communicate. Children with cognitive or intellectual disabilities are often unable to master some of these tasks, and children with hearing impairments may not learn to communicate. Children with motor impairments may not learn as much independence. Overprotection by family members may needlessly limit the child's independence. At this age, the preschooler's parents may not allow him or her to explore the environment. Reread the excerpts of Linda Pelletier and her appraisal of the effects of childhood overprotection on her adult life.

Many disabilities (and chronic illnesses) of children are relatively rare (also called *low-incidence disabilities*). Table 7.1 shows some selected conditions that are present in fewer than 1% of children. In spite of the fact that medical advances, such as neonatal medicine, have resulted in more babies' surviving with a disability, these types of disabilities are relatively rare.

J. M. Patterson (1988) explained:

> Unlike adults, where the type of chronic illnesses [disabilities] are few in number but are prevalent, each of the hundreds of different conditions in children is relatively rare. . . . Except for a few common disorders such as mild asthma, the prevalence of any single condition is less than 1 per 100 children. This low incidence rate of many types of disabilities in children means that many families must seek treatment in large metropolitan hospitals. Frequent travel, or perhaps moving the family residence, may be necessary in order to obtain treatment and services for the child with a disability.

Table 7.1

Estimated Prevalence of Low-Incidence Conditions in Children (Percentages)

Condition	Estimated prevalence per 1,000 children
Congenital heart disease	7.0
Seizure disorders	3.5
Cerebral palsy	2.5
Arthritis	2.2
Diabetes mellitus	1.8
Cleft lip/palate	1.5
Down syndrome	1.1
Blindness	0.6
Sickle cell disease	0.5
Cystic fibrosis	0.3
Deafness	0.1
Duchenne muscular dystrophy (males)	0.1

Note. The data in this table are from *The Future of Children*, a publication of the David and Lucile Packard Foundation, from 1991 to 2004. Available from www.futureofchildren.org

Low-incidence disabilities, as a rule, are more difficult to deal with than high-incidence disabilities. Since many congenital disabilities are low-incidence disabilities, it may become difficult to arrive at a diagnosis or a prognosis, which is stressful for parents. What are the best treatments for their child? What will be the course or the final prognosis? How does this child compare to other children with the same disabilities? These are questions which cannot be answered.

There are fewer accommodations and support groups for individuals with low-incidence disabilities. Parents of infants with low-incidence disabilities have no pioneers or history to which to refer. For example, many parents of children with Down syndrome (DS) express gratitude for parents from previous generations who advocated for their DS children, especially for the civil right of free and appropriate education. Today, parents of infants with DS are not required to fight these battles. Moreover, society has some familiarity for individuals of all ages with DS.

School-Age Children

School-age children begin to learn what Erikson terms *industry*, meaning that children learn to start and complete schoolwork. For young children, the completion of schoolwork is a major developmental task. School-age children also begin to emotionally separate from the family and develop peer relationships. Therefore, a disability that separates a child from peers can have a profound impact on the child's developmental progress. Disabilities that interrupt schooling or are visible (especially disfiguring disabilities) can make it difficult for the child to build peer relationships. There is stigma in attending "special" classes. Also, disabilities, such as cognitive or intellectual disabilities, that interfere with the child's self-concept as a competent student can make school, and any school-related activity, unpleasant and frustrating. Children with undiagnosed learning disabilities are often subjected to a great deal of punishment and criticism.

The actress Mia Farrow, in her memoir, *What Falls Away*, described the way in which the onset of her disability ended her childhood: "I was nine years old when my childhood ended" (p. 1). She contracted polio in 1954 at the age of 9.

Degenerating sensory loss is often discovered in the classroom. Eric Weihenmayer (2001) described his realization of his degenerating vision (and the difficulty of accepting this fact): "While I couldn't see well enough to . . . see an equation on the blackboard, I also couldn't accept myself as being blind" (p. 47).

David Wright, a poet in England, lost his auditory nerve from an illness when he was 7 years old. Jonathan Rée, in his 1999 book, *I See a Voice*, describes Wright's experience like so:

> Wright recalls that at first he did not realize what had happened: "How was I to know?" he says. "Nobody told me." He had to "deduce the fact of deafness through a process of reasoning." He heard guns, motorbikes, lorries [trucks], crowds and drills by touch: "there can't be much I miss," as he said, "of the normal orchestration of urban existence." He could appreciate music too, resting his finger on a piano or a loudspeaker. And in a room with a wooden floor he would listen to drum and string instruments through his feet. (p. 37)

Brenda Premo was born with a type of degenerating blindness. In this excerpt, she describes the way in which she assumes that all of the other schoolchildren's vision was like hers:

> The first time I remember understanding that my vision was different from other people was in the second or third grade when I realized other students could read the blackboard. Before then, I couldn't understand why the teacher would bother to write on the board. When it dawned upon me that other kids could read the board and I couldn't, it was one of those "aha" moments in my life. It was a new discovery. (Mackelprang & Salsgiver, 1999, p. 140)

Adolescence

The tasks of adolescence include (a) emotionally separating from parents and family; (b) beginning to develop occupational identity; (c) establishing intimate, romantic relationships; (d) establishing an adult identity; and (e) establishing a strong sexual identity. Adolescents with disabilities must forge their new identity as an adult, discovering their identity, their values, and their career choices. In addition, they must integrate the disability into this new adult identity. Often, there are few role models for these teenagers. Friends and peers, and the companionship and feedback they provide, are important to teenagers. Disabilities that are disfiguring, or are visible, often make peer relationships difficult. One female teenager with a therapeutic leg amputation (as a result of cancer) stated,

> I know young men, especially, really pay a lot of attention to looks and physical attractiveness. I wonder—will a boy accept me just the way I am? You hear them talking about how a girl's really built, or how she looks in a bathing suit and I hope they understand that they just amputated my leg, they didn't take my heart and soul and personality. I don't know if they'll ever accept me. (Darling, cited in Blumberg, Lewis, & Susman, 1984, p. 141)

As we can see in this statement, the treatment of illness and disabilities can be disfiguring. Gaining weight (a frequent side effect of medication), having tremors or spasticity, wearing hearing aids, or using a wheelchair can make teenagers self-conscious at a time in their life when they want to be attractive and fit in. Disabilities with unpredictable episodes of symptom manifestation can undermine the teenager's social confidence. Robert J. Neumann (1988) wrote about the effects of rheumatoid arthritis on his relationship, or lack of relationship, with girls:

> During my high school days, my social life was virtually nonexistent. Because I received physical therapy at home in the afternoon and because my stamina was poor in any event, I only attended school until about 1 p.m. This eliminated any possibility of interacting with peers in extracurricular activities. . . . Meanwhile, I unsuspectingly continued to . . . dream of the day I would start college and the active love life I had fantasized about for so long. Finally the big day arrived. Armed with a body of knowledge about women derived solely from TV, James Bond movies, and the *Playboy* magazines my younger brother smuggled in, I arrived at a small Midwestern college. . . . It took only a short while before I noticed my actual accomplishments with women were falling far short, not only of my expectations but also of the experiences of my friends. . . . [T]here was no need for me to call on social-sexual skills I had never learned. (p. 159)

Seizure disorders and epilepsy are unpredictable in that the individual cannot predict the time, frequency, or level of intensity of the seizures. Livneh and Antonak (1997) summarized,

> Psychosocial adaptation to epilepsy appears to have a complex curvilinear relationship with age of the individual, with increased risk of psychosocial maladaptation among adolescents and reduced risk among children and adults.

The same conclusion appears to apply to the relationship between psychoso-cial adaptation and age at onset of epilepsy. (p. 302)

Teenagers typically experience more independence and freedom than younger chil-dren because they are capable of performing more functions. For example, learning to drive a car is a very important milestone and a step toward more freedom and in-dependence. The child with epilepsy or intellectual disability probably will never be able to drive a car. For a teenager, this is more than a functional loss—it is a loss of in-dependence and normality. Every other 16-year-old is getting a driver's license. With the passage of the Americans With Disabilities Act (ADA), teenagers with disabilities are now afforded more with educational and career options. Before the ADA, these teenagers were often automatically excluded from high school career days or from in-terviews with visiting college and university representatives.

Teenagers are concerned about their future. When a teenager acquires a disability, such concerns are intensified: "Will I be able to have a baby?" "Will I be able to go to college?" "What kind of a career will I have?" and "Will anybody want to marry me?" are often asked (Hahn, 1993).

Schizophrenia is considered to be very disabling, in part because of its time of on-set. The symptoms of schizophrenia usually begin during late adolescence or in one's early 20s. Therefore, exactly when the individual is confronting lifelong questions of occupational choice, educational issues, and choices in partners, he or she becomes ill. Schizophrenia would not be such a disabling illness if the typical time of onset were, for example, during the elderly years. The treatment of schizophrenia often requires long periods of hospitalizations and medications with many visible side effects, making it difficult for the teenager to fit in with his or her peers.

Spinal cord injuries often occur during the teenage years. More than 50% of indi-viduals with spinal cord injuries acquired them between the ages of 15 and 24, and more than 80% of persons with spinal cord injuries are male (Livneh & Antonak, 1997). Most spinal cord injuries are caused by car accidents, falls, and stab and gunshot wounds.

Early Adulthood

The development tasks of young adulthood include establishing a family and begin-ning a career. The diagnosis or onset of a disability during young adulthood coincides with the peak years of career development and of assuming many social and economic responsibilities. "These factors maximize medical, social, and psychological problems that evolve and continue to grow over an extended period of time" (M. T. O'Brien, 1993, p. 124). One PWD recalled the diagnosis of his multiple sclerosis at age 25 as limiting his choices. He stated, "Anyone's early years out of school and in the world are all about empowerment. Confidence in the future suddenly was neutralized" (R. M. Cohen, 2004, pp. 26–27).

Sex and establishing intimate relationships are especially important in early adulthood. Many PWDs have internalized society's attitudes toward disability and, because of this, incorrectly think that no one would wish to date them. Society may teach PWDs to think of themselves as "damaged goods" (Wilson, 1990). Also, the risk of being turned down or ridiculed is often so great that the individual simply stays home or, at best, socializes in groups.

We have seen that there have been long-held beliefs that sexuality disappears with the onset of a disability, and these myths are difficult to eliminate. PWDs have expressed disappointment in physicians and other medical caregivers who did not discuss sexual and physical intimacy. In one survey conducted with individuals with spinal cord injuries and traumatic brain injuries (Putnam et al., 2003), the participants were asked to describe wellness factors in dealing with their disability and those aspects that did not promote wellness. The authors summarized:

> Participants also expressed aggravation at physicians who do not provide specific health and wellness issues relevant to their conditions. One woman said, "And I'm tired of people dancing around the information that we need to know. For instance, very specifically about sexual dysfunction ... why not tell us? Are we not all adults? Do most of us not have husbands and wives? Do we not have sex? Why can't you talk to us in plain English about things that are affecting us?" (Putman et al., 2003, p. 42)

Responding to the onset of a disability in early adulthood often includes not only the individual, but also his or her marriage partner. For example, the time of onset for multiple sclerosis usually occurs during the prime working years and, for a woman, during the childbearing years (Mairs, 1996). Therefore, the rehabilitation of individuals with this disability often includes family counseling to provide support to the spouse and children. Livneh and Antonak (1997) described the spouses of individuals with multiple sclerosis: "Spouses felt trapped, overwhelmed, and resentful" (p. 319). Disabilities that are acquired during the early years of marriage often require extensive assistance and custodial care of the partner with the disability. A wife of a man with a psychiatric disability summarized the experience by saying: "I feel like I've lost a partner and gained a problem child" (Mannion, 1996, p. 22). This type of custodial care may undermine the sexual relationship and render the partner with the disability sexually unattractive. Medications may interfere with sexual functioning. Further, a parent–child relationship can evolve when one partner acquires a disability. The partner without the disability becomes a parent to the partner with the disability. Issues of power and control in a marriage are complicated when one partner is a custodial caregiver to the other (e.g., "If you don't agree with me about decorating the living room, I won't bathe or feed you."). It is surprising that many insurance policies do not cover marriage therapy for individuals with disabilities.

Nonetheless, families have great restorative powers (Marsh & Lefley, 1996). Disability can provide the family with opportunities for constructive change. Family bonds can be strengthened. Family members often take pride in their mastery of the disability and report greater development of compassion, spirituality, and personal strength. One family member summarized, "I can now say that, like that old aluminum foil ad, I am 'oven tempered for flexible strength'" (Marsh & Lefley, 1996, p. 7). A study of caregivers whose spouses had multiple sclerosis showed that caregiver husbands and wives reported loving their spouse more than spouses in the normed sample (Perrone, Gordon, & Tschopp, 2006).

Family caregivers of an individual with a psychiatric disability are often required to assume an extra burden—that of being implicitly or explicitly blamed for the disability. Families with a member with a psychiatric disability may feel blamed, shamed, and unsupported (Mannion, Mueser, & Soloman, 1994). One man reported that his in-laws blamed him for his wife's depression (Mannion et al., 1994). Most spouse caregivers have been women, probably because of the longer life spans of women and the traditional roles assigned to women. However, many chronic illnesses are more prevalent among women; therefore, it is becoming more common for the caretaker spouse to be the husband. Researchers report that the problems of male caregivers may be different than the problems of female caregivers (Perrone et al., 2006). Men typically have fewer outside supports than women in similar roles and may not be as skilled at role flexibility as women.

Disabilities, acquired at any age, are financially stressful. For a young couple trying to establish a household, disability expenses can be devastating. Treatment and adaptive technology are expensive, and many times, as the individual ages with the disability, these types of costs continue to rise. Medical crises and unexpected technology breakdowns can make budgeting difficult. Putnam and colleagues (2003) interviewed individuals with spinal cord injuries, cerebral palsy, polio, and amputations in Portland, Oregon; Houston, Texas; and San Francisco, asking which factors contributed to their wellness and sense of well-being and which factors decreased their sense of well-being. The authors described one oft-mentioned concern.

> Many spoke about fears related to financing new equipment when their current devices needed replacing. Others relayed concerns about on-going maintenance expenses. One participant said, "Once my scooter gives up, what am I going to do? Once my van goes toes up, what am I going to do?" So, it's not so much . . . about obtaining the assistive devices the first time, but replacing them. Because once my scooter gives up, how do I walk? (Putnam et al., 2003, p. 42)

Pace-of-life issues are part of any marriage; one partner may be energetic, be hardworking, and enjoy activity and achievement, while the other may be relaxed, laid-back, and content to "kick back." Miles O'Brien, who had a therapeutic amputation of his left arm due to an accident, described his disability-imposed slower pace of life:

> Besides the pain, the biggest inconvenience about being one-armed isn't any individual task, but in the aggregate. I had a very busy overbooked life before I lost my arm. Now each thing I do takes longer—sometimes much longer. I could tell you about toasting a bagel, opening a new box of cereal, or changing the trash bag, but you get the idea. A morning routine that used to take 30 minutes now lasts more than an hour. At the end of the day, I have always done less than I expected to. This makes me cranky. (M. O'Brien, 2014, p. 37)

However, with some disabilities, such as multiple sclerosis or rheumatoid arthritis, fatigue and pain are common symptoms. Individuals with these types of disabilities learn to conserve their energy (Rustad, 1984). The spouse without a disability may not totally understand these symptoms or may resent the partner with the disability, feeling that life is not as fun as before. Symptom exacerbation is often unpredictable, and, therefore, scheduling for family activities is difficult. In addition, the partner with the disability often must spend considerable time treating or managing the disability.

The loss of job and career can be devastating. Hillyer (1993) wrote:

> Weekdays when I see other young women leaving for or returning from home I feel quite apart from the outside world. Whatever activities you take up, like painting, aren't the same. Nobody can convince you it's the same as being active within a normal work situation. (p. 16)

Another PWD explained the way in which her job loss affected her:

> I felt dreadful when I had to give up work. It was the most shattering experience I had had because going out to work you felt a part of society, you were contributing, you were earning your own money. You also had your friends that you went to work with, and then suddenly you were cut off. You were in the house alone. Also, of course, financially you are worse off. You were lonely, you felt useless, on the scrap heap, finished, and it really was a bad time. (Campling, 1981, p. 115)

Middle Adulthood

Since most individuals have established strong identities by middle adulthood, adjusting to the new identity as a PWD may pose certain questions. Middle adulthood is a time of peak achievement and career achievement. Indeed, many individuals in this period of life have reached their life goals and have gained some measure of status and prestige. Individuals now look forward to reaping the benefits of careful planning, hard work, and progressive success. In addition, marital happiness often increases in middle adulthood with the departure of the grown-up children from home. At this age, many individuals have resolved, or are in the process of working on, questions on the personal meaning of life. In short, middle adulthood is a time of life when personal satisfaction and feelings of mastery are greatest. Preparation for retirement also begins in this stage of life, and individuals begin to anticipate disengagement from the world of work.

The onset of a disability, for a man or a woman, during the middle adulthood years may prove to be interpreted as a loss of identity, status, and economic security. Because the individual in middle adulthood has established a strong, secure identity and a (perceived) place in society, a disability may appear to be an overwhelming shift in identity. Peak earning years may be gone, and the years that individuals looked forward to now may appear lost. Individuals with disabilities acquired earlier in life, such as arthritis or diabetes, may not have exhibited many symptoms, but with the advent of the aging process in the middle adulthood years, these symptoms frequently exacerbate, and functioning now becomes impaired. Perhaps physical disabilities are easier to accept for individuals in this age range, ages 25–65 years, because they have begun to subordinate the importance of their physical body and their physical appearance. This is a developmental task of all individuals in this stage of life.

The subsequent treatment, medical stabilization, and physical rehabilitation requires the adult to adjust to a new environment, new roles, and new experiences. An adult with a great deal of autonomy, freedom, and independence often has a difficult adjustment to hospital and rehab center life. Chuck Close, a well-known artist and art critic became a quadriplegic, paralyzed from his neck down. He was at Gracie Mansion, the home of the mayor of New York City, presenting an award when he experienced a collapsed spinal artery. The shock of acquiring an extremely impairing disability in an acute onset was compounded by his hospital experiences.

> Hospitals can be incredibly dehumanizing. A rehab hospital . . . is a very unusual kind of society. It has its own structure, its own crazy, wacky rules; you learn to live within it. If you try to beat the system, it can be very demoralizing and embarrassing . . . it is humiliating to be left in your own feces for hours. Even the choice to fight is interesting. You can try and get what you want by being—well, I tried to be especially nice, figuring that people would be more likely to give me what I needed if they liked me. Those people who fought harder for what they wanted—and they were absolutely justified—often didn't get a thing. Being nice paid off better. (Close, 1993, p. 18)

Middle adulthood is also a time when many individuals are involved in the care of elderly parents with disabilities. Most of this care is provided by women, for both their own parents and the parents of their husband. G. H. S. Singer (1996) stated, "Currently, a woman can expect to spend more years caring for a parent than looking after dependent children" (p. 13). Such caregiving demands on women are difficult because these women most often work outside the home and therefore have multiple role demands (Elliott, Shewchuk, & Richards, 1999; C. Vash, 1982). Indeed, Singer labeled the traditional caregiving responsibilities of women as "the role of women as sources of support for vulnerable people" (G. H. S. Singer, 1996, p. 13). Rather than enjoying the benefits of more time and money to themselves and freedom from the responsibility of raising children, women in middle adulthood frequently find themselves providing long-term care for elderly parents.

As Fine and Asch (1988) pointed out, women with disabilities are more likely to be cared for by strangers, while men with disabilities are more likely to be cared for by female family members. There are demographic explanations for this: (a) some women have never been married; (b) some women are divorced or widowed; and (c) women tend to marry older men. However, caring for family members has been viewed as a female gender role. Ties of obligation and love

> represent a defining aspect of femininity. Nurturing and connecting with others . . . evoke feminine associations. Many informants spoke of needing to be adaptable, invisible, and even subordinate. . . . These characteristics coincide with the generally tentative or inferior status traditionally available to women and, as such, contrast with the more fixed, visible, and dominant roles available to men. (Preston, 1994, p. 101)

Age 65 and Older

Despite the fact that disability onset is positively correlated with age, very few services have traditionally been provided to older PWDs. Until recently, there were few existing programs to meet the needs of elderly PWDs. This is a reflection of the Functional Model of disability in that paid employment is the only function considered. In other words, rehabilitation has been focused on job placement and vocational skill development because such services are regarded as investments that would be paid back when PWDs go to work, get off public assistance, and start paying taxes. Elderly PWDs are not of working age and therefore are not considered to be able to make a contribution to society. Often, old age itself is seen as a disability. Of course, there is a loss of physical and cognitive functioning associated with aging, and there is also prejudice and discrimination directed toward elderly individuals. Stein and Cutler (1998) remarked on the physical effects of aging:

> The normal wear and tear on the body takes its toll on the individual. Eyesight becomes weaker, hearing more difficult, range of movement in joints becomes limited, the muscles are not as strong, and the blood vessels begin to lose elasticity. (p. 204)

The increased life span of Americans puts them at greater risk (and longer risk) for acquiring a disability. Added to these physical changes are the losses and stresses of isolation from family, decreased income, vulnerability to crime, and a lack of usefulness to a society that stresses youth and physical fitness.

The acquisition of a disability during old age appears to be timelier in both social and chronological time. Loss occurs at any age, of course, but as people grow older, they experience more losses more frequently, and these losses have a cumulative effect. Indeed, the loss of energy for general functioning often leads to social isolation; the person simply does not have the energy to socialize. Therefore, reduced activity and mobility, and occasionally reduced cognitive ability, are viewed as part of old age. Further, the incidence of various stressful conditions often adds up cumulatively, reaching their peak as the individual ages. The major developmental task for individuals in the elderly stages of life is adaptation to loss. Erikson, and other developmental psychologists, viewed old age (older than the age of 65) as a time to avoid ego despair and disengagement from life's activities and relationships. Nonetheless, it should not be assumed that growing old means inevitable loss or that the normative physiological changes of aging *always* result in disabilities (Schienle & Eiler, 1984).

In addition to these physical losses, the elderly individual must deal with the ageism of a society that values youth, productivity, independence, achievement, and competition. Frequently, the knowledge and experience of elderly people are considered to be obsolete because of the fast pace of technological change. Much like PWDs, elderly people today may be viewed as burdens or drains because they no longer contribute to the economy (Zola, 1988).

Another manifestation of society's ageism is the fact that hypochondriasis is over-diagnosed in people who are elderly. (This is not to say that there are not elderly hypochondriacs who use their physical complaints to exert control; it is to say that medical professionals over-diagnose hypochondriasis.) It is logical for people of advanced age to be preoccupied with their bodies. Also, just as PWDs often incorporate society's handicapism into their self-identity, many elderly people accept ageism as a self-identifier (R. Young & Olsen, 1991).

There are two types of elderly people with disabilities: (a) those who acquired a disability early in life (Trieschmann, 1987) and (b) those who acquire a disability later in life (Verbrugge, 1989). Disabilities acquired in old age may have an acute onset (such as a heart attack or a broken hip) or may have an insidious onset (such as diabetes or Parkinson's disease). Acute-onset disabilities often move the individual quickly into old age. Insidious-onset disabilities, however, manifest symptoms that are difficult to distinguish from the natural changes of aging. To further complicate the picture, in some old–age-onset disabilities, the individual's cognitive abilities and personality fade away (Lubkin & Larsen, 1998).

Individuals who are elderly may have acquired disabilities earlier in their life. The aging process often interacts with the disability to produce complications or more severe decline in functioning. For example, individuals who acquired a spinal cord injury early in life experience greater loss of energy, strength, stamina, mobility, and flexibility at an earlier age than do their age-mates without a spinal cord injury. Growing older with a disability is often associated with an earlier decline in functioning. Nonetheless, growing older with a disability requires that the individual negotiate all the tasks of old age and, at the same time, manage the disability. Some disability scholars have theorized that living an adult life with a disability assists the individual in adjusting to the demands of old age.

Elderly people often feel that they have not been accorded any input into the design of agencies and programs intended to serve them (Szymanski & Trueba, 1994). This also parallels the disability experience, in that many programs for PWDs are developed and administered by PWODs. Also, elderly people are frequently reluctant to accept services from government agencies, viewing such services as charity or some sort of admission of failure or lack of control on the elderly individual's end. Seeking psychotherapy or counseling may be stigmatizing to these individuals. Because very few elderly people during their younger adult lives received such services, and because the people receiving psychotherapy were experiencing severe problems, elderly people today often avoid supportive counseling, viewing it to be unnecessary.

Despite the previous discussion, PWDs who are elderly are thought to respond to disability more positively than PWDs who are young adults. This positive response is thought to be a function of the following factors: (a) disability is often seen as normative for old age (i.e., everyone else one's own age has some sort of a disability); (b) elderly people often have fewer functional demands, such as a career or taking care of children; (c) elderly people have had a lifetime of transition and changes and have developed effective idiosyncratic ways in which to deal with them; and (d) elderly people are often less concerned with body image. Indeed, the onset of a disability may appear relatively minor to someone who has lived a successful and long life.

CHAPTER 8

TYPE OF ONSET AND THE INDIVIDUAL'S RESPONSE

✧ What are the differences between insidious-onset disabilities and acute-onset disabilities?

✧ What is the impact of a long prediagnosis period on the individual?

✧ Why can the unpredictable course of a disability be more disturbing than the actual symptoms?

✧ Why is symptom recognition culturally determined?

✧ What does this statement mean?: "As the course of the disability progresses, social support often disintegrates."

✧ What does *temporal disruption* mean in relation to a disability?

✧ What are the four phases of the course of a disability?

✧ Is there a relationship between the episodic course of some disabilities and *learned helplessness*?

✧ What does this statement mean?: "With each level of loss, the individual is faced with adjustment/response demands."

✧ Why is the importance of functional losses idiosyncratically and culturally defined?

✧ Why has the revolution in assistive technology changed the definition of functioning for many people with disabilities (PWDs)?

✧ What are the factors that determine the level of severity of a disability?

✧ Is there a clear-cut relationship between severity of disability and psychopathology?

✧ What is the difference between chronic pain and acute pain?

You will remember (from Exhibit 7.1) that there are 10 factors of a disability that influence an individual's response:

1. time of onset
2. type of onset
3. course of the disability
4. functions impaired
5. severity of the disability
6. degree of stigma
7. visibility of the disability
8. degree (if any) of disfigurement
9. prognosis
10. treatment required

Type of Onset

In this section, look for—

✧ two broad categories of type of onset:
   1. insidious
   2. acute

Thinking only of *onset* of disability (and not the time of *diagnosis*), we can conceptualize time of onset as falling within two broad categories: insidious onset and acute onset. An acute onset refers to a disability that has a sharp, definite beginning point (sometimes termed *clinical presentation*), and an insidious onset refers to a disability that begins in a subtle, stealthy manner. A spinal cord injury would be considered to have an acute onset, while diabetes is thought to have an insidious onset. Further, with many insidious-onset disabilities, it is the time of diagnosis that is referenced because no one can really accurately pinpoint the actual time of onset. Although, to be truly accurate, with many mental illnesses, the onset can be considered to be both acute and insidious. For example, the onset of schizophrenia is considered to be acute in that the individual has an intensification of symptoms that greatly impairs the individual's functioning and usually requires immediate hospitalization. Therefore, the onset is considered to be an acute emergency, requiring immediate treatment; but it is acknowledged that the onset was also insidious, meaning that symptoms, in reality, did not appear "out of the blue.")

Acute-Onset Disabilities

Acute-onset disabilities are considered to be medical emergencies; the individual is often required to disengage from his or her typical life activities, such as school, work, and family obligations, and the treatment of the disability becomes top priority. There is a sharp, decisive turning point for the individual, his or her family, and professional service providers. Rapid mobilization of medical, individual, and family resources is required (Chilman, Nunnally, & Cox, 1988; Lesak, 1986). Acute-onset disabilities, as would be expected, usually are a shock. Such events as accidents, disease presentation, or the birth of a baby with a congenital disability are unexpected, allowing no time for anticipatory and preparatory reaction. In the case of amputations, individuals with cancer or diabetes who were required to undergo a therapeutic amputation and who had only a few days' advance notice responded better to the amputation than did those individuals who experienced traumatic amputations. This makes intuitive sense because time for acceptance, even a few days, helps individuals to respond to the loss of a body part. (Most amputations are therapeutic amputations.) In contrast, individuals with traumatic amputations experience more problems with acceptance. In one sentence, a man tells of his acute-onset spinal cord injury with the accompanying feelings of suddenness, unexpectedness, and the need to deal with a medical diagnosis: "I was 22, a recent college graduate, and all of a sudden, I'm a T8 bilateral paraplegic, whatever the hell that is!" (Crewe, 1997, p. 32). This man, Roy, had gone on a graduation trip to the American West with friends. The driver fell asleep at the wheel and rolled the van. Roy was the only one seriously hurt.

Insidious-Onset Disabilities

Insidious-onset disabilities include such conditions as multiple sclerosis, diabetes, and rheumatoid arthritis. No one can definitively state the time of onset, not professional care providers nor the individual. More support is usually given for acute-onset disabilities because friends and family can clearly understand a sharp, sudden (often traumatic) onset. Insidious-onset disabilities appear to be more ambiguous than acute-onset disabilities. Frequently, individuals with insidious-onset disabilities (that have been diagnosed) must seek emergency medical care, undergo hospitalization, and disengage from their major life activities. For example, the diagnosis of depression or diabetes often requires that the individual go to the hospital for immediate treatment. Many people who experience insidious-onset disabilities speak about "something being not quite right for a long time," probably speaking of warning signs or prodromal symptoms, which at the time were not understood or acknowledged.

Implications and Cautions

Viewing onset of disability from this simple dichotomy leads to the following implications:

- We are not discussing *course* of the disability; only the beginning.
- We also are not discussing the *cause* of the disability, only the onset.
- We are not talking about the *visibility* of the disability; both acute-onset disabilities and insidious-onset disabilities can be either invisible or visible.
- Those with insidious-onset disabilities are less likely to seek treatment than those with acute-onset disabilities.
- An unknown time of onset (an insidious onset) can be stressful.
- A diagnosis leads to family support.
- For many psychiatric disabilities, knowing the onset of the disability can help in arriving at an accurate diagnosis.

Therefore, physicians will ask, "When did you first start having problems?" and "What happened next?" Many psychiatric and cognitive disabilities have similar symptoms but different types of onset; therefore, it is necessary to establish the type of onset to make the right diagnosis. Ziporyn (1992) stated: "Symptoms associated with more than one disease can underlie years of misdiagnosis" (p. 104). Parkinson's disease and a stroke have many of the same symptoms; however, the first disability is an insidious-onset disability, and the second is an acute-onset disability. Head injuries have an acute onset, while dementia has an insidious onset; yet, they share many of the same symptoms. Therefore, physicians will ask, "Have you been in a car accident or bumped your head in the last few weeks?" If the answer is "yes," then further probing for the presence of a head injury is warranted.

The Impact of a Long Prediagnosis Period

In this section, look for—

- ✧ the impact of prolonged uncertainty
- ✧ how individuals are given less support and validation
- ✧ how individuals are often labeled with negative diagnoses
- ✧ how people need diagnoses to receive services

Many disabilities with an insidious onset, such as multiple sclerosis, lupus, thyroid disease, Crohn's disease, and a host of autoimmune diseases, have a long prediagnosis period. When the diagnosis is finally made, the individual is torn between relief at having a name for the symptoms that he or she has been experiencing and the shock of having a serious disability. There is a simple and straightforward explanation for their symptoms (Ziporyn, 1992). However, the diagnosis can be a devastating disability (Donoghue & Siegel, 1992). Nonetheless, the diagnosis ends "a frightening array of possibilities" (Goodheart & Lansing, 1997).

These types of disabilities often present with the following symptoms: muscle weakness, fatigue, pain, sleep disturbances, numbness, and vision disturbance, all of which impair the individual's functioning but are also easily dismissed by physicians. Therefore, the individual undergoes an exhaustive, long diagnostic period while dealing with the symptoms. Even more important, the individual is often diagnosed as having psychological problems, drug abuse, or alcoholism. According to Donoghue and Siegel (1992), on average, from the first onset of symptoms to diagnosis of multiple sclerosis, an individual will endure 40 months of prediagnosis.

Rereading the definitions of *secondary gains* and *hypochondriasis*, we can see how easy it is for both professionals and family members to think that the individual is engaging in trying to obtain secondary gains (such as freedom from responsibility) or is being a hypochondriac. The doctor says, "The tests show nothing. There is nothing wrong with you." Friends and family often stop being supportive (and may, in fact, resent the individual for being such a "wimp"). However, those with less ambiguous disabilities and chronic illness are given support and validation, including medical care, time off from work, time to rest, flowers, cards, and the general solicitude of others. Further adding to the stress of the unknown problem are the negative labels given to the person. Physicians may accuse the individual of "doctor shopping," when in reality, the individual is trying to seek help for the debilitating symptoms. These individuals may be told to buy a new hat, take a vacation, have the fillings in their teeth replaced, take herbs and vitamins, or see a psychologist. Occasionally, spouses and other family members are aware of the effects of the symptoms on the individual, but their observations are discounted or dismissed by physicians. The cyclic or intermittent nature of some symptoms makes it difficult for others to understand their severity. After all, at times the individual seems "like himself [or herself]." However, because the individual has no medical diagnosis, he or she may overcompensate and overexert himself or herself during times of symptom remission. Indeed, "many energy depleting conditions have no visible manifestations, [but] they are nevertheless incapacitating" (Kohler, Schweikert-Stary, & Lubkin, 1998, p. 129).

For many, the time of diagnosis is a relief from the stress of not understanding the symptoms that the individual is experiencing. One expert in families with a member who has a mental illness terms the time of diagnosis as an "epiphany." She stated:

> After long periods of chaos and confusion, the nature of the problem suddenly seems clear. Family members, sometimes equally go for months or years of feeling anger, fear, confusion, and concern about a loved one's oppressive behaviors without being able to name them as illness. The point at which a person's troublesome behavior is transformed into a disease, via the pronouncements of medical experts, is typically a moment of epiphany. Such a moment of epiphany is, however, only the beginning of an ongoing interpretive process. (Karp, 2001, p. 49)

A college professor with multiple sclerosis described the unforgettable day of her diagnosis: "Every [person with] multiple sclerosis can remember the moment of diagnosis. It is one of those events which can be forever recalled in the most exquisite detail" (Toombs, 1995, p. 4). A woman with a husband with mental illness described her reaction to receiving her husband's diagnosis:

> I'll tell you one of the best days of my life was when I got a phone call from the hospital telling me what they decided was wrong with my husband, and they couldn't understand why I was so excited or happy. (Karp, 2001, p. 50)

An Englishwoman, Clare, received a diagnosis of multiple sclerosis; after this diagnosis, friends told Clare that they had previously thought she was simply lazy.

> One interesting piece of information that came to light after I told people that I had MS was the opinions that they and others had had of me. I guess that I was both hurt and mildly angry to discover that I had been seen as a lazy and work-shy person. . . . I was just left feeling betrayed by friends of many years. (J. Morris, 1991, p. 181)

Lack of a Diagnosis Does Not Mean Absence of Impairment

It is not uncommon for the individual who has an insidious-onset disability (which has not been diagnosed) to begin to wonder if he or she is "crazy." The pain, fatigue, and muscle weakness often work together to drastically change the individual's functioning and activities. Accordingly, these individuals devise coping devices, such as spending the entire weekend in bed to be able to go to work on Monday morning. Kohler and colleagues (1998) included an account of a woman with arthritis who found it difficult to accept her fatigue. She said:

> It's hard to justify my fatigue to friends and relatives; my husband often asks, "Why are you so tired?" It took an article in the *National Arthritis News* to finally help me to convince myself and him that my fatigue was real, physiologically, as well as emotionally. (p. 129)

Often, these individuals become "medical detectives," learning as much as possible about their symptoms and the best way in which to communicate the seriousness of these symptoms to physicians. As would be expected, some of these individuals become depressed (which, in itself, can lead to loss of energy). Without a diagnosis, without family support and validation, and with the symptoms and functional loss, these individuals often report their emotional responses to feeling like riding a roller coaster. The emotional roller coaster feels like helplessness, lack of control, and unpredictability. Furthermore, others (physicians, family members, and employers) perceive the individual as fully functional and, because of this, do not change their expectations of the individual. Donoghue and Siegel, in their book, *Sick and Tired of Feeling Sick and Tired*, referred to a study that examined the psychological impact of multiple sclerosis. To the researchers' surprise, the group of participants who reported the greatest distress and depression were men (with multiple sclerosis) who had few physical impairments. Indeed, these men were more depressed than others with more severe physical and functional impairments. The researchers determined that the ambiguity and stress of the prediagnosis period was associated with their depression. Many of these men reported low feelings of self-worth and the need to constantly defend and explain themselves to skeptical physicians and family members. These stressors, ambiguity and the skepticism of others, in this one study, were more depressing than physical impairments.

Tosca Appel (1988) wrote of her prediagnosis period before she was found to have multiple sclerosis. Her young age (11 years) may have contributed to some of the misdiagnoses since the typical age of onset for multiple sclerosis is about age 20. Note (a) that none of these symptoms were invisible, (b) the number of misdiagnoses, (c) the severity of the first symptom (her parents took her to the emergency room of the hospital), (d) the prolonged prediagnosis period, and (e) the negative labels given to her.

> I was 11 years, 9 months old when my first symptom appeared. My first attack of MS took the form of a lack of motor coordination of my right hand. I was unable to hold utensils and my hand was turned inward; my parents in their concern rushed me to the emergency room of the hospital. The intern who saw me at the emergency room told my parents, without any exam, that I had a brain tumor. . . . I was admitted to the hospital, where I stayed for 12 days. Ten days after the initial attack the symptoms abated. . . . The doctors had put the blame of the attack on a bad case of nerves. . . . My second attack occurred when I was 16 years old and in the 11th grade. . . . One day . . . my history teacher asked me a question. I stood up to answer and my speech came out all garbled. I was unable to string the words into a sentence. I was even unable to utter words. All that came out were sounds. I clutched my throat to help the words come out easier. . . . I remembered the teacher's look. He looked at me in utter surprise and a little bit helplessly. . . . Again, my parents rushed me to the emergency room where another intern did his initial workup on me. . . . The intern, in his wisdom, thought this behavior was an attention-getter. He thought I was faking the whole thing. (pp. 253–254)

Having discussed the onset and diagnosis of the disability and its meaning to the individual in the previous chapter, this chapter will begin with a discussion of the course of a disability, the physiological advancement of the disability, and the emotional and psychological responses to the progression of the disability.

The Course of the Disability

In this section, look for—

✧ three factors in the course of a disability:

- direction
- pace of movement
- degree of predictability

✧ the focus of (chronic) disabilities:

- controlling symptoms
- preventing secondary disabilities or complications
- maintaining the highest quality of life possible

Often termed the trajectory of the disability, the course of a disability includes three factors: (a) the direction (stays the same, improves, or deteriorates), (b) the pace of movement, and (c) the degree of predictability (N. White & Lubkin, 1998). The course is the way in which a disability or chronic illness advances, and, once again, it is the individual's *perception* and *response* to these stages that is most important. Reviewing Chapter 2 and the Biomedical Model of disability, it becomes apparent that the entire concept of the course of a disability is a relatively new approach since, for centuries, the practice of medicine involved only two outcomes—total cure or death. The idea that an individual would manage and treat a disability throughout his or her life span, working for the highest quality of life possible, is a new concept. We have also discussed that many people without disabilities, including physicians, do not consider people with disabilities, especially those with severe and multiple disabilities, to have any kind of quality of life. Occasionally, PWDs may believe in the capabilities of medicine to cure them. In this excerpt from a professor of English with multiple sclerosis, we can see that it took her some time to come to terms with the chronic, degenerating, and episodic nature of her disability.

> I was not going to get well—ever. Though I might have periods of remission, I would not (and could not) be cured. My expectation had been that (the profession of) medicine would restore me to health. Now, that expectation was dashed, along with my cherished illusion that I was in control of my life. The future disappeared. (Toombs, 1995, p. 4)

In the disability role, symptom control and prevention of complications and secondary disabilities are important. Further, while this chapter will be discussing the physiological and emotional responses to the stages or phases of the course of the disability, it should be remembered that the individual's developmental stage of life, his or her family resources, and his or her personal resources also affect the course of the disability. Finally, the course of the disability should not be confused with the stages of adaptation; although both involve movement and direction, and they certainly influence each other, the course of the disability is thought to be related more to physiological changes and symptom manifestation.

We have also discussed the stress, anxiety, and depression associated with ambiguity (Mishel, 1993). The individual with the disability, his or her family, and his or her caregivers feel more in control with a clear-cut, on-schedule, predictable course. The idea of planning for uncertainty is difficult to accept. For an individual who cannot explain the cause of his or her disability, or the course, the uncertainty may be more distressing than the actual symptoms of the disability. Humans demand explanations, and often, in disability, there are no explanations. Despite an inability to know for sure, individuals (both physicians and PWDs) try to predict the phases of the disability, the rate of the course, and symptom manifestation. Support groups can offer a newly diagnosed individual an opportunity to rehearse the later stages of his or her disability by seeing and talking with others with the same disability. The course of some disabilities is more variable than the course of others.

Complications and secondary disabilities must also be factored into this complex prediction. A straightforward example of unexpected complications is post-polio syndrome. Indeed, polio was considered to be a disability with a stable course in that once an individual reached medical stabilization, it was thought that he or she would continue to function at that level. However, 25% of polio survivors experience new symptoms of muscular weakness, severe fatigue, muscle and joint pain, and respiratory difficulties (Zola, 1988). Many of those who used braces or crutches must now use a wheelchair; many have been required to take early retirement from their careers. Physicians could not and did not predict post-polio syndrome, nor are physicians able to agree on the cause. Falvo (1991) told of the impact of post-polio syndrome: "Those who adjusted to and compensated for their disability, attaining active, independent lives, may find the occurrences of new symptoms and the limitations of post-polio syndrome difficult to accept. No specific treatment is available" (p. 196).

Factors such as the visibility of the symptoms influence the way in which the course of the disability is perceived. For example, for some disabilities, symptoms can progress to a very advanced stage and the individual may not be aware. High blood pressure and diabetes, conditions that can lead to serious disabilities and even death, often have invisible symptoms (Cott & Wilkins, 1993). Also, symptoms in remission are invisible symptoms, and some individuals may feel that they no longer have the disability and may terminate treatment and management. We have also learned that symptom recognition is influenced by the individual's culture and social class. Therefore, the course of an individual's disability is also culturally determined since it is the individual's recognition of symptoms and the meaning that he or she ascribes to the symptoms that regulate the course of the disability. In sum, *the individual's assessment* of symptoms is more important than the *physiological course* of symptoms.

Another factor in the course of a disability is the degree of social support offered at each phase. Usually, during the acute stage, friends and family rally to the aid of the PWD. However, as the course of the disability progresses, often this support disintegrates. In a study of individuals with brain injuries (Kozloff, 1987), it was found that with the passage of time after the injury, the size of the social network of the individual decreased. Friends disappeared. Kosciulek and Lustig (1998) commented, "As a result, the number of multiple relationships increased (i.e., family members served more functions as nonrelatives dropped out of the picture). The ultimate consequences of such changes was the social isolation of families" (p. 8). Randy Souders, a teenager who was paralyzed in a diving accident, described the gradual, one-by-one loss of friends:

> Of course, there are some things that I wish I could have changed. Initially, everyone rallies around you, you know—they're supportive. All of the friends I had at the time of the accident were right there—right at the beginning. Then, as time went on, one by one they kind of drifted away, slowly. I think it was because they obviously didn't know how to react to me—and I certainly didn't know how to make things easier on them. I was having a hard enough time trying to figure out what was happening to me. I don't know if I pushed them away or if they felt that I wasn't the same person. It was a very gradual thing, but most of them just kind of drifted off. And I drifted off into myself. (Souders, 1993, pp. 153–154)

The course of a disability can be fully known only in retrospect. The course can and should be predicted, but even the most predictable disabilities can be unpredictable. Disability scholars term this unpredictability *temporal disruption*, meaning that the PWD cannot accurately predict his or her future or the course of the disability. A disability usually disrupts the individual's future. "How long will this last?" "Will I be able to marry?" "Will I be able to have children?" "Will I have to go into a nursing home?" For the individual planning medical treatment, lifestyle changes, and family adaptations, the greater the predictability of the disability's course, the easier the adjustment. Temporal disruption also is associated with the predictability of the length of time of each stage.

The Phases or Stages of the Course of a Disability

In this section, look for—

♦ the four phases of the course of a disability:
  1. onset and diagnosis phase
  2. acute phase
  3. chronic phase
  4. symptom exacerbation phase (sometimes termed *relapse*)

Generally speaking, there are four phases of the course of a disability: (1) the onset and diagnosis; (2) medical stabilization; (3) chronic; and (4) symptom exacerbation, sometimes referred to as the crisis phase or relapse. Each of these phases or stages may be long or short in duration. All of these stages involve both a change in self-identity and role adaptation in addition to medical treatment. During the onset phase, the individual is required to think of himself or herself as a person with a disability; during the medical stabilization phase, the individual is required to think of himself or herself as a compliant patient or client. And, as we have discussed before, any change in self-identity is often viewed as both negative and stressful. During the onset and medical stabilization phases, the PWD learns to negotiate hospital life and begins to deal with the symptoms of the disability, which sometimes include pain. Both of these phases are regarded as acute emergencies, with available resources being marshaled. These resources include medical treatment and family care and support. During the chronic stage, however, the PWD is required to accept his or her permanently changed status and identity. The chronic stage is the day-to-day living with a disability.

Symptom exacerbation, or relapse, is common in many types of disabilities, especially psychiatric disabilities. Complications and secondary conditions are common in many types of physical disabilities, such as urinary tract infections in paraplegia or airway obstructions for those with muscular neurological conditions. Both of these examples can be fatal and, indeed, in the past, did result in the individual's death. Today, such complications or crises are carefully monitored and aggressively treated in order to prevent fatalities.

The Four Types of Courses

In this section, look for—

⬧ the four types of courses:
  1. stable course
  2. episodic course
  3. degenerating
  4. episodic, degenerating course

In rehabilitation, it is generally accepted that there are four broad categories of courses: (1) stable, (2) episodic (sometimes termed *recurring* or *relapsing*), (3) degenerating, and (4) degenerating episodic. A stable course is one in which, after medical stabilization, the symptoms are permanent, but they do not vary (assuming good management and treatment). Life is changed, and for most, there are limitations in functioning. Spinal cord injuries, intellectual disability, and deafness are considered to be stable disabilities. Disabilities with a progressive or degenerative course exhibit symptoms that worsen over time and require careful monitoring of present symptoms, the exacerbation of old symptoms, and the appearance of new symptoms. Multiple sclerosis and retinitis pigmentosa are types of degenerative disabilities. Relapsing and episodic disabilities include asthma, seizure disorders, and some types of mental illness. Episodic disabilities, as would be expected, are unpredictable, and yet the individual attempts to live a normal life. Simple graphs that illustrate each of these three types of courses are provided later in the chapter.

Stable Course Disabilities

It would appear that stable course disabilities would present fewer adjustment demands simply because the individual knows with what he or she is dealing. After diagnosis and medical stabilization, the individual reaches a plateau of functioning and symptom manifestation and is expected to continue at that level indefinitely. However, there are four factors to be considered. First, it is the individual's perception of the disability that determines his or her response to the disability, and, as we have discussed, one of the responses to a disability is denial, more specifically the denial of the stability of the disability (e.g., "I'm going to walk out of here."). Second, most disabilities are not stable in that secondary disabilities or complications often appear. Perhaps it should be stated that some disabilities have courses that are *more stable* than others. Third, for some disabilities, such as traumatic brain injury, the diagnostic period (even after an acute, traumatic onset such as an automobile accident) may take a long period of time—for some, up to 2 years (see Figure 8.1). Fourth, and perhaps most important, even when the disability is thought to have a stable course, changing life events happen to everyone, and for someone with a disability, minor and even positive variations can require additional coping responses. Disabilities, because they are chronic, do not have quick and easy solutions, nor are they limited.

Spinal cord injuries are considered to be stable course disabilities; however, individuals with these types of injuries experience (1) frequent genitourinary and respiratory infections; (2) sexual dysfunction, especially in males (Ducharme, Gill, Biener–Bergman, & Fertitta, 1993); (3) autonomic hyperreflexia, an abnormal stimu-

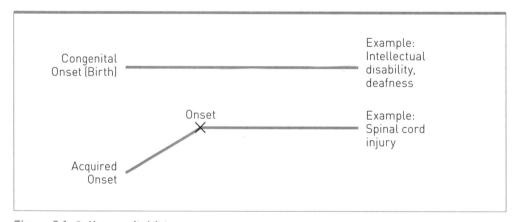

Figure 8.1. *Stable course disabilities.*

lation of the autonomic nervous system that results in headaches, sudden increase in blood pressure, decreased heart rate, sweating, nasal congestion, or blurred vision; (4) spasticity; (5) pain; and (6) decubitus ulcers, which are pressure sores that can become infected (Livneh & Antonak, 1997, p. 135). Jubala (1990) described the episodic course of these complications of spinal cord injury and the hospitalizations they require.

Jubala (1990) also explained autonomic dysreflexia:

> …a syndrome where neural stimulation below the level of injury causes dangerous autonomic processes to occur in the body. These include uncontrolled sweating and a significant increase in blood pressure that can lead to death if not treated. Furthermore, uncontrolled spasms of the paralyzed muscles are not uncommon, and at times can be severe enough to throw people from their wheelchairs. The spinal cord injured [sic] are very susceptible to skin pressure sores because of the long periods of sitting or lying without movement. Frequent weight shifts are necessary to prevent such complications. … It is not unusual for them to have several hospital admissions over the years because of breakdowns in the biological systems outlined above. (p. 230)

Episodic Course Disabilities

Disabilities with an episodic course are ambiguous for the individual, his or her family and friends, and society at large. Stated differently, episodic course disabilities usually have a great deal of unpredictability, which acts as a stressor (Gordon, Lewis, & Wong, 1994; Gulick, 1994). Therefore, stress over the prospect of symptom exacerbation may cause symptom exacerbation, and symptom exacerbation causes more stress. The individual feels a loss of control because he or she cannot predict when an episode will occur.

Nancy Mairs (1997a) described the episodic course (and the autoimmune nature) of her disability as "alien invaders." This analogy may also describe her feelings of lack of control.

> I have known that I have multiple sclerosis for about seventeen years now, though the disease probably started long before. The hypothesis is that the disease process, in which the protective covering of the nerves in the brain and in the spinal cord is eaten away and replaced by scar tissue, "hard patches," is caused by an autoimmune reaction to a slow-acting virus. Research suggests that I was infected by this virus, which no one has ever seen and therefore, technically doesn't even "exist," between the ages of four and fifteen. In effect, living with this mysterious mechanism feels like having your present self, and the past selves it embodies, haunted by a capricious and meanspirited ghost, unseen except for its footprints, which trips you even when you're watching where you're going, knocks glassware out of your hand, squeezes urine out of your bladder before you reach the bathroom, and weights your

whole body with a weariness that no amount of rest can relieve. An alien invader must be at work. But, of course, it's not. It's your own body. That is, it's you. (pp. 52–53)

A woman with a mental illness described the helpful way in which her physician described her disability and his recommendations for *management* and *control* (rather than recommendations for the cure.) Notice that it takes some time for the woman to accept the doctor's assessment.

> A California doctor once compared my mental illness to diabetes. "You have a chronic illness," he said. "You will have to take medication for it, probably for the rest of your life. But it will keep your illness manageable and under control." It took me several years and three more hospitalizations before I heeded that doctor's advice. . . . I would like to emphasize that only after I accepted the illness as a chronic one could I really do something about improving my life. I had to learn that I could not "wish" the illness: I could not "will it to be so." (Weingarten, 1997, p. 123)

Richard Cohen (2004), a journalist with multiple sclerosis, described the ambiguity as "shadow boxing": "Finally, I had been drafted, only this time into the army of 350,000 Americans who shadowbox with this neurological enemy they cannot see" (p. 23). In a single sentence, Cohen describes the way in which he did not choose multiple sclerosis (he was "drafted"), how he considers his disability an "enemy," and above all, the ambiguity—"an enemy that cannot be seen."

Most people try to reduce ambiguity in their lives; however, not *all* ambiguity can be eliminated. Almost everybody likes order, organization, and planning. Indeed, currently in the United States there is an entire industry built around time management and organizational management of one's plans, life, and possessions. Nonetheless, the unpredictable nature of episodic disability, with its intermittent and unpredictable relapses, often instills in the individual, and his or her family, feelings of chaos and lack of control. Two individuals who have spouses with mental illness describe the effect of the ambiguity on their lives:

> Our entire life together has been one big adaptation! I like things organized and planned. Life with mental illness has too many ups and downs with inability to concentrate on planned activities. (Mannion, 1996, p. 22)
>
> I guess I'm okay with it, but . . . I have tons of anger, not really to him— sometimes to him—but more to, you know, "Why me? Why did this happen to me? Why did my husband happen to be the one who got ill?" Because when we got married, we were the perfect little couple. . . . So yes, I've had to revise a lot. . . . I can't think far in advance any more. That is probably the biggest thing that has changed my life because I used to be a planner, all the time

planned—ten years ahead. . . . With an illness like this that runs in cycles. . . . I just think it's too much to put on yourself to expect things when you don't know what's going to happen. (Karp, 2001, p. 143)

However, many individuals with asthma, some types of mental illness, and other disabilities become very skilled in detecting prodromal symptoms (warning signs), such as fatigue and stress. For some disabilities, individuals can become proficient enough to *prevent* some of the relapses, while with other disabilities, the individual can only *predict* and therefore plan for the relapse. However, there are disabilities for which it is impossible to either predict or prevent symptom exacerbation.

Vocational placement, family life, and social life all become difficult. Repetitive recurrences of symptoms or relapses become burdensome for professional caregivers and family members. Compassion fatigue or burnout is quite common. The uncontrollable and unpredictable aspects of these disabilities may lead to learned helplessness (Peterson, Maier, & Seligman, 1993). Kohler and colleagues (1998) summarized the emotional response of some PWDs to episodic course disabilities:

> Clients have compared times of adjustment to riding a roller coaster; constantly challenged or angered by the uphill struggles, never knowing when another curve will come, and unable to stop the motion. During this period of mixed and conflicting emotions, they have a sense of instability, of bewilderment, and of helplessness. (p. 129)

Individuals with episodic course disabilities often hope for prolonged remissions and stabilization and fewer and shorter relapses. Each relapse or symptom exacerbation requires an emotional response. During a relapse, the individual may ask himself or herself many questions, including:

- "Will treatment be effective?"
- "Will this relapse be severe or moderate?"
- "How long will this episode last?"
- "Will I have my job when I come home from the hospital?"
- "Will there be residual effects?"
- "Will I return to my past level of functioning?"
- "Will my family take me back?"

Less serious than full-blown relapses are the fluctuating energy and fatigue levels of some disabilities. Also, chronic pain often varies from day to day. Individuals, their families, and their caregivers can feel overwhelmed by these fluctuations and the resulting lack of control. Family members also live with ongoing and permanent uncertainty (M. T. O'Brien, 1993).

Occasionally, family members and friends do not think that the individual with an episodic disability has a disability. The individual often (or most often) seems like herself or himself and can be highly adaptive and functional in periods of remission. Stefan (2001) completed a national survey of people with psychiatric disabilities, asking about their experiences. She summarized one of the findings:

> One of the most striking aspects of the survey responses was the percentage of people who described themselves as disabled but said that other people did not regard them as so, saying such things as: "Even the people who know of my psychiatric history do not know what a struggle it is for me to maintain my balance." Another wrote, "Friends and family—they don't understand my illness/disability—they think I am getting away with something—that there is nothing wrong with me." (p. 57)

Richard Cohen (2004) referred to the experience of his disability as "a lifetime of ambiguity" (p. 12). Toombs (1995) termed an episodic disability "global uncertainty" (p. 16), explaining:

> Our sense of who we are is intimately related to the roles we occupy, professional and personal . . . and to the goals we hold dear. Chronic, progressive disabling disease necessarily disrupted (or threatened to disrupt) my every role in ways that, at the outset, seemed to reduce my worth as a person. Moreover, the uncertainty of the prognosis transformed my goals and aspirations into foolishness. This sense of diminishment was accompanied by a sense of guilt. But still, in my heart of hearts, I felt in a myriad of ways that I was failing to do as I ought. (p. 16)

Even in times of symptom remission, when the individual lives a fairly normal life, he or she cannot afford to disregard the disability. Individuals with episodic disabilities (a) follow treatment regimens closely and (b) control their environment at all times with the understanding that symptom exacerbation could occur at any time. For example, individuals with seizure disorders take their antiseizure medication on time, do not engage in any activity that might trigger a seizure, wear a medical identification bracelet, and do not engage in dangerous activities alone (such as swimming). Naturally, if the PWD is a child, it is the parents who assume these treatment and management regimens.

The following two excerpts provide a clear picture of prodromal symptoms. The first account tells of antidepressants that stop working and describes the relapse as flames and fire. In the second account, Donna Orrin explained how she became aware of an impending relapse and then the steps she took to successfully avoid hospitalization.

> First, I had a mini-anxiety attack . . . and then I had trouble sleeping, and one morning, two weeks into my Kentucky trip, I woke up a madwoman again. The Prozac had simply stopped working. That's impossible. No, it's not. I

started to tap and touch things and to have to count until my mind clenched closed. Where are you, Prozac? Come home, come home. Back to my body again. . . . My mental illness came rushing back in. As fast as Prozac had once, like a sexy firefighter, doused the flames of pain, the flames now flared back up, angrier than ever and my potent pill could do nothing to quell the conflagration. (Karp, 2001, pp. 171–172)

I start to think squirrels are evil when I begin to become psychotic. Whenever I notice any symptoms, I call my therapist and psychiatrist immediately, so I can "nip my illness in the bud". . . . After a few days of increased medication, I have been able to return to my maintenance dosage. I used to decompensate quickly and my symptoms would escalate rapidly and I would land in the hospital. . . . I now act quickly enough to prevent that escalation. . . . I quickly get to a safe environment that is not overly stimulative and take care of basic needs. . . . After all those years of experience, I am now able to easily identify symptoms and take the appropriate actions quickly. (Orrin, 1997, pp. 142–143)

Read the following account of a woman with rheumatoid arthritis and how she deals with its episodic nature:

I have a handicap placard. . . . I feel so bad when I park in that spot, then I finally tell myself—I'm talking [about parking in] handicap spots—that on those days I'm so tired that I wonder how I even got out, it's all right to park in that spot. And on those good days, leave those spots for someone else. (Gordon, Feldman, & Crose, 1998, p. 8)

Another woman with rheumatoid arthritis described her relapses. (This is also an excellent description of an individual's definition of an autoimmune disease.)

I've been in the hospital every year—for a week or so. It's progressive. I know where it's heading. But I don't really think about it too often. I have termites and they're just eating, having a good time. That's how I describe juvenile rheumatoid arthritis—having termites eating away at my bones and joints. It's not something that can be fixed. You can't slow it down. Gold shots retard it a little bit, but they're still in there having a picnic. They're eating away at the shoulders, so I've lost the rotator cuffs. This hip has to be redone because the termites that eat the bone eat the glue. It just stinks. (Penn, 1993, p. 111)

Episodes are not only unpredictable; they also vary in frequency, duration, and intensity. An individual may have years without a relapse and then experience several relapses within a single year. Therefore, both the frequency and intensity of the relapses must be considered. If relapses occur very infrequently, are not very visible

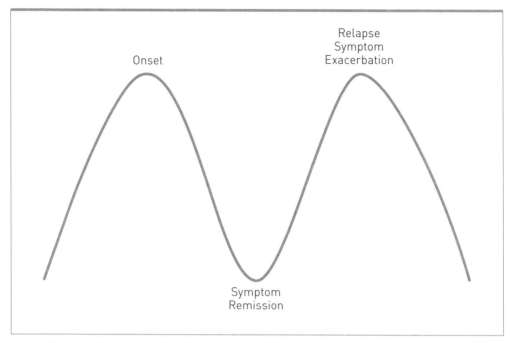

Figure 8.2. *Episodic course disabilities (e.g., seizure disorder).*

or impairing, or both, there are not many response demands. In summary, three factors of symptom exacerbation contribute to the individual's response: (a) the predictability, (b) the intensity of the symptoms (is the individual hospitalized?), and (c) the frequency (symptom exacerbations that occur once every 10 years would not impair an individual as much as those that occur every 2 weeks). As would be expected, researchers have found that those who expressed the highest degree of disability ambiguity—including course and treatment—were more likely to respond less positively (see Figure 8.2).

Although this chapter is discussing the *individual's* response to a disability, it is important to repeat that episodic disabilities elicit much more societal prejudice and discrimination than do chronic, stable disabilities. A legal scholar, Stefan (2001), summarized: "Society is most comfortable with disabilities that are permanent and chronic; either one is disabled or not. Even with people who sometimes have to use a wheelchair find themselves regarded with skepticism and suspicion bordering on hostility" (p. 10).

Stefan continued to describe this prejudice and discrimination as part of the larger legal and economic structures of the United States.

> The economic, mental health, and legal structures, however, cannot accommodate the central truth of alternating or concurrent crisis and functioning at all. The U.S. legal system, mental health system, and labor market are marked by a static and dichotomous vision: One is either disabled or not, and once identified as disabled, residence in the category is presumed permanent. There

is no place for the complexities and contradictions of people's real lives. . . . Defeats . . . are also not seen as temporary, but as permanent. One bad episode can mean the termination of parental rights, an involuntary commitment or involuntary medication. It is all or nothing in American society. (p. 59)

Because an individual's life is directly affected by the health care system and the legal system, a disability of any type, but especially an episodic disability, is difficult to negotiate. In addition, the American workplace is not responsive to individuals with episodic disabilities. As Stefan clearly points out, the lack of a simple dichotomy (disability or no disability) and the resulting ambiguity have created long-standing, institutionalized environmental barriers for individuals with episodic disabilities.

This institutionalized need for a clear-cut dichotomy, in this case, hospitalization or no hospitalization, can be seen in Donna Orrin's experience:

When I think about what I had to go through to get those medication reminder calls, it just infuriates me. I'm a pretty assertive person and, in fact I was on the Community Mental Health Board at the time. Yet they said I was trying to be "taken care of." That's like saying someone with a physical disability is asking to be taken care if they need a wheelchair. No, a wheelchair is a tool or instrument that enables them to have an independent life. A wheelchair is what they need to take care of themselves and move on in life. My medication calls were my tool and extremely cost effective—two one-minute phone calls a day compared to two months of hospitalization. It makes me wonder: if getting those calls was that difficult for me, what is it like for other(s) . . . when they ask for help they know they need. (Orrin, as cited in Mackelprang & Salsgiver, 1999, p. 184)

Degenerative Course Disabilities

With each level of loss, the individual is faced with adjustment and response demands and, often, the need to change his or her self-identity. In addition, the day-to-day living with a chronic disability must be managed, including the financial costs, costs of time, costs of seeking out accommodations and adaptations, and uncertainty of the future. Indeed, the result of several chronic degenerative course disabilities is the death of the individual.

Some degenerative disabilities have a steady rate of progression of symptoms without remission, while others have cyclic periods of symptom stability coupled with periods of degeneration. For most of these types of disability, there is no cure and no prevention, only treatment for symptom relief. Many autoimmune disorders, such as rheumatoid arthritis and lupus, are degenerative course disabilities. Not all degenerative course disabilities result in death. With these specific disabilities, the individual's life span is not shortened; however, 50% of those diagnosed with amyotrophic lateral sclerosis (ALS) die within 3 years of disease onset (see Figures 8.3 and 8.4.)

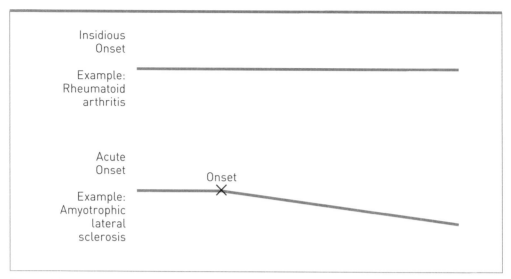

Figure 8.3. *Progressive course disabilities*

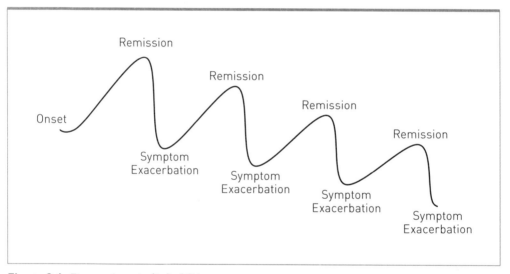

Figure 8.4. *Degenerating episodic disabilities.*

Robert Neumann (1988) described the progression of his rheumatoid arthritis:

> Early in 1960 I went to the Mayo Clinic, where my arthritis was diagnosed at last, and where more appropriate treatment was prescribed. Nonetheless, even this was not able to halt the progression of the disease to my other joints. First, it was my other knee, then my ankles, then my fingers, then my elbows, then my neck, then my hips, then. . . . With a sort of gallows humor, I'd say that I had joined the Joint-of-the-Month Club. But behind this facade, I was

terrified at how my body was progressively deteriorating right before my eyes. (p. 157)

A person with a degenerating disability typically is not born with the disability, nor does he or she experience an acute, sudden onset. Therefore, the course of the disability has a greater impact than the course of other types of disability, and the time of onset may be difficult to pinpoint. The loss of functioning and greater limitation is steady and inevitable. Accepting the realities of a progressive disability requires continual reevaluation of the loss and possible recycling through each of the stages of response.

Degenerating disabilities have steady downward courses, and although they are not as ambiguous as degenerating disabilities with a fluctuating course, they may appear ambiguous to others. In Jenny Morris's book, *Pride Against Prejudice* (1991), Edwina Fairchild related her experience as a young girl in England with degenerating vision. Her parents took her to various doctors, many of whom gave contradictory diagnoses. Nonetheless, over the years, the doctors eventually realized that she was experiencing a gradual vision loss. Edwina was not blind; neither was she fully sighted. Her parents chose to view Edwina as a sighted child:

> "Sighted" meant hope, rationality, capability, life. Given these choices, the adults around me tried to force me into the sighted mold. They did this partly by taking me to eye doctors who might be able to "cure" me, but mostly by simply denying that I could be anything but sighted. (J. Morris, 1991, p. 89)

Edwina's parents also imputed bad motives to her inability to see. Her family insisted that "she just sees what she wants to see" (p. 89). Fairchild spoke about being unfairly judged:

> Some deep part of me must have known it was wrong to be humiliated and punished for something that was a natural and unchangeable part of me. . . . Since I did not fit the acceptable category of "sighted" or even the less acceptable but still comprehensible category of "blind," I threw those who came into contact with me into confusion. I was a creature that existed between two concepts, and they strove to get me to fit into one or the other. (J. Morris, 1991, p. 89)

In addition, because her parents wanted to believe that she could see, Edwina probably was not given many accommodations that could have greatly assisted her functioning (especially in school).

As the disability degenerates, the environment becomes less and less accessible. Or stated more accurately, the environment remains inaccessible while the individual's disability degenerates. Michalko (2002) described his experience:

As my disability becomes worse, I am becoming less and less at home in the world. This is the world of the normal. The world of the normal is the background against which disability stands the figure of blindness. . . . Still, I belong here, but not naturally anymore. Now that I am blind, belonging is a struggle. (p. 38)

Degenerating Episodic Disabilities

In this section, look for—

- ✧ how some disabilities:
  - • are system-specific
  - • affect many systems of the body
- ✧ how the degree of impairment of cognitive functioning is important

A disability usually results in loss of function. Some functions, such as respiratory functions, are more important than others. Some disabilities affect many different systems of the body, while other disabilities are system-specific. Arthritis affects many different joints and thus affects functioning and mobility to a greater degree than does an amputation. Diabetes, often considered by the general public to not be a very limiting disability, affects all systems of the body and can result in many secondary disabilities and complications. The amputation of an arm is considered to be more disfiguring than the amputation of a leg but less of a loss of function. Of all amputations, 90% are lower-limb amputations.

Some disabilities affect functioning in many different areas of the individual's life. Intellectual disabilities, especially severe intellectual disabilities, affect academic, social, and vocational functioning. Fatigue, pain, and muscle weakness or numbness, while considered to be invisible to others, can affect functioning in many different areas of the individual's life. Fatigue, which has no direct relationship to physical activity, can render an individual totally immobile. The loss of functioning and greater limitation are steady and inevitable.

Richard Cohen (2004) described the experience of an episodic, degenerating disability: "I felt powerless, a passenger in a speeding car" (p. 26).

Communication Difficulties

In this section, look for—

- ✧ the problem of loss of communication:

- People with communication difficulties are often misdiag-nosed as having intellectual disability or behavior disorders.
- The Deaf Culture asserts that it is not the impairment of deafness that prevents communication but the lack of accommodations.

Communication is an important function that affects many different areas of an individual's daily life. As we have discussed, there are many ways in which to communicate other than via spoken language, but most people consider spoken language to be synonymous with communication. A great deal of learning (both formal and informal) uses spoken language. Daily interactions usually require communication, including interacting with family members. Therefore, parents, siblings, and spouses are affected by their family member's inability to communicate. Individuals with hearing impairments, cerebral palsy, speech disorders, and some developmental disabilities experience functional limitations in speaking and hearing. Often, the true cause of the individual's lack of ability to communicate is not diagnosed, and the individual is erroneously thought to have an intellectual disability or behavior disorders. Some individuals are able to hear and understand spoken language but cannot speak, such as those with cerebral palsy, while others can neither hear nor speak, which is the case with individuals who are profoundly deaf.

Those in the Deaf Culture state that it is not the functional limitations of the individual's hearing impairment that renders him or her unable to communicate; it is the lack of accommodations in the environment (Higgins & Nash, 1987). The Deaf Culture believes that people who are deaf can and do communicate; they simply use another language (Higgins, 1992b). Obviously, individuals who experience limitations in speaking, hearing, or both depend on visual channels of communication. Assistive technology, such as communication boards and visual or vibrating warning devices, are helpful.

Individuals who lose their hearing later in life often feel isolated and lonely because they have not learned sign language and because they are embarrassed to associate with people who speak. Further, these individuals may feel vulnerable because of their inability to hear sounds that alert them to danger, such as the honking of a car, a fire alarm, and so on. Naturally, those who have been deaf for the greater part of their lives have learned to use assistive devices.

Read the following account of two women in a nursing home. Ann (age 42) can walk, but her speech is difficult to understand, so she uses a communication board. Linda (age 52) uses a wheelchair and speaks very slowly. Notice also the lack of privacy:

> The attendants couldn't speak English and our speech is not so good so there was no communication. Also, we had no privacy. Men, women, anyone would just walk in at any time. They treated us like non-persons and I guess they felt that you can't intrude on a non-person. We were going crazy just

trying to be sane. Now I just use it [the communication board] when people don't understand me. Places like the doctor's office where it's important for people to understand me. It's really a last resort. I know myself and when I get anxious, I can't talk. (cited in Scherer, 1993, p. 96)

The Meaning of the Loss of Functioning

In this section, look for—

- ✧ the idiosyncratic meaning of functioning
- ✧ the degree of "intrusiveness"
- ✧ the importance of capitalizing on residual functioning and skills
- ✧ the revolution in assistive technology for PWDs

The importance of certain functions is also idiosyncratically defined. In other words, the individual's value system and lifestyle determine the importance of certain functions. For example, some individuals are adventuresome; enjoy outdoor, physical activities; and like taking risks. For such types of individuals, the loss of mobility may be felt as a great loss. However, the loss of mobility may not seem catastrophic to someone who enjoys intellectual pursuits. Stephen Hawking, an English physicist with amyotrophic lateral sclerosis (ALS), remarked that his disability gave him more time to think, and thinking is obviously an important function for a physicist. Indeed, many individuals with mobility impairments or sensory impairments have reported, "I escaped into my mind."

It is no coincidence that the leaders in the Disability Rights Movement have been intellectually gifted individuals. Justin Dart, Irving Zola, Paul Longmore, Judith Heumann, and Leonard Kriegel were or are survivors of polio, and their disability did not diminish their intellectual functioning. Livneh and Antonak (1997) used the term *intrusiveness* to describe the effects of a disability that interferes with an individual's functioning. The loss of valued activities (or *intrusiveness*) is idiosyncratically defined because valued activities are defined by the individual.

The example most often used to describe the importance of the idiosyncratic meaning of function was mentioned in Chapter 2: that of a piano player missing a little finger. For most people, the loss of a single finger would not be defined as a disability or as a loss of function. However, for an individual who had spent his or her life preparing to be a concert pianist, the loss of a single finger would greatly change his or her life. An individual's learning style can affect the unique meaning he or she ascribes to a loss of functioning. For example, auditory learners would experience difficulty in responding to late-onset hearing impairment, just as visual learners would have difficulty in responding to blindness. Personality characteristics, such as privacy and independence needs, also affect the meaning of the loss of certain functions. One woman with multiple sclerosis describes a particularly difficult loss of function:

> The loss of bowel and bladder control is much more than simply a mechanical or neurological dysfunction. Incontinence reduces an adult to the status of a helpless victim. One is no longer the master of even the most basic of bodily functions. So great is the threat of public humiliation that many afflicted patients simply choose to withdraw from society, rather than risk embarrassment. (Toombs, 1995, p. 18)

Functioning is also culturally and gender defined, meaning that both the loss of function and the role expectations of a PWD are, to some extent, determined by his or her culture and gender (Sasao & Sue, 1993; Sinacore-Guinn, 1995; Spector, 1991). For example, Alice Crespo, a court interpreter who is blind, remarked:

> My parents came from Puerto Rico.... There, women stay at home and raise babies. If you have a disability, it is assumed that you can't or won't have babies, but you stay home anyhow, being taken care of by your family. (Rousso, 1993, p. 101)

Lee Martin's father lost both his arms in a farming accident when Martin was 1 year old; therefore, Martin has no memory of his father with hands. Martin described trying to imagine his father with hands:

> When I look at photographs of my father before his accident, my eyes go immediately to his hands. I try to figure out whether they resemble my own, but I can never really decide. His appear to be small, his fingers shorter, but that may only be the perspective of the camera. All I can be certain of is the sadness that comes over me whenever I look at those photographs. I want to tell my father about that moment in the cornfield when the shucking box will clog. "Shut off the tractor," I want to tell him, but of course, I can't. He's there in the photographs, and I'm here over forty years later, recalling the cold steel of his hooks. (Martin, 2000, pp. 7–8)

For many individuals, it is not the onset of the disability that is most life-changing, but the related loss of function that may occur years after the diagnosis and onset of the disability. Many individuals with arthritis, multiple sclerosis, or muscular dystrophy report that the day they began to use a wheelchair was far more life-changing than the day they received their diagnosis. Other such functional losses include being required, because of a progressive disability, to move into an assisted living home, or wear hearing aids, or relinquish a driver's license.

When an individual loses the ability to function in one area, the solution is to use and develop and capitalize on his or her residual skills. Generally speaking, individuals with a broad range of interests and abilities are capable of responding more positively to a disability simply because they have more options. Individuals with unifocal interests, such as athletics and sports, often find responding to a loss of mobility to be difficult. However, individuals with a great deal of education, varied work skills and experience, and multifocal interests will be able to shift their functioning to the areas of their residual abilities and capabilities.

An example of a valued function that was idiosyncratically defined is presented in Marcia Scherer's (1993) book, *Living in the State of Stuck: How Technology Impacts the Lives of People With Disabilities*. Brian sustained a spinal cord injury in a motorcycle accident at age 17. Note the impact of an idiosyncratically defined function, attending a Grateful Dead concert.

> My friends came up to visit as usual and said that [my favorite group] the Grateful Dead were playing here in November. My mind was back, but I had to get my strength. The doctors said I would have to sit 4 to 5 hours straight if I were to go to the concert. Every time I got into the wheelchair, I blacked right out. Each day for only a short time, I would sit in a semireclined position determined to reach my goal. After a couple of days I was up to three hours. The day of the show I reached my goals and I was psyched. The concert was the first time I had been out of the hospital. I had reached my destination. (p. 22)

Before closing this discussion of loss of functioning, it is important to point out that assistive, or adaptive, technology has greatly decreased the loss of functioning that PWDs experience. Until the invention of computers, the design and use of assistive devices for PWDs changed little for hundreds of years. Before computers, these devices were simple mechanical equipment that were most often homemade. These included prosthetic devices such as artificial arms or legs, orthotic (straightening) devices such as braces, and mechanical wheelchairs (without power; Weisgerber, 1991). Now, most assistive technology is either computerized or electromechanical (Scherer, 1993). Examples of these newer technologies include power wheelchairs; Functional Electrical Stimulation (FES) that sends bursts of low-level electricity to paralyzed muscles; augmentative and alternative communication systems; environmental control computers that lock doors, turn on the furnace, and turn off the lights; and voice-activated computers that allow individuals who do not have the use of their hands to type. This revolution in assistive technology has changed the meaning of loss of function.

Severity of the Disability

In this section, look for—

✦ how some disabilities have clear-cut levels of severity

✦ how the level of severity of most disabilities is judged on several factors, including:

- the number of disabilities the individual experiences
- the number of areas of functioning affected
- the treatment necessary
- the degree of stigma directed at the individual

Some types of disabilities have clear-cut cutoff points between the categories of mild, moderate, and severe. For example, deafness is defined as the loss of hearing 80 decibels or greater; a severe impairment is the loss of hearing within the 60 to 80 decibel range; a moderate loss (sometimes called "hard of hearing") is defined as loss of hearing in the 40 to 60 decibel range, and a mild hearing loss is a loss of 25 to 40 decibels. Vision impairments also have numerical guidelines that designate categories. These types of categories are possible only when there is great diagnostic precision, usually using objective, standardized measuring instruments. Many disabilities do not have this diagnostic precision, and, therefore, it is more difficult to determine the medical treatment, educational placement, and living situation for individuals with these types of disabilities.

Up until 2013, with the fifth edition of the *Diagnostic and Statistical Manual of Mental Disorders* (DSM-5; American Psychiatric Association, 2013) levels of severity for intellectual disabilities were based on a range of I.Q. points. Mild intellectual disabilities included the range of I.Q. between 55 and 70; Moderate intellectual disabilities included the range of 40 and 55; Severe included the range of 25 and 40. An I.Q. score below 25 was considered Profound Intellectual Disability. Now, the DSM-5 determines level of severity based on adaptive functioning and the degree of support required, although individualized I.Q. testing, rendering numerical I.Q. scores, is still undertaken.

Disabilities that cannot be measured precisely are usually determined to be severe, moderate, or mild by several different standards. First, the number of disabilities an individual experiences can help to determine level of severity. For example, individuals who are both blind and deaf are considered to have a severe disability. Second, the number of areas of functioning affected can lead to a diagnosis of severity. An individual with quadriplegia would be considered to have a severe disability. Third, the treatment necessary can, in an indirect way, determine the level of severity. For example, an individual whose schizophrenia can be controlled by medication would not be considered to have as severe a disability as someone who must be institutionalized because he or she does not respond to the medication. Finally, the episodic nature of some types of disability often leads to a diagnosis of a severe disability, based on the premise that the individual's functioning is very impaired.

Degree of severity is never based on visibility of the disability; nor is degree of severity based on the level of prejudice directed toward the individual. Therefore, an individual with a heart condition (an invisible disability) could be considered to have a severe disability because the heart condition limits many different functions. Someone with a facial disfigurement, with few or any functional limitations, is also considered to have a severe disability as a result of the stigma and prejudice that limit the individual's functioning. Many people with facial disfigurements report that they stay at home, always. Individuals who wear eyeglasses (which restore their vision to full functioning) experience little prejudice and stigma. However, those who wear hearing aids (which improve their hearing) are subjected to prejudice and discrimination. Finally, it should be remembered that it is the individual's *judgment*, *assessment*, and *perception* of the disability that is most important. Further, the individual's judgment often differs from that of medical and educational professionals.

Quality of Life

In this section, look for—

- ⋄ how quality of life is both subjective and multidimensional
- ⋄ how minimum requirements usually include:
  - social and economic independence
  - freedom to function at one's highest level
  - social support
  - access to medical and psychological care
- ⋄ how, often, it is the lack of accommodations (and not the disability) that lowers the individual's quality of life

Disabilities can be categorized according to how much quality of life an individual with that type of disability enjoys. However, the concept of quality of life is subjective and multidimensional. Because there are more PWDs than ever before, and these individuals (like everyone else) continue to live longer, the already vague concept of quality of life becomes even cloudier. The chronic, long-term nature of disability coupled with longer life spans has done much to increase the *quantity* of life, and *quantity* can be measured. *Quality* of life cannot be measured, but is usually defined in terms of minimum requirements. For PWDs, quality of life is thought to be defined in terms of social and economic independence (within the limits of the disability); the freedom to function at one's highest level; social support, including family life; and the right to medical and psychological care. Others have felt that to have quality of life, an individual should be able to ascribe some sort of meaning or spiritual component to his or her life (Kilpatrick & McCullough, 1999; H. McCarthy, 1995; C. Vash, 1981; Yalom, 1980). We can see that included in these definitions are the concepts of having one's basic needs met, economic independence, social support, and self-actualization.

Often, it is the lack of accommodations, rather than the disability itself, that diminishes a PWD's quality of life. Accounts of PWDs tell of the day they received their van; their wheelchair; or, for one girl with legal blindness, a magnifying glass. The quality of life changed for these people. The prejudice, discrimination, and limited opportunities that PWODs direct toward PWDs also needlessly reduce the quality of life for PWDs. Accounts of PWDs tell of their first day at the neighborhood school, their first time in a movie theater, their first day on the job, their first paycheck, and their first date. Many PWODs cannot remember most of these "firsts," probably because these opportunities were automatically given to them. For many PWDs, these are memorable events, and, occasionally, some PWDs thought that they would never be able to experience them. Quality of life for PWDs can be limited by the disability itself, but it is safe to state that quality of life is more likely to be limited needlessly by PWODs. Sexual intimacy, considered to be a component of adult quality of life, may be altered, or the PWD's partner may leave after the onset of the disability (Ducharme et al., 1993). Partners who do stay in the relationship often report that they are hesitant to resume the sexual relationship.

Many PWDs report an increase in self-esteem and feelings of mastery and control because they are able to manage their disability. Barbara Waxman (J. Morris, 1991) reported that she is "quite skilled at being a disabled person":

> I don't think society understands anything about disability. People look at me and they ask me how do I live my life. I think what they're really saying is *why* do I live my life? They believe that the pain that I experience is derived from my functional limitations. What they don't understand is that the pain and rejection I've experienced have been purely socially based. I'm not depressed about being disabled. I'm quite skilled at being a disabled person. I'm quite proud of my identity as a disabled person. But the pain is social. (p. 62)

In contrast, read the following excerpt:

> I was born, educated, broke my neck, and I'll die and be buried just down the road here about half a mile, so my life hasn't been that much. . . . My life had no value. [The interviewer then asks, "Not even to you?"] No, because I didn't get a chance to do anything with it. It was not mine when I was a kid; it belonged to the parents. By the time I got to be 16, getting ready to go out and do something for myself, you break your neck, and that's it. You can't do anything. I suppose that a person could go to work; I mean, a lot of people do work that are handicapped [*sic*]; they earn money and have families—stuff like that. But once I was hurt, none of that applied to me any longer. I didn't care about it or think about it or nothing. I just kind of hunkered down for the long pull, I guess. You make the best of what you've got. There's nothing going to happen to me in life after that—not to me there wasn't. I knew that. (Crewe, 1997, p. 38)

The following are two more PWDs speaking of the quality of their lives:

I look at it like this, I was a 25-year-old hellion with a shaved head before my accident. I think I'm a better person than what I was then. I took life for granted, and boom, I got a big awakening. (B. B. Boswell, Dawson, & Heininger, 1998, p. 30)

It's like a gift ... over the years, I've evolved into thinking about the greater scheme and believing, that we all exist in our pigeonholes for a reason. And believing that, you can take this [disability] and be a burden with it. You can live with it as a burden or you can live with it as a gift. (B. B. Boswell et al., 1998, p. 30)

Pain and Trauma of the Disability

In this section, look for—

- ✧ how some disabilities involve or require:
  - pain
  - frequent surgeries
  - loss of income
  - loss of valued activities
  - expensive treatment
  - hospitalization or institutionalization

The treatment and management of a disability can be both time consuming and expensive. Often, sleep disturbances are part of the disability. PWDs often have to alter their lifestyle, relinquishing valued activities. If the PWD has been forced to give up his or her employment, there is a substantial loss of income, coupled with expensive medical and rehabilitation costs. Further, the money and time needed to manage the disability often use the PWD's disposable income and time. In other words, the individual must give up social opportunities and fun times to find the time and money to deal with the disability.

The treatment and management of some types of disabilities (for example, spina bifida) require repeated surgeries, prolonged medical treatment, and frequent hospitalizations. Indeed, for many PWDs, several hospital stays each year are typical. Fatigue and muscle weakness, both of which are invisible to others, limit the functioning of some PWDs. These individuals learn to conserve their energy for what they consider to be important activities. Read the following account of Zachary, a man with a spinal cord injury. Note the repeated surgeries, his limited functioning, and the goals he has set for himself:

The rods in my back were dissolving through a process of electrolysis. My doctor had no explanation—he said the metal was turning into bubble gum and axle grease. When we redid the rods, I was playing the perfect quad—I wouldn't get a glass of water; I wouldn't put any stress on them at all, and the second set still broke. The third set was actually a double operation, first anterior and then a week later, posterior. . . . The last 5 years has been "staying alive." I haven't really accomplished much that could be written down on paper except for staying alive. On April 11, I've been a quad for as many days as I was able-bodied. Right now I have no goals in my life other than that I want to leave this life consciously. (Crewe, 1997, p. 36)

Some disabilities result in the eventual death of the individual. For example, ALS is a rapidly progressing motor neuron disease, and 50% of diagnosed individuals die within 3 years. However, retinitis pigmentosa, a progressive type of blindness, does result in total blindness but not in death. Some types of disabilities are thought to have both degenerative and episodic courses, meaning that there are episodes of symptom exacerbation; however, when the symptoms remit, the individual does not return to the level of functioning he or she experienced before the relapse. In other words, the person does get somewhat better, but with each relapse, the individual returns to a lower level of functioning than before.

It would seem reasonable that severity of disability would be associated with psychopathology (D. W. Cook, 1991). In other words, those individuals with very severe disabilities would be maladjusted, depressed, lacking social skills, angry, or suicidal. Rehabilitation and disability researchers have sought, for more than 30 years, to find a relationship between severity of disability and degree of psychological impairment. Cook interpreted the research findings:

> In his extensive review of the literature, Shontz (1971) concluded that there is little support for the theory that severity of disability causes psychological maladjustment. In his review of research on emotional factors and disability. Based on their review, Roessler and Bolton (1978) also argued for a relationship, albeit complex, between severity of disability and degree of psychological impairment. (D. W. Cook, 1991, pp. 85–86)

It appears, therefore, that there are few researchers who would state that severity of disability is directly related to degree of psychopathology.

Chronic Pain

In this section, look for—

♦ how there is limited knowledge about pain
♦ the difference between acute pain and chronic pain

✧ how medical professionals often have negative stereotypes of
   individuals with chronic pain

Pain is a part of many disabilities, yet there is limited medical knowledge about "the specific mechanism for transmission and perception of pain" (Lubkin & Jeffrey, 1998, p. 149). Further clouding the diagnostic picture is the fact that pain is invisible, experienced subjectively, and impossible to measure objectively. Physicians ask patients questions about the location of the pain; the intensity of the pain using a numerical scale of 1 to 10; the onset, duration, variations, and rhythm of the pain; what relieves the pain; what causes or exacerbates the pain; and the effect of the pain on the individual's functioning. In spite of all this specificity, the experience of pain is impossible to describe fully.

Chronic pain, in contrast to acute pain, persists for a period of time, usually 3 to 6 months, or occurs at intervals for months or years (Bonica, 1990). Acute pain is a different experience: first, the individual knows that acute pain is temporary; second, acute pain subsides when healing occurs; and third, acute pain can usually be controlled by medications. Acute pain, therefore, is viewed as "having a purpose" and an end. In contrast, chronic pain usually is not related to any malignancy; rather, it is associated with musculoskeletal disabilities, such as lower back pain. There is no end to chronic pain.

Chronic pain can become the central focus of an individual's life, curtailing work, family life, and social activities. "The individual with chronic pain may undergo a change from being someone with multiple roles (worker, friend, family member, and so forth) to someone who only identifies with the pain" (Lubkin & Jeffrey, 1998, p. 153). Individuals often tire of defending themselves and trying to explain their pain to others. Indeed, they may even begin to question their own perceptions of the pain (e.g., "Maybe I *am* crazy."). In the United States, the most commonly reported cause of chronic pain is lower back problems. Chronic pain often leads to sleep disturbances, fatigue, depression, and poor concentration. Those who experience chronic pain often lead very restricted, dependent lives. Their lives are controlled by the pain. Family members take on additional responsibilities, trying at the same time to understand and respect the experience of chronic pain. Pain is both a physiological experience and an emotional experience. Additionally, like any other symptom, pain is culturally determined, and there have been cross-cultural and cross-national studies that have shown that one's cultural identification plays some part in the recognition and response to pain (Brena, Sanders, & Motoyama, 1990). According to R. M. Gallagher (2000), individuals who experience chronic pain are at high risk for depression. Gallagher stated the effect of depression: "Depression may lower both the pain threshold and tolerance" (p. 28). Therefore, it would appear that the relationship between pain and depression can become circular.

Medical professionals often have negative stereotypes of individuals with chronic pain. Thus, there is frustration and anger on the part of the physician and on the part of the patient. The physician cannot understand the pain, and the patient feels, justifiably, demeaned and devalued. The idea of pain, and the possibility that everyone may experience pain, gives the individual who does live with chronic pain an unpleasant reminder of an unpleasant possibility. Further, the ambiguity of chronic pain also contributes to the negative stereotypes of individuals who experience it. Pain is a private experience because there is no socially acceptable way to express it. No one wants to hear about someone else's pain and discomfort. Chronic pain often has no clear-cut cause; no end in sight; and, occasionally, no suitable relief (Bowman, 1994; Hadjistavropoulos & Craig, 1994). Everyone involved feels frustrated. Medical professionals often discount patients' reports of pain because of the following factors: (a) "Professionals do not always give credence to pain complaints unless there is some identifiable pathology"; (b) "Professionals also often assume that all clients have the same pain perception threshold and therefore perceive the same intensity of pain from the same stimuli"; and (c) "Many professionals have become desensitized to the client's pain experience and rate pain as less important than clients do" (Lubkin & Jeffrey, 1998, p. 151).

More About Pain

In this section, look for—

- ⬧ the widespread fear of pain
- ⬧ how, often, individuals who experience chronic pain are blamed for the following:
  - the pain itself
  - the management of the pain
  - reminding others of the human possibility of pain

Pain is invisible. Individuals who appear normal often experience chronic pain that effectively curtails many of their life functions. On the one hand, fear of pain can contribute to such problems as drug and alcohol addictions. On the other hand, society frequently lauds individuals, often athletes, who have overcome pain to accomplish some great goal. Neither view of pain—fearing all pain or ascribing hero status to those who overcome pain—is correct or helpful. Wendell (2006) described the first view of pain—that those who do not experience chronic pain ascribe much more power to the experience:

> People with painful disabilities can teach us about pain, because they can't avoid it and have had to learn how to face it and live with it. The pernicious myth that it is possible to avoid almost all pain by controlling the body gives the fear of pain greater power than it should have and blames the victims

of unavoidable pain. The fear of pain is also expressed or displaced as fear of people in pain, which often isolates those with painful disabilities. All this is unnecessary. People in pain and knowledge of pain could be fully integrated into our culture, to everyone's benefit. (p. 270)

D. B. Morris (1998) explained the second view of pain:

> Athletes are repeatedly praised by the media for overcoming extreme pain, like the astonishing Olympic gymnast from Japan who completed his dismount with a broken leg. Yet such praise and its implicit meaning (to overcome pain is heroic) leave a difficult legacy for chronic pain patients, who cannot surmount their affliction in a supreme moment of glory but must live with it, unpraised and often unobserved day after day. (p. 129)

In a study conducted with PWDs, Putnam and colleagues (2003) found that for some individuals, pain was interpreted as a positive sign: "A few individuals who experienced spinal cord injuries mentioned that pain in their lives, while difficult to tolerate, could be interpreted as a sign that their nerves were still working and therefore was a positive sign of health" (p. 39).

Perhaps the best writing on the experience of pain is Reynolds Price's book, *A Whole New Life* (1994). Price is a novelist and a professor at Duke University. After being diagnosed with spinal cancer, he underwent three surgeries and weeks of radiation. Price lost the use of his legs and was left in constant pain as a result of the damage caused by the surgeries and the radiation to his central nervous system. Price described his pain in great detail:

> The pain was high and all-pervading from the neck to the feet; it generally peaked in blinding storms late in the day if I was tired. It intensified in conditions of low barometric pressure; and for dozens of other mysterious reasons, by now it had seized frank control of my mind, my moods, and my treatment of friends. Patience had ebbed to its lowest reach. (Price, 1994, p. 151)

Eventually, Reynolds Price overcame the pain with biofeedback and self-hypnosis.

CHAPTER 9

MORE ON THE INDIVIDUAL'S RESPONSE TO DISABILITY

◆ What is the degree of stigma directed toward the disability?

◆ What is the degree of visibility of the disability?

◆ With invisible disabilities, why is choosing the point of disclosure important?

◆ What does the term *social death* mean?

◆ How is the treatment of disfiguring disabilities different from the treatment of other disabilities?

◆ What does the phrase "most enabling environment" mean?

◆ Does society foster dependence and helplessness for PWDs?

◆ How do PWDs redefine independence, autonomy, and control?

◆ What are the functions of support groups?

The Degree of Stigma Directed Toward the Disability

In this section, look for—

- ✧ how the PWD has two tasks:
    1. manage the disability
    2. deal with stigma
- ✧ stigma recognition
- ✧ stigma management

An individual with a disability has two tasks: he or she must (a) manage and treat the disability and (b) deal with the degree of stigma that others direct toward the disability. All PWDs, regardless of their type or severity of disability, personal achievements, or socioeconomic status, understand that they are members of a stigmatized and devalued group. However, it is safe to state that there is more stigma toward certain types of disabilities than toward other disabilities. We learned earlier that there is a hierarchy of stigma: individuals with physical disabilities experience the least degree of stigma, individuals with intellectual and cognitive disabilities experience more stigma, and individuals with psychiatric disabilities experience the most stigma.

Therefore, individuals with physical disabilities, such as blindness, mobility impairments, and chronic illness, experience less prejudice and less segregation and are allowed more choices than are individuals with schizophrenia (Fink & Tasman, 1992; Friesen, 1996; Garske & Stewart, 1999). If medical and rehabilitation care providers were to attempt to quantify the degree of impairment of a mobility impairment and the degree of impairment of schizophrenia, such considerations as functions impaired, residual capacities available to the individual, treatment and hospitalizations required, and impact on the individual's vocational functioning would be examined. However, even with a comprehensive review of these important factors, the experience of living with these two types of disabilities is very different. Probably the greatest difference between these two types of disabilities (orthopedic impairment and schizophrenia) is the prejudice and stigma that is directed toward one but not toward the other. In Chapters 3, 4, and 5, we discussed the concepts of prejudice, stigma, and discrimination from a societal viewpoint, looking at these concepts as a large group in power (society) holding prejudicial and stigmatizing views toward PWDs. In this chapter, the focus is on the individual's experience of stigma.

Stigma recognition and stigma management are two skills that PWDs are required to develop. Stigma recognition is the simple act of acknowledging that someone's judgments, appraisals, and actions are both inaccurate and hurtful. If the PWD is not able to recognize stigma and prejudice, he or she may be affected in the following ways: (1) engage in self-doubt, (2) feel angry, (3) feel depressed, or (4) feel humiliated (Holzbauer & Berven, 1996). Indeed, Holzbauer and Berven quoted an individual who felt the stigma to be justified, saying, "The worst part about it is that I felt it was my fault" (p. 481). Those PWDs who are adept at recognizing stigma may forgive the stigmatizer, thinking that he or she doesn't know any better or is having a bad day. Other PWDs may become angry. Most important, however, is that by recognizing stigma as inaccurate, the PWD does not internalize these types of judgments. In other words, the PWD does not believe the insults, and the insults do not become part of his or her self-concept. Naturally, a great deal of stigma recognition is dependent on the PWD's age (adults are better at stigma recognition than children) and his or her social skills and awareness. Stigma recognition becomes an even more difficult issue when the stigma (or handicapism) is unintentional. Remember the story of Sharon L., who was told by her high school counselor that she could be an artist because (1) she would not have to associate with others, and she could work alone and (2) those who purchased her art would never realize that it was "disabled art." Such attitudes are stigmatizing and hurtful, and yet, in this particular case, the professional career guidance was intended to be helpful. How should a PWD respond to such an unintentional stigma? Compare the counselor's view of "handicapped" art with the art of Randy Souders found in Chapter 6.

Stigma management can be handled with skillful humor, assertive and direct responses, or both. Of course, the PWD must be especially proficient at correcting misconceptions and refusing to be denied his or her rights. Often, the skillful humor and assertiveness backfire, and, as a result, the PWD has more stigma directed toward him or her.

Stigma management is also important in social situations and even more important in job interviews or admission interviews. Explaining accommodations (how they work, their expense, and how they would allow the PWD to do the job), explaining the disability and its impact (or lack of impact) on the job, or explaining the gap in a résumé because of a hospitalization all require skillful stigma management. Further, this type of stigma management has clear-cut effects for the PWD. Stigma is hurtful and stressful, and, in the case of PWDs, it is personally directed toward a single person. For someone who has been teased and harassed as a child, managing stigma as an adult can be overwhelming.

Filing formal complaints is a type of stigma management. A study that reviewed the complaints of discrimination by PWDs under the Americans With Disabilities Act (ADA) between 1992 and 1996 (McMahon, Shaw, & Jaet, 1995) found that the two disability categories with the highest numbers of complaints were mental illness and learning disabilities. Examining the records of the Equal Employment Opportunity Commission (EEOC), as McMahon and his colleagues did, supports the idea that there is more stigma directed toward cognitive and psychiatric disabilities. These researchers interpreted their findings: "Members of both groups have been erroneously perceived as having subaverage intelligence, and this and other respects are historically misunderstood by the general public. . . . This makes the matter of disability harassment appear all the more cowardly and insidious" (McMahon et al., p. 11).

Stigma by Association

Families with a member with a disability also experience stigma, only in this case it is termed "stigma by association." Leah Hager Cohen, Ruth Sidransky, and Lou Ann Walker wrote books about their parents who were deaf, and all spoke of the stigma of having relatives who are deaf and of the need to conceal their parents' deafness. It was felt that potential boyfriends or husbands did not want in-laws who are deaf or children who are deaf, and thus, dating and social opportunities for these women, all of whom were hearing, were unnecessarily limited. These authors relate many instances of stigma by association. Families with members with mental illnesses also feel stigma by association (Friesen, 1996), and many have responded to this by engaging in advocacy and educational efforts, such as the National Alliance for the Mentally Ill (NAMI). Reread the excerpt in Chapter 7 from the Westbrook and Legge Australian study. These family members thought the presence of a child with a disability in the family decreased the other children's chances of marriage.

Professionals who serve PWDs are often stigmatized by association. Professionals who have chosen to work with stigmatized individuals (PWDs) are thought to "lack initiative, training, and ambition" (Fink & Tasman, 1992, p. 204). Indeed, Fink and Tasman asserted that many talented psychiatrists leave the profession because they are aware of the stigmatization, feeling undervalued. Because psychiatrists treat patients with the most stigmatized disabilities (mental illness), these psychiatrists often feel themselves to be stigmatized. Also, professionals who work with individuals with intellectual disability are often thought to be less capable than professionals who work with higher functioning clients, students, or patients.

The Degree of Visibility of the Disability

In this section, look for—

- ✧ how there is no correlation between degree of visibility and degree of impairment
- ✧ how some episodic disabilities can be invisible during times of symptom remission
- ✧ how choosing the point of disclosure requires careful timing
- ✧ how, often, it is the PWD's family who wishes to keep the disability hidden

Some disabilities are readily apparent to others; other disabilities are not apparent to others unless the PWD chooses to disclose; and other types of disabilities are invisible even to the individual with the disability. Disabilities such as diabetes may be hidden from the individual for a prolonged period.

There is no correlation between degree of visibility and degree of impairment.

However, many PWODs, whether consciously or subconsciously, do view the degree of visibility to be related to the degree of severity. In other words, these PWODs mistakenly believe that invisible disabilities are not as severe as visible disabilities. Indeed, many individuals with invisible disabilities report, "You get tired of defending yourself all the time." Or, occasionally, individuals with invisible disabilities become angry and tell others, "It's none of your damned business." Often, PWODs do not consider these individuals to have a disability.

Disabilities with an episodic course are often visible only in times of symptom exacerbation or "flare-ups." Nonetheless, because most disabilities with an episodic course are unpredictable, it is difficult for the individual to hide the disability. For example, someone with a seizure disorder may have a difficult time explaining why he or she does not have a driver's license. A woman with rheumatoid arthritis, an episodic disability, described how she made daily decisions whether or not to disclose her disability. She said,

> I finally broke down and asked my doctor about a handicap sticker [parking sticker]. [Was that a big step for you?]. . . . yeah, well, I still didn't want the handicap license plate. The sticker, I can not use it or hide it or whatever. (Gordon, Feldman, & Crose, 1998, p. 8)

Both a parking sticker and a metal license plate are accommodations for the woman with rheumatoid arthritis. However, the parking sticker can be hidden when the woman is experiencing symptom remission.

In addition, legally (under the ADA) the individual with an invisible disability is required to disclose the disability to receive accommodations. If he or she chooses not to disclose, often functioning is sacrificed. Visibility of assistive technology, such as insulin pumps or hearing aids, can render a disability visible which heretofore was an invisible disability.

For many individuals with invisible disabilities, the question is not *whether* to disclose the presence of the disability, but *when* to disclose the disability. This is referred to as "choosing the point of disclosure." Individuals with these types of disabilities can allow relevant characteristics to be displayed, while establishing the relationship, and when they feel the time is right, they can tell others that they have a disability. For instance, the individual can settle into a new job and demonstrate his or her capabilities and productivity before informing his or her supervisor and coworkers of the disability. In this case, the job capabilities and productivity are the relevant characteristics and the individual with an invisible disability has availed himself or herself of the option to be viewed as an ordinary employee (i.e., an employee without a disability). As we have learned, many PWODs regard a disability to be the defining characteristic of the PWD; however, the individual with an invisible disability can avoid much of this labeling and stereotyping. In social relationships, the individual with an invisible disability can establish friendships and other types of relationships without the automatic and erroneous assumptions about disabilities interfering.

The timing of the disclosure requires a careful balance: The individual must judge when he or she has established his or her capabilities, but cannot take too long before disclosing, because others may feel betrayed. For example, in the case of a dating relationship, the individual with the invisible disability can wait until the relationship has become very serious and then reveal his or her disability. However, the dating partner may be angry that he or she was not told at the very beginning.

Michael Weisskopf, a reporter for *Time* magazine who acquired a disability while covering the war in Iraq, wrote an article titled, "How I Lost My Hand but Found Myself" (2006). He tells of his decision not to hide his disability:

> Before Iraq, the technology of arm prostheses hadn't changed much since World War II. The tiny population of amputees created little market incentive. Miguelez [the prosthetist] used the burst in demand from Walter Reed [hospital] to lean on manufacturers for progress. Before long, he was outfitting Iraq war amputees with an electronic hand that opened and closed 2½ times faster and could be programmed to function at different speeds and grip strength.
>
> The cosmetic arts also had improved. I received a silicone hand that was so lifelike it passed for real in social settings. But Pretty Boy, as I called it, kept tearing and afforded the precision of a boxing glove. It was too spongy to grasp anything small and too slippery to hold most objects for long.
>
> Function was only part of the problem. The idea of trying to pass had begun to trouble me. It made me feel as if I had something to hide or to be ashamed of. When I started to go bald, I shaved my head. No comb-overs, transplants or toupees for me. So why try to conceal a handicap? I was proud of how I had lost my hand. The stump had a story to tell. . . . (p. 37)

Also important in disclosure is *what* and *how much* to disclose. Should the PWD simply state that he or she has a medical condition? Of course, some individuals with invisible disabilities choose not to disclose at all. People with invisible disabilities often become very skilled in passing as someone without a disability. They learn to avoid situations in which their disability might be revealed. They are adept at idiosyncratic compensation methods. Michalko (2002) became legally blind while in high school, but he managed to convince his friends that he was fully sighted. The difficulty came at the time when all of his friends were obtaining driving licenses.

> The problem was having a "good reason" for not driving. . . . Thankfully, however, the culture that put so much pressure on me to pass as "normal," also presented me with the structure and organization from which I could create a "good reason" for not driving. I lived in a lower working-class area of the city where quasi-delinquent behavior was quite acceptable and even appropriate. It was not difficult for me to create a "good story" from the

building blocks of this social context. Caught drunk driving by the police and having the right to hold a learner's permit suspended for a year was a story that worked out well enough. (p. 74)

Richard Cohen was a television news reporter when he was diagnosed with multiple sclerosis at age 25. He is married to the television personality Meredith Viera. Cohen (2004) describes how he has wrestled with the decision to disclose, including weighing "what is at stake":

> I learned a valuable lesson then and there. Honesty is not the best policy. Candor about health problems works in the confines of academia and maybe in the movies. Full disclosure does not work so well in the real world. Hard times in a competitive industry at a tough moment in history leave little room for dealing fairly with a serious illness. People with serious problems can be perceived as weak candidates for employment in the dollars-and-cents world. The right thing to do has currency when nothing is at stake. . . . Don't tell nobody nuthin. . . . My stealth approach bothered me enough to write my private rulebook outlining when dishonesty went too far and when it was permissible. (pp. 54–55)

In addition, those who choose to hide their disability often are considered disloyal by others with the same disability. For example, many in the Disability Rights Movement label Franklin Roosevelt a "closet crip" because he hid and minimized his disability. Another cost is the stress of hiding both the disability and the accommodations or treatment of the disability. An individual may need time off from work during the day to attend Alcoholics Anonymous meetings, and his coworkers may think that he or she is goofing off. Another example is that of an individual with a psychiatric disability who has chosen not to disclose the disability and then must listen to friends' jokes about "fruitcakes," "wackos," and "psychos" and remain silent.

Cynthia Rich (as cited in J. Morris's 1991 book, *Pride Against Prejudice: Transforming Attitudes to Disability*) described two distinct types of "passing." The first type is that of a "consciously political tactic for carefully limited purposes," and for her, this type of passing does not have serious, pervasive, or long-term consequences for the individual. The second type of passing, in which the individual loses his or her own identity, has serious results:

> Passing—except as a consciously political tactic for carefully limited purposes—is one of the most serious threats to selfhood. We attempt, of course, to avoid the oppressor's hateful distortion to our identity and the real menace to our survival of his [*sic*] hatred. But, meanwhile, our identity is never acted out, can lose its substance, its meaning, even for ourselves. (p. 36)

It should be pointed out that others who have the same disability (or who have a great deal of experience with that type of disability) often are able to detect the disability, while most PWODs are not. Simply because these individuals are aware of the symptoms, limitations, treatments, and compensations of that particular disability, they can recognize the disability in others. They know what to look for. For example, people who wear contact lenses are usually aware of others who wear contact lenses, whereas most other people would not know. Individuals who have learning disabilities can often "pick up" on the adaptive techniques of others with learning disabilities simply because they know what to look for. People who wear prostheses are aware of others who wear similar prostheses. Others have no expectation or awareness of prostheses.

In today's age of technology and telecommunications, the concept of invisible disabilities has been changed. John Hockenberry, the news journalist in a wheelchair, worked in Los Angeles and did not tell his bosses in New York City that he had a disability. This is a single example that illustrates the changing definition of an invisible disability. Certainly, the people in Los Angeles saw the wheelchair, but Hockenberry decided that he wanted his bosses to see the quality of his work before disclosing his disability. (Hockenberry also had consequences for his refusal to disclose. He had no accessible bathroom at work.)

Looking at the Ann Landers letter, we can see that the writer chose to disclose the disability in the second paragraph, stressing both the disability and the functional limitations. Perhaps this would not be considered true disclosure, because it is an anonymous letter. Nonetheless, it is thought-provoking to consider what Ann Landers's response and the reader response would have been if the writer had chosen not to disclose the type of disability and the resulting limitations but simply stated, "I am handicapped, but one would never know it by looking at me."

Even in the case of an individual who has disclosed to his or her employer, the ADA requires that the employer maintain confidentiality. In these cases, the worker would be given accommodations, but his or her coworkers and clients would not know about the disability. The ADA provides for locked personnel file cabinets and other safeguards of the individual's privacy. Nonetheless, it is difficult to pass as a PWOD. Work absences for hospitalizations, the need to take medication on a strict schedule, or time off for support group meetings become difficult to explain. Further, as many people with invisible disabilities understand, the truth may be better than the negative implications that others often draw. In the case of the individual with a seizure disorder who does not have a driver's license, it may be wise to disclose the reason why he or she does not drive rather than have others believe the worst.

Refer to the chart on the cost–benefit ratio of disclosure (Exhibit 9.1). Perhaps the greatest cost of concealing a disability is the stress of hiding a characteristic that is central to one's identity. The individual may feel that he or she is always being a phony and being untrue to oneself and that no one really knows him or her. Reread Cynthia

Benefits of Disclosure

1. Accommodations are provided.
2. The truth is often better than negative assumptions.

Costs of Nondisclosure

1. No accommodations are given.
2. Negative characteristics are attributed to the individual with the disability.
3. Others with the same disability who have disclosed consider the person who "passes" as disloyal.
4. It is stressful to hide something that is part of one's self-identity.
5. The individual has lost an opportunity to advocate and educate others about the disability.
6. There might be more problems if the disability is discovered by others.
7. The individual sacrifices the solidarity, support, and understanding of associating with other PWDs.

Exhibit 9.1

Rich's excerpt above in which she refers to hiding a disability as "one of the most serious threats to selfhood."

Some individuals with invisible disabilities experience "heightened marginality" (Whitt, 1984). Speaking of the self-identity of children, Whitt explained:

> Some studies . . . report that children with diseases which produce little significant disability (e.g., epilepsy) may have more psycho-social problems than their physically disabled [*sic*] peers. Barker, Wright, Meyerson, and Gonick's (1953) concept of "marginality" acknowledged the heightened ambiguity experienced by children with minimal disabilities. These youngsters neither enjoy the benefit of being "normal" nor evoke the environmental support and allowances accorded more clearly handicapped [*sic*] children. (Whitt, 1984, p. 83)

Occasionally, it is not the PWD who wishes to hide or minimize the disability. Family members may encourage the individual with an invisible disability to keep the disability concealed. The family members understand the advantages of avoiding the "disabled role" for the PWD, and moreover, they may want to avoid the stigma by association for themselves. Weinberg and Sterritt (1991) explained the rationale:

> Many parents of children with physical disabilities would like to have their children develop a primary identification with the able-bodied world. Parents of children with disabilities know that society views people with disabilities as less acceptable, and that people with disabilities have difficulty in establishing satisfying social relationships and obtaining jobs. . . . To improve their children's chances of succeeding, parents may encourage their children to appear, and to behave, as able-bodied as possible. To the extent that children can "pass" as able-bodied, these parents believe that the likelihood of their children's being accepted and succeeding is increased. . . . (p. 68)
>
> Finally, if children with disabilities identify with and succeed in being a part of the able-bodied world, the parents' place in the able-bodied world is less disturbed. If, however, the parents have children who are unacceptable to able-bodied society, this reflects negatively on them, for they inevitably share their children's negative social identity. . . . (p. 69)

Weinberg and Sterritt (1991) also explained the effect on these children:

> In stressing the importance of "passing" as able-bodied, parents may also be communicating that being able-bodied is good and being disabled [*sic*] is bad. . . . Children with disabilities are thus being told, "As you are, you are inferior, and to the extent that you can emulate able-bodied people, this is the extent to which you can overcome your inferiority." Yet achieving full able-bodied status is inherently impossible, so children with disabilities may be condemned to always feel inferior, always to work to cover up their deficiencies, and always be on guard lest their disabilities show. They can rarely be at ease with who they are. (p. 69)

Facial cosmetic surgery for children with Down syndrome is one way in which parents are able to minimize the appearance of a disability. Proponents of this plastic surgery cite the advantages of social integration and greater opportunities for marriage. The surgery involves tongue reduction; implants in the bridge of the nose, chin, cheeks, and jaw; and reduction of the epicanthal fold in the eyelids. Nonetheless, in a study (Goeke, 2003) of 250 parents of children who have Down syndrome, 88% stated that they would refuse the surgery. A few parents said that they would refuse the surgery because the greatest stigma of Down syndrome is associated with intellectual disability and the related behavioral and social characteristics, none of which plastic surgery could ameliorate. However, most parents refused the surgery on the grounds that "society does not have the right to decide what is 'normal' or 'beautiful,' and by extension to determine who is a candidate for physical alteration" (p. 327). Others said that "to reconstruct a child's differences through painful surgery sends a strong message to both the child and the larger community that the parents do not accept their child's disability and that they find their child physically unattractive" (p. 328). Some parents "equated the decision to expose one's child to unnecessary surgery with child abuse," and several parents described it as "revolting" and "barbaric" (p. 329). This study shows that many parents are rejecting the societal expectation that PWDs must appear as normal as possible, and, perhaps more important, these parents have demonstrated that they consider their children's appearance as acceptable, many stating that they thought their children with Down syndrome were beautiful.

The Degree of Disfigurement of the Disability

In this section, look for—

  ⟡ how disabilities can be disfiguring
  ⟡ how symptoms of the disability can be disfiguring
  ⟡ how treatments can be disfiguring

Not all disabilities involve disfigurement. Amputations, facial disfigurements, and burns are examples of disabilities that are considered to be disfiguring. Others, such as myasthenia gravis, in which the individual's eyelids droop, or rheumatoid arthritis, in which the individual's joints are swollen and misshapen, are thought of as having disfiguring symptoms. Treatments can also be disfiguring. Medications often cause weight gain, radiation treatments cause the individual to lose his or her hair, and antipsychotic medications often have unpleasant and unattractive side effects. Disfiguring side effects of antipsychotic medications include perioral tremor ("rabbit syndrome"), in which the individual involuntarily moves his or her lips rapidly in movements that mimic a rabbit; and tardive dyskinesia—involuntary face, trunk, and limb movements, some of which are rocking, twisting, and jerking (Maxmen & Ward, 1995). (It is not difficult to understand why many individuals with psychiatric disabilities quit taking their medication.)

Disfigurements as Social Handicaps

In this section, look for—

  ⟡ disfiguring disabilities:
   • how age of onset (or stage of development) influences the individual's response
   • how pace of onset (acute or gradual) influences the individual's response.

Since an individual's body image is a reflection of how the individual thinks others perceive him or her, a disfiguring disability is truly a social handicap. Further, females and males respond differently to disfigurements because each gender thinks of body image in a somewhat different way. Finally, because an individual's body image evolves with each stage of development, the time of onset of a disfigurement is important (Rybarczyk, Nyenhuis, Nicholas, Cash, & Kaiser, 1995).

Disability scholars have used the term *social death* to describe the effect of a major disfigurement and the term *closet people* to describe individuals with these types of disfigurements. Closet people withdraw from all social contact and stay at home; therefore, they have experienced social death. These individuals feel they have no place in the world. Feminist disability scholars Adrienne Asch and Michelle Fine (1997) have asserted that women with disabilities, especially disfiguring disabilities, because they cannot attain the widely accepted standard of feminine beauty, often turn toward "male standards of achievement" (p. 251), which probably means career advancement. Another feminist disability scholar, Rosemarie Garland Thomson (1997c), stated that political subordination is linked "to the cultural valuing and devaluing of bodies on the basis of their appearance" (p. 297). Thomson also asserted that many feel that virtue is linked to feminine beauty and that "beauty brings fulfillment" (p. 299). Further, Thomson (1997b) stated that many believe that women with disfiguring disabilities must lead tortured, miserable lives.

Finally, the age of onset of the disfigurement is important. Those with congenital disabilities do not have to adjust their body image. "Children with congenital physical disabilities are only familiar with their already impaired bodies" (Livneh & Antonak, 1997). Generally speaking, it is adolescents who have the most difficulty in responding to a disfiguring disability simply because adolescence is a time when individuals are very concerned about their appearance and the opinions and judgments of others. Indeed, it can take years for adolescents (and some adults) to adjust their body image after the onset of a disfiguring disability. Elderly individuals may not feel a disfiguring disability to be a great challenge simply because they have already come to terms with physical losses and diminished attractiveness.

The pace of onset of the disfiguring disability influences the individual's response. Disabilities that have a slow and gradual onset, such as rheumatoid arthritis, are considered to present fewer adjustment demands on the individual's body image. Robert Neumann described his teenage experience with rheumatoid arthritis. Note the use of the third person—Neumann (1988) wrote of the person in the mirror as if the person were not himself.

> One day, almost by chance, I could avoid it no longer. I caught a good look at myself in a full-length mirror and was appalled at what I saw. I had remembered myself as having an able body. The person I saw looking back at me had a face swollen from high doses of cortisone, hands with unnaturally bent fingers, and legs that could barely support his weight. (p. 157)

However, the majority of disfiguring disabilities have acute onset, many of them traumatic (D. R. Patterson et al., 1993). For example, individuals who experience severe burns confront an unexpected, sudden change in body image (Weinberg & Miller, 1983). One little girl with facial burns remembered: "There were no mirrors in my house, so I wouldn't get scared" (Holaday & McPhearson, 1997, p. 354).

The Treatment of Individuals With Disfiguring Disabilities

In this section, look for—

♦ Treatment of disfiguring disabilities

- is a battle against societal reactions;
- usually does not concern itself with loss of function (mobility or sensory); and
- takes years of rehabilitation.

Treatment of individuals with disfiguring disabilities is different than other types of treatment or interventions. One disability scholar (Bernstein, 1989) described these different treatments and interventions as the result of three factors:

> First, treatment is a battle against societal values and community reactions. Second, it involves a problem of appearance and symbolism rather than a problem of mobility, pain, or sensory loss. And finally, there is an element of chronic grief over the situation. It is critical to be aware of time scale: for most of these individuals adjustment to a disfigurement takes years and rehabilitation takes years more—sometimes a lifetime. (pp. 155–156)

In their interviews, Holaday and McPhearson (1997) found that

> burn survivors insisted that patients also be told about normal and predictable emotional distress following a severe burn so that they could be prepared for the possibility of depression, sleep disorders, nightmares, and physical reactions to reminders of the burn or treatments. . . . "No one told me about the mood swings. I thought I was crazy. They should tell you these things. One of my daycare workers told me I was possessed because I had such terrible nightmares." (p. 353)

Individuals respond to their disfiguring disabilities in several ways (Goldstein, 1986). Some individuals develop compassion for the strangers who stare; one person with severe facial scars stated, "I'd stare if I saw someone like me too!" (Holaday &

McPhearson, 1997, p. 351). Some sequester themselves in their homes, while others decide that cosmetic devices, designed to make them appear more normal, are not worth the loss of function or the discomfort and inconvenience. Others do not incorporate the disfigurement into their identity, referring to their facial scarring as a "mask"; indeed, one woman insisted that she removed the mask when she was at home with her family (J. Morris, 1991). Beatrice Wright (1960) included a short excerpt from Katherine Butler Hathaway:

> Over and over I forgot what I had seen in the mirror. It could not penetrate into the interior of my mind and become an integral part of me. I felt as if it had nothing to do with me; it was only a disguise. But it was not the kind of disguise which is put on voluntarily by the person who wears it, and which is intended to confuse other people as to one's identity. My disguise had been put on me without my consent or knowledge like the ones in fairy tales, and it was on me for life. It was there, it was there, it was real. Every one of those encounters was like a blow on the head. They left me dazed and dumb and senseless every time, until slowly and stubbornly my robust persistent illusion of well-being and of personal beauty spread all through me again.... (p. 157)

The Importance of Social Support for Individuals With Disfiguring Disabilities

Anyone with any type of disability needs social support. However, individuals with disfiguring disabilities require even greater degrees of social support because their disability elicits a great deal of rejection and avoidance from others (Bernstein, 1990; Bernstein, Breslau, & Graham, 1988; Love, Bryne, Roberts, Browne, & B. Brown, 1987). During World War II, a group of English Royal Air Force (RAF) pilots who had acquired disfiguring disabilities (mostly burns) formed an organization. They all wore the same blazer and continued to meet 40 years after the end of the war. The importance of group solidarity, common understanding, and shared experiences filled a need for these men. (The blazer may have also served to inform others of the way in which they acquired their disfigurement: combat service in the RAF.)

Read the following excerpts. The first three are from individuals with severe burns. They all express the importance of social support.

> When I got burned at age 18, I found out who my real friends were: They were the ones who came to see me and they still are my friends. (Holaday & McPhearson, 1997, p. 349)
>
> They [friends] made me use my burned hand to play games like ping-pong, so it wouldn't get stiff. (Holaday & McPhearson, 1997, p. 349)
>
> Another severely burned interviewee (now a grandfather) . . . had been given the last rites and was expected to die. Against hospital rules, his wife brought their infant son into his room to say goodbye. It was at that moment

the new father decided that he would fight to live despite his injuries because he wanted to watch his son grow up. "My family became my motivation to survive." (Holaday & McPhearson, 1997, p. 348)

Nichols and Kosciulek (2014) interviewed individuals with TBIs (traumatic brain injuries). One of their conclusions was: "In some cases, the individual with TBI perceived that the injury had changed him or her and he or she felt that this change contributed to improvements in family relationships" (p. 25).

Read the lack of social support these individuals experienced:

Amy Hagadorn, a 9-year-old girl with cerebral palsy that limited the use of her fingers on her right hand and resulted in a limp and impairment in speech, wrote a letter to Santa Claus sponsored by a local radio station: "Kids laugh at me because of the way I walk and run and talk. I want just one day where no one laughs at me or makes fun of me." (Holzbauer & Berven, 1996, p. 479)

A vignette by Henry Viscardi, whose legs were congenitally deformed, on his first day of grade school: "My sister Terry took me to school the first day. Clutching her hand, I hoisted myself up the steps to the schoolyard. It was crowded with children. . . . I heard laughter. 'Hey, Louis, looka the ape man.' Three big boys came toward me. . . . The crowd of jeering boys had grown. One of them . . . came over and shoved me. I shoved back against his knee. 'Oh, you wanta fight, kid?'. . . . 'I want to go home.' I hung on Terry's arm, tears rolling down my cheeks. 'Sissy, sissy.'" (Holzbauer & Berven, 1996, p. 479)

Scapegoating of a family member with a disability can occur, sometimes with grisly consequences. . . . [A] young child who had been severely burned became a "whipping boy" to his poor, alcoholic, and dysfunctional family for many years. Nearly every evening his parents, two siblings, and two cousins would become drunk and make vicious fun of his disfigurement. One evening when the group had been more abusive than usual, he systematically lured each inebriated individual into a different room of the house, bludgeoning each of them to death. (Holzbauer & Berven, 1996, p. 479)

Susan Wendell (2006) theorized that if PWODs were to understand the experience of PWDs, including individuals with disfiguring disabilities, PWODs would no longer be "oppressed" by their bodies. She summarized:

Our physical ideals change from time to time, but we always have ideals. These ideals are not just about appearance; they are also ideals of strength and energy and proper control of the body. We are perpetually bombarded with images of these ideals, demands for them. . . . Idealizing the body prevents everyone, able-bodied and disabled, from identifying with and loving his/her real body. (p. 267)

Prognosis of the Disability

In the strictest sense, the definition of the word *prognosis* is the prospect of a cure or recovery; therefore, since disabilities are long-term chronic conditions, the concept of a prognosis does not actually apply to most disabilities. As you remember, the idea of a prognosis is that of two outcomes: cure or death. The idea of prognosis is probably considered in those few disabilities that do have a terminal course, such as muscular dystrophy (MD), AIDS, or cystic fibrosis. The key word in the last sentence is *course* because, as a result of the advances in medical science, individuals with these disabilities often live years after the onset.

Nonetheless, there are a few disabilities that eventually result in the individual's death. Some scholars have termed this experience "living with death," and, as would be expected, the tasks of the individual with this type of disability do not include long-term management of the disability or ensuring the highest quality of life, but emotionally preparing oneself and one's family for death. Certainly, the time of onset of these terminal disabilities has an impact on the individual's response. For example, MD is usually diagnosed by age 5, and the individual usually does not live beyond age 20 or 30 years. Therefore, the individual preparing for death is a child or a teenager. In contrast, ALS is a disability with a terminal course, but it is a late-onset disability, and the individual is usually elderly. Individuals with MD and their families report that emotional and psychological issues are greater concerns than are physical symptoms. This seems reasonable because it generally is more difficult for a child or young adult to die than it is for an elderly person.

In addition to age of onset, the duration of the period between the diagnosis and the death of the individual influences response. It is safe to state that many individuals who experience a period of years between diagnosis and death often deny the reality of their impending death. This long interval also allows the individual to undertake the typical developmental tasks, such as school, work, marriage, and family. For others, the interval between diagnosis and death is relatively short, and issues to be confronted are (a) pain, (b) fear of being separated from loved ones, (c) concern about being a burden on family, and (d) concern about family grieving after the death. Also, different types of disabilities require varied treatments during the final stages. Naturally, the living–dying interval is unique to each individual.

For many individuals with terminal disabilities, and their families, religious, spiritual, or philosophic questions and answers are of great importance. However, many professionals are not trained or experienced in supporting the individual's spiritual search for meaning. This is probably a result of the long-held view of the medical, psychological, and counseling professions that the spiritual, religious, or philosophical concerns of clients and patients are private, personal matters. Also, Freudian psychology has long been biased against religion, viewing it as an infantile escape from reality.

Indeed, until the fourth edition of the *Diagnostic and Statistical Manual* published by the American Psychiatric Association (1994), religious beliefs of patients and clients were either pathologized or ignored (D. W. Smart & J. F. Smart, 1997). In spite of this, Taylor, Jones, and Burns (1998) stated, "Spirituality is clearly a core dimension and critical determinant of health-related quality of life" (p. 215).

Many professionals (and others) assume that a disability with a terminal course brings only pain, suffering, and despair. However, many individuals with these types of disability experience a high-quality life and report a feeling of mastery and satisfaction, which often includes ascribing religious meaning and purpose to both the disability and their impending death.

Autonomy, Independence, and Control

In this section, look for—

- ⬥ the way in which society fosters dependence in PWDs
  - holds low expectations of PWDs
  - has institutionalized financial disincentives for work
  - often fails to provide accessible environments
  - often fails to provide assistive technology

- ⬥ the way in which many PWDs redefine independence and control
- ⬥ how PWDs want to define their own needs, including the need for assistance
- ⬥ the relationship between PWDs and assistive technology

American values often idealize independence and individualism, both on a national and on a personal level. We have also seen that the (false) ideal of total control over one's circumstances and future is so important that, for some individuals, death would appear preferable to losing this control. Asking for help may be viewed as a sign of weakness. Many PWODs cannot understand how PWDs can maintain their self-esteem and self-respect when they need help with so many of life's basic functions. Indeed, many PWDs have commented that it is humiliating to be dependent in a culture that worships independence (J. Morris, 1991). Longmore (2003) summarized:

> Autonomy and dependency and quality of life are highly value-laden concepts. They are rooted in American values that uphold complete physical self-sufficiency and absolute personal autonomy as cultural ideals. They express a myth, a myth that real Americans are rugged individualists who quite literally stand on their own two feet. The ideal, the authentic American is not

in any way dependent on others. To become sick or disabled in America is to
lose one's social validity. It is to acquire a relentlessly and radically negative
identity. It is to become the inversion of what a real American is supposed to
be. (p. 190)

Disabilities and their functional losses can and do make people dependent. Nonetheless, many disability scholars are clear in stating that society further and needlessly promotes the dependence and helplessness of PWDs. A society renders their
citizens with disabilities helpless and subordinate if it (a) holds low expectations of
PWDs; (b) has longstanding, institutionalized financial disincentives for work; and
(c) does not provide accessible environments, assistive technology, or personal care
attendants. Rather than viewing the needs of PWDs as situated in the relationship between the environment and PWDs, most PWODs consider these needs to be located
solely within an individual's body. Considering the great value Americans place on
independence and autonomy, it is ironic that American society fosters dependence in
a large segment of its population.

Accommodations and accessibility are often provided reluctantly and only after the
Americans With Disabilities Act has been invoked. Randy Souders (1993) is an artist
who became paralyzed after a diving accident when he was a teenager. He described
his experiences shortly after his accident and the way in which lowered expectations
(which he referred to as "underchallenge") and obsolete laws can foster dependence:

> It was the art that provided the motivation for me to get up every morning and
> do something instead of sitting in front of the TV. It's very easy to get sucked
> into a dependency routine—you know, this "give me, give me, give me" kind
> of attitude. Society has such limited expectations of the disabled [sic] person.
> It doesn't expect you to be able do much of anything. It (society) underchal-
> lenges us to perform. . . . And that's what I take the most pride in—the fact that
> what I'm doing today is well received all over, even with people who haven't
> a clue as to my physical condition. Then, when they learn about the paralysis
> and the story behind it, their mouths just drop and hang open. The gallery
> owners, for example, are flabbergasted that I can do anything. So that's what I
> take some measure of pride in: They don't say, "Gee, this is good, considering
> your condition . . . blah, blah," they say, "Boy, this is good, *period*." And they dig
> in their pockets and pull out their wallets. That, for me, is a kick. (p. 151)

An English disability scholar, Deborah Marks (1999), gave a straightforward explanation on the ways in which society makes PWDs dependent, subordinate, and
helpless:

> No person is completely self-reliant. Those people who are identified as be-
> ing particularly dependent are *made* this way because social organization and

distribution of resources are arranged in such a way that discriminates against them. For example, if steps rather than ramps are built at the entrance of buildings, then wheelchair users (or parents pushing prams) are made dependent on the assistance of others to carry them into the building. . . . In contemporary culture, dependence and independence often tend to be thought about in very narrow and mechanistic ways. (p. 96)

Society tends to define autonomy, control, and independence in very narrow ways; however, PWDs redefine these concepts. Indeed, many PWDs who consider themselves to be independent and productive may be seen by PWODs to be dependent and nonproductive (Phillips, 1991). Rather than viewing independence as the ability to perform particular functions, PWDs consider independence to have two components: (a) the capability to have one's needs met and (b) being a valued part of a larger system. Jenny Morris (1991) explained the first component:

We use the word [independence] in a practical and commonsense way to mean simply being able to achieve our goals. The point is that independent people have control over their lives, not that they perform every task themselves. Independence is not linked to the physical or intellectual capacity to care for oneself without assistance; independence is created by having assistance when and how one requires it, being able to choose when and how care takes place. (p. 140)

Morris was clear in stating the importance of the individual choosing when, where, and how the assistance is provided. PWDs have personally defined criteria and reject socially defined criteria. Not only do PWDs wish to identify their own problems and define their needs; they want to decide *how* these problems and needs will be addressed. In reading accounts of PWDs describing how they wish their needs to be met, the word *dignity* often appears. Cheryl Wade (1994) lives at home (rather than in an institution or nursing home) and requires the services of a personal care attendant. Wade related the importance of dignity:

But if our shame tells us that our needs lack dignity, then the next thing we hear our shame say is that it is more dignified to die than to live with these basic needs that take away our privacy and seem like such a burden. (p. 89)

The provision of personal care attendants in the individual's home has assisted many PWDs in leaving nursing homes and other institutions. Approximately 10 million people use personal care assistants; the majority of these assistants are unpaid family workers. Only 10% of personal care assistants are paid workers (Saxton et al., 2006). Thus, the accommodation of personal care assistants has released millions of individuals from a lifetime of institutionalization. Certainly, most individuals would rather live at home than in an institution.

While the woman in the following excerpt did not use the word *dignity*, she does state that accommodations that are dehumanizing will not be used.

> I'd love to be able to get into the spa. And they have a wonderful spa where I swim, but there is not a decent lift to get into it. They have a sling-type, which just doesn't work for us anymore. It's so fatiguing to use. It's so dehumanizing that it's just not worth it. (Putnam et al., 2003, p. 42)

Linton (1998) observed that society does not think PWDs should ask for luxuries or pleasure for three reasons: (a) PWDs are an economic drain on the system and therefore they really should not demand "non-necessities," (b) PWDs should be grateful for medical care, and (c) pleasure is not important for PWDs!

> Society's choice, and I see it as a choice, to exclude disabled [*sic*] people from social and cultural events that afford pleasure, or deny them sex education, sexual health care and, at times, marriage, privacy, and friendship are indications of the belief that pleasure is less consequential to disabled [*sic*] people than to nondisabled people. Yet that belief is likely a rationalization for more virulent impulses. Are disabled [*sic*] people denied access to pleasure by the unspoken notion that they are not entitled to it because they cause displeasure to others? . . . How dare we crippled, blind, and crazy folks ask for parity? Shouldn't we be satisfied with the provision of medical care and sustenance, and leave the luxuries for those who are thought to drain fewer resources from society? (Linton, 1998, p. 111)

We have seen how the concept of *normality* has quite literally been a stumbling block to PWDs. Many individuals were forced to undergo useless or harmful treatments, wear prostheses, and learn to speak and read lips simply because PWODs thought it important that PWDs appear as normal as possible. Often, PWDs were subjected to treatment or given assistive technology for very small gains. A recent oral history of Canadian World War II veterans with spinal cord injuries, entitled, "Going Back to Civvy Street," told of physicians who wanted the veterans to walk on crutches; however, after they discovered self-propelled wheelchairs, the veterans realized that using crutches was a wasteful expenditure of energy.

> It didn't make much sense spending all that energy covering a short distance (on crutches) . . . when you could do it quickly and easily with a wheelchair. . . . It didn't take long for people to get over the idea that walking was that essential. (Tremblay, 1996, p. 153)

Also, we have learned that many parents have refused facial plastic surgery for their children with Down syndrome, arguing that the surgery places the responsibility for adaptation on the individual, rather than on society as a whole. Of the parents surveyed, 88% rejected the cosmetic surgery. One parent stated, "As long as their physical appearance doesn't interfere with breathing, or seeing or eating, etc., then they are who they are. Beautiful people" (Goeke, 2003, p. 326).

When PWDs are in charge, assistance and accommodations are not viewed as undignified. In surveys of PWDs that have sought to determine their self-reported quality of life, many have stated that learning to do new things and learning to do former activities in a new way brought them a sense of self-worth and of autonomy. Indeed, respondents spoke about the need to reevaluate priorities and the perseverance required to retain their newly defined autonomy and independence (Putnam et al., 2003; Reid, 2004).

The second component in many PWDs' conception of independence and autonomy is a feeling of being a highly valued part of a larger system (Faull et al., 2004). Erik Weihenmayer (2001), who is blind, climbed Mt. Everest. Although climbing Mt. Everest is a rather unusual accomplishment, something that most people never accomplish, it is important to understand that Weihenmayer wished to be a highly valued part of a climbing team.

> I refused to be the weak link of the team. I wanted them to put their lives in my hands, as I would put mine in theirs. I would carry my share. I could contribute as any other team member. I would not be carried up the mountain and spiked on top like a football. If I were to reach the summit, I would reach it with dignity. (p. 5)

Assistive technology can be life-saving. Many PWDs speak of their assistive technology in terms of a relationship: the polio survivor who referred to the iron lung he has used for more than 40 years as his "second skin" (Fleischer & Zames, 2001, p. 132); the man who said that he "loved his first wheelchair with a passion that embarrasses me, now" (Kriegel, 1964, p. 52); and others who view their wheelchairs and other types of assistive technology "as a replacement for parts of themselves to get the job done" (Reid, 2004, p. 572). Some PWDs mark the date they received their technology as the beginning of their lives.

The Importance of Support Groups

In this section, look for—

- ✧ the functions of support groups:
  - reduce isolation

- normalize the experience of disability
- provide role models
- provide validity to the experience of disability
- challenge the way in which PWODs falsely view the lives of PWDs
- improve quality of life

Another type of treatment to be discussed is provided not by professionals but by mutual support groups. There are all types of mutual support groups, some for children, others for adults. Most mutual support groups are disability-specific—such as individuals with cancer or individuals with intellectual disability (Power & Rogers, 1979). Some groups comprise PWDs, whereas others comprise family members of PWDs. Also, the level of organization and goal attainment varies; some groups have clear-cut goals, while other groups are more informal and simply offer support. Once, mutual support groups were viewed as a challenge to the medical profession. Today, however, physicians recognize the value of such groups and encourage their patients to participate. Some of the benefits of these types of groups include the opportunity to learn about and associate with others who are living with the same type of disability. Often, those who have had the disability for a longer period of time are called veterans. Veterans can describe the likely course of the disability, help others to view their emotional responses as typical (this is referred to as *normalizing*), help others to establish realistic expectations, and assist others in accessing services and other resources in the community.

Commonality and support are the hallmarks of mutual support groups. Read Joan Tollifson's feelings about associating with other PWDs:

> After a lifetime of isolating myself from other disabled [*sic*] people, it was an awakening to be surrounded by them. For the first time in my life, I felt like a real adult member of the human community. Finally, identifying myself as a disabled [*sic*] person was an enormous healing. It was about recognizing, allowing, and acknowledging something that I had been trying to deny, and finding that disability does not equal ugliness, incompetence, and misery. (Tollifson, 1997, p. 107)

Support Groups Help to Reduce Isolation

Joan Tollifson (1997) described her life before she joined a support group of women with disabilities as a "private hell" (p. 107). In a well-known study by Clausen and Yarrow (1955), one third of the participants said they attempted to conceal the psychiatric disability of their family member by moving away or terminating relationships with extended family and friends. Clausen and Yarrow's study was completed more than 50 years ago, but it is safe to say that many families with disabilities of all types feel isolated. In a more recent study with women with various types of disabilities (Crawford & Ostrove, 2003), the authors reported the main finding:

> Participants spoke poignantly about their pervasive isolation and loneliness. Many participants espoused that their disabilities—or attitudes toward them—at least to some extent limited their ability to access meaningful social interactions. Participants' frustration with this situation was tied to their unwillingness to participate more actively in society at large. Thus a vicious cycle is activated which serves to further isolate individuals with disabilities and solidify stereotypes relating to their social maturity and competence. (p. 191)

It is important to note that the participants in Crawford and Ostrove's (2003) study used the phrase "meaningful social interactions." Obviously, PWDs do have social interactions (relationships) with PWODs and other PWDs, but they are stating that they do not have deep and satisfying associations.

One 57-year-old woman who is deaf told of her attempts to integrate herself:

> They [strangers] treat me like a ghost standing there. When I try to get into conversations, and oh this is the worst thing, they say this all the time. When I ask them what they are saying, they say, "Oh nothing, it's okay" and they won't repeat it because to them it is not worth repeating. To me, it is like gold. I still want to know. (Crawford & Ostrove, 2003, p. 187)

Crawford and Ostrove (2003) interpreted their findings by stating that the lack of social integration of PWDs, and their invisibility in the cultural life of the United States, have created difficulties for both PWDs and PWODs. In their opinion, "Lack of integration of individuals with disabilities prevents the daily interaction necessary for both disabled [sic] and able-bodied individuals to learn to negotiate the delicate balance between two cultures" (p. 191).

Family members also experience the isolation that a disability can bring. Solomon (2012) told of a father of a newborn baby with Down syndrome. The father reported having "crying jags" after the birth of his son with Down syndrome. He remembers the name of the woman who called them on the phone and honestly answered their questions about Down syndrome. Her name is Barbara Chandler, head of the Manhattan Parents Support Group. The mother asked Barbara, "Is there any joy at all in raising a child with Down syndrome?" Barbara answered that there was joy, but also a great deal of sorrow and difficulty. This honesty and support helped the father and mother move past the grieving stage. Ms. Chandler also told the family, "You're not alone" (Solomon, 2012, p. 215).

In another example, a woman relates her mother's difficulty in dealing with the daughter's psychiatric disability in the days before such support groups as the National Alliance for the Mentally Ill (NAMI) were available:

> At that time, one of the biggest problems was isolation [after her hospitalization]. People didn't know a lot. I couldn't talk to anyone about mental illness. My mother was frustrated; she didn't know where she could go for help, and she couldn't talk to any family members or friends about it because nobody was willing to talk to her. (Mackelprang & Salsgiver, 1999)

In Stefan's (2001) national survey of individuals with mental illness, the question was asked: "What are some examples of the worst discrimination you have experienced?" One respondent wrote, "I'm sick of losing friends," and another wrote, "friends who have abandoned me" (p. 14). One question asked if the psychiatric disability limited the individual in any way. One respondent simply wrote, "no job, no friends."

However, in the same survey, one woman wrote:

> A few years after my illness I met someone who permitted me to talk about my hospitalization. As I described the experience, I cried. A gentle touch that said, "It doesn't matter; we can still be friends," was worth years of therapy. That moment was an emotional breakthrough for me. (p. 14)

Remarkable in this excerpt is the fact that she did not find someone to whom she could share her experiences until years after her hospitalization, and, furthermore, she considers this conversation to be an unforgettable breakthrough. Stefan found that the most often cited sources of social support and community involvement were churches and synagogues; many respondents wrote that their church or synagogue was welcoming, friendly, and supportive and provided emotional and social sustenance.

Some participants in these surveys told of friends and family they deliberately avoided because they were not supportive or held negative, limited views of disability (Putnam et al., 2003). One woman said, ". . . there are certain people that I love dearly that I have to restrict association with, because they're not positive. . . ." (p. 41).

Often, the individual with a newly acquired disability has internalized all of the societal prejudices and discrimination against PWDs and, therefore, does not wish to associate with other PWDs. One individual refused to attend a support group because "sad stories bored him" (Goffman, 1963, p. 21). Polio survivors were encouraged not to associate with other polio survivors (Wilson, 1990). Marc Shell (2005) explained: "After release from the hospital, polios [survivors] usually isolated themselves from one another. They had internalized the doctrine that they should not 'fraternize' with one another after discharge but instead should get on with normal lives" (p. 118). Anne Finger had polio as a child and speaks of her first experience associating with other polio survivors at a conference on post-polio:

I sat for the first time in my life in a room filled with other disabled [*sic*] people. I remember how nervous I felt. I'd always gone to "regular" schools; I had been mainstreamed before there was a word for it. I had moved through the world as a normal person with a limp, and no thank you, I didn't need help, I manage just fine. And no, I was nothing like "them." I wasn't whiny, or needy, or self-pitying. (Finger, 1990, pp. 16–17)

Joan Tollifson (1997) remarked, "I joined a group of disabled [*sic*] women on the advice of my therapist. I hated the idea, but to my surprise, they were marvelous, dynamic women" (p. 107). Leslie Heller has cerebral palsy. Here she explains her fear of associating with other PWDs: "When I was growing up, I was terrified of walking into a room of people with disabilities and admitting that I was one of them. Now, I just love being in a community of people with disabilities" (Fleischer & Zames, 2001, p. 201).

Support Groups Normalize the Experience of Disability

Interacting with other PWDs allows individuals to feel normal. The word *normal*, as it is used here, simply means that the disability is considered to be ordinary and natural and the individual is not viewed as his or her disability. Actually, in a support group of individuals with the same type of disability, it would be impossible to identify a single individual only as his or her disability! In these types of support groups, PWDs feel comfortable and accepted as individuals. PWDs report that they feel relaxed around others who have had the same experiences, feeling that they could speak about their disability "without elaborate explanation" (Finger, 1990, p. 17). Carol, a woman who is deaf, was asked to name one PWOD who truly understood her experience as a deaf woman. The researchers described her reaction to the question as "bewilderment." Carol replied, "Who really understands my disability? My mother was determined to make me talk and she succeeded. But to understand deafness? I don't know, I don't know anybody that understands" (Crawford & Ostrove, 2003, p. 190). The authors summarized: "The vast majority of individuals who highlighted this lack of awareness coped by affiliating themselves primarily with the disability community" (p. 190). Support groups provide a setting in which PWDs feel neither "different" nor isolated.

In these types of support groups, the stress of dealing with the reactions of PWODs, including prejudice and discrimination, is eliminated. Indeed, often the discussion centers on the socially relevant, shared experience of prejudice and discrimination. Discussing similar experiences allows individuals to understand that the prejudice and discrimination are not a result of some personal fault, but that these prejudicial attitudes are widely held stereotypes. Realizing that other PWDs have experienced prejudice often results in a greater sense of self-worth and self-empowerment. Joan Tollifson (1997) told of "healing conversations" in that group of women with disabilities:

They shared so many of what I had always thought were my own isolated, personal experiences that I began to realize that my supposedly private hell was a social phenomenon. We had eye-opening, healing conversations. We discovered, for example, that we had all had the experience of being patronized and treated like children even though we were adults. It wasn't simply some horrible flaw in my own character that provoked such reaction, as I had always believed, but rather, this was part of a collective pattern that was much larger than any one of us. It was a stereotype that existed in the culture at large. Suddenly, disability became not just my personal problem, but a social and political issue as well. (p. 107)

A woman who is hearing impaired spoke about how relaxing it was not to worry about hiding her assistive technology:

> I remembered how relaxing it was . . . to be with people who took impaired hearing for granted. . . . How restful it would be to adjust the volume control on my transmitter without caring whether or not anyone was looking. To stop thinking, for a while, about whether the cord at the back of my neck was showing. What luxury to say out loud to someone, "Ye gods, my battery's dead!" (Goffman, 1963, p. 20)

Role models often normalize some of the emotions experienced by individuals who have recently acquired their disability.

> I didn't want to admit that I was also handicapped. . . . She [mentor] tells me that she felt like that, too, and that you get over this feeling. And you know that life goes on and that there's a lot out there that you can do, anything you want to do. . . . You can still be just as much of a person without [your legs]. (Veith, Sherman, Pellino, & Yasui, 2006, p. 293)

Of all the types of disabilities, the Deaf Culture has achieved the greatest group solidarity and common identity. The Deaf Culture also has the longest history of providing support and community for their members and their families. Much of this long history and solidarity are the results of a common language, sign language, and residential schools. Any language is the repository of a rich cultural tradition, and sign language has many expressions and jokes about handicapism and prejudice. Additionally, because most children who are deaf are born to hearing parents, many children cannot communicate with their families if the families do not learn sign language. Therefore, children who are deaf feel more at home among those individuals with whom they can communicate. The importance of having a social category, rather than remaining invisible, cannot be exaggerated.

Many PWDs in the Disability Rights Movement have observed that the hierarchy of stigma is reversed in disability groups—the more severe the disability, the greater the individual's stature and prestige.

Support Groups Provide Role Models

There have been few role models for PWDs. In the Disability History Project produced by National Public Radio (NPR), an individual recalls:

> One of the first people I saw working with a disability was the crippled newsie on the corner—the guy who couldn't use his legs who had a little knuckle board who dragged himself around to sell newspapers. I knew that except for the money my family had, that could very easily be me and it scared me to death. (NPR, 1998c)

Harold Russell lost his arms in World War II and starred in the movie, "The Best Years of Our Lives," for which he won an Academy Award. Russell was asked, "When you were a kid, did you ever know someone with a disability who worked?" Russell answered, "I never knew anybody with a disability before the war" (NPR, 1998a).

The former Assistant Secretary of the U. S. Department of Education, Judith Heumann, did not meet a role model with a disability until she was in her 20s. Heumann stated:

> When we go into most "establishment" organizations, we hardly meet any disabled [sic] individuals; there are no peers that we can look up to. I never met a disabled [sic] professional until I was in my twenties. I had only nondisabled role models—who were not role models to me because I am disabled. (Heumann, 1979, p. 17)

It is interesting that Judith Heumann has become a role model for many PWDs. One individual stated, "That was the turning point for me—when I met Judy Heumann and Ed Roberts. They acted and spoke like there was nothing wrong with them; that what was wrong was that doors were too narrow" (H. McCarthy, 2003, p. 216).

Role models for PWDs were absent in the media, with the exception of President Roosevelt (who worked very hard to hide his disability and possessed unlimited resources). Michalko (2002) remembered seeing characters who were blind on television and in the movies and reading about people who were blind when he was a teenager.

> They were all portrayed as victims of a misfortune. . . . When I saw blind people in the movies or on television and even when I saw the "real" ones, I saw incompetence, sadness, and poverty. And I saw misfortune. Whether my perception was accurate or not is irrelevant; that is just what I saw. What I did not see when I saw those blind people is just as significant as what I did see:

I did not see me. Still, when I saw them, I experienced a nebulous fear that I later understood was the fear of seeing myself. (p. 24)

Role models can also provide practical information and share their own experiences with a disability. A woman with a spinal cord injury related that she became less frightened as she received answers and information about her specific questions from someone else with a spinal cord injury (her mentor).

> . . . how [the mentor] got around and what had happened to her and how she dealt with cooking and how she dealt with her kids, how she had sex and what kind of bed she had. Lots of different questions [about] life and living. . . . Spasticity and, oh God, just everything. . . . And the more I learned, the less scared I got. (Veith et al., 2006, p. 291)

Other specific questions included, "How (can I) go through the day?" "How long might it take to go through my morning routine?" or "What might (I) be doing to cut it shorter?" Another individual stated, "The fear of the unknown was the biggest factor" (Veith et al., 2006, p. 291).

Other individuals who had recently acquired spinal cord injuries spoke of the importance of having a mentor or role model with whom they could identify:

> And then [the hospital staff] are showing people [with a spinal cord injury] in a $2 million yacht or on farms with 40 horses, you know; I mean that was for real? . . . [My mentor] is a real guy, you know, who lives a real life that's not easy and that's different than it was before. . . . Most of those things [in the video] are way out of reach for the average spinal-cord injured person [*sic*]. . . . It's not many Chris Reeves." (Veith et al., 2006, p. 294)

Services

In this section, look for—

✧ five general types of services
1. medical services
2. educational services
3. vocational services
4. residential services
5. mutual support groups

The last factor that influences an individual's response to a disability concerns the type of treatment and services the individual receives. As we have discussed, in the past, disability was thought to be a personal or family concern, meaning that the family took care of all of the PWD's needs. Moreover, it is safe to state that there are some people who continue to think that society should not concern itself with providing services to PWDs. Nonetheless, broadly speaking, these types of services can be conceptualized as falling within these categories: (a) medical services, (b) educational services, (c) vocational services, (d) residential services, and (e) mutual support groups. Because each of these five broad types of services is provided by different types of individuals and in different settings, it is important that services be comprehensive, continuous, and coordinated. As stated before, a perfect world is not a world without disabilities; it is a world in which (a) treatment and accommodations are provided to PWDs, and (b) there is full social, educational, vocational, and political integration of PWDs.

Medical treatment includes hospitals and regional rehabilitation centers where individuals, especially those with spinal cord injuries, learn the various skills and the use of assistive technology (B. B. Boswell, Dawson, & Heininger, 1998). Medical treatment also includes psychologists. Some PWDs, after the medical stabilization of their disability, will not use medical services more than anyone else. For other PWDs, there are symptom exacerbations, secondary disabilities, and complications that may require careful medical monitoring and treatment throughout the individual's life (Berkman, Weissman, & Frielich, 1978). Other PWDs take medication, thus requiring careful medical monitoring so as to maximize the therapeutic benefit while limiting side effects. As we have stated before, a PWD has two medical goals: (a) to manage and treat the disability, preventing complications, and (b) to maintain the highest quality of life possible. Rereading the section on the Biomedical Model of disability in Chapter 2, we can see that the relationship between the medical profession and PWDs has been ambivalent. On the one hand, medical practitioners and scientists have greatly improved the lives of PWDs, including saving their lives. On the other hand, medical providers have often not viewed their patients as individuals with social, familial, and vocational roles.

Institutionalized Work Disincentives

As we learned in Chapter 1, each agency and program has differing definitions of disability, and these differing definitions (and therefore eligibility requirements) can make continuity of services complex and difficult. For example, someone may have a disability that would be considered a disability by one agency or program but not considered a disability by another program. Indeed, some of the guiding foundations and purposes of these programs may be contradictory. The most clear-cut examples of these contradictory purposes are Social Security and VR. Social Security, derived from the Biomedical Model of disability, will not allow an individual to receive benefits if he or she earns more than a certain amount of money. Vocational Rehabilitation, derived from the Functional Model of disability, wants individuals to work—both for the benefits to the individual and for the benefits to the American government and economy. Attempts are under way (such as the Ticket-to-Work and Plan to Achieve Self-Support) to dismantle this archaic system of work disincentives.

One of the most interesting examples of work disincentives is the subject of Paul Longmore's (2003) essay, "Why I Burned My Book." Longmore contracted polio as a child and received Social Security Disability Insurance (SSDI). While the SSDI money never amounted to much, receiving SSDI made Longmore eligible for Medicaid, and without Medicaid benefits, he would be forced to live in a nursing home. Therefore, it was extremely important for Longmore to remain on SSDI. Longmore spent 10 years earning a PhD in American history (and he writes of the discrimination he experienced at these universities). Longmore also wrote a book, *The Invention of George Washington*, which was published by the University of California Press. Subsequently, he was offered a research fellowship at the world-renowned Huntington Library. However, the Social Security Administrator, in a letter, informed Longmore that if he accepted any book royalties, he would no longer be eligible for SSDI. Longmore also states in the essay that he would never earn enough as an academic to pay for all of his disability-related expenses. Longmore then carefully staged a book-burning demonstration with Disability Rights activists present and received television and newspaper coverage. Before the actual demonstration, he had practiced burning books because, "I didn't want to set *myself* on fire" (p. 251). Paul Longmore described his feelings:

> I somberly watched the fire consume my book. I had planned the protest. I had rehearsed how to burn the book. I had even thought about what sort of expression I should have on my face. But I could never have prepared for the emotional effect on me of the act itself. I was burning my own book, a book I had spent ten years of my life laboring over, a book that had earned me my Ph.D. in history, a book I felt proud of and, in fact, loved. It was a moment of agony. (p. 253)

Longmore concluded the essay:

> We, like all Americans, have talents to use, work to do, our contributions to make to our communities and country. We want the chance to work and marry without jeopardizing our lives. We want access to opportunity. We want access to work. We want access to the American Dream. (p. 258)

Conclusion

As these last four chapters have discussed, the many factors of a disability make each disability a unique experience. Even disabilities of the same type and severity will have different courses; the symptoms will present in different ways, may require somewhat different treatment, and will have varied prognoses. Carolyn Vash (1981), a disability scholar, developed a model of the factors that influence an individual's response to a disability, dividing these factors into three broad categories. These three categories are as follows: (a) factors in the individual, (b) factors in the environment, and (c) factors of the disability. As you will remember, factors in the individual include such aspects as the individual's coping abilities, level of education, and financial resources. The environment includes such aspects as family support, other social support, assistive technology available, services provided, and the amount of prejudice and discrimination in society. These last two chapters have focused on the 10 factors in the disability. We have only briefly discussed the three broad types of factor issues; nonetheless, it can be seen that each disability is a unique experience for the individual.

What Is Disability History?

John Hockenberry, a journalist who is paralyzed, asked:

> Why is it that a person would not be considered educated or privileged if he went through school and never learned there was a France or a French language? But if a person went through school and knew nothing about disability, never met a disabled person [*sic*], never heard of American Sign Language, he might be considered not only educated, but also lucky? (Fleischer & Zames, 2001, p. 205)

So it is with disability history. There have always been people with disabilities; however, society has chosen to view their experiences as a narrow, clinical concern, rather than a universal concern.

History gives voice to individuals and self-defined groups of people, typically those who have lived in the past, relating their experiences, accomplishments, contributions, perspectives, and accumulated wisdom and knowledge. PWODs have represented humanity. Disability history, like all history, is ownership of the past (Longmore, 2003). A group identity is necessary to compile and write the history of any collection of people. This last statement appears to be self-evident; however, in the case of PWDs, for centuries the only commonalities among PWDs were thought to be inferiority, prejudice, and discrimination. Because of these mistaken beliefs, PWDs did not form a group identity. Until recently, the persistence of the Biomedical Model of disability and the blame and shame of the larger culture worked in combination to keep individual PWDs from seeking each other out.

Disability scholars are justifiably ambivalent toward the Biomedical Model of disability. Medical professionals and scientists in the biological sciences have made many contributions to the lives of PWDs; however, as a *model* (rather than as specific individuals), the Biomedical Model has created the idea that disability is a *private, individual* concern and is pathological inferiority. These false but widely accepted views of PWDs have isolated PWDs from each other. Private concerns are not typically considered to be history. Neither is (falsely) perceived inferiority. After all, it is the winners and the ruling powers who write history. In the Disability History Project produced by National Public Radio (1998a, 1998b, 1998c), it is stated, "History is about successes and heroes. People who are isolated, hidden, incarcerated, and segregated do not write their history, nor are they considered to be heroes or successes." Furthermore, writers of history need institutionalized power, and PWDs have not had access to this type of power (Humphrey, 1999). However, recently, PWDs have been following the lead of Black Americans, Hispanic Americans, and women in reclaiming their right to be included in American history.

Of course, there have always been PWDs, so there has always been disability history. However, there has not been *written* and *recorded* history of PWDs written *by* PWDS. As we have seen throughout this book, PWDs do have common purposes; they share many of the same experiences, and many similar patterns and themes are found in diverse autobiographical works. This, then, is what disability history is. Millions of individuals have experienced a wide variety of disabilities throughout centuries, yet disability history is hidden from PWDs and, indeed, from everybody. Until recently, PWDs had no recorded history, and, therefore, students have not been required to study a nonexistent history. Both PWDs and PWODs have been deprived of disability history. A great historian (Wecter, 1985) remarked, "Ignorance . . . is bad citizenship" (p. 40).

One of the purposes of any type of history is to build a present and a future that are more equitable and moral. Self-criticism of our culture, society, and legal system is healthy and promotes growth. Disability history should be an integrated part of American life and of interest to everyone. Indeed, PWDs want their experiences, knowledge, and perspectives to become a valued part of ordinary public life (D. A. Young & Quibell, 2000).

As a nation, we observe the birthday of Dr. Martin Luther King, Jr., an American hero. Will we celebrate the birthday of Justin Dart? (Justin Dart is considered to be the father of the Americans With Disabilities Act.)

Why Has There Been No Disability History?

The medical professions and the media have dominated in representing PWDs to the public, and the media has used PWDs (or more accurately stated, the media's representations of PWDs) as a medium of exchange. The representation of PWDs to the public has been exploited to make money because disability appears to be deviant, alien, and exotic. The actor's (supposed) disability is never a secondary characteristic. Jenny Morris (1991), an English woman who is paraplegic, wrote:

> I could watch television for years, possibly a lifetime, without seeing my experience reflected in its dramas, documentaries, news stories. I could spend a

lifetime going to theatres, libraries, bookshops, reading newspapers, without finding any portrayal of a woman's life which speaks to my experience. (p. 84)

Every individual and every group of individuals claims the right to define themselves. Leonard Kriegel (1991), a polio survivor, summarized:

> But to be a cripple is to learn that one can be defined from outside. . . . What we invariably discover is that our true selves, our own inner lives, have been auctioned off so that we can be palatable rather than real. . . . [T]he only thing we can be certain of is that the world would prefer to turn a blind eye and a deaf ear to our selves—and that it will do precisely that until we impose those selves on the world. (p. 66)

Anne Emerman, former director of the New York City Office of People with Disabilities, stated:

> Our issues are always being discussed by people who are experts about us—politicians, policymakers, doctors, social workers—but not us. It's as if they thought, what do we know about ourselves? With all the enlightened thinking about disability, there's still that residue of paternalism. (Fleischer & Zames, 2001, p. 211)

Susan Wendell (2006) "fell ill overnight with what turned out to be a disabling chronic disease" (p. 260). As part of her attempts to identify as an individual with a disability, she relates:

> Some time ago, I decided to delve into what I assumed would be a substantial literature in medical ethics on the nature and experience of disability. I consulted *The Philosopher's Index,* looking under "Disability," "Handicap," "Illness," and "Disease." This was a depressing experience. At least 90 percent of philosophical articles on these topics are concerned with two questions: Under what conditions is it morally permissible/right to kill/let die a disabled person [sic] and how potentially disabled does a fetus have to be before it is permissible/right to prevent its being born? (p. 260)

As a university professor, Wendell turned to her research skills to help her learn about "the nature and experience of disability." She found very little disability history.

Marc Shell (2005), a polio survivor, wrote what might be termed a "metapathography" (Hawkins, 1993) of the experiences of hundreds of polio survivors. At the beginning of his book, Shell explained his research methods: "Authors of such autobiographical and biographical works (polio stories) usually seem unaware of one another; yet they often offer the same wise counsel about lifestyle, religion, love, and medical knowledge and the lack thereof" (p. 5). On the next page, Shell continued to describe the difficulties he experienced in simply *finding* these written accounts:

> *Polio and Its Aftermath* makes reference to hundreds of book-length first-person polio narratives. . . . Dozens of these polio narratives are referenced here for the first time anywhere. (Four dozen are not listed in a single library catalogue *anywhere* in the world. I found most of them at secondhand bookstores in Canada, the United States, Tasmania, Australia, South Africa, Zimbabwe, Singapore, Mexico, France, and Germany.) . . . Library materials about polios [survivors] from outside the usual commercial publishers' arena were especially difficult for me to find. Unpublished book manuscripts, self-published books, and even so-called children's books have been strangely "disappeared." Their absence from the libraries, as well as from the general histories of childhood and the sociology of childhood disease, mirrors not merely the commercial publishing practices of the past but also the general reception of polio literature and the general repression of the memory of polio. (p. 6)

Widespread knowledge and understanding of the American polio epidemics could serve to inform current debates. The U.S. experienced the greatest number of polio epidemics and the greatest numbers of people who contracted polio, became disabled, or died. These epidemics occurred because the U.S. had no "herd immunity" against polio, and, indeed, the only way in which the epidemics ended was when everyone had been exposed to polio. Today, we are discussing mass immunization and the importance of herd immunity to protect the few who refuse immunization.

Disability is thought of as deviation, not as human diversity or variation, and, because of this, few PWODs identify with PWDs. PWDs are thought to be "the other" and a relatively small and narrow population. Susan Wendell (2006), a disability feminist scholar, summarized: "Our culture idealizes the body and demands that we control it. . . . [T]he disabled are made 'the other,' who symbolize failure of control and the threat of pain, limitation, dependency, and death" (p. 260). Rather than viewing PWDs as ordinary people who share the concerns of family, education, work, and community life, PWODs view PWDs as deviant abnormals who should not be allowed to participate in family, education, work, and community life.

The Importance of Disability History

Disability history, written by those who have disabilities, should be integrated into cultural and social life. In other words, the experience of disability should be viewed as a valued, strengthening, and broadening diversity, with much to contribute to the wider culture. Disability is a rich and important part of life. Like any other cultural group, PWDs want their differences to be acknowledged, respected, and valued. They claim the right to self-identity. At the same time, they want others to view their differences and values to be an important part of human life, thus universalizing their experience. They no longer wish to be considered a narrowly defined minority.

Hockenberry (1995) stated that PWODs have been deprived of disability history. Those without disabilities have a great deal to learn from those who do have disabilities. Why haven't PWODs demonstrated interest in the disability experience? Perhaps it is the fear of acquiring a disability, or the idea that all disability is tragedy, or the historical tendency to segregate, institutionalize, and shun PWDs that has led to a lack of knowledge. It is probably a combination of all these factors. Liachowitz (1988) thinks that this fear of disability engenders more fear and that institutionalized segregation of PWDs leads to more segregation:

> Obviously, segregation affects people with physical handicaps [sic] and people with able bodies. . . . A major consequence of a segregated educational system is the fear that is fostered by ignorance. This kind of fear among those empowered to construct educational policy almost certainly engenders the justification of more segregation. (p. 111)

Nonetheless, everyone can benefit from the disability experience, including those who never acquire a disability. Joan Tollifson (1997), in a chapter titled "Imperfection Is a Beautiful Thing," explained:

> Imperfection is the essence of being organic and alive. Organic life is vulnerable; it inevitably ends in disintegration. This is part of its beauty. True meditation delves into this mystery of life and death, discovering (not intellectually, but experientially) how porous and momentary every thing is. (p. 106)

While most PWDs identify themselves as someone *with* a disability, most PWODs do not think of themselves as someone *without* a disability. Furthermore, because PWDs have been marginalized, most people without disabilities find it difficult to identify with someone with a disability. Susan Wendell (2006) explained: "Suffering caused by the body and the inability to control the body are despised, pitied, and above all, feared. This fear, experienced individually is also deeply embedded in our culture" (p. 267). Wendell considers this fear to be a barrier for PWODs to identify with PWDs. It will be difficult to integrate PWDs into the social and cultural life of society if the wider society maintains this fear and lack of ability to identify with PWDs.

Paul Longmore (2003) suggests that by learning and studying the disability experience, society will be able "to uncover cultural beliefs regarding such matters as body image, masculinity and femininity, personal autonomy and selfhood" (p. 39). Patricia Deegan (1991) considers it necessary to accept the fact that no one is exempt from acquiring a disability to understand the disability experience and PWDs: "To accept our own vulnerability is the first step to understanding the experience of the person with a disability. In so doing, we discover that we share a common humanity with PWDs and we are not 'worlds apart'" (p. 47).

Certainly, those with disabilities have experience and knowledge that are not available to those without disabilities; furthermore, these experiences and knowledge are important for those without disabilities. Thus, the disability experience is an important source of knowledge. If the experience of PWDs were incorporated into cultural life, the relationship between self and body would be viewed in a different way. By listening to those who have transcended pain, functional limitations, and uncertainty, much can be learned about adaptability, strength, and what it means to be human.

REFERENCES

Ablon, J. (1984). *Little People in America: The social dimensions of dwarfism*. New York, NY: Praeger.

Ablon, J. (1989). Families with dwarf children. In S. C. Hey, G. Kiger, & D. Evans (Eds.), *The changing world of impaired and disabled people in society* (pp. 350–358). Salem, OR: Society for Disability Studies and Willamette University.

A family portrait: Casey Roberts Dunham. (2005, Fall). *Tourette Syndrome Association Newsletter*. Bayside, NY: Author. Retrieved from http://www.tsa-usa.org/aPeople/LivingWithTS/Images/FamPor_Fal05_CRDunham.pdf

Affleck, G., Tennen, H., Pfeifer, C., & Fifield, J. (1987). Appraisals of control and predictability in adapting to a chronic disease. *Journal of Personality and Social Psychology, 53*, 273–279.

Agich, G. J. (1995). Chronic illness and freedom. In S. K. Toombs, D. Barnard, & R. A. Carson (Eds.), *Chronic illness: From experience to policy* (pp. 129–153). Bloomington: University of Indiana Press.

Albrecht, G. L., Seelman, K. D., & Bury, M. (Eds.). (2001). *Handbook of disability studies*. Thousand Oaks, CA: SAGE.

Alder, A. B., Wright, B. A., & Ulicny, G. R. (1991). Fundraising portrayals of people with disabilities: Donations and attitudes. *Rehabilitation Psychology, 36,* 231–240.

Allport, G. W. (1954). *The nature of prejudice*. Reading, MA: Addison-Wesley.

Allport, G. W. (1958). *The nature of prejudice* (2nd ed.). Garden City, NY: Doubleday Anchor.

Allport, G. W. (1986). *The nature of prejudice* (25th anniversary ed.). Reading, MA: Addison-Wesley.

Alter, J. (2006). *The defining moment: FDR's hundred days and the triumph of hope*. New York, NY: Simon & Schuster.

American Psychiatric Association (APA). (1994). *Diagnostic and statistical manual of mental disorders* (4th ed.). Washington, DC: Author.

American Psychiatric Association. (2000). *Diagnostic and statistical manual of mental disorders* (4th ed., text rev.). Washington, DC: Author.

American Psychiatric Association. (2013). *Diagnostic and statistical manual of mental disorders* (5th ed.). Washington, DC: Author.

Americans with Disabilities Act Amendments Act of 2008, 42 USCA § 12101 *et seq*. Retrieved from http://www.eeoc.gov/laws/statutes/adaaa.cfm

Americans with Disabilities Act of 1990, 42 U.S.C. § 12101 *et seq*. Retrieved from http://www.usdoj.gov/crt/ada/adahoml.htm

Amundson, R. (2000). Against normal functions. *Studies in the History and Philosophy of Biological and Biomedical Sciences, 31*, 33–53.

Anderson, G. R. (1987). Paternalism. In G. R. Anderson & V. A. Glesnes-Anderson (Eds.), *Health care ethics: A guide for decision makers* (pp. 177–191). Rockville, MD: Aspen.

Anderson, J., & Moller, J. (1997, August 26). Video foils insurance fraud. *Logan Herald Journal*. Retrieved from http://news.hjnews.com/allaccess/

Angier, N. (2001, May 27). Before the miracle. [Review of the books *The education of Laura Bridgman: The first deaf and blind person to learn language*, by E. Freeburg, and *The imprisoned guest: Samuel Howe and Laura Bridgman, the original deaf-blind girl*, by E. Gitter.] *New York Times*, pp. 12–13.

Anson, C. A., Stanwyck, D. J., & Krause, J. S. (1993). Social support and health status in spinal cord injury. *International Journal of Paraplegia, 31*, 632–638.

Antonak, R. F. (1980). A hierarchy of attitudes toward exceptionality. *Journal of Special Education, 14,* 231–241.

Appel, T. (1988). Personal statement: Living in spite of multiple sclerosis. In P. W. Power (Ed.), *Family interventions throughout chronic illness and disability* (pp. 253–257). New York, NY: Springer.

Artiles, A. J., & Trent, S. C. (1994). Overrepresentation of minority students in special education: A continuing debate. *The Journal of Special Education, 27,* 410–437.

Asch, A., & Fine, M. (1997). Nurturance, sexuality, and women with disabilities: The example of women and literature. In L. J. Davis (Ed.), *The disability studies reader* (pp. 241–259). New York, NY: Routledge.

Associated Press. (1997, September 10). Handicapped used as guinea pigs. *Logan Herald Journal,* p. A7.

Baesler, E. J. (1995). Persuasive effects of an involving disability role play. *Journal of Applied Rehabilitation Counseling, 26*(2), 29–35.

Barker, R. G., Wright, B. A., Meyerson, L., & Gonick, M. R. (1953). *Adjustment to physical handicap and illness: A survey of the social psychology of physique and disability* (rev. ed.). New York, NY: Social Science Research Council.

Barnard, D. (1995). Chronic illness and the dynamics of hoping. In S. K. Toombs, D. Barnard, & R. A. Carson (Eds.), *Chronic illness and the dynamics of hoping* (pp. 38–57). Bloomington: University of Indiana Press.

Barnartt, S., Schriner, K., & Scotch, R. (2001). Advocacy and political action. In G. L. Albrecht, K. D. Seelman, & M. Bury (Eds.), *Handbook of disability studies* (pp. 430–449). Thousand Oaks, CA: SAGE.

Barnes, C., Mercer, G., & Shakespeare, T. (1999). *Exploring disability: A sociological introduction.* Cambridge, England: Polity.

Barry, D. (2014, March 9). The 'boys' in the bunkhouse. *New York Times.* Retrieved from http://www.nytimes.com/interactive/2014/03/09/us/the-boys-in-the-bunkhouse.html?_r=0

Basheda, L. (2006, July). No arms, no legs—no worries. *Orange County Register, 1,* 7.

Batavia, A. I., & Schriner, K. (2001). The Americans with Disabilities Act as an engine of social change: Models of disability and the potential of a civil rights approach. *Disability Policy Studies Journal, 29,* 690–702.

Bauman, H. D. L., & Drake, J. (1997). Silence is not without voice: Including Deaf culture within the multicultural curricula. In L. J. Davis (Ed.), *The disability studies reader* (pp. 307–314). New York, NY: Routledge.

Baynton, D. C. (1997a, Spring). Disability: A useful category of historical analysis. *Disability Studies Quarterly, 17*(2), 81–87.

Baynton, D. (1997b). A silent exile on this earth: The metaphorical construction of deafness in the nineteenth century. In L. J. Davis (Ed.), *The disability studies reader* (pp. 128–150). New York, NY: Routledge.

Becker, G. S. (1999, August 2). Are we hurting or helping the disabled? *Business Week* 3635, 9.

Becker, H. S. (Ed.). (1963). *Outsiders: Studies in the sociology of deviance.* New York, NY: Free Press.

Beisser, A. R. (1989). *Flying without wings: Personal reflections on being disabled.* New York, NY: Doubleday.

Bendell, R. D. (1984). Psychological problems of infancy. In M. G. Eisenberg, L. C. Sutkin, & M. A. Jansen (Eds.), *Chronic illness and disability through the life span: Effects on self and the family* (pp. 23–38). New York, NY: Springer.

Berger, R. (2009). *Dreams on wheels: Disability and the competitive wheelchair athlete.* New York, NY: Routledge.

Berkman, A., Weissman, R., & Frielich, M. (1978). Sexual adjustment of spinal cord injured veterans living in the community. *Archives of Physical Medicine and Rehabilitation, 59,* 22–23.

Berkowitz, E. D. (1984). Professionals as providers: Some thoughts on disability and ideology. *Rehabilitation Psychology, 29,* 211–216.

Berkowitz, E. D. (1987). *Disabled policy: America's programs for the handicapped.* London, England: Cambridge University.

Bernstein, N. R. (1989). Psychological problems associated with facial disfigurement. In B. W. Heller, L. M. Flohr, & L. S. Zegans, (Eds.), *Psychosocial interventions with physically disabled persons* (pp. 147–161). New Brunswick, NJ: Rutgers University.

Bernstein, N. R. (1990). Objective bodily damage: Disfigurement and dignity. In T. F. Cash & T. Pruzinsky (Eds.), *Body images: Development, deviance, and change* (pp. 131–148). New York, NY: Guilford.

Bernstein, N. R., Breslau, J. J., & Graham, J. A. (Eds.). (1988). *Coping strategies for burn survivors and their families.* New York, NY: Praeger.

Berube, M. (1996). *Life as we know it: A father, a family, and an exceptional child.* New York, NY: Pantheon.

Berube, M. (1998). Foreword. In S. Linton (Ed.), *Claiming disability: Knowledge and identity* (pp. vii–xv). New York: New York University.

Bienvenu, M. J. (1989). Reflections of deaf culture in deaf humor. In C. J. Erring, R. C. Johnson, D. L. Smith, & B. D. Snider (Eds.), *The deaf way: Perspectives from the International Conference on Deaf Culture* (pp. 16–23). Washington, DC: Gallaudet University Press.

Bickenbach, J. E. (1993). *Physical disability and social policy.* Toronto, Ontario, Canada: University of Toronto.

Blumberg, B. D., Lewis, M. J., & Susman, E. J. (1984). Adolescence: A time of transition. In M. G. Eisenberg, L. C. Sutkin, & M. A. Jansen (Eds.), *Chronic illness and disability through the life span: Effects on self and the family* (pp. 133–163). New York, NY: Springer.

Bogardus, E. S. (1928). *Immigration and race attitudes.* Lexington, MA: D. C. Heath.

Bogdan, R. (1988). *Freak show: Presenting human oddities for amusement and profit.* Chicago, IL: University of Chicago.

Bogdan, R., & Taylor, S. J. (1987). Toward a sociology of acceptance: The other side of the study of deviance. *Social Policy, Fall,* 34–39.

Bok, S. (1979). *Lying: Moral choice in public and private life.* New York, NY: Vintage.

Bonica, J. J. (Ed.). (1990). *The management of pain.* Philadelphia, PA: Lea & Febiger.

Bordieri, J. E. (1993). Self-blame attributions for disability and perceived client involvement in the vocational rehabilitation process. *Journal of Applied Rehabilitation Counseling, 24*(2), 3–6.

Boswell, B., Knight, S., & Hamer, M. (2001). Disability and spirituality: A reciprocal relationship with implications for the rehabilitation process. *Journal of Rehabilitation, 67,* 20–25.

Boswell, B. B., Dawson, M., & Heininger, E. (1998). Quality of life as defined by adults with spinal cord injuries. *Journal of Rehabilitation, 64,* 27–32.

Bovard, J. (1997). The ADA defines disability too narrowly. In B. Stalcup (Ed.), *The Disabled (Current Controversies)* (pp. 47–53). San Diego, CA: Greenhaven.

Bowe, F. (1993). Preface. In M. J. Scherer (Ed.), *Living in the state of stuck: How technology impacts the lives of people with disabilities* (pp. xi–xvi). Cambridge, MA: Brookline.

Bower, E. M. (Ed.). (1980). *The handicapped in literature: A psychosocial perspective*. Denver, CO: Love.

Bowman, J. M. (1994). Experiencing the chronic pain phenomenon: A study. *Rehabilitation Nursing, 19*(2), 91–95.

Bradway, J. K., Malone, J. M., Racy, J., Leal, J. M., & Poole, J. (1984). Psychological adaptation to amputation: An overview. *Orthotics and Prosthetics, 38,* 46–50.

Bragg, B. (1989). *Lessons in laughter: The autobiography of a Deaf actor. As signed to Eugene Bergman.* Washington, DC: Gallaudet University.

Brault, M. W. (2012). *Americans With Disabilities: 2010.* Retrieved from http://www.census.gov/prod/2012pubs/p70-131.pdf

Brena, S. F., Sanders, S. H., & Motoyama, H. (1990). American and Japanese low back pain patients: Cross cultural similarities and differences. *Clinical Journal of Pain, 6,* 118–124.

Breslau, N. (1982). Psychiatric disorder in children with physical disabilities. *Journal of the American Academy of Child Psychiatry, 24,* 87–94.

Breslau, N., & Marshall, I. A. (1985). Psychological disturbances in children with physical disabilities: Continuity and change in a 5-year follow-up study. *Journal of Abnormal Child Psychology, 13,* 199–216.

Brew-Parrish, V. (2004, August 9). The wrong message—still. *Ragged Edge Online.* Retrieved from http://www.raggededgemagazine.com/focus/wrongmessage04.html

Brinckerhoff, L. C. (1997). Students with learning disabilities in graduate or professional programs: Emerging issues on campus and challenges to employment. In P. J. Gerbert & D.S. Brown (Eds.), *Learning disabilities and employment* (pp. 143–164). Austin, TX: PRO-ED.

Brown, D. (1997). Implications of cultural values for cross-cultural consultation with families. *Journal of Counseling and Development, 76,* 29–35.

Brown, S. C. (1991). Conceptualizing and defining disability. In S. Thompson-Hoffman & I. F. Storck (Eds.), *Disability in the United States: A portrait from national data* (pp. 1–14). New York, NY: Springer.

Brueggemann, B. J., & Burch, S. (Eds.). (2006). *Women and deafness: Double visions.* Washington, DC: Gallaudet University.

Burch, S. (2007). "Beautiful, though deaf": The Deaf American Beauty Pageant. In B. J. Brueggemann & S. Burch (Eds.), *Women and deafness: Double visions* (pp. 242–261). Washington, DC: Gallaudet University.

Burgdorf, R. (2002). *Americans With Disabilities Act: Supreme Court decisions thwart intent of ADA.* San Diego, CA: Center for an Accessible Society. Retrieved from http://www.accessiblesociety.org/topics/ada/index.html

Buss, D. M. (1999). *Evolutionary psychology: The new science of the mind.* Boston, MA: Allyn & Bacon.

Butcher, J. N., Dahlstrom, W. G., Graham, J. R., Tellegen, A., & Kaemmer, B. (2001). *Minnesota multiphasic personality inventory* (2nd ed.). Bloomington, MN: Pearson.

Byrd, E. K., & Elliott, T. R. (1988). Media and disability: A discussion of the research. In H. E. Yuker (Ed.), *Attitudes toward persons with disabilities* (pp. 82–95). New York, NY: Springer.

Byrom, B. (2004). A pupil and a patient: Hospital-schools in progressive America. In S. Danforth & S. D. Taff (Eds.), *Crucial readings in special education* (pp. 25–37). Upper Saddle River, NJ: Pearson.

Cameron, J. (1982). *For all that has been: Time to live and time to die.* New York, NY: Macmillan.

Campling, J. (1981). *Images of ourselves: Women with disabilities talking.* London, England: Routledge Kegan Paul.

Carroll, T. J. (1961). *Blindness: What it is, what it does, and how to live with it.* Boston, MA: Little, Brown.

Cate, I. M. P., & Loots, G. M. P. (2000). Experiences of siblings of children with physical disabilities: An empirical investigation. *Disability and Rehabilitation, 22,* 399–408.

Chang, J. C., Martin, S. L., Moracco, K. E., Dulli, L., Scandlin, D., & Loucks-Sorrel, M. B. (2003). Helping women with disabilities and domestic violence: Strategies, limitations, and challenges of domestic violence programs and services. *Journal of Women's Health, 12,* 699–708.

Charlton, J. I. (1998). *Nothing about us without us: Disability oppression and empowerment.* Berkeley: University of California.

Charlton, J. I. (2000). *Nothing about us without us: Disability oppression and empowerment* (New ed.). Berkeley: University of California.

Chilman, C. S., Nunnally, E. W., & Cox, F. M. (Eds.). (1988). *Chronic illness and disability: Families in trouble.* Newbury Park, CA: SAGE.

Chubon, R. A. (1994). *Social and psychosocial foundations of rehabilitation.* Springfield, IL: Thomas.

Chubon, R. A., & Moore, C. T. (1982). The cocoon syndrome: A coping mechanism of spinal cord injured persons. *Rehabilitation Psychology, 27,* 87–96.

Clanton, L. D., Rude, S. S., & Taylor, C. (1992). Learned resourcefulness as a moderator of burnout in a sample of rehabilitation providers. *Rehabilitation Psychology, 37,* 131–140.

Clausen, J., & Yarrow, M. R. (1955). The impact of mental illness on the family. *Journal of Social Issues, 11,* 1–65.

Clendinen, D., & Nagourney, A. (1999). *Out for good: The struggle to build a gay rights movement in America.* New York, NY: Simon & Schuster.

Close, C. (1993). Chuck Close. In J. K. Smith & G. Plimpton (Eds.), *Chronicles of courage: Very special artists* (pp. 14–28). New York, NY: Random House.

Cohen, L. H. (1994). *Train go sorry: Inside a Deaf world.* Boston, MA: Houghton Mifflin.

Cohen, R. M. (2004). *Blindsided: Lifting a life above illness: A reluctant memoir.* New York, NY: Harper Collins.

Cole, S. S. (1984). Facing the challenge of sexual abuse in persons with disabilities. *Sexuality and Disability, 7,* 71–88.

Cole, S. S. & Cole, T. M. (1993). Sexuality, disability, and reproductive issues through the lifespan. *Sexuality and Disability, 11,* 189–201.

Coleman, B. C. (1994, July 12). Study: Girls' weight, boys' height affect future earning power. *Standard-Examiner,* p. A4.

Coleman, L. M. (1997). Stigma: An enigma demystified. In L. J. Davis (Ed.), *The disability studies reader* (pp. 216–231). New York, NY: Routledge.

Conrad, P. (2004). The discovery of hyperkinesis: Notes on the medicalization of deviant behavior. In S. Danforth & S. D. Taff (Eds.), *Crucial readings in special education* (pp. 18–24). Upper Saddle River, NJ: Pearson.

Conway-Giustra, F., Crowley, A., & Gorin, S. H. (2002). Crisis in caregiving: A call to action. *Health and Social Work, 27,* 307–311.

Cook, D.W. (1991). Disability, psychopathology, and vocational adjustment. In M. G. Eisenberg & R. L. Glueckauf (Eds.), *Empirical approaches to psychosocial aspects of disability* (pp. 85–105). New York, NY: Springer.

Cook, S. W. (1978). Interpersonal and attitudinal outcomes in cooperating interracial groups. *Journal of Research in Developmental Education, 12,* 97–113.

Corrigan, P.W., & Penn, D. L. (1999). Lessons from social psychology on discrediting psychiatric stigma. *American Psychologist, 54,* 765–776.

Cott, C., & Wilkins, S. (1993). Aging, chronic illness and disability. In M. Nagler (Ed.), *Perspectives on disability* (2nd ed.) (pp. 363–377). Palo Alto, CA: Health Markets Research.

Couser, G. T. (1997). *Recovering bodies: Illness, disability, and life writing.* Madison: University of Wisconsin.

Craine, L. S., Henson, C. E., Colliver, J. A., & McLeland, D. G. (1988). Prevalence of a history of sexual abuse among female psychiatric patients in a state hospital system. *Hospital and Community Psychiatry, 39,* 300–304.

Crawford, D., & Ostrove, J. M. (2003). Representations of disability and the interpersonal relationships of women with disabilities. *Women and Therapy, 26,* 179–194.

Crespo, A. (1993). Alice Crespo, court interpreter. In H. Rousso (Ed.). *Disabled, female, and proud!* (pp. 95–104). Westport, CT: Bergin & Garvey.

Crewe, N. M. (1997). Life stories of people with long-term spinal cord injury. *Rehabilitation Counseling Bulletin, 41,* 26–42.

Curry, R. L. (1995). The exceptional family: Walking the edge of tragedy and transformation. In S. K. Toombs, D. Barnard, & R. A. Carlson (Eds.), *Chronic illness: From experience to policy* (pp. 24–37). Bloomington: University of Indiana.

Dailey, S. F., Gill, C. S., Karl, S. L., & Minton, C. A. B. (2014). *DSM-5: Learning companion for counselors.* Alexandria, VA: American Counseling Association.

Darke, E. (1993). The Elephant Man: An analysis from a disabled perspective. *Disability and Society, 9,* 327–343.

Davis, L. J. (1995). *Enforcing normalcy: Disability, deafness, and the body.* London, England: Verso.

Davis, L. J. (1997a). Constructing normalcy: The bell curve, the novel, and the invention of the disabled body in the nineteenth century. In L. J. Davis (Ed.), *The disability studies reader* (pp. 307–314). New York, NY: Routledge.

Davis, L. J. (Ed.). (1997b). *The disability studies reader.* New York, NY: Routledge.

Deal, M. (2003). Disabled people's attitudes toward other impairment groups: A hierarchy of impairments. *Disability & Society, 18,* 897–910.

Deegan, P. E. (1991). Recovery: The lived experience of rehabilitation. In R. P. Martinelli & A. E. Dell Orto (Eds.), *The psychological and social impact of disability* (3rd ed.) (pp. 47–54). New York, NY: Springer.

Deegan, P. E. (1997). Recovery: The lived experience of rehabilitation. In L. Spaniol, C. Gagne, & M. Koehler (Eds.), *Psychological and social aspects of psychiatric disability* (pp. 92–98). Boston, MA: Boston University, Center for Psychiatric Rehabilitation.

DeJong, G., & Lifchez, R. (1983). Physical disability and public policy. *Scientific American, 248*(6), 40–49.

DeLoach, C. & Greer, B. G. (1981). *Adjustment to severe disability: A metamorphosis.* New York, NY: McGraw-Hill.

DeLoach, C. P. (1994). Attitudes toward disability: Impact on sexual development and forging of intimate relationships. *Journal of Applied Rehabilitation Counseling, 25,* 18–25.

Disability Rights Education and Defense Fund (DREDF). http://www.dredf.org.

Doherty, B. (1997). ADA compliance is too expensive. In B. Stalcup (Ed.), *The disabled, current controversies series* (pp. 54–61). San Diego, CA: Greenhaven.

Donoghue, P. J., & Siegel, M. E. (1992). *Sick and tired of feeling sick and tired: Living with invisible chronic illness.* New York, NY: Norton.

Ducharme, S., Gill, K., Biener-Bergman, S., & Fertitta, L. (1993). Sexual functioning: Medical and psychological aspects. In J. DeLisa (Ed.), *Rehabilitation medicine: Principles and practices* (2nd ed.) (pp. 763–782). Philadelphia, PA: Lippincott.

Dunn, D. S. (1996). Well-being following amputation: Salutary effects of positive meaning, optimism, and control. *Rehabilitation Psychology, 41,* 285–302.

Dunn, M. (1996). Subscale development of the Rehabilitation Situations Inventory. *Rehabilitation Psychology, 41,* 255–264.

Edwards, M. L. (1997). Deaf and dumb in ancient Greece. In L. J. Davis (Ed.), *The disabilities studies reader* (pp. 29–51). New York, NY: Routledge.

Education for All Handicapped Children Act of 1975, 20 U.S.C. § 1400 et seq.

Elliott, T. R., Shewchuk, R. M., & Richards, J. S. (1999). Caregiver social problem-solving abilities and family member adjustment to recent onset physical disability. *Rehabilitation Psychology, 44,* 104–123.

Equal Access to Software and Information. (1999). Retrieved from http://easi.cc

Erikson, E. H. (1963). *Childhood and society* (2nd ed.). New York, NY: Norton.

Erikson, E. H. (1968). *Identity and crisis.* New York, NY: Norton.

Esses, V. M., & Beaufoy, S. L. (1994). Determinants of attitudes toward people with disabilities. *Journal of Social Behavior & Personality, 9,* 43–64.

Estroff, S. E. (1995). Whose story is it anyway? Authority, voice, and responsibility in narratives of chronic illness. In S. K. Toombs, D. Barnard, & R. A. Carson (Eds.), *Chronic illness: From experience to policy* (pp. 77–102). Bloomington: University of Indiana.

Evans, H. (1998). *The American century.* New York, NY: Alfred A. Knopf.

Evans, A. D., & Falk, W. W. (1986). *Learning to be deaf.* Berlin, Germany: Mouton de Gruyter.

Falvo, D. R. (1991). *Medical and psychosocial aspects of chronic illness and disability.* Gaithersburg, MD: Aspen.

Farber, B. (1968). *Intellectual disability: Its social context and social consequences.* Boston, MA: Houghton Mifflin.

Farber, B., & Lewis, M. (1976). Compensatory education and social justice. *Peabody Journal of Education, 49,* 85–96.

Farrow, M. (1997). *What Falls Away: A Memoir.* New York: Bantam.

Faull, K., Hills, M. D., Cochrane, G., Gray, J., Hunt M., & McKenzie, C. M. (2004). Investigation of health perspectives of those with physical disabilities: The role of spirituality as a determinant of health. *Disability and Rehabilitation, 26*(3), 129–144.

Feinstein, A. R., & Chapman, H. (2002). *Principles of medical statistics.* Boca Raton, FL: CRC Press.

Fenigsen, R. (1997). Euthanasia of disabled infants is not morally acceptable. In B. Stalcup (Ed.), *The disabled* (pp. 160–164). San Diego, CA: Greenhaven.

Fichten, C. S., Compton, V., & Amsel, R. (1985). Imagined empathy and attributions concerning activity preferences of physically disabled college students. *Rehabilitation Psychology, 30,* 235–239.

Fine, M., & Asch, A. (1988). *Women with disabilities: Essays in psychology, cultural, and politics.* Philadelphia, PA: Temple University.

Fingarette, H. (1988). *Heavy drinking.* Berkeley: University of California.

Finger, A. (1990). *Past due: A story of disability, pregnancy, and birth.* Seattle, WA: Seal Press.

Finger, A. (1993). Toward a theory of radical disability photography. *Disability Rag, November,* 29–31.

Fink, P. J., & Tasman, A. (Eds.). (1992). *Stigma and mental illness.* Washington, DC: American Psychiatric Association.

Fisher, B., & Galler, R. (1988). Friendship and fairness: How disability affects friendship between women. In M. Fine & A. Asch (Eds.), *Women with disabilities: Essays in psychology, culture, and politics* (pp. 407–413).

Fitzgerald, J. (1997). Reclaiming the whole self: Self, spirit, and society. *Disability and Rehabilitation, 19,* 407–413.

Fleischer, D. Z., & Zames, F. (2001). *The disability rights movement: From charity to confrontation.* Philadelphia, PA: Temple University.

Fox, M. (2007). *Talking hands.* New York, NY: Simon & Schuster.

Frances, A. (2013). *Essentials of psychiatric diagnosis: Responding to the challenge of DSM-5* (Rev. ed.). New York, NY: Guilford.

Frank, A. W. (1991). *At the will of the body: Reflections on illness.* Boston, MA: Houghton Mifflin.

Frank, A. W. (1995). *The wounded storyteller: Body, illness, and ethics.* Chicago, IL: University of Chicago.

Frese, F. (1997). Twelve aspects of coping for persons with serious and persistent mental illness. In L. Spaniol, C. Gagne, & M. Hoehler (Eds.), *Psychological and social aspects of psychiatric disability.* Boston, MA: Center for Psychiatric Rehabilitation, Boston University.

Friedlander, H. (1995). *The origins of Nazi genocide: From euthanasia to the final solution.* Chapel Hill: University of North Carolina.

Fries, K. (Ed.). (1997). *Staring back: The disability experience from the inside out.* New York, NY: Plume.

Friesen, B. J. (1996). Family support in child and adult mental health. In G. H. S. Singer, L. E. Powers, & A. L. Olson (Eds.), *Redefining family support: Innovations in public-private partnerships* (pp. 259–274). Baltimore, MD: Brookes.

Galambos, C. M., & Rosen, A. (2000). The aging are coming and they are us. In S. M. Keigher, A. E. Fortune, & S. L. Witkin (Eds.), *Aging and social work: The changing landscapes* (pp. 13–19). Washington, DC: NASW Press.

Gallagher, H. G. (1985). *FDR's splendid deception.* New York, NY: Dodd and Mead.

Gallagher, H. G. (1990). *By trust betrayed: Patients, physicians, and the license to kill in the Third Reich.* New York, NY: Henry Holt.

Gallagher, R. M. (2000). Treating depression in patients with comorbid chronic pain, Part 1. *Directions in Rehabilitation Counseling, 1,* 15–32.

Garske, G. G., & Stewart, J. R. (1999). Stigmatic and mythical thinking: Barriers to vocational rehabilitation services to persons with severe mental illness. *Journal of Rehabilitation, 65,* 4–8.

Gartner, A., & Joe, T. (Eds.). (1987). *Images of the disabled, disabling images.* New York, NY: Praeger.

Gawande, A. (2007). *Better: A surgeon's note on performance.* New York, NY: Picador.

Gawande, A. (2014). *Being mortal: Medicine and what matters in the end.* New York, NY: Metropolitan Books/Henry Holt.

Gellman, W. (1959). Roots of prejudice against the handicapped. *Journal of Rehabilitation, 40,* 115–123.

Gerber, P. J., & Brown, D. S. (Eds.). (1997). *Learning disabilities and employment.* Austin, TX: PRO-ED.

Gill, C. J. (2000). Health professionals, disability, and assisted suicide: An examination of relevant empirical evidence and reply to Batavia (2000). *Psychology, Public Policy, and Law, 6*(2), 526–545.

Gill, C. J. (2001). Divided understandings: The social experience of disability. In G. L.

Albrecht, K. D. Seelman, & M. Bury (Eds.), *The handbook of disability studies* (pp. 351–373). Thousand Oaks, CA: SAGE.

Gist, N. R., & Dworkin, A. G. (1972). *The blending of the races: Marginality and identity in a world perspective.* New York, NY: Wiley Interscience.

Glueckauf, R. L., & Quittner, A. L. (1984). Facing physical disability as a young adult: Psychological issues and approaches. In M. G. Eisenberg, L. C. Sutkin, & M. A. Jansen (Eds.), *Chronic illness and disability through the life span: Effects on self and the family* (pp. 167–183). New York, NY: Springer.

Goeke, J. (2003). Parents speak out: Facial plastic surgery for children with Down syndrome. *Education and Training in Developmental Disabilities, 38,* 323–333.

Goffman, E. (1948). *Stigma: Notes on the management of spoiled identity.* Englewood Cliffs, NJ: Prentice Hall.

Goffman, E. (1963). *Stigma: Notes on the management of spoiled identity.* Englewood Cliffs, NJ: Prentice Hall.

Goffman, E. (1997). Selections from stigma. In L. J. Davis (Ed.), *The disability studies reader* (pp. 203–215). New York, NY: Routledge.

Goldstein, R. K. (1986). Adjustment of the burned patient. In D. W. Krueger (Ed.), *Emotional rehabilitation of physical trauma and disability* (pp. 87–104). New York, NY: Pergamon.

Goodheart, C. D., & Lansing, M. H. (1997). *Treating people with chronic disease: A psychological guide.* Washington, DC: American Psychological Association.

Gordon, P. A., Feldman, D., & Crose, R. (1998). The meaning of disability: How women with chronic illness view their experiences. *Journal of Rehabilitation, 64,* 5–11.

Gordon, P. A., Lewis, M. D., & Wong, D. (1994). Multiple sclerosis: Strategies for rehabilitation counselors. *Journal of Rehabilitation, 60,* 34–38.

Gouvier, W. D., Coon, R. C., Todd, M. E., & Fuller, K. H. (1994). Verbal interactions with individuals presenting with and without physical disability. *Rehabilitation Psychology, 39,* 263–268.

Graliker, B. V., Fishler, K., & Koch, R. (1962). Teenage reaction to a mentally retarded sibling. *Journal of Mental Deficiency, 66,* 838–843.

Grealy, L. (1997). *Autobiography of a face.* New York, NY: Perennial.

Greenberg, M. T. (1980). Hearing families with deaf children: Stress and functioning as related to communication method. *American Annals of the Deaf, 125,* 1063–1071.

Groce, N. (1985). *Everyone here spoke sign language: Hereditary deafness on Martha's Vineyard.* Cambridge, MA: Harvard University.

Gulati, S. (2003). Psychiatric care of culturally Deaf people. In N. S. Glickman & S. Gulati (Eds.), *Mental health care of deaf people: A culturally affirmative approach* (pp. 33–107). Mahwah, NJ: Erlbaum.

Gulick, E. E. (1994). Social support among persons with multiple sclerosis. *Research in Nursing and Health, 17*(3), 195–206.

Hadjistavropoulos, H. D., & Craig, K. D. (1994). Acute and chronic low back pain: Cognitive, affective, and behavioral dimensions. *Journal of Consulting and Clinical Psychology, 62,* 341–349.

Hahn, H. (1988a). Can disability be beautiful? *Social Policy, 18,* 26–32.

Hahn, H. (1988b). The politics of physical differences: Disability and discrimination. *Journal of Social Issues, 44,* 39–47.

Hahn, H. (1991). Foreword. In R. P. Marinelli & A. E. Dell Orto (Eds.), *The psychological and social impact of physical disability* (3rd ed.) (pp. ix–x). New York, NY: Springer.

Hahn, H. (1993). Can disability be beautiful? In M. Nagler (Ed.), *Perspectives on disability* (2nd ed.) (pp. 213–216). Palo Alto, CA: Health Markets Research.

Hahn, H. (1997). Advertising the acceptable employment image: Disability and capitalism. In L. J. Davis (Ed.), *The disability studies reader* (pp. 172–186). New York, NY: Routledge.

Hahn, H. (2005). Academic debates and political advocacy: The U.S. disability movement. In G. E. May & M. B. Raske (Eds.), *Ending disability discrimination: strategies for social workers* (pp. 1–24). Boston, MA: Pearson.

Hannah, M. E., & Midlarsky, E. (1987). Differential impact of labels and behavioral descriptions on attitudes toward people with disabilities. *Rehabilitation Psychology, 32,* 227–238.

Hardman, M. L., Drew, C. J., Egan, M. W., & Wolf, B. (1993). *Human exceptionality: Society, school, and family* (4th ed.). Boston, MA: Allyn & Bacon.

Harper, D. C. (1999). Social psychology of difference: Stigma, spread, and stereotypes in childhood. *Rehabilitation Psychology, 44,* 131–144.

Harris, R. W. (1992). Musings from 20 years of hard-earned experience. *Rehabilitation Education, 6,* 207–211.

Havighurst, R. J. (1951). *Developmental tasks and education.* New York, NY: Longman Green.

Hawking, J. (2007). *Travelling to infinity: My life with Stephen.* Surrey, UK: Alma Books.

Hawkins, A. H. (1993). *Reconstructing illness: Studies in pathography.* West Lafayette, IN: Purdue University.

Head, D. W., Head, B., & Head, J. (1985). Life or death of severely disabled infants: A counseling issue. *Journal of Counseling and Development, 63,* 621–624.

Heiney, R. W. (1976). Renaissance or retreat for special educators: Issues to explore before 1984. *The Journal of Special Education, 10,* 415–425.

Heller, A., Rafman, S., Zvagulis, I., & Pless, I. B. (1985). Birth defects and psychosocial adjustment. *American Journal of Diseases of Children, 139,* 257–263.

Helms, J. E. (1992). Why is there no study of cultural equivalence in standardized cognitive ability testing? *American Psychologist, 47,* 1083–1101.

Henderson, G., & Bryan, W. V. (1997). *Psychosocial aspects of disability* (2nd ed.). Springfield, IL: Charles C. Thomas.

Henoff, N. (1996, May 21). Class warfare to the death. *Village Voice,* 12.

Herrmann, D. (1998). *Helen Keller: A life.* New York, NY: Knopf.

Heumann, J. (1979). *Disability: Our challenge.* New York, NY: Columbia University.

Heumann, J. (1999). Personal narrative. In R. Mackelprang & R. Salsgiver (Eds.), *Disability: A diversity model in human service practice* (pp. 51–54). Pacific Grove, CA: Brooks/Cole.

Hevey, D. (1997). The enfreakment of photography. In L. J. Davis (Ed.), *The disability studies reader* (pp. 332–347). New York, NY: Routledge.

Higgins, P. C. (1992a). *Making disability: Exploring the social transformation of human variation*. Springfield, IL: Thomas.

Higgins, P. C. (1992b). *Outsiders in a hearing world: A sociology of deafness*. Newbury Park, CA: SAGE.

Higgins, P. C., & Nash, J. E. (Eds.). (1987). *Understanding deafness socially*. Springfield, IL: Thomas.

Hillyer, B. (1993). *Feminism and disability*. Norman: University of Oklahoma Press.

Himmelstein, D. U., Woolhandler, S., & Wolfe, S. M. (1992). The vanishing health care safety net: New data on uninsured Americans. *International Journal of Health Services, 22,* 381–396.

Hiranandani, V. (2005). Rethinking disability in social work: Interdisciplinary perspectives. In G. E. May & M. B. Raske (Eds.) *Ending discrimination in social work: Strategies for social workers* (pp. 71–81). Boston, MA: Allyn & Bacon.

Hockenberry, J. (1995). *Moving violations: War zones, wheelchairs, and declarations of independence.* New York, NY: Hyperion.

Hofsiss, J., & Laffey, M. (1993). Jack Hofsiss and Maureen Laffey. In J. K. Smith & G. Plimpton (Eds.), *Chronicles of courage: Very special artists* (pp. 78–87). New York, NY: Random House.

Holaday, M., & McPhearson, R. W. (1997). Resilience and severe burns. *Journal of Counseling and Development, 75,* 346–356.

Holcomb, L. P. (1990). Disabled women: A new issue in education. In M. Nagler (Ed.), *Perspectives on disability* (pp. 381–388). Palo Alto, CA: Health Markets Research.

Holcomb, R. (1977). *Hazards of deafness.* Northridge, CA: Joyce Media.

Holzbauer, J., & Berven, N. (1996). Disability harassment: A new term for a longstanding problem. *Journal of Counseling & Development, 74,* 478–483.

Home, M. D. (1988). Modifying peer attitudes toward the handicapped: Procedures and research issues. In H. E. Yuker (Ed.), *Attitudes toward persons with disabilities* (pp. 203–222). New York, NY: Springer.

Houck, C. K. (1984). *Learning disabilities: Understanding concepts, characteristics, and issues.* Englewood Cliffs, NJ: Prentice Hall.

Hubbard, R. (1997). Abortion and disability: Who should live and inhabit the world? In L. J. Davis (Ed.), *The disability studies reader* (pp. 187–200). New York, NY: Routledge.

Humphrey, J. C. (1999). Disabled people and the politics of differences. *Disability & Society, 14,* 17–188.

Hursh, N. C. (1995). Essential competencies in industrial rehabilitation and disability management practice: A skills-based training model. In D. E. Shrey & M. Lacerte (Eds.), *Principles and practices of disability management in industry* (pp. 303–354). Winter Park, FL: GR Press.

Hurst, R. (1998). Forget pity or charity: Disability is a rights issue. *Disability International, 5*(3), 14–16.

Huston, A. M. (1987). *Common sense about dyslexia.* New York, NY: Madison.

Imrie, R. (1996). *Disability and the city: International perspectives.* New York, NY: St. Martin's Press.

Ivey, A. E., & Ivey, M. B. (1998). Reframing the *DSM-IV:* Positive strategies from developmental counseling and therapy. *Journal of Counseling and Development, 76,* 334–350.

Jacoby, S. (2002). Living better, longer. *American Association of Retired Persons Bulletin, 11,* 14.

Janicki, M. P. (1970). Attitudes of health professionals toward twelve disabilities. *Perceptual & Motor Skills, 30,* 77–78.

Jankowski, K. A. (1997). *Deaf empowerment: Emergence, struggle and rhetoric.* Washington, DC: Gallaudet University.

Johnson v. Thompson, 971 F. 2d 1487 (1992).

Johnson, A. G. (2001). *Power, privilege, and difference* (2nd ed.). New York, NY: McGraw Hill.

Johnson, H. M. (2003, February 16). Should I have been killed at birth? The case for my life. *New York Times,* 50–55.

Johnson, H. M. (2005, March/April). Too late to die young. *American Association of Retired Persons Bulletin, 44,* 46, 99.

Johnston, R. B. (1987). *Learning disabilities, medicine, and myth: A guide to understanding the child and the physician.* Boston, MA: Little, Brown.

Jones, M., Sanford, J., & Bell, R. B. (1997). Disability demographics. How are they changing? *Team Rehab Report, 38,* 36–44.

Joseph P. Kennedy, Jr. Foundation. (1991). *Facts about intellectual disability.* Washington, DC: Author.

Jubala, J. A. (1990). Spinal cord injuries. In M. Hersen & V. B. Van Hasselt (Eds.), *Psychological aspects of developmental and physical disabilities* (pp. 229–245). Thousand Oaks, CA: SAGE.

Karp, D. A. (2001). *The burden of sympathy: How families cope with mental illness.* Oxford, UK: Oxford University.

Kaye, H. S., LaPlante, M. P., Carlson, D., & Wenger, B. L. (1997). Trends in disability rates in the United States, 1970–1994, #17 *Disability statistics abstract.* San Francisco: University of California at San Francisco. Retrieved from http://www.dsc.ucsf.edu

Kaye, J., & Raghavan, S. K. (2002). Spirituality in disability and illness. *Journal of Religion & Health, 41,* 231–242.

Kendall, E., & Buys, N. (1998). An integrated model of psychosocial adjustment following acquired disability. *Journal of Rehabilitation, 64*(3), 16–21.

Kessler Foundation/National Organization on Disability. (2010). *The ADA 20 years later: Survey of Americans with disabilities.* Retrieved from http://www.2010disabilitysurveys.org/pdfs/surveyresults.pdf

Keydel, C. (1988). The impact of a handicapped child on adolescent siblings: Implications for professional intervention. In P. W. Power, A. E. Dell Orto, & M. B. Gibbons (Eds.), *Family interventions throughout chronic illness and disability* (pp. 201–215). New York, NY: Springer.

Kiesler, D. J. (1999). *Beyond the disease model of mental disorders.* Westport, CT: Praeger.

Kiger, G. (1992). Disability simulations: Logical, methodological, and ethical issues. *Disability, Handicap, & Society, 7,* 71–78.

Kilpatrick, S. D., & McCullough, M. E. (1999). Religion and spirituality in rehabilitation psychology. *Rehabilitation Psychology, 44,* 388–402.

Kirk, S. A., & Kutchins, H. (1992). *The selling of the DSM: The rhetoric of science in psychiatry.* New York, NY: Degruyter.

Kisor, H. (1990). *What's that pig outdoors? A memoir of deafness.* New York, NY: Hill and Wang.

Kleege, G. (2006). *Blind rage: Letters to Helen Keller.* Washington, DC: Gallaudet University.

Kleinman, A. (1988). *The illness narratives: Suffering, healing, and the human condition.* New York, NY: Basic.

Klobas, L. (1988). *Disability drama in television and film*. Jefferson, NC: McFarland.

Kluger, J. (2014). A preemie revolution: Cutting-edge medicine and dedicated caregivers are helping the tiniest babies survive and thrive. *Time, 183*(21), 24–31.

Knickerbocker, B. (2006, August 29). In Iraq, fewer killed, more are wounded. *The Christian Science Monitor*. Retrieved from http://www.csmonitor.com/2006/0829/p03s02-usmi.html

Kohler, K., Schweikert-Stary, T., & Lubkin, I. (1998). Altered mobility. In I. M. Lubkin & P. D. Larsen (Eds.), *Chronic illness: Impact and interventions* (4th ed.) (pp. 122–148). Sudbury, MA: Jones & Bartlett.

Kosciulek, J. F., & Lustig, D. C. (1998). Predicting family adaptation from brain injury-related family stress. *Journal of Applied Rehabilitation, 29*(1), 8–12.

Kouzis, A. C., & Eaton, W. W. (2000). Psychopathology and the initiation of disability payments. *Psychiatric Services, 15*, 908–913.

Kozloff, R. (1987). Networks of social supports and the outcome from severe head injury. *Journal of Head Trauma Rehabilitation, 2*, 14–23.

Krause, J. S. (1998a). Changes in adjustment after spinal cord injury: A 20-year longitudinal study. *Rehabilitation Psychology, 43*, 41–55.

Krause, J. S. (1998b). Dimensions of subjective well-being after spinal cord injury: An empirical analysis by gender and race/ethnicity. *Archives of Physical Medicine and Rehabilitation, 79*, 900–909.

Krause, J. S., & Anson, C. A. (1997). Adjustment after spinal cord injury: Relationship to participation in employment or educational activities. *Rehabilitation Counseling Bulletin, 40*, 202–214.

Krause, J. S., Coker, J., Charlifue, S., & Whiteneck, G. G. (1999). Depression and subjective well being among 97 American Indians with spinal cord injury: A descriptive study. *Rehabilitation Psychology, 44*, 354–372.

Kriegel, L. (1964). *The long walk home*. New York, NY: Appleton-Century.

Kriegel, L. (1982). Claiming the self: The cripple as American male. In M. G. Eisenberg, C. Griggins, & R. J. Duval (Eds.), *Disabled people as second-class citizens* (pp. 52–63). New York, NY: Springer.

Kriegel, L. (1987). The cripple in literature. In A. Gartner & T. Joe (Eds.), *Images of the disabled, disabling images*. New York, NY: Praeger.

Kriegel, L. (1991). *Falling into life*. San Francisco, CA: North Point.

Kriegel, L. (1997). Falling into life. In K. Fries (Ed.), *Staring back: The disability experience from the inside out* (pp. 37–50). New York, NY: Plume.

Kübler-Ross, E. (1969). *On death and dying*. New York, NY: Macmillan.

Lane, H. (1992). *The mask of benevolence: Bio-power and the Deaf community*. New York, NY: Knopf.

Lane, H. (1996). The hearing agenda I: To mitigate a disability. In H. Lane, R. Hoffmeister, & B. Bahan (Eds.), *A journey into the deaf-world* (pp. 334–366). San Diego, CA: Dawn Sign Press.

Lane, H., Hoffmeister, R., & Bahan, B. (1996). *A journey into the deaf-world*. San Diego, CA: Dawn Sign Press.

Langer, E. J. (1983). *The psychology of control*. Beverly Hills, CA: SAGE.

Langer, E. J., Bashner, R. S., & Chanowitz, B. (1985). Decreasing prejudice by increasing discrimination. *Journal of Personality and Social Psychology, 49*, 113–120.

Langer, K. G. (1994). Depression and denial in psychotherapy of persons with disabilities. *American Journal of Psychotherapy, 48*, 181–194.

LaPlante, M. P. (1991). The demographics of disability. In J. West (Ed.), *The Americans with Disabilities Act: From policy to practice* (pp. 55–80). New York, NY: Milbank Memorial Fund.

LaPlante, M. P. (1993). State estimates of disability in America. *Disability statistics abstracts No. 3.* Washington, DC: National Institute on Disability and Rehabilitation Research.

LaPlante, M. P. (1996). Health conditions and impairments causing disability. *Disability statistics abstracts No. 16.* Washington, DC: National Institute on Disability and Rehabilitation Research.

LaPlante, M. P. (1997). How many Americans have a disability: #5. *Disability Statistics Abstract.* San Francisco: University of California at San Francisco. Retrieved from http://www.dsc.ucsf.edu

Lee, A. (1948). *My soul more bent.* Minneapolis, MN: Augsburg College.

Leete, E. (1991). The stigmatized patient. In P. J. Fink & A. Tasman (Eds.). *Stigma and mental illness* (pp. 17–25). Washington, DC: American Psychiatric Association Press.

Lefley, H. P. (1991). The stigmatized family. In P. J. Fink & A. Tasman (Eds.), *Stigma and mental illness* (pp. 127–138). Washington, DC: American Psychiatric Association Press.

Lehr, D. H., & Brinckerhoff, J. (1996). Bases of practice for young children with disabilities who challenge the system. In D. H. Lehr & F. Brown (Eds.), *People with disabilities who challenge the system* (pp. 3–22). Baltimore, MD: Brookes.

Lerner, W., & Belts, H. (2005). Striving for equity. *Modern Healthcare, 35*(36), 20.

Lesak, M. D. (1986). Psychological implications of traumatic brain damage for the patient's family. *Rehabilitation Psychology, 31,* 241–250.

Liachowitz, C. H. (1988). *Disability as a social construct: Legislative roots.* Philadelphia: University of Pennsylvania.

Lifchez, R., & Wade, C. (1982). What every architect should know. In M. G. Eisenberg, C. Griggins, & R. J. Duval (Eds.), *Disabled people as second class citizens* (pp. 88–102). New York, NY: Springer.

Linton, S. (1998). *Claiming disability: Knowledge and identity.* New York: New York University.

Livneh, H. (1980). Disability and monstrosity: Further comments. *Rehabilitation Literature, 41,* 280–283.

Livneh, H. (1982). On the origins of negative attitudes toward people with disabilities. *Rehabilitation Literature, 43,* 338–347.

Livneh, H. (1986a). A unified approach to existing models of adaptation to disability: I. A model of adaptation. *Journal of Applied Rehabilitation Counseling, 17*(1), 5–16, 56.

Livneh, H. (1986b). A unified approach to existing models of adaptation to disability: II. Intervention strategies. *Journal of Applied Rehabilitation Counseling, 17*(2), 6–10.

Livneh, H., & Antonak, R. F. (1990). Reactions to disability: An empirical investigation of their nature and structure. *Journal of Applied Rehabilitation Counseling, 21*(4), 13–21.

Livneh, H., & Antonak, R. F. (1997). *Psychosocial adaptation to chronic illness and disability.* Gaithersburg, MD: Aspen.

Logan Herald Journal. (2014, August 10). Modern day freak show, p. A7.

Long & sorry history of discrimination against people with disabilities in the United States—and its likely causes. (2000, September/October). *Ragged Edge Online.* Retrieved from http://www.raggededgemagazine.com/garrett/causes.htm

Longmore, P. K. (1985). Screening stereotypes: Images of disabled people. *Social Policy, 16,* 31–37.

Longmore, P. K. (2003). *Why I burned my book and other essays on disability.* Philadelphia, PA: Temple University.

Love, B., Bryne, C., Roberts, J., Browne, G., & Brown, B. (1987). Adult psychosocial adjustment following childhood injury: The effect of disfigurement. *Journal of Burn Care and Rehabilitation, 8,* 280–285.

Lubkin, I., & Jeffrey, J. (1998). Chronic pain. In I. M. Lubkin & P. D. Laresen (Eds.), *Chronic illness: Impact and interventions* (4th ed.) (pp. 149–178.) Sudbury, MA: Jones and Bartlett.

Lubkin, I. M., & Larsen, P. D. (Eds.). (1998). *Chronic illness: Impact and interventions.* Sudbury, MA: Jones & Bartlett.

Lubkin, I. M., & Larsen, P. D. (Eds.). (2006). *Chronic illness: Impact and interventions* (6th ed.). Sudbury, MA: Jones & Bartlett.

Ludwig, E. G., & Adams, S. D. (1968). Patient cooperation in a rehabilitation center: Assumption of the client role. *Journal of Health and Social Behavior, 9,* 328–336.

Lynch, R. T., & Thomas, K. R. (1994). People with disabilities as victims: Changing an ill-advised paradigm. *Journal of Rehabilitation, 69*(1), 8–11.

Mackelprang, R., & Salsgiver, R. (1999). *Disability: A diversity model approach in human service practice.* Pacific Grove, CA: Brooks/Cole.

Madrigal, A. (2014). Making babies: Five predictions about the future of reproduction. *The Atlantic, 313*(5), 32–34.

Mairs, N. (1996). *Waist-high in the world: A life among the nondisabled.* Boston, MA: Beacon.

Mairs, N. (1997a). Carnal acts. In K. Fries (Ed.), *Staring back: The disability experience from the inside out* (pp. 51–61). New York, NY: Plume.

Mairs, N. (1997b). Foreword. In G. T. Couser (Ed.), *Recovering bodies: Illness, disability, and life writing* (pp. ix–xiii). Madison: University of Wisconsin.

Mannion, E. (1996). Resilience and burden in spouses with mental illness. *Psychiatric Rehabilitation Journal, 20,* 13–24.

Mannion, E., Mueser, K., & Soloman, P. (1994). Designing psychoeducational services for spouses of persons with serious mental illness. *Community Mental Health Journal, 30,* 177–189.

Marks, D. (1999). *Disability: Controversial debates and psychosocial perspectives.* London, England: Routledge.

Marsh, D. T. (1992). *Families and mental illness: New directions in professional practice.* New York, NY: Praeger.

Marsh, D. T., & Lefley, H. P. (1996). The family experience of mental illness: Evidence for resilience. *Psychiatric Rehabilitation Journal, 20*(2), 3–13.

Martin, L. (2000). *From our house: A memoir.* New York, NY: Dutton.

Maxmen, J. S., & Ward, N. G. (1995). *Psychotropic drugs: Fast facts* (2nd ed.). New York, NY: Norton.

May, G. E. (2005). Changing the future of disability: The disability discrimination model. In G. E. May & M. B. Raske (Eds.), Ending discrimination in social work: Strategies for social workers (pp. 82–98). Boston, MA: Allyn & Bacon.

McBrien, M. (1997). Maybe you'd rather die than be me. *DIA Activist, January,* 3.

McCarthy, H. (1993). Learning with Beatrice A. Wright: A breath of fresh air that uncovers the unique virtues and human flaws in us all. *Rehabilitation Education, 10,* 149–166.

McCarthy, H. (1995). Understanding and reversing rehabilitation counseling's neglect of spirituality. *Rehabilitation Education, 9,* 187–199.

McCarthy, H. (2003). The disability rights movement: Experiences and perspectives of selected leaders in the disability community. *Rehabilitation Counseling Bulletin, 46,* 209–223.

McCarthy, M. (1999). Consent, abuse, and choices: Women with intellectual disabilities and sexuality. In R. Traustadottir & K. Johnson (Eds.), *Women with intellectual disabilities: Finding a place in the world* (pp. 133–155). Philadelphia, PA: Kingsley.

McColl, M. A., Bickenbach, J., Johnston, J., Nishihama, S., Schumaker, M., Smith, K., et al. (2000). Spiritual issues associated with traumatic-onset disability. *Disability and Rehabilitation, 19,* 555–564.

McFarlane, J., Hughes, R. B., Nosek, M. A., Groff, J. Y., Swedlend, N., & Mullen, P. D. (2001). Abuse Assessment Screen-Disability (AAS-D): Measuring frequency, type, and perpetrator of abuse toward women with physical disabilities. *Journal of Women's Health & Gender-Based Medicine, 10,* 861–866.

McMahon, B. T., Shaw, L. R., & Jaet, D. N. (1995). An empirical analysis: Employment and disability from an ADA litigation perspective. *NARPPS Journal and News, 10*(1), 3–14.

Mee, C. L. (1977). *A visit to Haldeman and other states of mind.* Lanham, MD: M. Evans.

Mee, C. L. (1999). *A nearly normal life: A memoir.* Boston, MA: Little, Brown.

Mental disorders are not diseases. (2000, January). *USA Today,* pp. 30–31.

Michalko, R. (2002). *The difference that disability makes.* Philadelphia, PA: Temple University.

Mikata, S. (1995, November). Difficult, but not tragic. Presentation given at the annual meeting of the Utah Rehabilitation Association, Salt Lake City.

Miller, J. (1988). Personal statement: Mechanisms for coping with the disability of a child—A mother's perspective. In P. W. Power, A. E. Dell Orto, & M. B. Gibbons (Eds.), *Family interventions throughout chronic illness and disability* (pp. 136–147). New York, NY: Springer.

Mims, B. (1998, January 24). Mentally disabled worker files $10M suit charging Smith's co-workers ridiculed him. *Salt Lake Tribune,* pp. B1, B5.

Mishel, M. (1993a). Reconceptualization of the uncertainty in illness theory. *Image: The Journal of Nursing Scholarship, 22,* 256–262.

Mishel, M. (1993b). Uncertainty in illness: Nursing theory. Retrieved from http://www.authorstream.com/Presentation/cgannon-276275-uncertainty-illness-theory-212mishelfinal presen-education-ppt-powerpoint/

Montgomery, C. (2006). "Little acts of degradation": Ragged Edge Online launches Project Cleigh. Retrieved from http://www.raggededgemagazine.com/departments/closerlook/000713.html

Morris, D. B. (1998). *Illness and culture in the postmodern age.* Berkeley: University of California.

Morris, J. (1991). *Pride against prejudice: Transforming attitudes towards disability.* London, England: The Women's Press.

Morrison, J. (2014). *DSM-5 made easy: The clinician's guide to diagnosis.* New York, NY: Guilford.

Murphy, R. F. (1987). *The body silent.* New York, NY: Henry Holt.

Murphy, R. F. (1990). *The body silent in America: An anthropologist embarks on the most challenging journey of his life: Into the world of the disabled.* New York, NY: Norton.

Murphy, R. F., Scheer, J., Murphy, Y., & Mack, R. (1988). Physical disability and social liminality: A study in the rituals of adversity. *Social Science and Medicine, 26,* 235–242.

National Organization on Disability (June 24, 2004). "Landmark survey finds pervasive disadvantages." [Press Release]. Washington, DC: NOD. Retrieved from http://nod.org/research

_publications/surveys_research/harris

National Organization on Disability/Harris Survey of Americans with Disabilities. (2004). New York, NY: Harris Interactive.

National Public Radio. (1998a, May). Inventing the poster child. On *The disability history project* [Radio documentary]. Retrieved from http://www.npr.org/programs/disability/ba_shows .dir/index_sh.html

National Public Radio. (1998b, May). The overdue revolution. On *The disability history project* [Radio documentary]. Retrieved from http://www.npr.org/programs/disability/ba_shows .dir/index_sh.html

National Public Radio. (1998c, May 4). Tomorrow's children. On *The disability history project* [Radio documentary]. Retrieved from http://www.npr.org/programs/disability/ba_shows .dir/index_sh.html

National Research Council. (1996). *Understanding violence against women.* Washington, DC: National Academy Press.

Naugle, R. I. (1991). Denial in rehabilitation: Its genesis, consequences, and clinical management. In R. P. Marinelli & A. E. Dell Orto (Eds.), *The psychological and social impact of disability* (3rd ed.) (pp. 139–151). New York, NY: Springer.

Navarro, M. (2007, May 17). Clearly, frankly, unabashedly disabled. *New York Times.* Retrieved from http://www.nytimes.com/2007/05/13/fashion/13disabled.html?pagewanted=all& _r=0

Nelson, J. L., & Berens, B. S. (1997). Spoken daggers, deaf ears, and silent mouths: Fantasies of deafness in early modern England. In L. J. David (Ed.), *Disability studies reader* (pp. 52–74). New York, NY: Routledge.

Neumann, R. J. (1988). Personal statement experiencing sexuality as an adolescent with rheumatoid arthritis. In P. W. Power, A. E. Dell Orto, & M. B. Gibbons (Eds.), *Family interventions throughout chronic illness and disability* (pp. 156–163). New York, NY: Springer.

Nichols, J. L., & Kosciulek, J. (2014). Social interactions of individuals with traumatic brain injury. *Journal of Rehabilitation, 80,* 21–29.

Nielsen, K. E. (2006). Was Helen Keller deaf? Blindness, deafness, and multiple identities. In B. J. Brueggemann & S. Burch (Eds.), *Women and deafness: Double visions* (pp. 21–39). Washington, DC: Gallaudet University.

Nixon, C. D. (1993). Reducing self-blame and guilt in parents of children with severe disabilities. In G. H. S. Singer & L. E. Powers (Eds.), *Families, disability, and empowerment: Active coping skills and strategies for family interventions* (pp. 175–201). Baltimore, MD: Brookes.

Norden, M. F. (1994). *The cinema of isolation: A history of disabilities in the movies.* New Brunswick, NJ: Rutgers University.

Nordqvist, I. (1980). Sexual counseling for disabled persons. *Sexuality and Disability, 3,* 193–198.

O'Brien, M. (2014). My new life with one arm. *The Week, July 18,* 36–37.

O'Brien, M. T. (1993). Multiple sclerosis: Stressors and coping strategies in spousal caregivers. *Journal of Community Health Nursing, 10,* 123–135.

Oldenburg, A. (2014, March 16). Defined by determination. *USA Today, B7–B8.* Retrieved from http://usatoday30.usatoday.com/LIFE/usaedition/2014-03-17-Amy-Purdy-feature_ST_U .htm

Olkin, R. (1999). *What psychotherapists should know about disability.* New York, NY: Guilford.

Ong, W. A. (1993). *Asian American cultural dimensions in rehabilitation counseling.* San Diego, CA: San Diego State University, Rehabilitation Cultural Diversity Initiative (RCDI).

Orrin, D. (1997). Past the struggles of mental illness, toward the development of quality lives. In L. Spanoil, C. Gagne, & M. Hoehler (Eds.), *Psychological and social aspects of psychiatric disability* (pp. 138–144). Boston, MA: Center for Psychiatric Rehabilitation. Boston University.

Panek, W. C. (1992). Visual disabilities. In M. G. Brodwin, F. Tellez, & S. K. Brodwin (Eds.), *Medical, psychosocial, and vocational aspects of disability* (pp. 217–230). Athens, GA: Elliott & Fitzpatrick.

Panzarino, C. (1993). Connie Panzarino: Art therapist. In H. Rousso (Ed.), *Disabled, female, and proud!* (pp. 107–118). Westport, CT: Bergin & Garvey.

Patterson, D. R., Everett, J. J., Bombardier, C. H., Questad, K. A., Lee, V. K., & Marvin, J. A. (1993). Psychological effects of severe burn injuries. *Psychological Bulletin, 113,* 362–368.

Patterson, J. M. (1988). Chronic illness in children and the impact upon families. In C. S. Chilman, E. W. Nunnally, & F. M. Cox (Eds.), *Chronic illness and disability* (pp. 69–107). Beverly Hills, CA: SAGE.

PBS. (1998). *A Paralyzing fear: The story of polio in America* (Item no. PFPA 401) [Television documentary]. Arlington, VA: Author.

Peele, S. (1989). *The diseasing of America.* Boston, MA: Houghton Mifflin.

Pelka, F. (1997). *The ABC-CLIO companion to the disability rights movement.* Santa Barbara, CA: ABC-CLIO.

Pelletier, L. (1988). Personal statement: The challenge of cerebral palsy: Familial adaptation and change. In P. W. Power, A. E. Dell Orto, & M. B. Gibbons (Eds.), *Family interventions throughout chronic illness and disability* (pp. 54–59). New York, NY: Springer.

Penn, A. (1993). Audrey Penn. In J. K. Smith & G. Plimpton (Eds.), *Chronicles of courage: Very special artists* (pp. 109–117). New York, NY: Random House.

Perduta-Fulginiti, P. S. (1996). Impact of bowel and bladder dysfunction on sexuality and self-esteem. In D. M. Krotoski, M. A. Nosek, & M. A. Turk (Eds.), *Women with physical disabilities: Achieving and maintaining health and well-being* (pp. 287–298). Baltimore, MD: Brookes.

Perkins, R. (1996). *Talking to angels: A life spent in high latitudes.* Boston, MA: Beacon.

Perrone, K. M., Gordon, P. A., & Tschopp, M. K. (2006). Caregiver marital satisfaction when a spouse has multiple sclerosis. *Journal of Applied Rehabilitation Counseling, 37,* 26–32.

Peterson, C., Maier, S. F., & Seligman, M. E. P. (1993). *Learned helplessness: A theory for the age of personal control.* New York, NY: Oxford University.

Petty, D. (1979). What is it like to be deaf-blind? *Consumers Contemporary, 1,* 10–11.

Pfeiffer, D. (1989). Disability simulation using a wheelchair simulation. *Journal of Post Secondary Education & Disability, 7,* 53–60.

Phillips, M. (1991). "Try harder": The experience of disability and the dilemma of normalization. In P. M. Ferguson, D. L. Ferguson, & S. J. Taylor (Eds.), *Interpreting disability: A qualitative reader* (pp. 213–227). New York, NY: Columbia Teachers College.

Poole, W. C., Jr. (1927). Social distance and personal distance. *Journal of Applied Sociology, 11,* 114–120.

Pope, A. M., & Tarlov, A. R. (Eds.). (1991). *Disability in America: Toward a national agenda for prevention.* Washington, DC: National Academy Press.

Power, P. W., & Rogers, S. (1979). Group counseling for multiple sclerosis patients: A preferred mode of treatment for unique adaptive problems. In R. G. Lasky & A. E. Dell Orto (Eds.),

Group counseling and physical disability (pp. 115–127). North Scituate, MA: Duxbury.

Powers, L. E. (1993). Disability and grief: From tragedy to challenge. In G. H. S. Singer & L. E. Powers (Eds.), *Families, disability, and empowerment: Active coping skills and strategies for family interventions* (pp. 119–149). Baltimore, MD: Brookes.

Powers, L. E., Curry, M. A., Oschwalk, M., Maley, S., Saxton, M., & Eckels, K. (2002). Barriers and strategies in addressing abuse: Survey of disabled women's experiences. *Journal of Rehabilitation, 68,* 4–13.

Preston, P. (1994). *Mother father deaf: Living between sound and silence.* Cambridge, MA: Harvard University.

Price, R. (1994). *A whole new life: An illness and a healing.* New York, NY: Atheneum.

The problem with 'challenge.' (1985). *Ragged Edge Online.* Retrieved from http://www .raggededgemagazine.com/archive/challenge.htm

Pugach, M. C., & Seidl, B. L. (1996). Deconstructing the diversity connection. *Contemporary Education, 68,* 5–8.

Putnam, M., Greenen, S., Powers, L., Saxton, M., Finney, S., & Dautel, P. (2003). Health and wellness: People with disabilities discuss barriers and facilitators to well being. *Journal of Rehabilitation, 69,* 37–45.

Rée, J. (1999). *I see a voice: A philosophical history of language, deafness, and the senses.* New York, NY: Harper Collins.

Reed, P. G. (1991). Toward a nursing theory of self-transcendence: Deductive reformulation using developmental theories. *Advances in Nursing Science, 13(4),* 64–77.

Reid, D. (2004). Impact of the environment on role performance in older stroke survivors living at home. *International Journal of Therapy and Rehabilitation, 11,* 567–573.

Rodger, S., & Tooth, L. (2004). Adult siblings' perceptions of family life and loss: A pilot case study. *Journal of Developmental and Physical Disabilities, 16,* 53–71.

Roessler, R., & Bolton, B. (1978). *Psychosocial adjustment to disability.* Baltimore, MD: University Park Press.

Rolland, J. S. (1994). *Families, illness, and disability: An integrative treatment model.* New York, NY: Basic.

Rosin, H. (2014, March). Letting go of Asperger's. *The Atlantic.* Retrieved from http://www .theatlantic.com/magazine/archive/2014/03/letting-go-of-aspergers/357563/

Rossides, D. W. (1990). *Social stratification: The American class system in comparative perspective* (2nd ed.). Englewood Cliffs, NJ: Prentice-Hall.

Rousso, H. (1993). *Disabled, female, and proud: Stories of ten women with disabilities.* Westport, CT: Bergin & Garvey.

Rustad, L. C. (1984). Family adjustment to chronic illness and disability in mid-life. In M. G. Eisenberg, L. C. Sutkin, & M. A. Jansen (Eds.), *Chronic illness and disability through the life span: Effects on self and the family* (pp. 222–242). New York, NY: Springer.

Rutkow, I. (2010). *Seeking the cure: A history of medicine in America.* New York, NY: Scribner.

Rutter, M. (1989). Intergenerational continuities and discontinuities in serious parenting difficulties. In D. Cicchetti & V. Carlson (Eds.), *Child maltreatment: Theory and research on causes and consequences of child abuse and neglect* (pp. 317–348). Cambridge, England: Cambridge University.

Ryan, J., & Thomas, F. (1980). *The politics of mental handicap.* Harmondsworth, England: Penguin.

Rybarczyk, B., Nyenhuis, D. L., Nicholas, J. J., Cash, S. M., & Kaiser, J. (1995). Body image, perceived social stigma, and the prediction of psychosocial adjustment to leg amputation. *Rehabilitation Psychology, 40,* 95–110.

Sacks, O. (1989). *Seeing voices.* Berkeley: University of California.

Sacks, O. (2010). *The mind's eye.* New York, NY: Knopf.

Safran, S. P. (1998). The first century of disability portrayal in film: An analysis of the literature. *The Journal of Special Education, 31,* 467–479.

Sailor, W., Kleinhammer-Tramill, J., Skrtic, T., & Oas, B. K. (1996). Family participation in new community schools. In G. H. S. Singer, L. E. Powers, & A. L. Olson (Eds.), *Redefining family support: Innovations in public-private partnerships* (pp. 313–332). Baltimore, MD: Brookes.

Santelli, B., Turnbull, A. P., Lerner, E., & Marquis, J. (1993). Parent to parent programs: A unique form of mutual support for families of persons with disabilities. In G. H. S. Singer & L. E. Powers (Eds.), *Families, disabilities, and empowerment: Active coping skills and strategies for family interventions* (pp. 27–57). Baltimore, MD: Brookes.

Sasao, T., & Sue, S. (1993). Toward a culturally anchored ecological framework of research in ethnic-cultural communities. *American Journal of Community Psychology, 21,* 705–772.

Sawyer, H. W., & Clark, W. D. (1980). Disability simulation as a strategy for attitude change. *Journal of Applied Rehabilitation Counseling, 11,* 132–135.

Saxton, M., Curry, M. A., McNeff, E., Limont, M., Powers, L., & Benson, J. (2006). We're all little John Waynes: A study of disabled men's experience of abuse by personal assistants. *Journal of Rehabilitation, 72,* 3–13.

Scheer, J., & Groce, N. (1988). Impairment as human constraint: Cross cultural and historical perspectives on variation. *Journal of Social Issues, 44,* 23–37.

Scherer, M. J. (1993). *Living in the state of stuck: How technology impacts the lives of people with disabilities.* Cambridge, MA: Brookline.

Schienle, D. R., & Eiler, J. M. (1984). Clinical intervention with older adults. In M. G. Eisenberg, L. C. Sutkin, & M. A. Jansen (Eds.), *Chronic illness and disability through the life span: Effects on self and the family* (pp. 245–268). New York, NY: Springer.

Schmelkin, L. P. (1988). Multidimensional perspectives in the perception of disabilities. In H. E. Yuker (Ed.), *Attitudes toward persons with disabilities* (pp. 127–137). New York, NY: Springer.

Schur, E. M. (1971). *Labeling deviant behavior: Its sociological implications.* New York, NY: Harper and Row.

Schur, E. M. (1979). *Interpreting deviance.* New York, NY: Harper and Row.

Schur, E. M. (1983). *Labeling women deviant: Gender, stigma, and social control.* Philadelphia, PA: Temple University.

Scotch, R. K. (1984). *From good will to civil rights: Transforming federal disability policy.* Philadelphia, PA: Temple University.

Scott, R. (1969). *The making of blind men: A study of adult socialization.* New York, NY: Russell Sage Foundation.

Shakespeare, T., Gillespie-Sells, K., & Davies, D. (1996). *The sexual politics of disability: Untold stories.* London, England: Caswell.

Shapiro, J. P. (1993). *No pity: People with disabilities forging a new civil rights movement.* New York, NY: Times Book.

Shapiro, J. P. (1997). Assisted suicide devalues the lives of disabled people. In B. Stalcup (Ed.), *The disabled* (pp. 170–178). San Diego, CA: Greenhaven.

Shell, M. (2005). *Polio and its aftermath: The paralysis of culture.* Cambridge, MA: Harvard University.

Shontz, F. C. (1971). Physical disability and personality. In W. S. Neff (Ed.). *Rehabilitation psychology.* Washington, DC: American Psychological Association.

Shontz, F. C. (1975). The psychological aspects of physical illness and disability. New York, NY: MacMillan.

Shontz, F. C. (1977). Physical disability and personality: Theory and recent research. In J. Stubbins (Ed.), *Social and psychological aspects of disability: A handbook for practitioners* (pp. 333–353). Baltimore, MD: University Park Press.

Shontz, F. C. (1991). Six principles relating to disability and psychological adjustment. In R. P. Marinelli & A. E. Dell Orto (Eds.), *The psychological and social impact of disability* (3rd ed.) (pp. 107–110). New York, NY: Springer.

Sidey, H. (1997, April 28). A monumental mistake. *Time, 149*(17), 4.

Sidransky, R. (1990). *In silence: Growing up hearing in a deaf world.* New York, NY: St. Martin's Press.

Simpson, G. E., & Yinger, J. M. (1985). *Racial and cultural minorities: An analysis of prejudice and discrimination* (5th ed.). New York, NY: Plenum.

Sinacore-Guinn, A. L. (1995). The diagnostic window: Culture and gender-sensitive diagnosis and training. *Counselor Education and Supervision, 35,* 18–32.

Sinason, J. (1992). *Mental handicap and the human condition.* London: Free Association Books.

Singer, G. H. S. (1996). Introduction: Trends affecting home and community care for people with chronic conditions in the United States. In G. H. S. Singer, L. E. Powers, & A. L. Olson (Eds.), *Redefining family support: Innovations in public-private partnerships* (pp. 3–38). Baltimore, MD: Brookes.

Singer, G. H. S., & Irvin, L. K. (1989). Family caregiving, stress, and support. In G. H. S. Singer & L. K. Irvin (Eds.), *Support for caregiving families* (pp. 3–25). Baltimore, MD: Brookes.

Singer, G. H. S., Powers, L. E., & Olson, A. L. (Eds.). (1996). *Redefining family support: Innovations in public-private partnerships.* Baltimore, MD: Brookes.

Singer, P. (1981). *The expanding circle: Ethics and sociobiology.* New York, NY: Farrar, Straus, & Giroux.

Singer, P. (1994). *Rethinking life and death: The collapse of our traditional ethics.* New York, NY: St. Martin's Press.

Singer, P. (2000). *Writings on an ethical life.* New York, NY: Ecco/Harper Collins.

Sinick, D. (1969). Training, job placement, and follow-up. In D. Malikin & H. Rusalem (Eds.). *Vocational rehabilitation of the disabled: An overview* (pp. 129–153). New York: New York University Press.

Smart, D. W., & Smart, J. F. (1997). *DSM-IV* and culturally sensitive diagnosis: Some observations for counselors. *Journal of Counseling and Development, 75,* 392–398.

Smart, J. F. (2004). Models of disability: The juxtaposition of biology and social construction. In T. F. Riggar & D. R. Maki (Eds.), *Handbook of rehabilitation counseling* (pp. 25–49). New York, NY: Springer.

Smart, J. F. (2005a). Challenges to the Biomedical Model of disability: Changes to the practice of rehabilitation counseling. *Directions in Rehabilitation Counseling, 16*(4), 33–43.

Smart, J. F. (2005b). The promise of the International Classification of Functioning, Disability, and Health (ICF). *Rehabilitation Education, 19,* 191–199.

Smart, J. F. (2006). Challenging the biomedical model of disability. *Advances in Medical Psychotherapy and Psychodiagnosis, American Board of Medical Psychotherapists, 12,* 41–44.

Smart, J. F. (2012a). *Disability across the developmental lifespan.* New York, NY: Springer.

Smart, J. F. (2012b). The power of models of disability. *Journal of Rehabilitation, 75,* 231–240.

Smart, J. F., & Smart, D. W. (1997). The racial/ethnic demography of disability. *Journal of Rehabilitation, 63,* 9–15.

Smart, J. F., & Smart, D. W. (2006). Models of disability: Implications for the counseling profession. *Journal of Counseling and Development, 84,* 29–40.

Sobsey, D. (1994). *Violence and abuse in the lives of people with disabilities: The end of silent acceptance.* Baltimore, MD: Brookes.

Sobsey, D., & Doe, T. (1991). Patterns of sexual abuse and assault. *Sexuality & Disability, 9,* 243–260.

Sobsey, D., & Mansell, S. (1993). The prevention of sexual abuse of people with developmental disabilities. In M. Nagler (Ed.), *Perspectives on disability* (2nd ed.) (pp. 283–292). Palo Alto, CA: Health Markets Research.

Solomon, A. (2012). *Far from the tree: Parents, children, and the search for identity.* New York, NY: Scribner.

Souders, R. (1993). Randy Souders. In J. K. Smith & G. Plimpton, (Eds.), *Chronicles of courage: Very special artists* (pp. 147–155) New York, NY: Random House.

Spechler, J. W. (1996). *Reasonable accommodation: Profitable compliance with the Americans with Disabilities Act.* Delray Beach, FL: St. Lucie Press.

Spector, R. E. (1991). *Cultural diversity in health and illness* (3rd ed.). Norwalk, CT: Appleton & Lange.

Stalcup, B. (Ed.). (1997). *The disabled, current controversies series.* San Diego, CA: Greenhaven.

Stefan, S. (2001). *Unequal rights: Discrimination against people with mental disabilities and the Americans with Disabilities Act.* Washington, DC: American Psychological Association.

Stein, F., & Cutler, S. K. (1998). *Psychosocial occupational therapy: A holistic approach.* San Diego, CA: Singular Publishing Group.

Stewart, J. R. (1994). Denial of disabling conditions and specific interventions in the rehabilitation counseling setting. *Journal of Applied Rehabilitation Counseling, 25*(3), 7–15.

Stokoe, W. C., Croneberg, C., & Casterline, D. (1965). *Dictionary of American Sign Language* (2nd ed.). Washington, DC: Gallaudet College.

Stonequist, E. V. (1937). *The marginal man: A study in personality and culture conflict.* New York, NY: Scribner & Sons.

Stonequist, E. V. (1961). *The marginal man: Reprinted.* New York, NY: Russell and Russell.

Stubbins, J. (1988). The politics of disability. In A. E. Yuker (Ed.), *Attitudes toward persons with disabilities* (pp. 22–32). New York, NY: Springer.

Sullivan, D. M. (1998). Hunting and fishing: Ways of life in rural America. In T. S. Smith (Ed.), *Rural rehabilitation: A modern perspective* (pp. 292–312). Amaudville, LA: Bow River.

Suter, S. (1993, August). *Women with disabilities: How to become a boat rocker in life.* Paper presented at the Ethics in Rehabilitation Conference, New Zealand Rehabilitation Organization, Dunedin, NZ.

Szasz, T. S. (1961). *The myth of mental illness.* New York, NY: Harper.

Szymanski, E. M., & Trueba, H. T. (1994). Castification of people with disabilities: Potential disempowering aspects of classification in disability services. *Journal of Rehabilitation, 60*(3), 12–20.

Taylor, E. J., Jones, P., & Burns, M. (1998). Quality of life. In I. M. Lubkin & P. D. Larsen (Eds.). *Chronic illness: Impact and interventions* (4th ed.) (pp. 207–226). Sudbury, MA: Jones & Bartlett.

Thomas, A. (2000). Stability of Tringo's hierarchy of preference toward disability groups: Thirty years later. *Psychological Reports, 86,* 1155–1156.

Thomas, S. A., Foreman, P. E., & Remenyi, A. G. (1985). The effects of previous contact with physical disability upon Australian children's attitudes toward people with physical disabilities. *International Journal of Rehabilitation Research, 8,* 69–70.

Thompson-Hoffman, S., & Storck, I. F. (Eds.). (1991). *Disability in the United States: A portrait from national data.* New York, NY: Springer.

Thomson, R. G. (1996). *Freakery: Cultural spectacles of the extraordinary body.* New York: New York University.

Thomson, R. G. (1997a). *Extraordinary bodies: Figuring physical disability in American culture and literature.* New York, NY: Columbia University Press.

Thomson, R. G. (1997b). Feminist theory, the body, and the disabled. In L. J. Davis (Ed.), *The disability studies reader* (pp. 279–292). New York, NY: Routledge.

Thomson, R. G. (1997c). Integrating disability studies into the existing curriculum: The example of "women and literature" at Howard University. In L. J. Davis (Ed.), *The disability studies reader* (pp. 296–311). New York, NY: Routledge.

Tollifson, R. (1997). Imperfection is a beautiful thing: On disability and meditation. In K. Fries (Ed.), *Staring back: The disability experience from the inside out* (pp. 105–112). New York, NY: Plume.

Toombs, S. K. (1995). Sufficient unto the day. In S. K. Toombs, D. Barnard, & R. A. Carson (Eds.), *Chronic illness from experience to policy* (pp. 2–23). Bloomington: University of Indiana.

Toombs, S. K., Barnard, D., & Carson, R. A. (Eds.). (1995). *Chronic illness: From experience to policy.* Bloomington: University of Indiana.

Torriero, E. A. (2006, September 3). Foes of Lewis telethon most uncharitable. *Chicago Tribune.* Retrieved from http://articles.chicagotribune.com/2006-09-03/news/0609030246_1_satellite-telethon-locations-housing-and-employment-possibilities-south-coast-hotel-casino

Tremblay, M. (1996). Going back to civvy street: A historical account of the Everest and Jennings wheelchair for Canadian World War II veterans with spinal cord injuries. *Disability and Society, 11,* 146–169.

Trieschmann, R. B. (1987). *Aging with a disability.* New York, NY: Demos.

Tringo, J. L. (1970). The hierarchy of preference toward disability groups. *The Journal of Special Education, 4,* 295–306.

Tucker, B. P. (1998). Deaf culture, cochlear implants, and elective disability. *Hastings Center Report, 28*(4), 6–15.

Turner, V. (1979). Betwixt and between: The liminal period in rites of passage. In W. Lessa & E. Z. Vogt (Eds.), *Reader in comparative religion* (4th ed.) (pp. 234–243). New York, NY: Harper & Row.

Tuttle, D. W. (1984). *Self-esteem and adjusting with blindness: The process of responding to life's demands.* Springfield, IL: Thomas.

Ulicny, G. R., White, G. W., Bradford, B., & Matthews, R. M. (1990). Consumer exploitation attendants: How often does it happen and can anything be done about it? *Rehabilitation Counseling Bulletin, 33,* 240–246.

Van Cleve, J. V., & Crouch, B. A. (1989). *A place of their own: Creating the Deaf community in America.* Washington, DC: Gallaudet.

Vash, C. (1981). *The psychology of disability.* New York, NY: Springer.

Vash, C. (1982). Women and employment. In L. Perlman (Ed.), *Women in rehabilitation: The sixth Mary E. Switzer memorial seminar monograph* (pp. 15–24). Alexandria, VA: National Rehabilitation Association.

Vash, C. & Crewe, N. M. (2003). *Psychology of disability* (2nd ed.). New York, NY: Springer.

Veith, E. M., Sherman, J. E., Pellino, T. A., & Yasui, N. Y. (2006). Qualitative analysis of the peer-mentoring relationship among individuals with spinal cord injury. *Rehabilitation Psychology, 51,* 289–298.

Verbrugge, L. (1989). Gender, aging, and health. In K. Markides (Ed.), *Aging and health: Perspectives on gender, race, ethnicity, and class* (pp. 55–75). Newbury Park, CA: SAGE.

Vermeij, G. (1997). *Privileged hands: A scientific life.* New York, NY: Freeman.

Vernellia, R. R. (1994). Impact of managed care organizations on ethnic Americans and underserved populations. *Journal of Health Care for the Poor and the Underserved, 5,* 224–237.

Wade, C. (1994). It ain't exactly sexy. In B. Shaw (Ed.), *The Ragged Edge: The Disability Experience from the Pages of the First 15 Years of the Disability Rag.* Louisville, KY: Avocado.

Walker, L. A. (1986). *A loss for words: The story of deafness in a family.* New York, NY: Harper.

Walkup, J. (2000). Disability, health care, and public policy. *Rehabilitation Psychology, 45,* 409–422.

Warren-Leubecker, A., & Bohannon, J. N. (1989). Pragmatics: Language in social contexts. In J. Berko-Gleason (Ed.), *The development of language* (pp. 327–368). Columbus, OH: Merrill.

Watkins, K. E., & Podus, D. (2000). Alcohol and drug abuse: The impact of terminating disability benefits for substance abusers on substance abuse and treatment participation. *Psychiatric Services, 51,* 1371–1381.

Waxman, B. F. (1991). Hatred: The unacknowledged dimension in violence against disabled people. *Sexuality and Disability, 9,* 185–199.

Wecter, D. (1985). How to write history. In *A sense of history: The best writing from the pages of American Heritage* (pp. 38–45). New York, NY: American Heritage.

Weihenmayer, E. (2001). *Touch the top of the world: A blind man's journey to climb farther than the eye can see.* New York, NY: Dutton.

Weinberg, N., & Miller, N. J. (1983). Burn care: A social work perspective. *Health and Social Work, 8,* 97–106.

Weinberg, N., & Sterritt, M. (1991). Disability and identity: A study of identity patterns in adolescents with hearing impairments. In M. G. Eisenberg & R. L. Glueckauf (Eds.), *Empirical approaches to psychosocial aspects of disability* (pp. 68–75). New York, NY: Springer.

Weingarten, R. (1997). How I've managed my mental illness. In L. Spanoil, C. Gagne, & M. Hoehler (Eds.), *Psychological and social aspects of psychiatric disability* (pp. 123–129). Boston, MA: Center for Psychiatric Rehabilitation, Boston University.

Weisgerber, R. A. (1991). *Quality of life for persons with disabilities: Skill development and transitions across life stages.* Gaithersburg, MD: Aspen.

Weisskopf, M. (2006, October 2). How I lost my hand but found myself. *Time,* 28–37.

Wendell, S. (2006). Toward a feminist theory of disability. In L. J. Davis (Ed.), *The disability studies reader* (2nd ed.) (pp. 243–256). New York, NY: Routledge.

West, T. G. (1997). Slow words, quick words—Dyslexia as an advantage in tomorrow's work place. In P. J. Gerber & D. S. Brown (Eds.), *Learning disabilities and employment* (pp. 349–370). Austin, TX: PRO-ED.

Westbrook, M. T., & Legge, V. (1993). Health practitioners' perceptions of family attitudes toward children with disabilities: A comparison of six communities in a multicultural society. *Rehabilitation Psychology, 38,* 177–185.

Westbrook, M. T., Legge, V., & Pennay, M. (1993). Attitudes towards disabilities in a multi-cultural society. *Social Science & Medicine, 36,* 615–623.

White, M., & Gribbin, J. (1993). *Steven Hawking: A life in science.* New York, NY: Penguin.

White, N., & Lubkin, I. (1998). Illness trajectory. In I. M. Lubkin & P. D. Larsen (Eds.), *Chronic illness: Impact and interventions* (4th ed.) (pp. 53–76). Sudbury, MA: Jones & Bartlett.

White, P. H. (2002). Access to healthcare: Health insurance considerations for young adults with special health care needs/disabilities. *Pediatrics, 110,* 1328–1336.

Whitney, C. R. (1993, January 19). Germans fear they'll be the next target. *New York Times.* Retrieved from http://www.nytimes.com/1993/01/19/world/disabled-germans-fear-they-ll-be -the-next-target.html

Whitt, J. K. (1984). Children's adaptation to chronic illness and handicapping conditions. In M. G. Eisenberg, L. C. Sutkin, & M. A. Jansen (Eds.), *Chronic illness and disability through the life span: Effects on self and family* (pp. 69–102). New York, NY: Springer.

Widmer, T. (2006, May 7). Magic man: How Franklin D. Roosevelt brought America back from the brink. [Review of the book *The defining moment: FDR's hundred days and the triumph of hope,* by J. Alter.] *New York Times.*

Wilson, D. J. (1990). *Living with polio: The epidemic and its survivors.* Chicago, IL: University of Chicago.

Winzer, M. A. (1993). Education, urbanization, and the Deaf community: A case study of Toronto, 1870–1900. In J. V. Van Cleve (Ed.), *Deaf history unveiled: Interpretations of the new scholarship* (pp. 127–145). Washington, DC: Gallaudet University.

Wolbring, G. (2001). Where do we draw the line? Surviving eugenics in a technological world. In M. Priestley (Ed.), *Disability and life course* (pp. 38–48). Cambridge, UK: Cambridge University.

Wolfensberger, W. (1972). *The principle of normalization in human services.* Toronto, Canada: National Institute on Intellectual disability.

Wolfensberger, W. (1981). The extermination of handicapped people in World War II Germany. *Intellectual disability, Vol. 1–7.* Toronto, Ontario, Canada: National Institute on Intellectual Disability.

Wolfensberger, W., & Tullman, S. (1982). A brief outline of the principle of normalization. *Rehabilitation Psychology, 27*(3), 131–145.

Wolfensberger, W., & Tullman, S. (1991). A brief outline of the principle of normalization. In M. G. Eisenberg & R. L. Glueckauf (Eds.), *Empirical approaches to the psychosocial aspects of disability* (pp. 202–215). New York, NY: Springer.

Woodward, J. (1991, November/December). Getting rid of special. *The Disability Rag,* pp. 35–41.

World Health Organization (WHO). (2001). *International classification of functioning, disability and health.* Geneva, Switzerland: Author.

World Health Organization (WHO). (2015). *The international statistical classification of diseases and related health problems* (10th rev.). Geneva, Switzerland: Author. Retrieved from http://apps.who .int/classifications/icd10/browse/2015/en

Wright, B. A. (1960). *Physical disability: A psychological approach.* New York, NY: Harper & Row.

Wright, B. A. (1975). Sensitizing outsiders to the position of the insider. *Rehabilitation Psychology, 22,* 129–135.

Wright, B. A. (1983). *Physical Disability—A psychosocial approach.* New York, NY: Harper and Row.

Wright, B. A. (1991). Labeling: The need for person–environment individuation. In C. R. Snyder & D. R. Forsyth (Eds.), *Handbook of social and clinical psychology: The health perspective* (pp. 469–487). New York, NY: Pergamon.

Wright, D. (1994). *Deafness: An autobiography.* New York, NY: Mandarin.

Yalom, I. D. (1980). *Existential psychotherapy.* New York, NY: Basic Books.

Yelin, E. H. (1992). *Disability and the displaced worker.* New Brunswick, NJ: Rutgers University.

Yoshida, K. K. (1993). Reshaping of self: A pendular reconstruction of self and identity among adults with traumatic spinal cord injury. *Sociology of Health & Illness, 15,* 217–245.

Young, D. A., & Quibell, R. (2000). Why rights are never enough: Rights, intellectual disability, and understanding. *Disability and Society, 15,* 747–764.

Young, I. (1990). *Justice and the politics of difference.* Princeton, NJ: Princeton University.

Young, R., & Olsen, E. (1991). Introduction. In R. Young & E. Olson (Eds.), *Health, illness, and disability in later life: Practice issues and interventions* (pp. 1–7). Newbury Park, CA: SAGE.

Yuker, H. E. (Ed.). (1988). *Attitudes toward persons with disabilities.* New York, NY: Springer.

Zavirsek, D. (2002). Pictures and silences: Memories of sexual abuse of disabled people. *Journal of Social Welfare, 11,* 270–285.

Ziporyn, T. (1992). *Nameless diseases.* New Brunswick, NJ: Rutgers University.

Zola, I. K. (1972). Medicine as an institution of social control. *Sociological Review, 20,* 487–504.

Zola, I. K. (1982). *Missing pieces: A chronicle of living with a disability.* Philadelphia, PA: Temple University.

Zola, I. K. (1988). Policies and programs concerning aging and disability: Toward a unifying agenda. In S. Sullivan & M. Lewin (Eds.), *The economics and ethics of long-term care and disability* (pp. 90–130). Washington, DC: American Enterprise Institute for Public Policy Research.

Zola, I. K. (1991). Communication barriers between "the able-bodied" and "the handicapped." In R. P. Marinelli & A. E. Dell Orto (Eds.), *The psychological and social impact of disability* (pp. 157–164). New York, NY: Springer.

Zola, I. K. (1992). "Any distinguishing features?" The portrayal of disability in the crime-mystery genre. In P. M. Ferguson, D. L. Ferguson, & S. J. Taylor (Eds.), *Interpreting disability: A qualitative reader* (pp. 233–250). New York, NY: Columbia University

Zola, I. K. (1993). Disability statistics: What we count and what it tells us. *Journal of Disability Policy Studies, 4,* 9–39.

AUTHOR INDEX

SUBJECT INDEX

ABOUT THE AUTHOR

Julie Smart, PhD, LPC, CRC (ret.), LVRC, NCC, is professor and former director of the Rehabilitation Counseling program at Utah State University. Her first career was as a college teacher of Spanish, and she has continued to utilize her Spanish language skills by translating and field-testing rehabilitation instruments, such as *The Acceptance of Disability Scale* and *Client Satisfaction with Rehabilitation Services Scale.* She has authored or co-authored more than 45 articles in rehabilitation and general counseling journals and also has written 10 book chapters, and two books, *Disability across the Developmental Lifespan* and *Disability, Society, and the Individual.* Her research interests include the rehabilitation of racial and ethnic minority individuals with disabilities, and models of disability. In 1989–1990, Dr. Smart was the recipient of a postdoctoral research fellowship, the Mary E. Switzer Award, from the National Institute on Disability and Rehabilitation Research (NIDRR).